The New Guide to
North Carolina Beaches

The New Guide to

All You Need to Know to Explore and Enjoy
Currituck, Calabash, and Everywhere Between

North Carolina Beaches

GLENN MORRIS

The University of North Carolina Press
Chapel Hill

A SOUTHERN GATEWAYS GUIDE

© 2019 The University of North Carolina Press

Designed by Jamison Cockerham
Set in Scala, Payson, and Kododa
by Tseng Information Systems, Inc.

Manufactured in the United States of America

The University of North Carolina Press has been a member
of the Green Press Initiative since 2003.

Cover illustration: *Outer Banks Beach at Sunrise from the
Sand Dunes*, © iStockphoto.com/RickSause.

LIBRARY OF CONGRESS CATALOGING-IN-PUBLICATION DATA
Names: Morris, Glenn, 1950– author.
Title: The new guide to North Carolina beaches : all you need to know to explore
    and enjoy Currituck, Calabash, and everywhere between / Glenn Morris.
Other titles: Southern gateways guide.
Description: Chapel Hill : The University of North Carolina Press, [2019] |
    Series: A southern gateways guide | Includes bibliographical references and index.
Identifiers: LCCN 2018049777 | ISBN 9781469651736 (pbk : alk. paper) |
    ISBN 9781469651743 (ebook)
Subjects: LCSH: Beaches—North Carolina—Guidebooks. |
    Recreation areas—North Carolina—Guidebooks.
Classification: LCC F252.3 .M656 2019 | DDC 917.5604—dc23
LC record available at https://lccn.loc.gov/2018049777

Southern Gateways Guide™ is a registered trademark
of the University of North Carolina Press.

For Griffin, Sutton, and Lawson Wiles

Be Curious

Contents

FEATURE ARTICLES

Hurricane Florence

An Unwelcome Visitor, September 14–16, 2018

Hurricane Florence, a sprawling maelstrom, roared toward southeastern North Carolina as this book entered final editing. It made landfall at Wrightsville Beach as a Category 1 storm on September 14. While the storm punched the island beachfront communities between Cape Lookout and Cape Fear with less impact than predicted, its lingering inland track brought historic, record-setting rainfall and flooding. Floodwater closed roads to Wilmington, swamped Fayetteville, and drowned Lumberton.

Every island dune line between Cape Lookout and Cape Fear took a beating, but the majority of oceanfront homes weathered the assault intact. Returning vacationers will see new roof shingles, new decking, and a swash line that is much closer to the front-row homes than before. Sand dunes will be newly replenished, and dune crossovers are likely to be brand new or still under construction. If past storm recovery can serve as an indicator, homeowners will repair as quickly as possible in time for the summer season.

Recovery will be much slower for inland communities such as Harkers Island and eastern Carteret County. The Core Sound Waterfowl Museum & Heritage Center was vacated for repairs; the road to Harkers Island needed to be rebuilt. Flooding was horrific to some of the Downeast communities between Cedar Island and Beaufort. The same was true for New Bern and low-lying coastal communities north and west of Topsail Island, Wrightsville Beach, and Southport.

The natural islands—Cape Lookout National Seashore, Bear Island, Lea-Hutaff Island, Masonboro Island, and Bird Island, prominent among others—rolled with the storm's punch. Bear Island lost much of its primary dune line; a few of the concessionaire cabins in Cape Lookout were repaired or replaced as needed.

Hurricanes such as Florence destroy property, upend lives, and crush dreams, but it is difficult to believe that these storms, when they spin up to threaten, are ever completely a surprise. Instead, they troll out of sight and out of mind, buried deep in the fine print of living close to the edge of the sea.

Swim Safely

Going to the beach assumes playing in the waves, but the ocean can be a fickle, dangerous playmate. Swimming at a beach with a lifeguard and understanding and obeying the posted warnings can help you make sure that your vacation stays a vacation. Fortunately, an operating network of on-line surf-condition alerts is growing. Here's how to connect.

Surf Conditions for Dare County and Cape Hatteras National Seashore Text this number, 30890, with the following message: Join OBXBeachConditions. After the second text, enter the sending number under contacts.

Learn about Rip Currents and Specific Beach Warnings Go to www.weather .gov/safety/ripcurrent. On the navigation bar, click on Surf Forecasts, then click on the city closest to your location.

For rip currents in general: www.ripcurrents.com.

Check the Beach Forecast In 2018, this experimental website premiered: www.weather.gov/beach/mhx.

The New Guide to
North Carolina Beaches

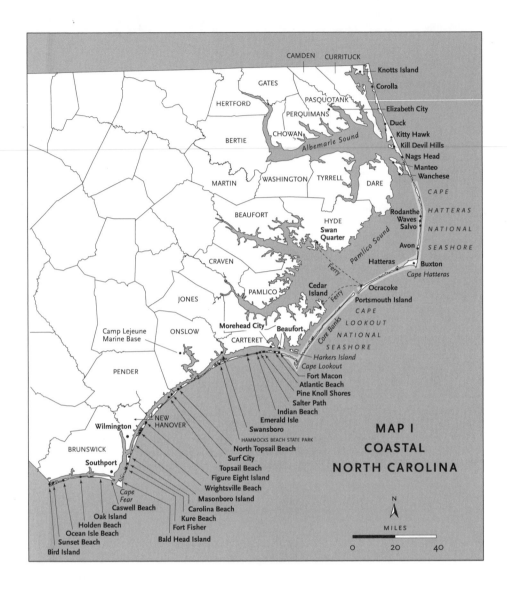

CAMDEN CURRITUCK

GATES

HERTFORD

PASQUOTANK

PERQUIMANS

CHOWAN

BERTIE

Albemarle Sound

Knotts Island

Corolla

Elizabeth City

Duck

Kitty Hawk

Kill Devil Hills

Nags Head

Manteo

Wanchese

MARTIN WASHINGTON TYRRELL

DARE

CAPE

HATTERAS

BEAUFORT

HYDE

Swan
Quarter

Rodanthe
Waves
Salvo

NATIONAL

Pamlico Sound

Avon

SEASHORE

CRAVEN

PAMLICO

Hatteras

Buxton

Cape Hatteras

Cedar
Island

Ferry

Ocracoke

Portsmouth Island

JONES

Morehead City

Beaufort

Ferry

CAPE

LOOKOUT

Camp Lejeune
Marine Base

ONSLOW

CARTERET

Core Banks

NATIONAL

SEASHORE

Harkers Island

Cape Lookout

Fort Macon

Atlantic Beach

Pine Knoll Shores

Salter Path

Indian Beach

Emerald Isle

Swansboro

HAMMOCKS BEACH STATE PARK

North Topsail Beach

Surf City

Topsail Beach

Figure Eight Island

Wrightsville Beach

Masonboro Island

Carolina Beach

Kure Beach

Fort Fisher

Bald Head Island

PENDER

Wilmington

NEW
HANOVER

BRUNSWICK

Southport

Cape
Fear

Caswell Beach

Oak Island

Holden Beach

Ocean Isle Beach

Sunset Beach

Bird Island

MAP I

COASTAL

NORTH CAROLINA

N

MILES

0   20   40

Introduction

Welcome to the fourth edition of *North Carolina Beaches*, a companion for a journey along the state's 326-mile-long coast. North Carolina is blessed with a unique resource—a series of sandy peninsulas and barrier islands that stand offshore between the mainland and the Atlantic Ocean. A map shows how unusual this feature is compared to other southeastern coastal states: nowhere else in the nation do barrier beaches exist so distant from the mainland.

These barrier islands are the reasons for the great natural sounds, comparatively shallow bodies of water between the barrier islands and the mainland. North to south the sounds are Currituck, Albemarle, Roanoke, Croatan, Pamlico, Core, and Bogue Sound. Together these form the second-largest estuary in the nation, after the Chesapeake Bay. Land and water meet in an astonishing array of complex edge patterns: pine savannas, hardwood forests, sweeps of salt marsh, low and high swamps, and even abrupt bluffs touch the wide, brackish water of the sounds, bays, and estuaries.

The far-flung isles known as the Outer Banks, properly celebrated and widely known, are exceptional. The majority of North Carolina's ocean frontage is closer to the mainland and easily accessible. This book is about all the beaches near and far.

There are natural differences among the coast's many islands. There are differences, too, in those islands' communities. This book looks at the traits that give a location its personality—the natural setting, the architectural character, the recreational opportunities, the rhythm and pulse of daily life. These sorts of things add up to the tone and feeling of place, something that is difficult to determine from afar and even from online resources such as travel guides and real estate brochures. The intention of this book is to help in sifting through this type of material to provide a sense of place, perhaps enough to entice a visit. One place may be a great fit for some but not for others. The difference between a great vacation and a week at the beach is finding a place that pushes all the right buttons.

This edition mirrors the coast of 2018, where the pattern of islands and inlets remains just about the same as it was 15 years ago. A gull's-eye view of the coast reveals some inevitable, gradual change. Some inlets—Old Topsail, Corncake, and Mad Inlet—are permanently closed, and some parts of islands have gained sand, while parts of other islands battle chronic erosion that threatens roads and houses. (The widely reported formation of Shelly Island off Cape Point in Buxton in 2017 was certainly dramatic, but the island subsequently grafted to the point and "disappeared.")

What has changed the most is the growth of tourism and how communities and organizations have engaged with and responded to that growth. New cultural and educational venues have opened; existing venues have expanded or renovated facilities and programming. A wonderful example of this kind of outreach is that visitors can now climb all of the great lighthouses on the coast (don't tarry; arrive early). While some beach locations are sleepier than others, they generally offer more side trips and adventures to enjoy when not on the beach. Sadly, there are fewer fishing piers now, but each section of the coast has at least two options to enjoy this peaceful way to idle time—or just to go for a long walk.

Earlier editions emphasized public access locations because that information was not consistently available at every location. This is no longer the case. Resort communities recognize that public access and lifeguarded beaches are highly family friendly. Access information is readily available at every resort community, and general access information is included here. Since reliable access information is online, both relevant "Search" shortcuts and web addresses to online maps are listed (in the e-editions, these are hyperlinks).

There is an amazing amount of information online. Local tourism bureaus have splashy, informative websites that provide outstanding local guidance, as do real estate brokers. The web is a great way to find accommodations, dining, and recreation opportunities. General, reliable sites for tourism information are offered. Deference is given to local community websites, and the search criteria and addresses provided offer a solid starting point for a broader, personal research effort. The assumption is that public or municipal websites do not favor vendors but provide listings equitably.

WHAT'S IN THIS BOOK

The book proceeds from north to south along the coast from Virginia to South Carolina, organized by the eight coastal counties—Currituck, Dare, Hyde, Carteret, Onslow, Pender, New Hanover, and Brunswick—and two national seashores, Cape Hatteras and Cape Lookout. The seashores have listings distinct from their host counties and are placed in the book as they are encountered in north-to-south travel.

Each entry begins with a general county (or seashore) introduction, followed by a Search key listing websites for additional information. Access is briefly noted at the end of the text; a Search key is provided for access maps. The maps reveal the access site's location, the number of parking spaces, and other features.

The web addresses provided are linked to public agencies. Private websites are noted as such when no public websites are available. The list cannot possibly be all-inclusive, but is intended to be a filter to the most reliable website that can be available for follow-up queries.

Within each county, specific entries occur as they would during a north-to-south line of travel. The same hierarchy for additional information is used for each entry within a county. The Search entry is omitted if there is no corresponding website.

The maps correlate with the text, noting major landmarks, regional access sites, and the major routes serving a location. They should guide you directly to the places mentioned here.

Although every effort has been made to provide the most accurate, up-to-date information (particularly URL addresses), changes may of course occur after this book is published. Unfortunately, dates and hours of operation, admission fees, phone numbers, and other site-specific information can change as well. Clever searching on the internet may be the best way to confirm these details.

A FEW NOTES ON ACCESS

North Carolina provides grants to local communities to create or improve access locations as land becomes available. The North Carolina Division of Coastal Management provides an interactive map online locating and describing access locations along the entire coast. (To see the map, search NC Beach Access; click the NC DEQ Beach and Waterfront Access Map link; at the bottom of the second column, click "Go to Beach Access Locator"; zoom in to find access sites.)

The access site hierarchy is:

Regional access sites. These are the largest, with parking for 40 to 200 cars, restrooms, outside showers, a gazebo or seating area, a dune crossover (a controlled route through the dunes) with access ramp, beach lifeguards in summer, and accessible to all users. (Easy to find; in summer, arrive early.)

Neighborhood access sites. Midsize, with parking for 10 to 50 cars, a dune crossover, and trash receptacles. Lifeguards availability varies by municipality.

Local access sites. For neighborhoods. Limited if any parking. A dune crossover.

Mobility-impaired or wheelchair access. Regional access sites are fully accessible, as are all National Park Service Visitor Centers. All North Carolina Ferry Terminals are accessible, and most sound crossing vessels are too, but it is best to confirm accessibility when making ferry reservations.

Most resort communities can provide a wide-wheeled chair suitable for the beach with advance notice. Check with the local fire department or emergency response office for availability.

Access North Carolina. Search Access in North Carolina, choose the www.nc.gov/services/access-north-carolina site, then click the www.ncdhhs .gov/document/access-north-carolina link for a PDF file detailing the accessibility of public parks, recreation areas, tourism destinations, and historic sites across the state.

PARKS, PRESERVES, RESERVES, AND REFUGES

Many government agencies and some private organizations have landholdings on the coast. Nearly all of them welcome visitors. Some have interpretive facilities and regular programming, while others have few roads and only restricted or difficult access. These properties provide a different perspective because of their natural, historical, and cultural importance. They have separate listings in the text.

Cape Hatteras and Cape Lookout National Seashores are the most prominent public lands on the coast. Between them, they protect nearly one-half of the state's oceanfront mileage.

The U.S. Fish and Wildlife Service has its North Carolina Coastal Plain

Refuge Complex in Manteo. This office overseas multiple coastal wildlife refuges, five of which—Mackay Island, Currituck, Alligator River, Pea Island, and Cedar Island—abut the North Carolina coast. Several others, such as Mattamuskeet, Pocosin Lakes, and Swanquarter National Wildlife Refuge, are easily visited en route.

The U.S. Department of Defense has huge acreage in its military bases, target ranges, and landing fields. The largest is the Marine Corps Base Camp Lejeune and New River Air Station at Jacksonville. There is also Cherry Point Marine Air Station at Havelock. The multiservice target range at Stumpy Point and the Naval Auxiliary Landing Field at Bogue can provide some high-energy entertainment when in use. Visitation policies at the military sites vary.

The U.S. Coast Guard maintains active bases to serve the state's major inlets. The coast guard stations are open to the public and occasionally offer programs. Oregon Inlet Station is worth approaching just to see the main building's historically respectful architecture. The coast guard also maintains the lights in the lighthouses.

The State of North Carolina manages five parks, seven natural areas, three aquariums, one pier, four maritime museums, four historic sites, and an underwater archaeological preserve. It also manages 10 reserves under the supervision of the North Carolina Coastal Reserve system, a little-known but very successful state program established to protect the wild and natural coast.

The reserve system originated in 1982, when the National Oceanic and Atmospheric Administration (NOAA) funded five years of acquisition for the National Estuarine Sanctuary Program. In North Carolina, NOAA accepted four sites: Currituck Banks, Rachel Carson, Masonboro Island, and Zeke's Island. In 1988 this program became the National Estuarine Research Reserve, which managed the use of the lands for research, education, and compatible recreational activities. Each is a walk on the wilder side of the coast.

BICYCLING OPTIONS

North Carolina's coast is great country for cycling, and the state is actively involved in roadway improvements to make cycling safer. The resort communities are well aware of how bicycling is both a family activity and a safe and easy way to explore locally.

Paved recreational trails thread through the communities, so bringing bicycles will not be a wasted effort. There are plenty of vendors offering bicycles to rent for the day if bringing bikes from home is not practical.

Longer trips, such as bicycling the Outer Banks, present different challenges, particularly given the heat and traffic of summer. NC 12, the highway serving the Outer Banks, is frighteningly narrow (there are bicycle side trails in Rodanthe and Avon) and throbbing with vacation traffic hurtling along. While experienced cyclists may be able to adjust expectations to these conditions, choosing another time of year might make such a trip safer and more enjoyable. Spring and fall months offer a better mix of cooler temperatures and lower traffic for Outer Banks roads.

The North Carolina Department of Transportation Division of Bicycle and Pedestrian Transportation provides an online map that highlights recommended bicycle routes statewide. The details of the routing may be printed from the website. Five out of eight designated bicycling trails make use of highways passing through coastal locations. These include portions of the Mountains to Sea, Ports of Call, Cape Fear Run, Ocracoke Option, and North Line Trace Trails.

The Interactive Bicycle Route website is www.ncdot.gov/bikeped/nc bikeways/. Select a numbered trip, then use the "Plan Your Trip" highlighted bar to switch to an interactive map for each numbered route. Highlight the route segment to print the detailed directions. The longest coastal bicycling route is the Ports of Call route, which covers portions of the historic colonial trade routes from South Carolina to Virginia.

Social network websites are also excellent sources of detailed bicycle route information. Map My Ride (www.mapmyride.com/us/nc/) and Strava (www.strava.com) are two such sites that provide routing information.

BEACH RIGHTS ISSUES

Although a landowner may legally deny access across his or her property to the beach, when on the beach, there is a clear, legal right to be there. North Carolina case law has repeatedly upheld the right of citizens to use the "foreshore," that is, the wet sand beach, which is covered by the reach of high tide and exposed by the retreat of low tide. This portion of the oceanfront is reserved by the doctrine of public trust for the use of all. A 1983 ruling of the North Carolina Supreme Court reaffirmed this principle: "The longstanding right of the public to pass over and along the strip of land lying between the high-water mark and low-water mark adjacent to respondents' property is established beyond the need of citation. In North Carolina private property fronting coastal water ends at the high-water mark and the property lying between the high-water mark and the low-water mark known as the 'foreshore' is the property of the state."

In December 2016, the North Carolina Supreme Court dismissed an oceanfront homeowner's appeal of a unanimous North Carolina Court of Appeals ruling in favor of the state. The plaintiff had sued, contending that the Town of Emerald Isle regulation forbidding permanent structures in an area 20 feet seaward from the base of the primary dunes amounted to an illegal taking. The Court of Appeals judges who heard the case stated that the "public right of access to dry sand beaches in North Carolina is so firmly rooted in the custom and history of North Carolina that it has become a part of the public consciousness."

This ruling not only ended a specific case affecting Emerald Isle but also is an important affirmation of the doctrine of public trust along the coast.

OUTER BANKS ORIGINS

What makes the Outer Banks geologically special is their distance from the mainland. Most barrier islands on the East Coast are closer, and their origin, shape, and existence are better understood. The geological story of the Outer Banks is more complicated.

Around the world, barrier islands exist wherever any gently sloping coastal plain borders the ocean. In the United States, every southeastern state has barrier islands. Exceptions to this rule (along South Carolina's Grand Strand, for example) are unusual.

Coastal geologists theorize that the ancient Outer Banks formed when the gradually rising sea level forced a landward migration of ancient dune ridges that had become islands. The island building probably began approximately 12,000 years ago, after the last period of massive glaciers. Sea level may have been as much as 200 feet lower than today, and our prehistoric beaches at least 90 miles east.

The melting glaciers raised sea level steadily, and as sea level climbed, the shoreline inched landward, moving vast quantities of sand before it in the form of beach deposits. River sediments from coastal plain deltas were pulled into the wave zone and also moved along the shore. Eventually the sea level rise slowed, and by 4,000 to 5,000 years ago—the start of the

Holocene, an age of comparative stability—it was within a few meters of the present level.

Sea level remained steady during this period, and wind and waves shaped these masses of sand and sediment into the precursors of our present barrier islands. At that time, in the early Holocene, these islands were considerably wider than they are today. Landward of the prehistoric beach was a gently sloping, forested coastal plain carved by the Cape Fear, Neuse, Tar, Roanoke, and Chowan Rivers and their principal tributaries.

Two thousand years ago, sea level began to rise again, though at a much slower rate. The ocean breached the formative barrier islands to flood the forested coastal plain and the floodplains of the ancient coastal riverbeds. This breach and flooding created the sounds.

This hypothesis, known as "barrier ridge drowning," seems to explain the geological idiosyncrasies of the Outer Banks. Fossils of an extinct species of oyster that lived in brackish water have been recovered on the ocean side of the barrier islands. The likely reason is that the islands migrated gradually landward over once-inland oyster beds. Also, the mainland coast has the intricate patterning characteristic of flooded river valleys.

The islands "migrated" landward, retreating before the rising sea level. This sequence of steps is repeated today, and we can see it in the sharp cut of a sand dune or a fan of sand spreading into an inland marsh after a storm has surged over an island. When the ocean breaches the islands, it fills in the shallow sound waters with sand and sediment. If left alone, this new fill will support pioneering vegetation and with enough time will become forested. Wind and waves push the dune line landward: the wind blows the dune sand, and it covers the established forest (as happens on the west side of Jockey's Ridge State Park), filling in the soundside marsh. Think of a Slinky crawling over itself down a flight of stairs. In a similar set of movements, the entire barrier island rolls over, retreating before the rising sea.

Over decades (though sometimes overnight), the shape of an entire island may change. Ironically, without a fixed reference, such as houses or lighthouses, islands would appear stationary and unchanged. If nobody lived on an island and it migrated naturally, would anybody notice or care?

On barrier islands, "permanent" is a relative term, and over decades, houses, docks, roads, and even lighthouses serve as landmarks to the coastal movement. Geological processes push against permanence and vividly illustrate that people are renters, not owners. The Cape Hatteras Lighthouse ruled 1,800 feet of beach in 1870, but by the 1990s it had to be moved.

At present, scientists can document that sea level is rising at a rate far faster than has been previously observed. This acceleration is caused by a rise in the general global average temperature that is sufficient to cause melting of global ice fields and glaciers. These incremental changes in sea level can have profound effects on the nearly flat slope of North Carolina's coastal plain, where an inch of sea level rise can result in many feet of mainland drowning. (See "Just What Is Level about the Sea?" [p. 55]). While we may cling to our castles built on these magnificent sands, unless we commit to change as a global community, all we can do is rail at the heavens in protest.

COASTAL HISTORICAL TOUCHSTONES

When the first English-speaking peoples attempted settlement on Roanoke Island in 1585, Native Americans had fished, hunted, and farmed on nearly every island along the coast. Because they had no written language, they left no written record. Our knowledge of them comes from either firsthand accounts of explorers or the investigations of archaeologists and anthropologists.

John White, an artist on the 1585 expedition who documented in drawings the first glimpse of the New World, reported more than 20 Native American villages near Roanoke Island. These were most likely allied with or related to the Hatteras tribe, the first group to meet the European explorers and settlers. According to White, the Native Americans cleared villages out of the maritime forests of the islands. They centered the village on a sweat lodge, which served as a common gathering place. Evidence favors the theory that while these local peoples were self-sufficient and traded minimally, the sounds and rivers in no way restricted their mobility.

The English settlement attempts followed Spanish efforts. Spain had an early advantage exploring and settling what would become North Carolina. In 1520, Pedro de Quexoia sailed to the Cape Fear region. A passenger on that voyage, Lucas Vázquez de Ayllón, returned in 1526 with 500 men, women, slaves, and livestock to settle the "Rio Jordan," thought to be the Cape Fear River. In the face of disease, the settlement soon withdrew to the South Carolina coast, but illness killed Ayllón in October 1526, and the 150 survivors boarded ships and sailed to Santo Domingo.

In 1524, Florentine navigator Giovanni da Verrazano recorded the first exploration of the North Carolina coast. He landed in the Cape Fear region and made detailed observations as far north as Hatteras, producing a glowing report for Francis I of France. In 1582, Englishman Richard Hakluyt published the account under the title *Divers Voyages touching the Discoverie of America and Islands Adjacent.*

Hakluyt's report sparked English ambition for the profitable possibilities in the "New World." On March 25, 1584, Queen Elizabeth I granted Sir Walter Raleigh a patent for the exclusive rights to and rewards of a New World colony. Raleigh secured investors and supplied a two-ship expedition commanded by Philip Amadas and Arthur Barlowe and piloted by the Portuguese navigator Simón Fernandez. The expedition entered Pamlico Sound through "Wococon" Inlet (present-day Ocracoke Inlet) on July 4, 1584. Barlowe soon sailed north to an island Native Americans called "Roanoke." The first encounter with Native Americans went well, and on the expedition's return to England, Manteo and Wanchese sailed along, becoming the first Native Americans to visit England.

Barlowe's subsequent report fired Raleigh's appetite for colonization of the area, which by now had been named "Virginia" in honor of the unwed Elizabeth I. He found new investors, and on April 9, 1585, Sir Richard Grenville set sail from Plymouth, with Ralph Lane along as "lieutenant gourvernour," in a fleet of seven ships with 108 men. The fleet reached Hatteras on July 22, 1585, and by August 17 had disembarked on Roanoke Island. Ten months later, Sir Francis Drake evacuated the colony, which was pressed for food and supplies and beset by deteriorating relations with the indigenous peoples. He left behind 18 men to guard the fort they had built.

The Lane group's report intrigued Raleigh, who again organized an expedition. This attempt would differ by attempting to farm and build a community in the deepwater region of Chesapeake Bay. Raleigh enlisted John White, the artist of the 1585 expedition, as "Governor" of the "Citie of Ralegh in Virginia." Women, children, livestock, and supplies were part of this package.

Raleigh's "second colonie" left England in the spring of 1587 led by the *Admirall*, piloted by Fernandez, a temperamental personality who clashed with White about continuing to the Chesapeake Bay. They reached Hatteras on July 22, 1587, and quickly proceeded to Roanoke Island to pick up Grenville's men, but they had disappeared and the fort was destroyed. Fernandez refused to sail north as planned, so White ordered the colonists to disembark on Roanoke Island.

It was a struggle from the start, but not without its joys and benchmarks. On August 18, White's daughter Eleanor and her husband, Ananias Dare, gave birth to Virginia, the first child of English-speaking parents born in the New World. But the colony quickly ran low on food. White reluctantly agreed to sail to England for provisions, and the colonists promised to leave a sign if they abandoned Roanoke Island.

White returned to the threat of European war and could not sail again to Roanoke Island until 1590. There he found the settlement in disarray and the letters CRO, believed to indicate the Indian village of Croatan, carved in a tree. The colonists were never found; the colony was lost. (In 2016, archaeological evidence inland revealed artifacts consistent with a relocation of some of the colonists.) White returned to England, and colonization attempts on North Carolina soil ended. In 1607 colonization successfully shifted north to Jamestown in the Chesapeake region.

North Carolina's population grew slowly, disadvantaged by treacherous ocean waters, shoaling inlets, shallow sounds, and the lack of deepwater ports except for the Cape Fear River. Early settlement spilled over from Virginia, where there was reliable deepwater access.

The oldest communities in the state were settled along the sounds in the eighteenth century. The town of Bath incorporated in 1706, followed by New Bern in 1710 and Beaufort in 1723; each was a port town with no reliable access to the open ocean.

Pirates plagued the coast early on: Stede Bonnett and Edward Teach, better known as Blackbeard, had their pirating terminated on the North Carolina coast. Blackbeard's flagship, the *Queen Anne's Revenge*, sunk off of Beaufort Inlet, is a National Historic Landmark and a star exhibit at the North Carolina Maritime Museum in Beaufort.

Growth quickened in the Cape Fear River region at Brunswick, established in 1725, and Wilmington, established around 1735. As early as 1732, the population of Brunswick was 1,200. Wilmington thrived on its deepwater port. Newcomers pushed inland.

The coastal region continued to grow and prosper, tied firmly to dependence on agriculture, large landholding patterns, and slave labor. Agriculture, timber products (particularly naval stores), and fishing became the economy of eastern North Carolina until the Civil War.

By 1861 North Carolina had two major ports, Wilmington and Morehead City, each linked to the Piedmont by rail. Fort Macon guarded the channel serving Morehead City and was quickly seized by the Confederacy. Confederate forces moved swiftly to construct Fort Fisher in order to secure the more reliable deepwater port of the Cape Fear River.

Union ships blockaded the North Carolina coast beginning around 1862, but the erratic shoreline provided refuge for shallow-draft blockade-runners that smuggled arms and supplies across the sounds. There were skirmishes along the Outer Banks at Hatteras Island, and Roanoke Island was captured in 1862. The famous Union ironclad ship *Monitor* swamped while being towed from Hampton Roads, Virginia, and sank offshore from Cape Hatteras; it has been located, and archaeological recovery operations continue.

In the 1870s, the sparsely populated barrier islands caught the eye of two different groups of people: wealthy northern industrialists and mariners who sailed the outlying waters. The industrialists discovered the seasonal waterfowl populations in Currituck and Pamlico Sounds and purchased thousands of acres for private sport.

Meanwhile, the loss of life due to shipwrecks spurred the federal government to improve the lighthouses and to establish the U.S. Life-Saving Service. Beginning with the first stations in 1874, the lifesaving service eventually established a network along the entire length of North Carolina's barrier islands. The stations and their crews (and the post offices that followed) put the barrier island hamlets on the official U.S. postal map. Their rescues became the stuff of legend on the Outer Banks.

In 1900 two brothers named Wright arrived from Ohio and began their quest for heavier-than-air flight at Kitty Hawk.

Significant change came to the Outer Banks with the bridges and ferries of the 1930s and the beginning of World War II. Through 1942, German U-boats ravaged merchant shipping off Cape Hatteras, giving the area the nickname "Torpedo Junction." After the war, new bridges, the increasingly commonplace automobile, more leisure time, inexpensive land, and a solidly growing economy started the second wave of settlement on the barrier islands.

HIGHWAYS TO THE COAST

I-95 is the major north–south interstate in eastern North Carolina. There are easy connections to US 158, US 64, US 264, US 70, and I-40, the east–west routes serving the coast.

From Raleigh, I-40 runs nearly due south to Wilmington. North Carolina Highways 24, 41, 50, 55, 111, and 210 intersect I-40 and go to the coast. Older routes—US 421 south from Dunn, NC 87 from Fayetteville, and NC 211 from Lumberton—are lazier and less monotonous, but still lead to the coast.

Travelers starting in Virginia take US 17 south to Elizabeth City before following the northern edge of Albemarle Sound to New Bern. From South Carolina, it moves inland to Wilmington and then parallels the coast as far north as Jacksonville. This route threads through the historical heart of coastal North Carolina. The appeal of history makes the route worthy of its own tour.

US 158 and US 64/264 serve the Outer Banks. US 158 intersects I-95 at Roanoke Rapids and goes to the Currituck mainland. This is a scenic, usually lightly traveled road until Elizabeth City. East of Elizabeth City, at Barco, US 158 merges with NC 168 from Virginia, and traffic thickens noticeably. The road turns south, crosses the Intracoastal Waterway at Coinjock, and heads to the Wright Memorial Bridge and the Outer Banks.

US 64 intersects I-95 west of Rocky Mount, 136 miles from Manteo. The road is the major east–west artery from the Piedmont, linking Raleigh with Manteo and the beaches of Dare County. It is the fastest route from the North Carolina Piedmont cities to the Outer Banks.

US 264 sort of parallels US 64 as it sweeps along the mainland adjacent to Pamlico Sound. It is lightly traveled and offers an alternate route to Manteo from cities south of Washington and Greenville. It passes through several wildlife refuges and winds near Bath, a refreshing historical side trip. US 264 also passes Swan Quarter, where there is a ferry depot to Ocracoke.

The major highway to Carteret County and Cape Lookout National Seashore is US 70, which links with I-95 20 miles west of Goldsboro. This is an excellent, well-traveled route. East of Beaufort, US 70 becomes part of the Outer Banks National Scenic Byway and is a route with extraordinary panoramas. It sweeps through the farms and woodlands of Carteret County, linking up with NC 12 for the trip to Cedar Island and the ferry to Ocracoke.

Travelers on US 70 going to southern Carteret County or the Onslow or Pender County resorts should use US 258 or US 58 from Kinston. US 258 goes to Jacksonville to connect with US 17 or NC 24; US 58 is a "blue highway" alternative from Kinston to Bogue Banks and can be crowded on summer weekends.

Licenses and Permits

Two traditional North Carolina beach activities, fishing and driving on the beach, are still permitted but with restrictions and legal requirements.

FISHING All anglers 16 years and older must have a saltwater recreational fishing license. This license is also required for crabbing, cast netting, and oyster and clam gathering. Everybody in a boat with fishing tackle should probably have a license. Also, carry another form of identification, such as a driver's license.

See "Hook, Line, and Rulebook" (p. 259) for more details.

The licensing agencies are at these websites: www.ncwildlife.org
/Licensing/Licenses-and-Regulations; portal.ncdenr.org
/web/mf/recreational-fishing-licenses-and-permits.

DRIVING ON THE BEACH Any vehicle to be driven on the beach must comply with all relevant vehicle licensing, inspection, and insurance requirements. Any driver must be licensed. All North Carolina motor vehicle laws apply to driving on the beach.

See "Rods, Reels, 'n' Wheels: Driving on North Carolina Beaches" (p. 24) for extensive details.

Nearly every resort community or land management agency permits driving on the beach with a proper local permit. The cost of the permit varies from community to agency. Most beaches are closed to motor vehicles during the summer months and during the nesting season for pelagic turtles, from April 1 until October 1. Cape Hatteras and Cape Lookout National Seashore permit driving but will restrict access as needed to protect wildlife and the habitat. ORV permits may be purchased at all National Park Visitors Centers or online at https://www.recreation.gov.

Inquire about local permits at town offices.

Currituck County

CURRITUCK COUNTY, the state's northeasternmost county, has almost 27 miles of nearly wild and wildly popular coastline. This sandy magnet for vacationers extends south from the Virginia border as a narrow, windswept, and once nearly desolate peninsula, a barrier between Currituck Sound and the Atlantic Ocean.

In one generation—since 1984, when NC 12 was paved to the center peninsula community of Corolla—the entire character of this oceanfront transformed from remote and unpopulated to one of the most seasonally populated and sought-after beach destinations in the state. More has changed on Currituck Banks in the last two decades of the twentieth century than did in perhaps the previous two centuries.

Such rapid development can sometimes be jarring, but the Currituck oceanfront remains highly appealing. The almost continuous single-family resort developments are sufficiently sequestered behind native vegetation to soften the passage along the two lanes of NC 12, the only road serving Currituck's banks.

To be sure, there are lots of houses, but for the most part the Currituck oceanfront doesn't look like a group of subdivisions plopped on a beach. Add to this surprisingly nestled appearance some particular attractions— the easy access to water recreation on the sound and oceanfront, some one-of-a-kind historical attractions, and the romantic allure of driving on the beach—and the vacation appeal beckons far and wide.

The vacation center is Corolla (pronounced "*Cuh*-rah-la," accent on the first syllable), a village about 24 miles north of the Wright Memorial Bridge and at the approximate midpoint of the Currituck Banks. Twenty-four miles does not seem like a great distance, but the traffic can be demoralizing in high summer "change-over days," when the seasonal renters come and go. State highway officials seek to reinstate active planning for a 7-mile, two-lane Mid-Currituck Toll Bridge crossing Currituck Sound between Aydlett on the mainland to a location south of Corolla. Completion is not likely until early in the 2020s.

Still, for all the crowding even on the nonroad parts of the barrier, known as the 4x4 (Four-Wheel-Drive or 4WD) Beaches, the famed "wild horses" of Currituck still roam freely, a concession to history and tourism appeal. Even with the ongoing press of development, extensive acreage of Currituck's banks remain as wild as they have ever been: there are immense actively moving sand dunes, thickets of stable maritime forest, and thousands of acres of marshy wetlands.

Those marshy wetlands edge the waters of Currituck Sound. This shallow embayment, approximately 30 miles long by 4 miles wide at its greatest width, is the central physical feature here. It has jigsawed the geography into three distinct parts: the mainland to the west of the sound, Knotts Island protruding into the north-central waters, and the peninsula barrier oceanfront.

Traditional livelihoods in Currituck—before tourism—were often a blend of mainland agriculture supplemented by the waterman's life of fishing and hunting in Currituck Sound. This pattern held well into the seventh decade of the twentieth century, a function of the then-clear shallow water favoring the growth of aquatic herbs and grasses that provided superb habitat for fish and excellent forage for waterfowl. Native Americans ordered their lives on the abundant natural resources, establishing permanent and temporary settlements here. The county name is a corruption of the Algonquian word *coratank* (wild geese).

European settlers followed the Algonquin pattern of farming, fishing, and hunting. Although fully one-sixth of the Atlantic Flyway's migratory waterfowl population comes to Currituck County in fall and winter, the numbers pale next to those of the nineteenth century. Starting in the mid-1800s, locals hunted or guided for a living and wealthy sportsmen from across the nation purchased land and marsh for pleasure hunting.

By the early twentieth century, private hunt clubs owned much of the 27-mile peninsula barrier beach between the Virginia state line and Duck in Dare County. Remnants of these extensive holdings became the core lands of the several national wildlife refuges and private refuges that comprise much of the open space on the Currituck Banks. The story is wonderfully recounted in a must-visit attraction: the Outer Banks Center for Wildlife Education in Corolla.

It may seem unlikely today, but Currituck oceanfront land primarily served as open range for grazing livestock owned by the few people who lived here in the nineteenth and early twentieth centuries, when this setting was still very remote. Before the hunt clubs employed residents as caretakers, cooks, and guides, the only steady paycheck on the oceanfront came by working for the U.S. Lighthouse Service or as a surfman at one of the four stations built by U.S. Life-Saving Service (a forerunner of the U.S. Coast Guard).

The peculiarities of North Carolina geography and demographics place the mainland portion of Currituck County "out of the way" for most North

Carolina residents who want to visit the county beaches. The two main highways, NC 168 and US 158, link and course directly along the high, well-drained agricultural land between Currituck Sound to the east and the swamps of the North Landing River to the west. These roads are the commercial lifeline of the county, carrying goods, services, and vacationers to and from Tidewater Virginia. In summer, vehicles on these roads sport license plates from Virginia to Pennsylvania and New York passing through on the way to the Outer Banks beaches.

Services along these roads cater to residents of the local communities but also provide seasonal produce shopping for vacationers. A summertime stop can offer a bounty of farm-to-market produce. In 2017 an expansive water park opened at Powell's Point, perhaps the vanguard recreational enterprise marking a change in the type of commerce along this primary route to the vacation beaches. Closer to the Virginia border, mainland Currituck has a rural, agricultural character peppered with local community services and few enterprises serving vacationers. At the southern end of the mainland, commercial ventures are definitely geared to vacation traffic. The drive south from Virginia on NC 168 and US 158 reveals the still-rural feeling of the mainland but has come to be treated more like a passageway. The resonant community names—Moyock, Sligo, Currituck, Maple, and Barco, among others—punctuate the passage with a singsong cadence. The older commercial hearts and history of these communities can be glimpsed along the passage.

Knotts Island, in north central Currituck, is a county outlier. It is actually a peninsula extending southeast from Virginia. All roads tie it to that state; its link to mainland North Carolina is principally by boat or an absolutely delightful ferry. The island is two-thirds marsh, most of which is Mackay Island National Wildlife Refuge, and one-third coastal plain forest and farmland. It is sleepy, quiet, very flat, and filled with possibilities for fishing, hiking, wildlife viewing, and bicycle riding.

The beaches of Currituck County gained popularity because they had fewer houses and even fewer year-round residents. But the isolation fueling part of that appeal vanishes in high summer. The summer rental success impedes convenient access to goods and services: that is, the goods and services that exist here are not always immediately or easily accessible. It can be really crowded. Traffic does not move at internet speeds in July and August: travel time to reach Corolla destinations can dissolve eager anticipation into a puddle of frustrated resolve, particularly when it comes, as it frequently does, at the end of a long drive from, say, the Northeast. Many folks believe that the destination definitely rewards the journey. There is plenty of space to spread a towel and much more to see and do when you finally arrive. In July and August, this is a good thought to keep in mind.

Search Visit Currituck or enter www.visitcurrituck.com.

For Your Bucket:
> Climb the Currituck Beach Lighthouse
> Visit the Outer Banks Center for Wildlife Education
> Tour the Whalehead Club
> See the wild horses of Corolla
> Ride the ferry to Knotts Island
> See the snow geese at MacKay Island (winter)
> Kayak or canoe Currituck Sound

KNOTTS ISLAND

At the north end of Currituck County, surrounded by the waters of Back Bay to the north, Knotts Island Channel and Bay to the east, and the North Landing River to the west, is the peninsula Knotts Island. It is an overlooked and underappreciated corner of North Carolina, served only by ferry from the mainland town of Currituck or by road from Virginia. It is possible but highly improbable to stumble upon Knotts Island. One has to aim to get there, and any trip will bring particular low-key rewards.

To configure the geography further: Princess Anne Road from Virginia becomes NC 615 at the North Carolina state line. It crosses a waterway known as Corey's Ditch, a narrow tidal creek linking the North Landing River and Back Bay, the western and northern estuaries surrounding the high ground of Knotts Island. That tidal creek makes it an island.

Most of the island's high acreage, forested or farmed or residential, is along the eastern third, fronting Knotts Island Channel and Knotts Island Bay. The larger part of the peninsula is marshland, the highly valuable waterfowl habitat that comprises the Mackay Island National Wildlife Refuge. The land is flat, the roads well-paved, and the island drivers courteous. In fact, NC 615 from the Virginia Line to the ferry terminus on the island is part of

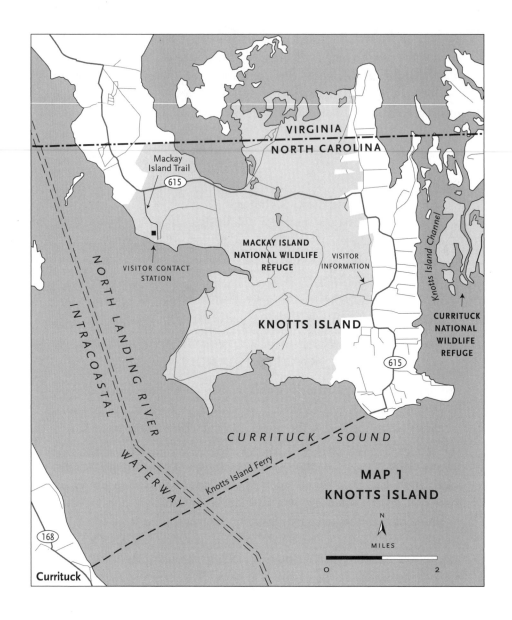

MAP 1
KNOTTS ISLAND

the North Line Trace, a North Carolina Department of Transportation Bike Route, which highlights passage through the wildlife refuge.

The settled part of the island includes a post office, several small stores, an elementary school, a beautiful white wooden United Methodist church, and a mix of residences and second homes placed among farmed or wooded land. It has a settled rural character, and the fewer, newer second homes are obvious. There is a community park with water access off of Brimley Road, and off of Parker Road there is a large Zen garden sponsored by the International Federation of Yoga Teachers. It is a young garden and a curiosity.

Knotts Island is a tight-knit community. As described by a member of the ferry crew, people are either "Been Heres or Come Heres"—that is, folks with a long island lineage or the recently moved.

Even though the island sits in a direct line for the sprawl of Virginia Beach, it still has the feeling of a waterman's island: quaint, literally and figuratively insular, and charming for its out-of-the-mainstream perseverance in a simpler pace of life. The number of Virginia commuters is increasing, but many of these are islanders pursuing better jobs in Tidewater Virginia. Corey's Ditch, humble though it is, seems to be an effective moat . . .

Essential equipment for a Knotts Island outing might be a bicycle, binoculars, hiking/running shoes, and a small pack to carry water. There are guide services to host fishing and hunting trips, and there's a pick-your-own peach orchard with a vineyard. The ferry ride to the island is delightful; the multiple twists and turns to drive to the island from North Carolina wind through gorgeous marsh and river land and by large farms. There is no urban life on Knotts Island, and that is its own reward.

Knotts Island is easily reached by free ferry from Currituck. Driving directions that weave a course through beautiful Tidewater farms and woods in Virginia and North Carolina are below. The directions begin on NC 168 at Currituck.

> Head north on NC 168 through Moyock, to the Expressway stoplight
> Right turn onto Gallbush Road; travel 1.6 miles
> Left turn onto Sanderson Road; travel 0.8 miles
> Right turn onto Hungarian Road; travel 2.6 miles
> Left turn onto Blackwater Road; travel 0.8 miles
> Right turn onto Pungo Ferry Road: travel 2.7 miles
> Right turn onto Princess Anne Road: travel 4.8 miles
> Virginia/North Carolina State line: enter Knotts Island
> (It is 9.0 miles from here to the ferry dock.)

KNOTTS ISLAND FREE FERRY

The free ferry between Knotts Island and the Currituck mainland holds approximately 20–22 cars. In 1984 the ferry was literally cut in half and expanded to include a large weatherproof cabin for the Knotts Island children who attend upper schools on the mainland. Accordingly, the ferry schedule reflects the school calendar. Boarding is first-come, first-served from a new ferry visitor center in Currituck. The location is clearly signed from NC 168.

The ride takes 50 minutes and provides total decompression, with distant views of the Currituck Banks and close-up views of nesting ospreys. During the school year, from Monday to Friday there are six round-trip departures from Currituck beginning at 6 AM and ending at 5:30 PM. Knotts Island returns depart approximately 1 hour later. The summer schedule of five round trips begins June 9 and continues through August 6, with the first Currituck departure at 6 AM and the last at 4:30 PM. Knotts Island returns are adjusted accordingly.

Search NC Ferry or enter www.ncdot.gov/divisions/ferry.

MACKAY ISLAND NATIONAL WILDLIFE REFUGE

A boat and binoculars may be the best equipment to bring to Mackay Island National Wildlife Refuge. No boat? A bicycle and binoculars is perhaps the next-best combination, but binoculars and good hiking boots do the trick as well. The distant corners and wildlife of this magnificent preserve are better brought into view by binoculars, and the various transportation options help you discover its more than 12 square miles of multiple habitats. There are many places that cars cannot go.

Mackay Island National Wildlife Refuge is a big place encompassing the northern and western two-thirds of Knotts Island. The 8,219 acres (854 acres of marsh are in Virginia) are a mosaic of several coastal plain ecotypes: tidal freshwater marsh, moist soil flatland, estuarine fringe loblolly forest, and the more familiar coastal plain pine flatlands, with its mix of pine, maple, sweet gum, and American holly.

More than 180 species of birds have been sighted at Mackay Island, including a spectacular wintering population of greater snow geese. The waterfowl season begins populating in late December. The snow geese, which feed voraciously on all types and parts of vegetation, settle in for the winter along with black ducks and some tundra swans.

The practical northern limit of the refuge is the NC 615 causeway, the main road to Knotts Island and one of the best locations for bird-watching. The roadway passes through the vast expansive stretches of tawny marsh grass. An elevated viewing stand that is part of the commemorative Charles Kuralt Trail is beside the causeway in a fine location for viewing the marsh ponds to the north and south, which quack and honk with ducks and geese beginning in fall. The Great Marsh Trail, located along the causeway, is a one-third-mile loop for year-round hiking and bird-watching. The refuge office is located off of NC 615 and is open all year, 8 AM to 4:30 PM weekdays.

White-tailed deer, raccoon, nutria, and mink are also resident. The management team permits limited trapping and hunting within the refuge to manage populations. The refuge is closed to nonhunting activities on hunting days. The schedule of closure is posted on the refuge website. Hunters must have all necessary licenses and permits.

History stands tall here, as the core of the refuge holdings came indirectly from the estate of Joseph Palmer Knapp, publisher and outdoor sportsman. In the early twentieth century Knapp constructed a mansion, since torn down, overlooking the North Landing River on Mackay Island and spent many winter hours hunting and fishing Currituck Sound. He was a great benefactor to the county and its people and maintained an environmental vigil over the shallow sound waters. Committed to conservation and game management, he established the More Game Birds in America Foundation in 1930. This organization evolved into Ducks Unlimited.

Visitors may drive the Mackay Island Road and walk or bicycle the Mackay Island Trail (4 miles) or the Live Oak Point Trail (6.5 miles) from March 15 to October 15 during daylight hours.

Search Mackay Island Refuge or enter www.fws.gov/refuge/Mackay_Island.

4X4 BEACHES

Once literally and figuratively the end of the road, the North Beach Access Ramp, where the NC 12 pavement stops, is today the beginning of a wonderful adventure. The North Beach Ramp provides entry to Currituck's highly popular 4x4 Beaches. No other stretch of the North Carolina coast offers such an unusual combination of separation, wildness, and surprising luxury.

It is visually stunning—a smooth strand, varying in width with the tide cycle, backed by a substantial dune line, a welcome relic constructed in the early twentieth century. Landward of the dunes there is the thick vegetation

Rods, Reels, 'n' Wheels:
Driving on North Carolina Beaches

Driving on the beach is part of beach recreation in North Carolina. It is an inseparable part of surf fishing, indispensable on the many miles of both national seashores. Most drivers are laser-focused, well-intended anglers, and their vehicle is their tackle shop/campsite on wheels.

Beach driving is generally allowed, but there can be calendar restrictions and closures to protect beach-nesting wildlife. Cape Hatteras and Cape Lookout National Seashores, which have the greatest lengths of drivable beach, frequently have seasonal and wildlife restrictions.

Here's where it gets serious. **All North Carolina motor vehicle laws apply to driving on the beach**—every one of them, including the requirement of wearing a seat belt and the prohibition on open alcoholic beverages in the cab of the car. The vehicle must be registered, currently licensed, and inspected. The driver must have a valid driver's license or learning permit and must carry minimum liability insurance.

Most municipalities and government agencies require permits and have access limitations and restrictions. Oceanfront municipalities usually forbid beach driving within a time window between April and November. Government and agency websites will post their regulations on relevant websites or publish these in tourism material.

Areas that permit year-round access (and may post some seasonal restrictions) include Currituck's 4x4 Beaches, north of Corolla; Cape Hatteras and Cape Lookout National Seashores; Carolina Beach Freeman Park (local permit required); and Fort Fisher State Recreation Area (permit required).

CURRITUCK COUNTY Visitors and residents must drive on the beach north of Corolla in Currituck County to reach rental homes along the isolated waterfront. The county is serious about beach driving safety. Here is an abbreviated version of the current regulations and recommendations.

- The beach is regarded by the state as an unpaved portion of NC 12. It is a state-recognized "road" or Public Vehicular Area (PVA).
- The vehicle must be registered, properly licensed, and insured to legally drive on the beach or on the roads behind the dunes.
- All motor vehicle laws apply, including age restrictions and DWI thresholds.

- The speed limit on the beaches of Corolla is 35 mph but **drops to 15 mph** if within 300 feet of any person or animal.
- The tires **must not** be inflated to a pressure greater than **20 pounds per square inch**.
- Do not park or unload in the North Beach Access Ramp Area.
- Do not park on the beach in the first mile north of the North Beach Access ramp (approximately milepost 14).
- Do not park or set up tents or chairs in the designated fire, emergency, and vehicular traffic lanes: the hard-packed sand landward of the surf run and the tracked sand seaward of the dune line.

Additional considerations:

- Do not attempt to drive on the beach without **four-wheel drive** and elevated clearance.
- Carry a shovel and a tow strap for emergencies.
- Fill the gas tank before driving onto the beach. There are no gas stations in the four-wheel-drive area.
- Know the ocean tide table before going.
- Do not stop until you are clear of all posted No Parking/No Stopping zones. Rule of thumb: park where roofs are visible beyond the dune line.
- Do not set up "camp"—sunshades, blankets, chairs, coolers, fishing lines—or dig holes or trenches in the foreshore or the travel lane at the foot of the dunes.
- The law requires that individuals fill all ruts and holes and level any sand structures they have created.
- Do not approach or attempt to feed the horses. It is against the law to approach closer than 50 feet. You may take their picture from a distance.
- Remove all gear by dusk. The entire beach becomes driving area after dark.
- Both Winks Grocery and Twiddy Real Estate offices have courtesy tire inflation pumps.
- Stuck? It happens! A friend or friendly resident can help but cannot tow or charge for the assistance.

Search Currituck Beach Driving to download
a PDF file with additional detail.

CAPE HATTERAS NATIONAL SEASHORE The National Park Service regulates beach driving in Cape Hatteras National Seashore. Applicable state vehicle registration, insurance, inspection, and licensing requirements apply to all vehicles.

Permits for Cape Hatteras are available in person at the three park visitor centers: Bodie Island Lighthouse and Visitors Center; Cape Hatteras Lighthouse and Visitors Center; and the Ocracoke Visitors Center. Permits may also be purchased online at the Cape Hatteras ORV site at www.recreation.gov. In 2018, fees were $50 for a 10-day pass and $120 for an annual pass.

CAPE LOOKOUT NATIONAL SEASHORE All cars must be transported to Cape Lookout by National Park Service–licensed ferry concessions. Applicable state vehicle registration, insurance, inspection, and licensing requirements apply to all vehicles. Cape Lookout requires drivers to obtain an ORV **Education Certificate** at no charge in order to drive on the beach. The certificate may be obtained in advance online or is available at the offices of the licensed auto ferry operators. Transportation fees are separate.

Search Cape Lookout ORV or enter www.nps.gov
/calo/planyourvisit/orv.htm.

CAROLINA BEACH FREEMAN PARK Applicable state vehicle registration, insurance, inspection, and licensing requirements apply to all vehicles. As of 2018, the following permits were available: daily, $30; holiday (Easter, Memorial Day, Fourth of July, and Labor Day), $50; annual pass, $150. Daily and holiday passes may be purchased at the park entrance; annual passes must be purchased off-site. See Freeman Park website for current locations.

Search Freeman Park Carolina Beach or enter www.carolinabeach.org
and use the "Visitors" drop-down menu.

FORT FISHER STATE RECREATION AREA Registered vehicles with valid park-issued permits are allowed in the four-wheel-drive access area. (Trailers are NOT allowed.) Beach vehicle access permits are for sale at the park's visitor center daily; cash, money orders, or personal checks accepted with proper identification. Annual and family pass holders are still required to register at office. Permits are $15 weekdays and $25 weekends. An annual pass is $60, a family pass $100.

of maritime forests or the new shingled facades of impressively large ocean-front homes.

On any given warm-weather day, a nomadic beach party sets up camp from their neatly parked four-wheel-drive vehicle. This is a beach-driving day-trippers dream—imagine sunshades and beach chairs. Pick your spot and park according to the rules.

Currituck Banks is a beach of dreams, offering the simple essentials: there is little there but sun, sea, and sand. It is not easily accessible, but it offers the double bonus of remoteness and exclusivity. And the area is fast proving that if you build it—no matter how big and extravagant—plenty of people will come to rent it.

On the south side of the North Beach Access Ramp is a fence designed to keep the famed wild horses of Currituck from wandering south, onto the paved roads and into the danger of auto traffic. There is another similar fence nearly 12 miles north, excluding the peripatetic herds from Virginia's neighboring Back Bay National Wildlife Refuge.

Between the fences, Currituck Banks is comparatively untamed. This has always been a wild, unruled stretch of beach—it is nearly 12 miles to the Virginia border—and while there are platted, signed streets, none are paved. The separation from modernity ends there, however, because a surge of vacation home building has introduced a rustic form of luxury along the shore. There are now hundreds of homes luxuriating in all the amenities offered in paved-road vacation communities. Yes, there are swimming pools, but don't forget the coffee . . .

While much less lonely than before, Carova Beach, North Swan Beach, and Swan Beach, the named communities that comprise the 4x4 Beaches, are havens for beach isolationists.

If you can drive on the sand (see the sidebar titled "Rods, Reels, 'n' Wheels: Driving on North Carolina Beaches"), these places are easy to reach, but very much out of the way. Folks who plan vacations around amusements, shopping, and restaurant dining might find these locations more than slightly removed from convenient.

There are attractions: the drive north passes beside preserves of the Currituck Beach Estuarine Research Reserve and the upland portion of the Currituck National Wildlife Refuge. This is the destination of choice for photographing the wild horses that are frequently seen on the beach.

The drive passes Lewark's Hill (also known as Penny's Hill), one of the great moving Outer Banks sand dunes that has pushed its way over the aban-

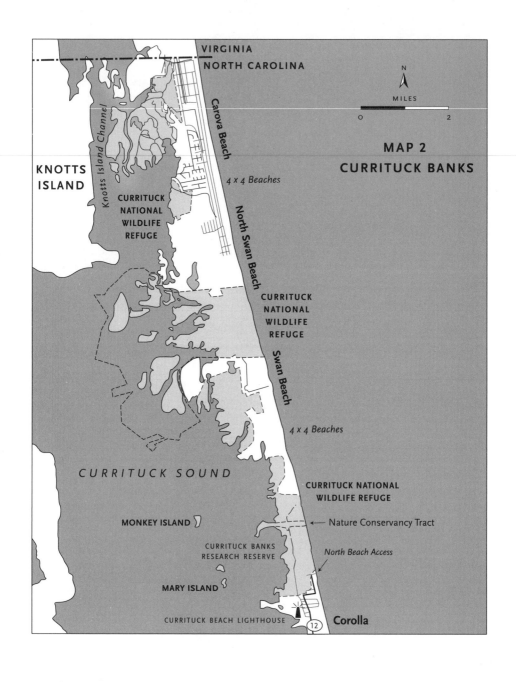

VIRGINIA
NORTH CAROLINA

N

MILES

0   2

MAP 2
CURRITUCK BANKS

Carova Beach

KNOTTS
ISLAND

Knotts Island Channel

4 x 4 Beaches

CURRITUCK
NATIONAL
WILDLIFE
REFUGE

North Swan Beach

CURRITUCK
NATIONAL
WILDLIFE
REFUGE

Swan Beach

4 x 4 Beaches

CURRITUCK SOUND

CURRITUCK NATIONAL
WILDLIFE REFUGE

MONKEY ISLAND

← Nature Conservancy Tract

CURRITUCK BANKS
RESEARCH RESERVE

North Beach Access

MARY ISLAND

CURRITUCK BEACH LIGHTHOUSE

12

Corolla

In 2007 Doug and Sharon Twiddy of Twiddy & Company reconstructed the 1917 boathouse in front of the restored U.S. Coast Guard Station in Wash Woods on the 4x4 Beaches. The watchtower was reconstructed in 2011. (Photo courtesy of Twiddy & Company)

doned community of Seagull, which thrived when New Currituck Inlet was open in the nineteenth century.

Another landmark is Wash Woods, the stumps of a drowned forest emerging from the beach. Visibility varies with tides and time of year.

Slightly more than 7 miles north of the ramp is the restored historic Wash Woods Coast Guard Station at 1994 Sandfiddler Road. This handsome building with a detached kitchen and reconstructed watchtower has been carefully restored by Twiddy and Company to serve as the 4x4 Beaches rental office for their clients.

Mostly there are miles of gently undulating shoreline, marked by vehicle tracks as vacationers have a chance to use the four-wheel-drive options of their sport utility vehicles.

Parking is prohibited for the first 1.5 miles (milepost 14) once you cross the ramp and where National Wildlife Signs indicate refuge lands.

CURRITUCK NATIONAL WILDLIFE REFUGE

The 4x4 Beaches are buffered to the west in several locations by the separate segments of the 4,110-acre Currituck National Wildlife Refuge. In fact, approximately 44 percent of the acreage north of the access ramp at Corolla is part of the refuge.

There are 418 acres of beach/dune habitat in the refuge, and the boundaries are plainly signed above the tide line with the National Wildlife Refuge logo. As you drive on the beach, look to the west; if you do not see houses behind the dunes, it is likely that you are traveling on or adjacent to refuge or protected land. The first refuge section encountered is about three-quarters of a mile north of the ramp.

The Currituck refuge protects the full range of habitats existing on the northern banks. This includes beach, dune fields, grassy flats, maritime shrub thickets, maritime forests, and marsh and wetlands. Nearly half of the refuge is in marsh and wetlands, highly important acreage for wading birds and migratory waterfowl.

The land is typical of the North Banks, a transitional area between northern and southern maritime vegetation. For example, both bayberry (*Myrica pensylvanica*) and its southern relative, wax myrtle (*M. cerifera*), grow here. The higher elevations and forested portions of the site support deer, fox, raccoon, feral hogs, and horses. The marsh is habitat for muskrat, river otters, mink, and a portion of the Atlantic flyway waterfowl population that winters in Currituck. Refuge managers have confirmed nesting of the piping plover, an endangered species, in the dunes within the refuge, prompting them to closely monitor vehicular traffic there during the nesting season, June through July.

The refuge also provides a haven for the wild horses that have been prohibited from roaming in Corolla by an ocean-to-sound fence separating them from paved-road automobile traffic.

The wild horse tours make a direct line to the refuge property, since that is typically where the horses will be visible on the beach.

Though good for tourism, the horses, a non-native species, pose a conflict with ideal refuge management for native species. Management has enclosed a 150-acre flat area behind the frontal dunes about 5 miles north of the ramp to provide a horse-free area to compare and contrast vegetation growth inside and outside the fence.

In 2014 the Fish and Wildlife Service joined Currituck County, the

Corolla Wild Horse Fund, and the North Carolina National Estuarine Research Reserve in the Wild Horse Management Plan to help resolve the complex conflicts surrounding the horse herds. The horses will remain, but the size of the herd will be maintained at around 130 animals.

The refuge was established in 1984 from separate parcels of land purchased by the Nature Conservancy. Much of the acreage was purchased from the holdings of hunt clubs.

One such club was Monkey Island, a small island in Currituck Sound. The northern portion of the island is one of the largest egret rookeries in the state, and when the birds are on the nest, it looks as if sheets are drying in the trees. Part of the island was a summer fishing base and burial ground for Native Americans centuries prior to Currituck's settlement

Currituck National Wildlife Refuge is accessible by boat or four-wheel-drive vehicle. The headquarters and staff are at Mackay Island National Wildlife Refuge on Knotts Island.

Hiking, photography, wildlife watching, hunting, and fishing are encouraged. Visitors should carry water and insect repellent.

Search Currituck Wildlife Refuge or enter www.fws.gov/refuge/currituck/.

CURRITUCK BANKS NORTH CAROLINA
NATIONAL ESTUARINE RESEARCH RESERVE

Drivers crossing the North Beach Access Ramp enter the Currituck Banks Component of the National Estuarine Research Reserve, a 960-acre sea-to-sound holding that is part of a state and national system of dedicated coastal research acreage. This is the place to visit if you want to gain a modest understanding of barrier beach environments.

The reserve is the southernmost of three properties. To the north are a sea-to-sound Nature Conservancy tract and the Monkey Island Unit of the previously described Currituck National Wildlife Refuge; together these control the approximately 1.5 miles of beach. The consecutive tracts appear as one large all-natural parcel. All properties are open, but there is no parking on their oceanfront.

However, there is easy access to the research reserve by way of a 9-space car park on the left side of NC 12 just before the access ramp. The parking area is the entrance to trails threading the reserve.

A boardwalk penetrates the upland habitat of the preserve, poking through the maritime shrub thicket to continue into a maritime hardwood forest. It then crosses seasonally flooded sinks or sloughs before finishing above the marsh and waters of Currituck Sound. The 0.3-mile-long board-walk (wheelchair accessible) is a delightful stroll that takes about 15 minutes each way, longer if you stop to study the interpretative displays that inform the differences in the habitats along the trail.

A sandy footpath departs the north side of the boardwalk about midway. The 1.5-mile trail penetrates deeper into the reserve's upland acreage and provides a more varied inside look at the maritime forest and shrub thickets.

The upland terrain you will see exhibits the typical mid-Atlantic vegetation pattern: a dense shrub thicket and some maritime forest thriving behind the artificial dune line created by the Civilian Conservation Corps in the 1930s on a flat, harsh sandy environment. The dune line created a windbreak that thwarted damaging salt spray. This in turn permitted shrubby vegetation and trees to grow.

During the warmer months there is a lot of beach activity at the southern boundary of the preserve where it adjoins the private property of the Ocean Hill subdivision to the south.

Search Currituck Reserve or enter www.nccoastalreserve.net.

COROLLA

Everyone who goes to the Outer Banks should go to Corolla; it is obvious from the summer crowds that many people agree. In high summer Corolla plays to the crowds teeming its shores about as well as can be expected from any 12-mile-long waterfront destination served by only a two-lane highway. The fact is, it is worth the trip in any season.

Corolla (locally pronounced "*Cuh*-rah-la"), offers an appealing mix of old and new—history, outdoor recreation, shopping, dining, and an amazing range of accommodations, most of which are single-family homes to rent. While this is a familiar resort recipe, the development that hammered its way to the historic village beginning in 1984, when NC 12 was paved, has settled into Currituck Banks nicely. Trees have grown, and native evergreen shrubs—and a few exotics—buffer the highway, cloaking the many houses. The once-sandy flats that stretched from the Dare County line to the Currituck Beach Lighthouse now sport a lot of green. When you look to the west,

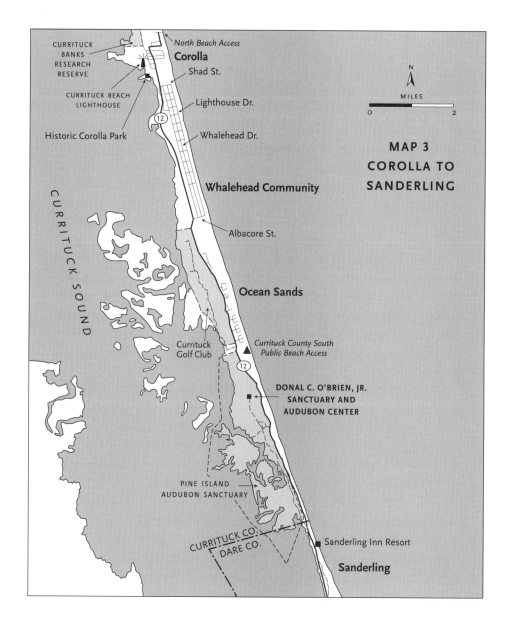

CURRITUCK
BANKS
RESEARCH
RESERVE

North Beach Access

Corolla

Shad St.

CURRITUCK BEACH
LIGHTHOUSE

Lighthouse Dr.

Historic Corolla Park

12

Whalehead Dr.

Whalehead Community

N

MILES

0   2

**MAP 3
COROLLA TO
SANDERLING**

Albacore St.

Ocean Sands

C U R R I T U C K   S O U N D

Currituck
Golf Club

*Currituck County South
Public Beach Access*

12

**DONAL C. O'BRIEN, JR.
SANCTUARY AND
AUDUBON CENTER**

PINE ISLAND
AUDUBON SANCTUARY

CURRITUCK CO.
DARE CO.

■ Sanderling Inn Resort

Sanderling

most development is tucked behind a screen of vegetation, particularly near the original village center. NC 12 takes a winding course, doing its part to nudge visitors into vacation mode.

This stretch of coast, the southernmost part of Currituck County, provides easy access to both the Atlantic Ocean and Currituck Sound. This in

Currituck County

turn fosters all the water sports that come with such proximity. Lifeguard stations are sprinkled along its length during summer to help visitors safely enjoy the ocean.

Currituck Banks is mostly less than one-half mile wide from sound to shore (and quite a bit skinnier than that in some places). The beaches are ample and gently sloped. The early morning sun (a terrific sight) and sunsets over Currituck Sound can be exquisite.

A bit of recent (but vanished) history: in the 1980s only a washboard dirt track wandered north to Corolla from where the pavement of NC 12 stopped just at the Currituck/Dare County boundary (just north of the Sanderling Resort). In 1984 that road was paved, and most of what you see along the drive from the Dare County line has been built since then.

Certainly Corolla is no longer isolated or remote as it was for much of its history, but it is still out of the way. There is everything needed to supply and resupply a weeklong family beach vacation—groceries, distilled and nondistilled beverages, ATMs, and so on. It's a great place to lose momentum because commuting to and from attractions in Kitty Hawk, Kill Devil Hills, Nags Head, and Manteo is not quickly or easily done in the high season—mid-June to mid-August.

Since 1875, the landmark of old Corolla has been the handsome redbrick tower of the Currituck Beach Lighthouse. It emerges from a forest to tower above Corolla Village Road, which stretches between an oceanfront-access parking lot across NC 12 to the still-sleepy forested area where the earliest residents settled. Carotank Drive, School House Lane, and Persimmon Street frame the grid of the longest-settled part of Corolla.

The lighthouse, which is privately owned by Outer Banks Conservationists (the working light is maintained by the U.S. Coast Guard), is worth the stop and the spiral climb to the observation deck about 150 feet above the grounds. The $10 entry fee goes toward the continuing restoration of the lighthouse complex, which includes the lightkeeper's house (initially hauled by barge to the site precut) and outbuildings.

Search Currituck Light or enter www.currituckbeachlight.com.

Just north of the lighthouse, at the corner of Schoolhouse Lane and NC 12 on a slightly elevated site, is the sales office of Twiddy and Company, a real estate sales and management firm. A sign above the door reads: "U.S. Life-Saving Station."

The building began as the original Kill Devil Hills Life-Saving Station, constructed in 1878. The crew from this station witnessed the Wright Brothers' first flight. Surfman John T. Daniels snapped the photograph of the twentieth century—the now-famous picture of the first motorized airplane flight.

Realtor Doug Twiddy purchased the building and moved it here in 1986, preserving a valuable structure in lifesaving station history. Twiddy restored the station to its original condition (the sign on the front is a duplicate of the original on display inside) and showcases first-flight historical items as well as artifacts from lifesaving days, including several Lyle guns and a Breeches Rescue Buoy. The Twiddy Company does accommodate visitors.

As a courtesy to vacationers and renters, Twiddy and Company provides tire air pressure stations at its rental headquarters behind the sales office on School House Lane. (This is an important stop for those who must deflate their tires to drive on the beach.)

Twiddy also renovated the old Corolla schoolhouse at the corner of Schoolhouse Lane and Corolla Village Road. And as you continue along Corolla Village Road, there are other well-preserved original houses and outbuildings refurbished for commercial and/or residential use.

On the western side of Corolla Village Road is the historic Corolla Chapel, the front part of which was constructed in 1885. By 1958 the use had dwindled. In 1962 longtime U.S. Postmaster John H. Austin purchased the chapel at a tax sale. In 1988 Pastor John and Ruth Strauss began holding year-round services. The family of John Austin gifted the structure to the ministry with the stipulation that it be used as an interdenominational Christian church.

Regular services are held in the chapel and visitors are welcome. Should you attend, take note of exquisite Legend of the Pelican stained glass window commissioned by Pastor John Strauss to honor his late wife. The chapel is entered through the oldest section.

Search Corolla Chapel or enter www.corollachapel.com.

Farther north on NC 12 is Wink's Grocery, a local institution. Opened in 1957, Wink's used to be the only store to stay open between Labor Day and Memorial Day before the vacation growth surge. If you are staying at a house on the 4x4 Beaches, this is the last (or first) stop for what you forgot.

The Village Shops at Corolla are nearly opposite the entrance to Historic Corolla Park on the east side of NC 12. They have comfortable dining and a mix of recreation and retail vendors. The complex also provides public restrooms.

Farther south, the Corolla Light resort community spreads between NC 12 and the oceanfront, and there is some additional development west of the highway on the sound. The resort has the full expected range of rental homes and amenities. Soundside, the Inn at Corolla Light is one of the few places offering nightly lodging that is near the old village. The inn is an idiosyncratic hostelry because in an earlier life the complex of soundside rooms housed a boutique retail complex. What was once shops are now spacious rooms, some with a view, some not. The inn has a pool and a gazebo on the sound.

Corolla Access

The following public access areas are in Corolla. These are listed north to south. Green street signs reading "Public Access" indicate locations along NC 12.

> Carova Beach Public Park (4x4 Beaches)
> North Beach Access Ramp (four-wheel-drive vehicles only)
> Currituck Banks Research Reserve, North Beach Access Road
> Corolla Village Road Beach Access (Bath House)
> Corolla Village Road Sound Access
> Whalehead Club Heritage Park
> Whalehead Community: 13 access areas at the east end of the
> following streets: Shad, Tuna, Sturgeon, Barracuda, Herring,
> Perch, Mackerel, Bonito, Coral, Sailfish, Marlin, Dolphin, and
> Albacore. Southern County Public Beach Access, near Yaupon
> Street (Bath House)
> The Corolla Village Shoppes provides public restrooms.

Lifeguards

Lifeguards are on duty from 9:30 AM until 5:30 PM daily. Roving patrols (four-wheel-drive trucks and ATVs) travel from the county line north to Penny's Hill (a 4x4 beach) for your assistance.

For lifeguard tower locations, search Corolla Beach Rescue or
enter www.corollabeachrescue.com/Home/TowerMap.

The Corolla Fire Department loans a beach wheelchair
with advance notice by calling 252-453-3242.

CURRITUCK BEACH
LIGHT STATION AND MUSEUM

Start a visit to Corolla by winding up the stairs of the Currituck Beach
Lighthouse. It is an energizing (innervating?) ascent of 220 steps, an ever-
tightening spiral that leads to the observation platform. The view from the
observation deck 150 feet above the ground is spectacular. Notice how tree
covered much of Corolla appears.

Then take a look at the historical photographs in the anteroom. Photographs taken during the nineteenth century and early in the twentieth show
few trees. The vegetation on the lighthouse grounds is a comparatively new
feature of the site, perhaps no more than 70 years old. Up until the 1940s,
Currituck Banks was open range for grazing cattle. Prior to the war years,
as many as 6,000 cattle and wild horses cropped the vegetation along the
Outer Banks. The Great Depression of the early twentieth century brought
significant change.

In the 1930s, Works Progress Administration and Civilian Conservation
Corps teams were given the task of stabilizing the dunes of the Outer Banks.
They bulldozed sand into an artificial (and arbitrary) dune line, planted it
with beach grass and sea oats, and planted pine trees inland. Once the pines
survived the grazing and sheltered the landward side of the island, other
plants could successfully germinate and grow. Looking down from the light,
you may be startled by the amount of green below, the thickness of the
soundside woods, and the composition of the island—dune to flats to shrub
thicket to maritime forest to marsh.

When first lighted on December 1, 1875, the Currituck Beach light completed the network of major beacons on North Carolina's Outer Banks. It
filled the gap between Cape Henry at the entrance to Chesapeake Bay and
Bodie Island at Oregon Inlet, giving mariners a series of lights to guide
them along the coast from Cape Lookout north. This light, maintained by
the U.S. Coast Guard, is a first-order Fresnel lens. It has a 20-second flash
cycle: 3 seconds on, 17 seconds off.

Since North Carolina's other major beacons were daymarked in the black-and-white patterns familiar today, officials decided not to paint the new beacon to distinguish it. At the base of the 162-foot-tall tower (measured to the very top), the walls are 5 feet 8 inches thick—all brick. The wall thickness tapers to a mere 3 feet at the top—still all brick.

Outer Banks Conservationists, Inc., has been responsible for the careful restoration of the lighthouse and outbuildings since being granted a long-term lease in 1980.

The ornate Victorian keeper's house was precut, hauled across the Currituck Sound by barge, and assembled on-site in 1876. It is a state property and listed on the National Register of Historic Places.

In July 2003 the Department of the Interior rewarded the organization's hard work with the deed to the lighthouse under the provisions of the National Historic Lighthouse Preservation Act of 2000. Fees for the climb go to maintaining and restoring the grounds, including a smaller outbuilding that now serves as a gift shop.

At the west end of the parking area, slightly south of the turn in Corolla Village Road, is a boardwalk that penetrates about 300 yards through the maritime forest, a freshwater cattail swamp, and the adjoining marsh, and out into Currituck Sound. Although the walk can be buggy, it provides access not only to spectacular sunsets but also to the incredible evening song arising from the many unseen inhabitants.

Search Currituck Light or enter www.currituckbeachlight.com.

HISTORIC COROLLA PARK

After climbing the lighthouse bright and early, enjoy the offerings in Historic Corolla Park south of the lighthouse across Corolla Village Road. A visit rewards a few hours of looking, learning, and lazing about on the 29-acre public setting. The story of Currituck Sound—its wildlife, watermen, and wealthy guests—unfolds elegantly in two remarkable facilities: the new Outer Banks Center for Wildlife Education and the magnificent, historic Whalehead Club. The one sets a simple stage for the extravagance of the other.

Opened in 2006, the Outer Banks Center for Wildlife Education is one of three education centers operated by the North Carolina Wildlife Commission. The center presents the ecology of Currituck Sound and explains how the waters and wetlands became a haven for wildlife both feathered and scaled. This in turn shaped the lives of the people who lived on its shores and worked on its waters. Admission is free.

In the late nineteenth and early twentieth century, Currituck Sound was home to some of the most extraordinary populations of wintering waterfowl in the country. A cottage industry grew around hunting and guiding. The center's introductory 30-minute film artfully describes the history of wings and water and its impact on the lives of Currituck residents.

It is not a static story. Currituck Sound and the vegetation it supports, crucial as food and habitat, have changed dramatically—and the people who live there have adapted to the ecological dynamics.

The film serves as gateway to an interpretive display room that details many stories of the watermen of the Outer Banks, from decoy carvers to boatbuilders and guides. The exclamation point on the tour is an 8,000-gallon aquarium that lets you peek beneath and above the waters to view some of the inhabitants of the watery environment. The center offers child-friendly activities, scheduled more frequent during summer.

Even if it did not sit on a superb waterfront location, the Whalehead Club would still be a stunning architectural statement. It is perhaps the embodiment of extravagance brought about by a confluence of waterfowl abundance, fashion, and Gatsby-like wealth. Regardless, it is a treasure worth the price of admission.

Restored to its original opulence, the Whalehead Club stands as the most lavish of the hunting clubs built around Currituck Sound. It strains the imagination to comprehend that it entered service as a hunting "cottage."

Pennsylvanian industrialist Edward Collins Knight Jr. had two loves late in life: Marie-Louise LeBel and duck hunting. He brought them together in eclectic, near-fantastic art nouveau style at a place he called Corolla Island. Between 1922 and 1925, barge after barge crossed the sound ferrying laborers and materials to the site. About $383,000 later, the railroad magnate's 21,000-square-foot gift to his wife was complete.

It still shows off the dash of the time: a copper roof, cork flooring, an exterior of cypress wood, interior corduroy walls, Tiffany chandeliers, and the original grand piano. There were little comforts too—a generator, an Otis elevator, art nouveau window pulls, spectacular door and window moldings, and an exquisite art nouveau clock, since replaced in kind.

The Knights named their cottage Corolla Island.

The parklike grounds are shaded by live oaks and highlighted by a hand-

Currituck Beach Lighthouse is visible behind the picturesque bridge at Whalehead. (Photo by Chip Henderson, courtesy of VisitNC.com)

some arched bridge over an artificial lagoon where kayakers may dock and a boathouse. The bridge is a prime site for a souvenir photograph with the Whalehead Club backdrop. The bridge and boathouse design are thought to be a reconstruction of structures noted by Knight's wife on a trip to Europe. The Knights sailed through the Depression with guns and party lights blazing, but both died in 1936, only seven years after the home's completion.

Since their heirs had little use for the property or interest in duck hunting, it was eventually sold in 1939 for $25,000.

It was the second owner, Ray T. Adams, who named it the Whalehead Club. From that year until 1992, when Currituck County bought it for preservation, the building steadily lost ground to the elements as it cycled through a variety of uses, including housing for the U.S. Coast Guard, as a private academy and then as a rocket-testing station. The nearly 30-

year effort to restore it brought detailed authenticity gleaned from histori-cal photographs, inside and out. The self-guided audio tour is an upstairs/downstairs peek at great wealth and the social divisions of the times, which were bridged somewhat by a shared love of Currituck waterfowl.

Search Outer Banks Wildlife Center or enter www.ncwildlife.org /Learning/Education-Centers/Outer-Banks.

Search Whalehead Club or enter www.whaleheadwedding.com.

The drive south from Corolla Historic Park winds past Corolla Light Resort, the Inn at Corolla Light on the sound, and the resort's gym facili-ties. The road veers soundside at the commercial center of Monterey Plaza, and then the fairways of the Currituck Club become visible. The 1996 Rees Jones links-style course is open to the public. The golf course weaves among the residential homes of a now-gated community.

The course acreage belonged to the Currituck Shooting Club when pur-chased. At that time the club was the oldest continually operated hunt club in the country. Founded in 1857, the Currituck Shooting Club was on the National Register of Historic Places and front and center in the sporting his-tory of the county. The club owned more than 2,000 acres of undeveloped land in this location that formed the nucleus of the exquisite golf course named Currituck Club. That history went up in smoke in April 2003; the club burned to the ground in a confirmed accident.

Search Currituck Golf or enter www.clubcorp.com.

DONAL C. O'BRIEN JR. SANCTUARY AND AUDUBON CENTER AT PINE ISLAND

The next big woods on the west side of NC 12 is the uplands of the Donal C. O'Brien Jr. Sanctuary, a significant and historic setting that is now an Audu-bon Sanctuary.

In the early 1970s, the land was turned over the Audubon Society by the owner of the historic Pine Island Club, a neighboring hunt club to the Currituck Shooting Club. The Pine Island tract once extended from sound to the oceanfront. The oceanfront parcel is the site of private homes and the Hampton Inn and Suites.

The mission of the preserve is to provide sanctuary for wintering water-fowl in the marsh and waters that it manages.

At the southern end of the property is a sign for the Pine Island Racquet and Fitness Club. This facility, which sits on the sanctuary grounds, is open to the public and has indoor and outdoor tennis courts, a fitness center, and showers. The club is also the parking area for the entrance to the 2.5-mile (one way) nature trail of the sanctuary that routes over the historic road between Duck and Corolla.

The trail wanders beneath a bower of trees in the maritime forest—loblolly pines and sculpted, twisted live oaks. There are vistas into the extensive sound marsh and a rare red bay swamp. Prime viewing for waterfowl is the fall and winter, but wading birds and ospreys may be seen year-round. Binoculars and insect repellant are recommended.

Search Pine Island Sanctuary or enter pineisland.audubon.org.

Search Pine Island Racquet Club or enter www.pineislandrc.com.

Dare County

DARE COUNTY has an unmatched stature in North Carolina's history and its oceanfront tourism. Roanoke Island is the site of the first English-speaking colony in America, settled in 1585; Kitty Hawk on the oceanfront hosted Wilber and Orville Wright as they successfully completed the first motorized airplane flight in 1903. At distant Buxton, the tallest brick lighthouse in North America is available for climbing (after being moved inland to a safer location in the summer of 1999). It is a masonry exclamation point to the nearly 60 miles of oceanfront preserved as the 28,000-acre Cape Hatteras National Seashore, the first national seashore park in the country.

Those are a few of the big draws in a county that has more square miles of water than it does land. Yet it is the Dare County oceanfront, a small percentage of that total land, which has an outsized presence and scores national name recognition.

A satellite photograph of North Carolina's coast shows an irregular beige and green bracket that gradually loses proximity to the mainland as it bows far into the Atlantic Ocean. It then shifts direction, returning to again hug the mainland. This bracket, of course, is North Carolina's Outer Banks, and the islands that comprise it belong to four counties: north to south, Currituck, Dare, Hyde, and Carteret. The salient, a shape you can imitate by extending the thumb and forefinger of your right hand, belongs to Dare County.

This particularly far-flung parcel is Hatteras Island—the outermost of the low, sandy islands historically known as sand banks or sea banks. The term "Outer Banks" is well-known but sometimes arbitrarily inclusive. It is generally understood to include the oceanfront communities of Currituck and Dare Counties and the miles of Hatteras and neighboring Ocracoke Islands included in Cape Hatteras National Seashore.

The Outer Banks label should not stop there, however. Geographically speaking, that term should also embrace the islands of Cape Lookout National Seashore: Portsmouth, North and South Core Banks, and Shackleford Banks, which are in Carteret County. The bustling beachfront communities on Bogue Banks in Carteret County are also properly considered part of the Outer Banks.

(Although it is an obvious descriptor, the term "Outer Banks" lacks a precise etymology. It may have been used in the earliest proposals to preserve these islands as parkland in the 1930s.)

The peninsula (extending south from Virginia) and Outer Banks of Dare County are reasonably uniform in their physical characteristics. These are low islands (and many times were in different island configurations), and along much of their length the dune line built by the Civilian Conservation Corps in the 1930s offers some of the highest ground. There are exceptions, though. The unusual stands of hardwood maritime forest on older dune ridges in Nags Head and Buxton are important natural features that have been purchased and preserved in their unaltered condition. Another notable exception is the massive sand dunes like Jockey's Ridge of Nags Head and Big Kill Devil Hill in Kill Devil Hills.

Dare County rightly and smartly markets and derives the benefits of these marvelous beaches. Their catchy moniker—which has been condensed to a three-letter abbreviation, OBX—scores high on place recognition. For all practical purposes, Outer Banks has come to embrace much of the extended peninsula from Virginia south to Oregon Inlet and the islands of the Cape Hatteras National Seashore.

The widespread Outer Banks buzz of today grew steadily with access to the oceanfront. Pre–Civil War hotels and cottages established on the sound side of the banks at present-day Nags Head gave way to oceanfront homes there after the problem of the half-mile-long soft-sand island crossing was solved. The first oceanfront homes were built beginning in the 1870s.

Second home construction accelerated rapidly after the first Wright Memorial Bridge (wooden) opened in the 1930s and the first 18 miles of what would eventually become NC 12 were paved. Improved roads and bridges inland brought more people seeking hotels and building second homes. The oceanfront portion of the communities of Kitty Hawk, Kill Devil Hills, and Nags Head grew steadily. Each evolved an individual character that is distinguishing even if clear demarcations between them are less so. In a colloquial nod to origins, the phrase "going to Nags Head" long served as the vacation declaration for all the Dare County beaches.

There are 26 miles of oceanfront communities in Dare County between the Currituck County line and the oceanfront parcels of Cape Hatteras National Seashore. About 10 of those miles are north of the parallel spans of the Wright Memorial Bridge that routes US 158 from the mainland to the oceanfront. North of the bridge are Sanderling (a resort community), Duck, and Southern Shores.

The Wright Memorial Bridge marks the northern limit of Kitty Hawk and the beginning of the 16-mile expanse south through Kitty Hawk, Kill Devil Hills, and Nags Head.

In the 1980s, Sanderling was a nearly sequestered oasis poised at the

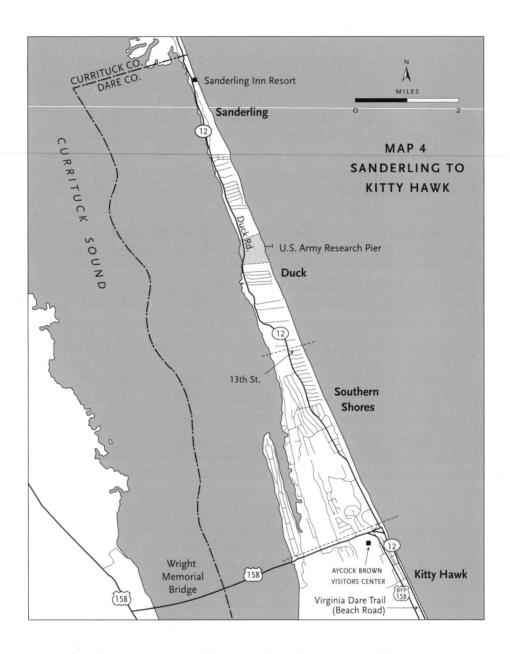

MAP 4
SANDERLING TO
KITTY HAWK

peninsula's narrowest spot. To the south, Duck was a joyous four-letter syn-
onym for laid-back chic vacations. Duck was signaled on the northward drive
by an unexpected S-curve in NC 12 that drew cars close to Currituck Sound
before whisking them back past the water tower to mid-peninsula—the eastern side streets serving ocean rentals.

Today Sanderling is slightly hemmed in, and while Duck is still Duck, the brisk whisk is gone during the high summer season. On Saturday, the usual rental change day, traffic moves with the speed of the tides as folks ply their way through Duck and to Duck.

The boundaries of Southern Shores span from Duck to the north side of US 158. It is a private community comprising a series of residential subdivisions reached from NC 12. The oceanfront lots are spacious, and the homes back of the dunes are large and stylish. Although one may also catch a glimpse of the original signature "Florida-style" flat-roofed, cinderblock, stucco-covered homes originally constructed here in the late 1950s, prosperity has rolled over iconic Southern Shores architecture with a tidal wave of vacation home style. Southern Shores is plush.

The southern edge of town (and the northern edge of Kitty Hawk) is US 158 as it leaves the Wright Memorial Bridge. It cuts across the island heading directly east to a chaotic intersection. The landing of US 158 is the final taxiway for vacationers turning left onto NC 12 to travel north through Southern Shores to Duck and Corolla. Unfortunately, this is where many vacation dreams stall at the traffic light. High summer Saturday traffic can back up across the Wright Memorial Bridge.

Other vacationers veer right, or south, on US 158, here named the Croatan Highway. It is a five-lane inland bypass serving Kitty Hawk, Kill Devil Hills, and Nags Head before reconnecting to NC 12, which serves Cape Hatteras National Seashore. Ignore the five-lane bypass and follow the dialed-down route that continues straight. This road, NC 12, rounds a gentle curve to head south just behind the front-row cottages and dunes. The highway is locally referenced as Virginia Dare Trail (and also known as Beach Road).

Regardless of the route, the 15 miles of oceanfront between the US 158/ NC 12 intersection and Whalebone Junction, the intersection of NC 12 and US 64, is the primary bustle of Dare County's tourism. Kitty Hawk, Kill Devil Hills, and Nags Head line up north to south from sea to sound. Along Virginia Dare Trail, the ocean, even if not directly visible, always feels immediate and accessible.

These communities are crazy quilts offering every gradation between neon, unabashedly beach-commercial spots and sun-bleached, weathered-by-the-sea summer places. A romanticized attraction rooted in tradition lures vacationers and underlies a debate on how to receive the increasing numbers and not abandon the qualities that initially attracted them.

What exists today is a sort of holiday sampler of hostelries, houses, and recreation options. Mile for mile, the mix of patina, past, and personality of the resort cities and the public preserves is a collection of opportunities that can't be matched elsewhere.

City demarcations are low key and nearly indiscernible. The three resort towns share a bleached, weathered look, worn in by the maritime conditions—shiny and new do not last long here. Years by the sea is what distinguishes and flavors the several blocks of "ocean-close" commercial and residential development in Kitty Hawk, Kill Devil Hills, and Nags Head. Yes, there is newer development—US 158 is mostly a commercial strip that could be anywhere, with the exception of certain attractions. The interior blocks between commercial buildings fronting the bypass and Virginia Dare Trail (NC 12, locally known as Beach Road) hold an eclectic mix of vacation cottages and smaller commercial ventures. But what spreads west from the beach is the core of communities that are still flavored by a simpler time with simpler vacation wants.

Presently, Kitty Hawk, Kill Devil Hills, and Nags Head share powerful development and ocean erosion pressure. Each has responded differently, and each offers a different flavor of seaside. There is a kind of weathered serendipity that drapes over the oldest core of each, where buildings have an indigenous look, as though they just belong.

The historical center of these communities is buried in the thick maritime forests west of US 158. Exploring these inland roads reveals an environment of very different character, one that would be safer for permanent settlement than the uncertain of life exactly at the edge of the sea.

Cape Hatteras National Seashore begins south of Whalebone Junction. The border introduces a significant character change for the next 60 miles of Dare County's oceanfront. There is an early hint of the intoxicating mix of solitude and wildness that NC 12 gracefully sways through. As native vegetation obscures the roofs of South Nags Head homes, the road seems to be a gray ribbon framed by maritime shrubs, marsh, and sky. The remainder of the route will alternate between vast expanses of sky and water and the historic communities Rodanthe, Waves, and Salvo. These are followed by Avon, Buxton, and Frisco, and, at the end of the road, Hatteras.

The Oregon Inlet crossing reveals the vulnerable truth of living on the narrow sandy islands. Land and sea are in an endless struggle for relative position, and that which is fixed in place—roads and houses, for example— is not guaranteed to remain so. (One guesstimate of permanent population may be extrapolated from utility accounts: there are approximately 7,600 accounts in the electrical cooperative serving Hatteras Island, and some of those are businesses. Hatteras is not the permanent home of many.)

The miles of preserved, unpopulated oceanfront and marsh are the prime attractions of the seashore. Natural recreation abounds: from bird-watching at Pea Island National Wildlife Refuge to camping, swimming, fishing, kayaking, and windsurfing. Greater than the lure of these activities is the unmatchable drive. There are lengths of roadway that become elemental: sand and sky and sea. Cape Hatteras National Seashore harbors such vast spaces; the sea-to-sound expanse diminishes self-importance in a mesmerizing manner.

Away from the oceanfront, Roanoke Island hosts a full day and part of another with superlative attractions. Fort Raleigh National Historic Site, a site of national significance, should be at the top of any list. This is the site of the first attempt at English-speaking settlement in the New World. Adjacent to it is the Waterside Theater, home to the popular outdoor drama *The Lost Colony*, and the commemorative Elizabethan Gardens. One of the three outstanding North Carolina Aquariums is on the island's west side. Adjoining charming Manteo's harbor, a short walk from town center, is Roanoke Island Festival Park, which holds the *Elizabeth II*, a full-scale replica of a sixteenth-century sailing vessel. In summer the festival park brims with a steady offering of interpretive programs, concerts, and entertainment.

Roanoke Island was once the gateway island to the Outer Banks. The early routing of US 64/264, the pre-interstate east–west highway that extends to Tennessee, came through Manns Harbor on the mainland crossing Croatan Sound on the William B. Umstead Bridge. It then routed nearly the entire length of Roanoke Island before crossing Roanoke Sound over the Washington Baum Bridge. This is the scenic route today.

Built to interstate standards, the newer US 64 Bypass routes over the Virginia Dare Memorial Bridge and shoots straight to Whalebone Junction. The new highway cuts through the top of mainland Dare County, a huge peninsula containing more than 350 square miles of nearly impenetrable forests and swamps.

The Albemarle, Croatan, and Pamlico Sounds surround it on the north and east; the Alligator River forms its western boundary. It is vast and un-populated, crisscrossed by timber roads that once served the largest community in Dare County: Buffalo City, an early twentieth-century logging town deep in the mainland woods.

In 1984 nearly the entire mainland portion of Dare County was donated to the U.S. Fish and Wildlife Service to establish the Alligator River National Wildlife Refuge. It protects one of the most pristine tracts of coastal forest and swamp remaining in the Southeast and confirmed the Department of Interior as the largest landowner in Dare County.

US 264, an alternate on the mainland, skirts the eastern edge of the Alligator River refuge, leading to Engelhard, Swan Quarter, and eventually Washington. (This route passes very close to the Dare County Bombing Range, a multiservice target range west of Stumpy Point.)

Yes, mainland Dare County gets little respect from the average family, except when its sweetbay magnolia and Gordonia are blooming and filling the air with floral perfume. It is territory for the committed hunter, angler, kayaker, or bird-watcher. Everybody else hurries by this vast preserve on the way to the beaches.

Search Outer Banks or enter www.OuterBanks.org.

For Your Bucket:
Walk the Duck Boardwalk
Take a lazy drive on Beach Road
Climb Big Kill Devil Hill
See sunset from atop Jockey's Ridge
Take a hang-gliding lesson
See the historic Nags Head Cottages
Visit Roanoke Island Festival Park
See Fort Raleigh National Historic Site
Attend *The Lost Colony* at Waterside Theater

Access

The individual municipalities and management agencies provide beach access. A pamphlet published by the Outer Banks Visitors Bureau, *Exploring the Outer Banks*, details locations, facilities, and lifeguards at each. The access locations are clearly signed along NC 12; regional access sites are signed along US 158 bypass.

Beach access sites are listed in the community sections.

Search NC Beach Access; click the NC DEQ Beach and
Waterfront Access Map link; at the bottom of the second
column, click "Go to Beach Access Locator."

Bicycling: search Dare County Bicycle or enter www.outerbanks.org
/things-to-do/on-land/biking/ or xfer.services.ncdot.gov
/gisdot/DOTBikeMaps/Dare/Welcome_Locator_Map.pdf.

Surf Conditions text alert for Dare County: text the number
30890 with the message "Join OBXBeachConditions." After the
second text received, enter the number under contacts.

DUCK

Duck got its tourism mojo a generation ago, in the very early 1980s, before
chatter about extending two-lane NC 12 to Corolla became pavement on the
ground. (It seems incredible today that until 1984 a guardhouse on NC 12
at the Dare County line restricted access farther north to property owners
and their guests.)

Duck quickly grew from a quiet outpost (current year-round population
520) with a handful of stores huddled around the S-swerve in NC 12 to an
extended series of residential "neighborhoods" and an expanded cluster of
thoughtfully designed retail, dining, and recreation businesses attracting a
summer population of about 20,000 people.

Like any resort, it fits some folks better than others. It has an inherent
appeal that arcs more toward Topsiders served with french fries. That non-
sensical simile is close, but does not fully capture its quirky personality.

As an unincorporated and highly desirable location, Duck attracted a lot
of vacation homebuilding, and it turned out well. Early on, after much tur-
moil it rejected a large grocery chain and built on its state designation as a
"Beautification District." It used the taxes permitted under the latter to place
utilities underground. This permits native trees and shrubs to cloak NC 12.

In most cases, individual developers respected the maritime forest
when building the resort homes—most subdivision streets disappear into
the woods, headed for the ocean. This approach capitalizes on the unusually deft routing of NC 12. Duck does not present itself all at once. The road
snakes and winds; commercial clusters are distinct and somewhat buffered
by vegetation. Satisfied with the look and amount of local commercial services, Duck continued to grow one subdivision at a time.

Along the way, a distinctive flair was injected into the commercial archi-

The Waterfront Shops at Duck have a beautiful boardwalk along Currituck Sound. (Photo by Chip Henderson, courtesy of VisitNC.com)

tecture. Scarborough Faire Shopping Village, a 1984 clustering of individual buildings linked with boardwalks, was built in the maritime forest around many existing live oaks. Boardwalks thread among the trunks and connect the separate retail units. The complex is weathered and settled; natural leaf litter covers the ground. It set a high bar for retail.

In a different way, the Waterfront Shops handsomely exploit their Currituck Sound location, opening to a boardwalk that wraps the western side of the multiple-boutique vendor center. (Duck's Cottage Coffee & Books opened at the Waterfront Shops on July 22, 2002. The building is the former Powder Ridge Gun Club, a hunting cottage built in 1921, one of Duck's oldest buildings.)

That same boardwalk is part of a 7-mile trail that continues its wandering ways as a waterside attraction of the town. The soundside peregrinations weave past the town amphitheater behind City Hall and City Hall Green.

When Duck finally incorporated on May 1, 2002, it was, as far as land development goes, finished. The new town's boundaries stretched from sea to sound and slightly more than 6 miles, from Southern Shores in the south to the Dare/Currituck line. Duck, for the most part, was done.

The peninsula is narrowest at Duck's northern end. This used to be the site of Caffey's Inlet. Today it is the site of the Palmer's Island Club, an exclusive subdivision with only one row of houses, all oceanfront homes with unobstructed views of Currituck Sound.

When Sanderling, a residential enclave slightly south of Palmer's Island, opened in 1985, it turned out to be a marriage of place and attitude that started out right and has been carrying on strong ever since. There are bike trails, and a dense planting of live oaks, Elaeagnus, and wax myrtle shields the homes from the views of passersby.

In a tip of the hat to history, the resort restored the 1899 Caffey's Inlet Life-Saving Station and renovated it to become a restaurant, The Lifesaving Station. U.S. Life-Saving Service artifacts and the story of the station are on display inside. It is one of the few accessible buildings of that service still standing and open to the public. (The original sign from the Caffey's Inlet Life-Saving Station is in the hands of the owners of Owens' Restaurant in Nags Head, which is housed in a building constructed to resemble the old station house at Whalebone Junction.)

The last large parcel of undeveloped land in Duck belongs to the U.S. Army. This is the U.S. Army Corps of Engineers Coastal Engineering Research Center's Field Research Facility, and it houses the Coastal and Hydraulics Laboratory, where scientists monitor physiographic changes along the coastline. The working end of the station is a massive 1,884-foot-long concrete pier that stabs into the Atlantic from the center of the 176-acre oceanfront site.

The pier is one of a limited number of sites nationwide where scientists gather the data used to compute the long-term trends in sea-level fluctuation. It serves as an official tide-monitoring station.

Occasionally you may see the Coastal Research Amphibious Buggy (CRAB), a remarkable self-powered three-legged tower that rolls along the nearshore making precise measurements of the sea floor just beyond the breaking waves.

The site was acquired from the U.S. Navy in 1973. Along with it came some unusual naval artifacts—unexploded ordinance.

Signs advise the following: Danger. No Trespassing. Ammunition Dud Area. Items May Explode When Handled. Removal of Items Prohibited by Penalty of Law.

The facility is closed to the public.

While Duck is generally easy, it does come with some challenges. High summer traffic is notorious, and left turns onto or off of NC 12 may require the benevolence of a fellow vacationer. "Shoulder season" and off season present fewer traffic issues. There is no grocery store in Duck; restocking requires driving to Corolla or Southern Shores.

Access

There is no public beach access. Beach access has been privately provided as residential developments were constructed. There are summer lifeguards on the beach, and the Town of Duck provides a map showing their locations.

Driving on the Beach

Vehicles are not permitted on the beach between May 1 and September 30. Beach driving is permitted the remainder of the year by using PRIVATE vehicular access points. There are no public access points in Duck.

Search Outer Banks or Town of Duck or enter
www.outerbanks.org or www.townofduck.com.

SOUTHERN SHORES

Southern Shores, one of the oldest planned communities on the Outer Banks, is private and almost completely residential and possesses a low-key, sequestered charm. Vacationers traveling north on NC 12 to reach other destinations may overlook its well-planned features. A mile wide from sound to sea and 4 miles long north to south, it harbors approximately 2,600 full-time residents, many in the shaded neighborhoods tucked into the maritime forest inland. In summer the population increases to about 10,000.

Renowned illustrator Frank Stick launched Southern Shores in 1946–47. He began developing the approximately 2,900 acres on his own, although development per se was managed through the Kitty Hawk Land Company. The community grew slowly, becoming a tight-knit enclave that established a civic association to monitor parks, beach access, and community appearance.

NC 12 routes directly behind the oceanfront row of homes, and two things are immediately apparent: the oceanfront lots and mirroring inland lots are very generous, and the homes are large, fairly new, and stylish. Peeking from behind established shrubbery are a few distinctive, flat-roofed

Just What Is Level about the Sea?

We calibrate the elevation of mountains in feet or meters using the level of the sea as the reference base, considering sea level "zero." But the ocean is not constant, so exactly how is this base determined?

The beach is the best place to wrestle with the notion that sea level is neither constant everywhere nor static over time. It not only varies from sea to shining sea but has also fluctuated greatly through much of prehistory. Present evidence indicates that sea level is incrementally rising, and any science-based argument is about how fast that is happening and where it might stop.

The National Ocean Service uses a device known as a tide gauge to determine a base sea-level measure. A mechanical tide gauge is simple but seems complicated. It consists of a float inside a perforated pipe. Wire links the float to a pulley, which in turn drives a screw-operated stylus that marks a clock-operated drum. The markings on the drum provide a time graph of the level of the sea. The perforations in the pipe are below tide level to minimize float movement from passing waves. To further reduce wave interference, geologists place tide gauges at the ends of piers extending several hundred feet from the shoreline. There are about 150 such locations throughout the United States. There is one at the U.S. Army Research Pier in Duck.

Scientists have been recording this data for decades, and analysis reveals that tidal action varies within a month, between months, and from year to year. Because the longest cycle of tidal variation takes about 18.75 years, there needs to be a continuous recording from a tidal gauge for at least 19 years to qualify its readings as a determinant of sea level at the station of record.

Mean sea level, our base measuring reference for heights, is the average height from such a series of recordings.

This is literally a starting point. Precise surveying extends this base level across land. Eventually, it is possible to compare a carefully surveyed elevation from one location with a survey based on data obtained independently at another location. The results can be astonishing: for example, sea level on the western coast of the Florida peninsula is 7 inches higher than that on Florida's East Coast beaches. Also, the Pacific coast averages 20 inches higher than the Atlantic. (In theory, to travel west in the Panama canal is to sail upwater, climbing nearly a foot from Atlantic to Pacific.)

This is unleveling, to say the least, and there is no completely satisfactory reason for the variation. Water temperature and barometric pressure can chip away at constancy—because water expands when heated, its level rises when the atmospheric pressure is low. Prevailing winds, water density differences caused by salinity, and the shape of the nearshore ocean bottom can add up to a not-so-sea-level start to a cross-country measuring trip. Add in the spin from the earth's rotation and its effects on currents such as the Gulf Stream (which is lower on the east side than on the west), and this is another way water piles up in locations, altering sea level. Each of these factors has varying effects in different locations—in other words, they are local, but still contribute to some of the intracontinental variations.

Just when it seems like there is solid ground for grasping the nuances in the process, one must account for the geological complication that some coastlines are sinking because of the weight of deposited sediment. Where it occurs, this sinking obviously exacerbates the rate of sea level rise. (This is occurring in Tidewater Virginia and northeastern North Carolina.)

As noted earlier, data indicates that sea level is rising (and/or the land where any given tidal gauge is fixed is subsiding). A worldwide rise in sea level is called a eustatic change.

There's no simple explanation here either. In fact, several factors or a combination of factors might be responsible, such as a change in the amount of water held on land in the form of ice, snow, lakes, and streams; a change in the capacity of the ocean basin through deformation, sedimentation, or volcanism; and changes in the total amount of water on the earth.

Meteorologists and coastal geologists cite a global climatic warming trend that is reducing the water held as ice and snow as the most likely cause. If this is so, then it is an inexorable, unstoppable, and unmanageable change that will shake things up along the coast.

Although such a transformation is generally a long-term change, telltale signs will show. One of them could be the persistent erosion of beaches as water relentlessly nibbles, trifling the sand away.

Though we act as if the surface of the ocean is constant, it is not. It is on the move—higher. With this in mind, take a North Carolina geography pop quiz: How high is Mount Mitchell? It is 6,684 feet above mean sea level—for now.

concrete-block "Florida homes." Solid-looking, with brightly painted trim, the few that remain evoke the earlier-era Florida retirement homes that inspired them. At one time they lined the oceanfront.

When Highway 12 turns inland, the route moves through the distinctive highlands composed of old dune ridges and enters the maritime forest. The northern end of Southern Shores is a series of neighborhood streets winding through these established woodlands. Thirteenth Street signals the northern limit of Southern Shores and the beginning of Duck.

Access

There is no public access. Parking and beach access are reserved for residents and their guests.

AYCOCK BROWN WELCOME CENTER

Southbound traffic from the Wright Memorial Bridge onto US 158 Bypass will have a right-lane exit to the Aycock Brown Welcome Center, operated by the Outer Banks Visitors Bureau. Built in a shingle architectural style reminiscent of the early lifesaving stations, the center sits atop a dune with an impressive view of northern Kitty Hawk. The welcome center offers destination advice, brochures, reservation assistance, and updated travel information on the Outer Banks communities and Cape Hatteras National Seashore. It also has restrooms and picnic sites.

Namesake journalist and photographer Aycock Brown became the Outer Banks' first director of tourism in 1950. His work in this capacity brought nationwide attention to these shores and communities.

The welcome center is officially located at Milepost 1; milepost numbers get higher as you travel south. Most destinations in publications are located by reference to mileposts that are signed along both US 158 Bypass (Croatan Highway) and NC 12 (Virginia Dare Trail or Beach Road).

Access

Aycock Brown Welcome Center is open and fully accessible from 9 AM to 5 PM daily, year-round except Thanksgiving and Christmas Day.

Search Outer Banks Welcome.

MONUMENT TO A CENTURY OF FLIGHT

On a windy November 8, 2003, in advance of the celebration of the centennial of the Wright Brothers' first flight, December 17, 1903, nearly 600 people gathered to dedicate the Monument to a Century of Flight. It is a contemplative, inspiring, and educational gift to the soaring spirit and technological innovation of humanity.

This new public park perches on top of a sand dune adjacent to and overlooking the Aycock Brown Welcome Center. It features a bold design: 14 stainless steel wing-shaped pylons increasing in height from 10 to 20 feet are set in a curve measuring 120 feet, symbolizing the length of the Wright Brothers' first flight.

The pylons are faced with black granite etched with the 100 most significant advances in aviation during the first century of flight.

The Monument to a Century of Flight is open to visitors year-round.

Search Monument to Flight or enter
www.monumenttoacenturyofflight.org.

KITTY HAWK

Kitty Hawk is the northernmost and smallest community of the historic Dare County resort beaches. It is one town with two characters: unpretentious, modest cottages close to the oceanfront; and a blend of traditional homesteads and medium-density second homes in the forested western half, where the community originated. It is completely casual in appearance and personality—as laid-back as the origin of the idiosyncratic name, possibly a corruption of a Native American word, *chicahuack* or *chickahawk*, meaning "a place to hunt geese."

Travelers arriving from the north cross the Wright Memorial Bridge to enter the northern limits of Kitty Hawk. On Saturdays in peak summer, this is a frustrating passage because of traffic waiting to head north on NC 12. Once you're past this intersection, the approximate 3.5 miles of Kitty Hawk oceanfront begins with a new landmark, the Hilton Garden Inn Kitty Hawk. Visible to the north of the hotel are the truncated remnants of the Kitty Hawk Fishing Pier, long the visual northern limit of the beach. Hurricane Isabel in 2003 ended the pier's long history; in a good-faith gesture,

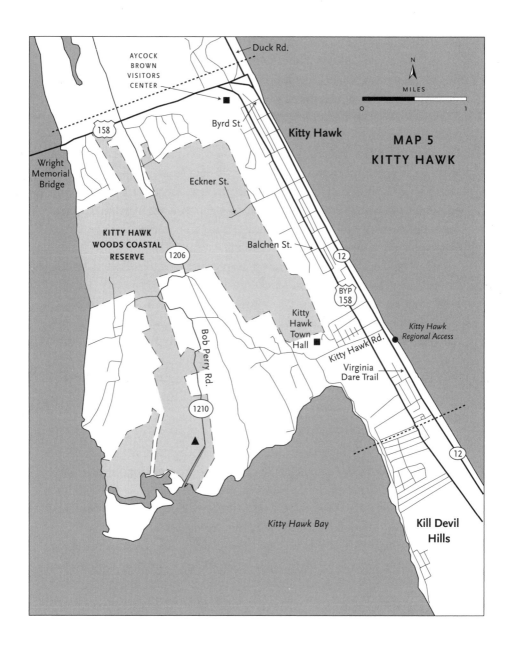

AYCOCK
BROWN
VISITORS
CENTER

Duck Rd.

N

MILES

0   1

Byrd St.

Kitty Hawk

**MAP 5
KITTY HAWK**

158

Wright
Memorial
Bridge

Eckner St.

**KITTY HAWK
WOODS COASTAL
RESERVE**

1206

Balchen St.

12

BYP
158

Kitty
Hawk
Town
Hall

*Kitty Hawk
Regional Access*

Bob Perry Rd.

Kitty Hawk Rd.

Virginia
Dare Trail

1210

Kitty Hawk Bay

**Kill Devil
Hills**

12

the Garden Inn incorporated the remainder to start a new, abbreviated story at the same location.

Virginia Dare Trail curves past the hotel and begins an uncluttered drive south through a resort that recalls a simpler, less lavish era. The Kitty Hawk oceanfront extends steadily south to the border at Kill Devil Hills, just beyond milepost 5. (The DeCharmarnel Travel Trailer Court at East Sibbern Drive is the informal landmark of the southern city limits.)

Virginia Dare Trail provides a cruise that can be tedious if you're squeezed for time or a calming decompression if you're enjoying an unhurried drive along the oceanfront. The road threads between unadorned, residential cottages on the west side and modest weather-beaten oceanfront homes to the east. There are few business on this route, and the houses are small because the lots were platted with a 50-foot frontage. In recent years sand has been piled high, blocking the ocean view, and there are gaps in the continuous row of houses. Kitty Hawk has been in a heady tussle with the sea, which has clawed inland, gobbling homes and, during severe storms, overwashing and destroying the pavement.

These storm impacts are the latest chapter in a much older story. In the late nineteenth and early twentieth centuries the only permanent housing on the sandy flats behind the beach belonged to the U.S. Life-Saving Service—no one else "lived" seaside. One of the seven original stations along the Outer Banks was originally located approximately at Kitty Hawk Road and Virginia Dare Trail—just about milepost 4. You can still get the flavor of that era by dining at the Black Pelican Restaurant, the converted lifesaving station, which had a telegraph, at the corner of Virginia Dare Trail and Kitty Hawk Road.

The black pelican theme echoes the legend that such a bird was repeatedly seen prior to a shipwreck and so became a harbinger of rescue. W. D. Tate, the station's original keeper or captain, supposedly logged this association. Inside, photographs and nautical artifacts build on the station's history, which is notable. After their historic flight in 1903, the Wright Brothers came here to telegraph their success to the world.

On the west side of Beach Road, one-quarter mile south of the Black Pelican, is the 1899 Kitty Hawk Lifesaving Station. The companion to the restaurant in lore and history, it too was originally east of Beach Road, but is safely set back and elevated as a private residence. It is recognizable by its distinctive architecture and a sign that declares its lineage as Kitty Hawk Life-Saving Station No. 2.

Kitty Hawk spills from the oceanfront into the 2-mile-wide maritime forest known as Kitty Hawk Woods west of US 158. Historically, the community settled first in the shelter of the woods, closer to the sound, where early inhabitants made their living. Bound together by an informal cohesion of place, Kitty Hawk finally incorporated in 1981.

Kitty Hawk Road, SR 1208, loops inland from US 158 bypass through the oldest part of Kitty Hawk and connects with Woods Road, SR 1206, deep in the extensive maritime forest, a portion of which is owned by the town. Preservation of this substantial wooded character has been firmly established by a 461-acre town holding that is included in the 1,824 acres of Kitty Hawk Woods, part of both the North Carolina Coastal Reserve and the National Estuarine Research Reserve.

Sturdy frame houses, some of which are pre-twentieth century, are still visible on roads in the forest. These are older country homes, durably built for year-round housing by the watermen and tradespeople who made Kitty Hawk home. The Wright Brothers stayed safely in the woods in such a home while working toward their dream of flight on the sandy hills and flats to the east.

Newer developments have come to the woods: the Sea Scape golf community, along the west side of US 158, peeks from the edge of the older sequestered community. The Kitty Hawk municipal center is also on the eastern edge of the sheltering forest setting.

Search Kitty Hawk NC or enter www.kittyhawknc.gov.

Access

There is public parking and access at the following streets: Balchen, Bennett, Bleriot, Fonck, Hawks, Lillian, Maynard, and Wilkins.

Byrd Street has a bathhouse, shower, and parking.

There is a regional access site at Kitty Hawk, south of Kitty Hawk Road on Virginia Dare Trail.

There are fixed lifeguard stands staffed by Kitty Hawk Ocean Rescue personnel at the Byrd Street, Eckner Street, and Kitty Hawk Bath House access sites. Roving lifeguards on ATVs patrol from 10 AM to 6 PM Memorial Day to Labor Day. The town also has a handicap-accessible public sound access at Windgrass Circle.

KITTY HAWK WOODS COASTAL RESERVE

In the middle of the village of Kitty Hawk is the magnificent Kitty Hawk Woods, a component of the North Carolina Coastal Reserve. A total of 1,824 acres of maritime forest, deciduous swamp, and marsh has been set aside for safekeeping and research. The town of Kitty Hawk, with a conservation easement with the state, owns 461 acres. It is an investment in Kitty Hawk's future by saving one of the most important ecological habitats of its past.

The preserve includes upland forest on ancient dune ridges and lowland freshwater swamps between the ridges. The height of the dune ridges shields plants from the damaging effects of salt spray. Plant types found in the forest include some normally found no closer than 100 miles west, as well as plants more common in the sandy oceanside environment. The rare (for this area) hop hornbeam is also found here and in nearby Nags Head Woods.

The wildlife population is equally diverse: the upland areas have gray fox, raccoon, and white-tailed deer; the marsh environment includes nutria, muskrat, and river otter. Birding in Kitty Hawk Woods presents the possibility of seeing warblers, woodpeckers, and hawks. Wrens and other songbirds are also abundant. Deep swales provide habitat for wood ducks and the full range of familiar marsh visitors—herons, egrets, geese, ducks, swans, and rails.

Most of all, there is incredible peace and quiet in Kitty Hawk Woods, with several walking trails that provide access to the interior of this important coastal reserve.

Access

From US 158, a half mile east of the Wright Memorial Bridge, turn south on Woods Road, SR 1206, and park at a small playground a quarter mile from US 158 next to Dominion Power. A multiuse path parallels Woods Road.

There is also public access from the west end of Eckner Street and at the end of Amadas Road and Birch Lane. Parking is limited.

Search NC Coastal Reserve or enter
www.nccoastalreserve.net. Click reserve sites.

KILL DEVIL HILLS

Kill Devil Hills is the most populous municipality in Dare County. The year-round population is more than 7,200, and that swells to more than 40,000 during peak summer weeks. That seasonal growth is a by-product of a broad community embrace of beach tourism in all forms and duration. The US

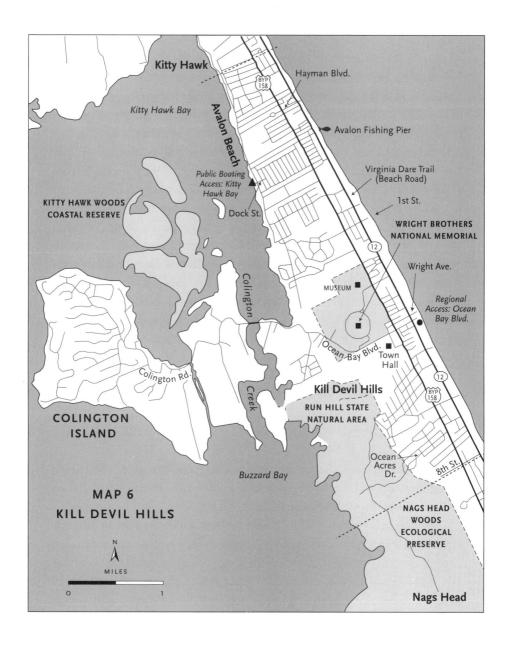

Kitty Hawk

Hayman Blvd.

BYP 158

Kitty Hawk Bay

Avalon Beach

Avalon Fishing Pier

Public Boating
Access: Kitty
Hawk Bay

Virginia Dare Trail
(Beach Road)

KITTY HAWK WOODS
COASTAL RESERVE

Dock St.

1st St.

WRIGHT BROTHERS
NATIONAL MEMORIAL

12

Wright Ave.

Colington

MUSEUM

Regional
Access: Ocean
Bay Blvd.

Ocean Bay Blvd.

Town
Hall

Colington Rd.

Creek

Kill Devil Hills

12

BYP 158

COLINGTON
ISLAND

RUN HILL STATE
NATURAL AREA

Ocean
Acres
Dr.

8th St.

Buzzard Bay

MAP 6
KILL DEVIL HILLS

NAGS HEAD
WOODS
ECOLOGICAL
PRESERVE

N

MILES

0   1

Nags Head

158 bypass is a thriving commercial road with shopping centers, boutique stores, and recreation outlets. Restaurants, among them familiar national names, are plentiful. This tilt toward service enterprises is noticeable in Kill Devil Hills and is part of its attraction as a destination.

There are charming touches as well. The Glenmere Avenue Beach Access off of Virginia Dare Trail, just south of Prospect Avenue, which leads west to the Wright Brothers National Memorial, is the site of Hope Access—Home of the Little Red Mailbox. It is exactly that: a bright red mailbox set on a piling next to the gazebo by Kill Devil Hills resident Sue Goodrich. Inside are a bound journal, pens, and the opportunity to leave a personal message of hope. It is a wonderful chance to give and receive in kind.

Kitty Hawk and Kill Devil Hills share a lengthy history as early resort communities. Kill Devil Hills was long a township of Kitty Hawk. In 1953 Kill Devil Hills incorporated and began to shape a new town identity.

Its 4.7 miles of Virginia Dare Trail (Beach Road) feel and look more like a vacation destination than a community of private family homes. The Kill Devil Hills oceanfront is open for the beach vacation business. This difference in character and tone is noticeable but still on a comfortable human scale. The view of the strand from atop Big Kill Devil Hill at the Wright Brothers National Memorial reveals a Monopoly board silhouette—houses, hotels, houses, and hotels. There is no wall of hotel rooms continuously blocking the view of the ocean. There's a mix and the variety is appealing.

Along with this mix in the size and scale of buildings comes a noticeable uptick in community tempo. The beach is wonderful, and it is possible to choose accommodations welcoming visitors for less-than-weekly stays. There is a caveat, however—a single weekend night in summer is hard to find. An informal policy requiring two-night weekend rentals in summer prevails.

These differences are not abruptly evident when you enter town along Virginia Dare Trail from Kitty Hawk. One town eases into another, and then hotels appear, as would be expected at a beach resort.

The origin of the name of Kill Devil Hills may have been a comment attributed to William Byrd dating from 1728: he reported that a New England rum favored by the inhabitants on these sandy and isolated shores of the Outer Banks was strong enough to "kill the devil." This remark, combined with the unusually large hills of sand dominating the barrier island, possibly led to the naming of the largest hill as "Kill Devil Hill" on an 1808 map.

The area has always been dependably windy, so much so that the community and its massive hills were vegetation free from the maritime forest to the ocean. The massive sand hills (Big Kill Devil Hill was stabilized with a grass planting in 1928) migrated to and fro, back and forth, south to north, with the annual cycle of steadily prevailing winds. Vegetation could not root in the moving sand. In the late nineteenth and early twentieth centuries there were constant winds and a soft sandy place to land, and there was nobody around to scoop a secret project. The only thing the Wright Brothers really had to avoid was the Kitty Hawk Life-Saving Station.

The mix was ideal and appealing to Wilber and Orville Wright. In 1900 they brought their dream and determination to Kitty Hawk and established a workshop at the base of the 90-foot summit of Big Kill Devil Hill. They obtained all the solitude and time they needed, and the primary witnesses to three years of trials and errors and their eventual success were the crew members of the Kitty Hawk Life-Saving Station. They occasionally assisted the brothers in their experiments. That story is well told at the Wright Brothers National Memorial. (The original boathouse from the Kitty Hawk station has been relocated and repurposed in Corolla as an office for Twiddy and Company Realty. See Corolla in the Dare County chapter.)

Kill Devil Hills is verdant today by comparison to its sandy early years, the result of a Great Depression stabilization program in the 1920s and 1930s. The U.S. Army Corps of Engineers not only stabilized Big Kill Devil Hill but also constructed a line of dunes along the oceanfront. The stabilization and dune line enabled the maritime vegetation to anchor and grow.

The substantial tract of inland maritime forest and stable soundside locations makes Kill Devil Hills attractive for permanent homes in addition to oceanfront vacation homes.

Since the local economy hinges on tourism, the town actually markets its beach access program and provides clearly marked sites. During the summer season, though finding a single room for one weekend night is difficult, access to the beach is convenient.

Search KDHNC or enter www.kdhnc.com.

Access

Kill Devil Hills has 28 public beach accesses, starting with Arch Street in the north and ending with Eighth Street at the southern city limits. The locations are clearly signed from Virginia Dare Trail; several provide parking.

Ten access sites provide restrooms as shown on a city map. They are, north to south, Hayman Boulevard, Asheville Drive, Prospect Avenue, Woodmere Avenue, Ferris Avenue, Raleigh Avenue, Carlow Avenue, Clark Street, Martin Street, and Atlantic Street.

Several ramps serve off-road vehicles. Between October 1 and April 30 you may drive on the beach.

The North Carolina Wildlife Resources Commission maintains fishing and boating access on Kitty Hawk Bay at Avalon Beach, a half mile west of US 158 on Dock Street.

WRIGHT BROTHERS NATIONAL MEMORIAL

Yes, this is the exact location of one of the most important achievements of humankind, but the background story of the multiyear run-up to the Wright Brothers' success—the inventing, crafting, kiting, gliding, and crashing before flying—is why you should visit. It is not the story of what went (W)right but of what went wrong and how they overcame the setbacks.

The narrative is told in interpretive talks by the park service rangers, and it breathes history into this memorial. Otherwise, what offers continuity here with those historic years is mostly the prevailing winds.

The Kitty Hawk location that the Wright Brothers chose was very different than the memorial site today. At the dawn of the twentieth century, there were no trees, no grass, and, for their purposes, no people with contact to the outside world. There was sand all the way to the sea for soft landing and steady winds for loft. The lack of people, beyond landlords who offered housing and U.S. Life-Saving Service personnel who frequently assisted, assured privacy. There was also Big Kill Devil Hill, the massive 100-foot-high dune that served as their runway and launching pad.

What the park service rangers describe with masterful narration is the genius and persistence that really propelled the Wright Brothers' quest for powered, heavier-than-air flight. In one such talk—these engaging lectures are regularly scheduled at the memorial—a ranger speculated that it may have been the brothers' childhood fascination with a rubber band propelled "bat" toy that launched their dream of flight. Perhaps true, but indisputably intriguing. All presentations make clear that what carried the brothers to success was their unrelenting curiosity, mechanical intuition and aptitude, and methodical experimentation. They spent five years building, crashing, and repairing at this place and inventing in Ohio to achieve their success. They pursued the challenge with a relentlessness that bordered on obsession.

Roll Tide Roll

The moon commits gravity on the high seas, and by another name, it is the tide. This is a wild concept: the sun and moon move the sea molecule by molecule, and each molecule/droplet moves on cue. The sea crawls up and back on the beach, moving to a heavenly metronome. This is done with cunning, not muscle: what moves the waters is not the mass of the sun but the proximity of the moon.

You have to hang around the coast to appreciate this daily dance. The moon sleeps late, rising later each day by an average of 50 minutes. So does the tide. The full tidal cycle is 24 hours and 50.4 minutes. As the moon passes through its phases, waning from full to new then waxing to full again, the tidal rise corresponds; it's highest on the full and new moon phases.

The big tides, called spring tides, come when the moon, earth, and sun are aligned during the full and new moons. On these syzygies, the combined gravitational pull of the sun and moon summons the ocean to its greatest flood, usually 20 percent greater than normal.

In addition, the moon's elliptical orbit carries it closer to the earth once every revolution. If this minimal orbital distance coincides with the time of a new or full moon, then the result is the perigean spring tides—the highest of the cyclical tidal flows.

The lowest tides occur during the quarter phases of the moon. When the gravitational pull of the moon and sun are perpendicular to each other, the lowest, or neap, tides occur. There are 14 days between spring tides and neap tides, corresponding to the time between full and new moons.

This is the astral mechanism behind the tides, but as with much about the ocean, the tidal picture is not so simply explained. On North Carolina's jigsawed coast, there are local fluctuations in tide times. It's never high tide everywhere at once. High tide differs because the shape of the shoreline modifies the tidal effect.

When, as Ocracokers say, it is "hoigh toid on the sound soid," it is not high tide on the mainland at Swan Quarter. The tides are different in the shifting inlets of the Outer Banks, affected by the slope of the offshore ocean and the sound basin, the width of an inlet, and the depth of the inlet's channel. The tide has to move through inlets. This passage delays the tide schedule on inland shores in larger increments as the distance increases.

The U.S. Coast and Geodetic Survey is armed with all these local differences and can predict the time and approximate height of the tide at any given location. Commerce at the coast moves on this information.

North Carolina's semidiurnal or twice-daily tidal rhythm—two high tides and two low tides each day—is normal for the Atlantic coast. The highs and lows are very similar, covering or failing to cover approximately the same amount of beach as the previous pair in the tidal cycle. Not so on the Pacific coast, where a high high tide and then a low low tide are followed by a lower high tide and a higher low tide.

Along the Gulf Coast, tidal change is minimal during a given day—one swelling for a high and one exhalation for a low. Since the different tidal patterns cannot be attributed to changes in the moon and sun, other factors must govern this rhythm—factors that are perplexingly complex.

Keep tidal management simple: low tides are for clamming and shelling, high tides are for fishing and inlet travel. Don't lose sleep over the tides—this is, after all, the beach.

Today the granite pylon dedicated to the first motor-powered airplane flight dominates the west horizon of Kill Devil Hills, sitting high atop Big Kill Devil Hill. In 1928, 25 years after the historic first flight, the federal government planted grass to stabilize the once-sandy Big Kill Devil Hill. One could say they caught it just in time, because by then the prevailing winds had moved Big Kill Devil Hill 450 feet southwest of where the Wright Brothers launched their epic flight. Granite markers mark the exact location and the humble distances of humankind's first four powered flights.

Behind the hill is full-scale bronze and stainless steel sculpture replicating the famous first-flight photograph taken December 17, 1903, by John Daniels, a surfman with the Kitty Hawk U.S. Life-Saving Station. It is a fabulously detailed addition to the memorial.

Renovations to the National Historic Landmark visitors' center were completed in the fall of 2018. The renovated display space is home to a full-scale replica of the 1903 flyer, and all exhibits are new and updated. The memorial is open 9–5 daily except Christmas Day. There is an admission fee.

Search Wright Brothers Memorial or enter www.nps.gov/wrbr.

RUN HILL STATE NATURAL AREA

There is a massive, often-overlooked natural feature behind First Flight Elementary and Middle Schools on Veteran's Drive: Run Hill State Natural Area. Run Hill is one of the remaining medaños, or massive unvegetated moving sand dunes, historically found on the northern Outer Banks (Big Kill Devil Hill was once one; nearby Jockey's Ridge, a state park, is another). The Nature Conservancy helped arrange the transfer of the 123-acre Run Hill from Kill Devil Hills to the state park system in 1995. As a North Carolina State Natural Area, it is supposed to be protected in its natural state with no improvements. As such, it is a quiet retreat little known beyond the city limits of Kill Devil Hills.

As with Jockey's Ridge, prevailing winds shift the dune along a northeast–southwest alignment. The opposition of prevailing winds has enabled the massive accumulation of sand that is the existing dune. The shift of winds from winter (northeast) to summer (southwest) also contributes to the steep faces of the dunes on the northeast and southwest sides.

As it moves, it engulfs whatever might be in its path. Run Hill is encroaching on Nags Head Woods to the southwest, and it spills steeply into the vestigial forest as strong northeast winds roll sand over the top to abruptly fall down the lee side of the dune.

Run Hill reveals all the intricate ecological stories of the great moving dunes without the crowds. It is low-key and invites contemplative observation. Visitors are on their own to make sense of what they observe in this living remnant of an unpopulated Outer Banks. No interpretive information or facilities are available at the site.

Run Hill State Natural Area is west of First Flight Elementary and Middle Schools, 107 Veterans Drive, Kill Devil Hills, NC.

NAGS HEAD WOODS ECOLOGICAL PRESERVE

The pent-up enthusiasm for ocean and beach propels visitors past more than 1,200 acres of original Outer Banks habitats: Nags Head Woods Ecological Preserve. It is a nationally significant reserve—a mix of dunes, interdune ponds, hardwood forests, swamps, marshes, and shoreline—an environmental smorgasbord of rarely altered Outer Banks ecology. Few places comparable to Nags Head Woods remain, and it is one of the largest examples of a once-prevalent mid-Atlantic maritime hardwood forest. Visitors from inland cities of the mid-Atlantic might find that the preserve "looks just like home," and this is one key to its rarity. It is a mosaic of ordinarily distant plant and animal communities nested and thriving on a sandy barrier peninsula.

As such it is a superb counterpoint in appearance, mood, and appeal to the beachfront of the resorts. Nags Head Woods offers shade, serenity, and the hush of an isolated forest cove. In autumn it boasts exquisite sequestered fall color, a seasonal expression decidedly rare on the Outer Banks.

The woods sprawls on the peninsula's western edge, from Run Hill State Natural Area in Kill Devil Hills south to Jockey's Ridge State Park in Nags Head. The Nature Conservancy manages the 1,200-plus acres, which is threaded by hiking trails up to several miles long. The trails vary in length and hiking challenge. Several are short and easily walked by families with small children. There is a half-mile-long Americans with Disabilities Act–approved trail constructed as a boardwalk with paved surfaces suitable for wheelchairs and strollers. It provides access and viewing to one of the many interdunal ponds, the maritime forest swamp, and a brackish marsh overlook. Some of the more challenging trails have constructed steps to minimize trail wear on steep dune faces. The trails dispel any preconceived notion that barrier islands are flat, sandy, and boring. In fact, hikers can discover building foundations and burial plots from the earliest days of Nags Head, when the resort community first formed on the sound side of the peninsula. Nags Head Woods is many things, but it is not boring.

The woods was recognized as a National Natural Landmark in 1974, a designation that fueled the Nature Conservancy's effort to protect it, starting with an initial purchase of a 420-acre tract in 1978. Several purchases and dedications of land through the 1980s resulted in a sustainable preserve managed by the Nature Conservancy. Trails are open during daylight hours. Dogs must be leashed and are restricted to designated trails.

A sign, approximately at milepost 10 on US 158 bypass, directs visitors onto Ocean Acres Drive through a residential neighborhood to the visitor center. There is a stoplight with a McDonald's that marks the turn west onto Ocean Acres Drive. When the pavement ends, keep going; the road in the preserve is not paved.

Search Nature Nags Head Woods or enter www.nature.org and click through geographically sorted headings to find the home page.

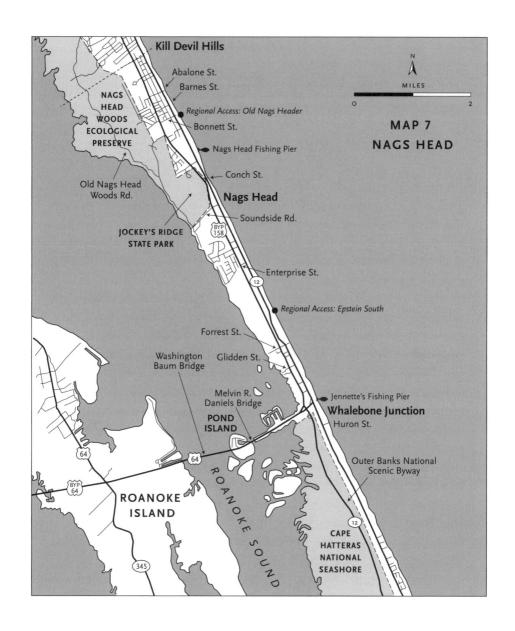

Kill Devil Hills

Abalone St.
Barnes St.

NAGS
HEAD
WOODS
ECOLOGICAL
PRESERVE

● Regional Access: Old Nags Header
Bonnett St.

● Nags Head Fishing Pier

Old Nags Head
Woods Rd.

Conch St.

Nags Head

Soundside Rd.

JOCKEY'S RIDGE
STATE PARK

BYP
158

12

Enterprise St.

● Regional Access: Epstein South

Forrest St.

Washington   Glidden St.
Baum Bridge

Melvin R.
Daniels Bridge

POND
ISLAND

64

● Jennette's Fishing Pier

Whalebone Junction
Huron St.

Outer Banks National
Scenic Byway

64

BYP
64

ROANOKE
ISLAND

ROANOKE SOUND

12

CAPE
HATTERAS
NATIONAL
SEASHORE

345

N

MILES

0   2

MAP 7
NAGS HEAD

Access

Trails are open during daylight hours.

Address: Nags Head Woods Ecological Preserve, Visitor Center, 701 West Ocean Acres Drive, Nags Head, NC 27948. Phone: 919-441-2525.

NAGS HEAD

Nags Head, with its 11-mile beachfront, has two unique and defining features. One is a landmark—Jockey's Ridge—and the other an imprint: the weathered and unpainted oceanfront cottages that date from the early years of the resort's history. These two particularities anchor Nags Head in place and time.

Jockey's Ridge, part of an eponymous state park, is a medaño, a massive, unvegetated, continually shifting sand dune, large enough that five-lane US 158 had to be routed around it. It is the tallest active sand dunes on the East Coast, and in its wandering it has gobbled houses, forests, and even a miniature golf course long since buried. It is a dominating, enthralling feature, all the more so for the hang gliders and kite flyers regularly cavorting on its gritty slopes.

The architecturally distinctive beach cottages lining Virginia Dare Trail epitomize Nags Head's unpretentious origins as the first resort in Dare County. They are easily visible from atop Jockey's Ridge as sentinels at the dunes' edge. The summering tradition on the Outer Banks began here before the Civil War when planters from inland counties migrated to the coast to enjoy ocean breezes and escape the seasonal miasma of their permanent homes. Amazingly, Nags Head has homes that can be linked directly to this nineteenth-century origin. They are included in an informal Nags Head Beach Cottage Historic District.

Until the middle of the twentieth century, the historic district homes set a tone for the town's growth and appearance. Today they are admired for the simpler times they evoke and their longevity. (See "Serenity by the Sea: Nags Head Beach Cottage Historic District.")

Nags Head stayed exclusive and virtually inaccessible until the 1930s. The construction of the Wright Memorial Bridge initiated the big change. The bridge brought US 158 to the island. That route directly served the northeastern agricultural communities that pioneered summering here. In addition, the state paved the first 18 miles of what would become NC 12. Shortly thereafter, the post office moved over from the mainland and the development of the Nags Head oceanfront began in earnest.

Nags Head beachfront extends from Kill Devil Hills south to the oceanfront of Cape Hatteras National Seashore, almost half the distance to Oregon Inlet. The community is narrow; the greatest width is slightly more than a mile at the northern city limits with Kill Devil Hills, denoted by Eighth Street.

Except for Jockey's Ridge State Park and Nags Head Woods, the town between Kill Devil Hills and Whalebone Junction, where US 64 begins (or ends), is a scramble of commercial and residential development.

South of Whalebone Junction, Virginia Dare Trail veers west, and the road that splits off to follow the oceanfront is Old Oregon Inlet Road. It continues south through 5 miles of residential development sandwiched between a relentlessly encroaching ocean and the maritime shrub and marsh habitat of Cape Hatteras National Seashore to the west.

The community is home to 2,800 year-round residents. Visitors stay and play along the oceanfront east of Virginia Dare Trail that has hotels, single-family vacation homes, and two fishing piers. The oceanfront remains mostly residential, and multiple dune crossovers provide beach access. The architectural character of the oceanfront housing is in flux as the modest, single-family cottages-by-the-sea of the mid-twentieth century (and earlier, of course) yield to massive, lavishly styled, multiple-family accommodations. The business of vacation rental is thriving, and the newer homes serving the multifamily/special event market command the oceanfront in a grander manner than their humbler predecessors.

On the other side of Virginia Dare Trail, restaurants, recreation, and commercial enterprises spread west until they create a solidly commercial corridor with malls and strip shopping centers along US 158. The corridor is a commercial hub that in peak summer has a fevered pace.

In recent years Nags Head (and communities to the north) turned to beach nourishment to replace sand and reclaim a greater width of foreshore. Diminishing beach is not a new story here. Several of the homes in the historic district have retreated multiple times for this reason. (The houses were built for this contingency.) South Nags Head has been found to be particularly vulnerable to erosion.

Visitors will find a fine strand, and the town provides ample access with dune crossovers approximately every one-half mile. There are multiple lifeguard stations along the beach between Memorial Day and Labor Day.

Even nonanglers can respect the long-running saga of the Nags Head Fishing Pier at 3335 South Virginia Dare Trail (milepost 11.5) slightly south of Bainbridge Street. The original pier was built in 1947, and 10 years later a hurricane removed 300 feet from the end. It was rebuilt, and two years later a hurricane blew a wrecked ship through the middle. The infamous 1962 Ash Wednesday storm—possibly the worst storm ever—completely destroyed the pier and pier house (and pretty much everything around it).

Today the pier reaches 740 feet into the Atlantic over a sandy bottom. It offers a full tackle shop and full-service restaurant. In summer there is live music. The pier is open to strollers, of course.

A North Carolina historical marker at the Bladen Street access area hints at the compelling story of the wreck of a naval gunship, the USS *Huron*.

On November 24, 1991, the 114th anniversary of the shipwreck of the USS *Huron*, citizens of Nags Head and state officials gathered to mark the establishment of the first North Carolina Historic Shipwreck Preserve.

The preserve honors a horrible event: on November 24, 1877, the USS *Huron*, a naval ship that had been repaired and resupplied and was bound for Cuba, sailed too close to shore and ran aground here in Nags Head at 1:30 AM. The location corresponds roughly to milepost 11.5. Ninety-eight of the 134 men aboard perished. Although there was a U.S. Lifesaving Station less than 2 miles away, it was closed until December, so there was no one to help the men. The wreck is about 250 yards offshore in 20 feet of water and approximately even with the end of the Nags Head Fishing Pier visible to the south.

This shipwreck and the subsequent wreck of the passenger steamer *Metropolis* near Corolla, costing 85 lives, prompted Congress to fully fund and staff the U.S. Life-Saving Service in North Carolina.

Mixed with such salt-bleached charm are the seasonal businesses and enterprises that thrive between Memorial Day and Labor Day. Across from Jockey's Ridge State Park is Kitty Hawk Kites, the self-proclaimed largest selection of kites in the East, and Kitty Hawk Kites' Hang Gliding Training Center is the place to learn to fly. School will be in session right across the street.

There are other classic and enduring enterprises in Nags Head that bridge eras. Owens' Restaurant at milepost 16.5 on Beach Road is the longest-running family restaurant on the beach (since 1946). It is modeled on the shingle style of the old lifesaving station and sports the original sign of the Caffey's Inlet Station north of Duck.

On the causeway to Manteo is Basnight's Lone Cedar Café, where folks come early for the waterside setting and fresh seafood that is purchased and

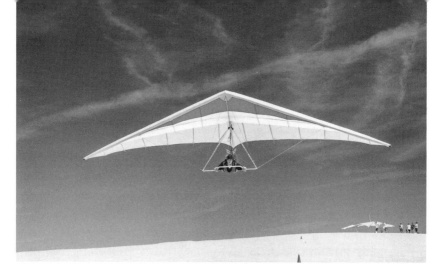

Jockey's Ridge is the tallest active sand dune on the East Coast and home of the world's largest hang-gliding school. (Photo by Bill Russ, courtesy of VisitNC.com)

cleaned daily at the restaurant—emphasis on local and fresh. Early dining guarantees the daily specials will be available.

Search Nags Head or enter www.nagsheadnc.gov.

Access

The Town of Nags Head lists 43 signed access sites along Virginia Dare Trail, beginning with Eighth Street at the northern city limits and extending to the park service access site 10 miles to the south. Most east–west streets provide beach access, but not always parking. In season there are lifeguards at several locations.

Nags Head originally named east–west streets alphabetically north to south. Each letter corresponded to a milepost marker. At the northern city limits, milepost 10, the street names began with the letter *A*—Abalone, Albatross, and so forth. At milepost 11, the street names began with *B*; at milepost 12, the letter *C*; and so on. While the practice has faded, it is useful to remember that Whalebone Junction, where I-64 starts (or ends), corresponds to Gulfstream Street. Addresses farther down the alphabet will be south of Whalebone Junction and off of Old Oregon Inlet Road (aka Beach Road).

Bathhouses are located at Bonnett Street, Epstein South (about milepost 15.25), Jennette's Pier, and Hargrove Street south of Whalebone Junction.

JOCKEY'S RIDGE STATE PARK

Anyone could reasonably assume that something the size and age of Jockey's Ridge—one of the largest sand dunes on the East Coast, wavering between 80 and 100 feet tall and noted on eighteenth-century navigation maps—would be enduring and beyond man-made threat. It almost wasn't. In 1973 bulldozers had begun to flatten a side of the dune for a subdivision when a highly motivated local resident, Carolista Baum, took action. First she stopped the bulldozers by jumping in front of them, and then she helped form a committee to save this historic playground. In short order the immense living dune was designated a National Natural Landmark, the North Carolina General Assembly authorized it to become a park and purchased 152 acres, and the Nature Conservancy nearly doubled the park's size, to 266-plus acres. Today 420 mostly sand-covered acres comprise this landmark state park.

Jockey's Ridge is considered a living dune—it is constantly shaped by the wind, but never so much so that it travels too far from its historical vicinity. It has shifted more than 1,000 feet southwest since the 1970s, covering some forest in the process.

There are few finer laboratories for witnessing the tug of war between wind and sand than Jockey's Ridge. Prevailing summer winds from the southeast nudge the sand to the northeast, and prevailing winter winds from the northeast push it back. So it goes, year after year. Seasonal changes in breezes roll the sand from one side to the other, and although thousands of visitors climb the dune each year, their tracks are simply erased. From the top of the dune you can see how mobile its surface is. For many years, an adjoining novelty-golf concession would have to dig out of winter's loess to open the summer season.

Jockey's Ridge is not unique on the Outer Banks. It is one of a series of noteworthy dunes that includes nearby Run Hill State Natural Area, Big Kill Devil Hill (now stabilized with grass), Poyners Hill in Currituck County, and others of local lore, such as Engagement Hill, Pin Hill, and Seven Sisters. Despite its mobility, the dune has changed comparatively little in size or configuration since 1949, as revealed by aerial photographs of that time.

You can climb the dune and fly a kite or run down its side or slide down its side or roll down its side, then splash in the rainwater trapped in the hollows. It's certainly one place where your children can run free—and barely get out of eyesight.

Serenity by the Sea: Nags Head
Beach Cottage Historic District

Beginning at Conch Street, approximately milepost 12.5, and extending south for about a mile (milepost 13.5) along Virginia Dare Trail are 60 properties mapped on the town website as an informal "Nags Head Cottage Historic Area." The district is clearly signed on Virginia Dare Trail. This is not a city-administered zone; no official zoning protection or restriction legally preserves these homes. It is part cachet but mostly reverence for place and history that inspires owners to maintain their distinctive look. Nine of these homes date from the nineteenth century.

The National Register of Historic Places officially recognized these weathered, idiosyncratic, shingled cottages for their distinctive architectural character in 1977. But even for decades prior, the homes had been known as the "Unpainted Aristocracy." They are monuments to simpler times and simpler pleasures and the origins of Nags Head and, subsequently, Outer Banks tourism.

Author David Stick writes that a planter from Perquimans County, North Carolina, purchased 200 acres in the soundside woods and built a house in 1838. He then sold lots to others. A hotel followed soon thereafter. Visitation increased but was hindered by an arduous walk to the beach—one-half mile through sand—and water too shallow for passenger schooners. Both problems were solved with an extended pier and a mule cart "railroad." Antebellum Nags Head became a social gathering spot during July and August, the miasma months of summer heat and humidity.

The Civil War interrupted these happy times, ultimately dismantling the economy that supported such leisure, but by the late 1870s Nags Head bustled again. In this new wave of summering, a family built a house on the oceanfront approximately 300 yards away from the breakers. By 1885, there were 13 cottages along the ocean's edge slightly north of the once-lonely Nags Head Life-Saving Station.

The resort "officially" went seaside in the 1930s, following the construction of the Wright Memorial Bridge, which brought US 158 to the banks, and the paving of the first 18 miles of what would become NC 12. Shortly thereafter, the post office moved east and the development of the Nags Head oceanfront took off.

Between 1920 and 1940, the beachfront houses evolved a distinctive, environmentally adaptive style attributed by architectural historian Catherine Bisher to the remodeling and construction handiwork of Elizabeth City builder Stephen J. Twine, who did much of his work in a 1-mile length of beach. Twine also worked on St. Andrews by the Sea, the Episcopal Church on Virginia Dare Trail.

The genteel quality of their purpose, simple shelter by the sea, set a stylistic tone adopted by guesthouses such as the First Colony Inn, a vintage inn at milepost 16. Threatened at its oceanfront location 3 miles north in 1988, the Lawrence family saved the inn by sawing it into thirds, relocating it, and restoring it. The inn is on the National Register of Historic Places.

The view from Jockey's Ridge is magnificent, especially for sunsets. The dune is more comfortably climbed in the early or late hours of the day. On hot days, shoes are a must, particularly for children. On very windy days, sunglasses or other eye protection is recommended. Leave the dune if a thunderstorm is imminent; it is the highest location around and a frequent target of lightning strikes.

Hang-gliding enthusiasts trudge their wings to the top for a flight with a sure soft landing, in compliance with park restrictions. Watch for low-flying people.

It's not all sand all the time: the soundside access parking offers sunbathing, wading, and paddling in Roanoke Sound, plus a 1-mile nature trail with access to wetlands, grassy dunes, and maritime thickets.

Search Jockey's Ridge or enter www.ncparks.gov/jockeys-ridge-state-park.

Access

Parking and restroom facilities are located off of the US 158 bypass, marked by a stoplight and brown park sign. The park opens at 8 AM. The visitor center closes at 5 PM, 6 PM in summer. The park closes at 9 PM May–September.

By calling ahead 24 hours in advance, mobility-impaired visitors can schedule an ATV ride to the top of the dunes. Phone number: 252-441-7132.

Jennette's Pier at Whalebone Junction has aquariums and static exhibits along its length. (Photo by Bill Russ, courtesy of VisitNC.com)

JENNETTE'S PIER

In 2011 Jennette's Pier reopened as an educational ocean pier, a new attraction of the North Carolina Department of Natural and Cultural Resources. The 1,000-foot-long concrete pier extends into the ocean from the original 5-acre site occupied since 1939, slightly north of Whalebone Junction. The North Carolina Aquarium Society pursued this idea and purchased the pier in 2003. Hurricane Isabel then arrived to destroy the just-purchased and (many times rebuilt) wooden structure.

Today Jennette's Pier is open for fishing, with an expected and indispensable tackle shop and snack bar. Anglers pay a daily fee that also covers the required North Carolina saltwater fishing license. Visitors may walk the pier for a nominal fee. The pier features live animal exhibits and educational programs and has a reception and meeting center for hire.

There is also public beach access at this location.

Search Jennette's Pier or enter www.ncaquariums.com/jennettes-pier.

WHALEBONE JUNCTION

There is a stoplight at this most curiously named intersection where US 158 ends its eastward North Carolina arc; US 64/ launches its westward, cross-country trek, and the Outer Banks National Scenic Byway, charming NC 12, begins its mesmerizing 163-mile-long journey south over land and water.

The name harks back to the 1930s, well before paving. In those days the firmest ground available each day became the route most traveled along the Outer Banks, eventually arriving in this vicinity. A service station that stood at the intersection back in the day, and closed around the time the US 158 bypass was built, displayed the bleached bones of a beached leviathan. Although the landmark is now gone, the best intersection nickname in the state survives.

North from Whalebone Junction, a sign designates NC 12 as the Marc Basnight Highway, honoring a longtime Speaker of the House in the North Carolina General Assembly. Postal addresses will refer to NC 12 by its older name, Virginia Dare Trail. In local conversation the route is sometimes known as Beach Road.

WASHINGTON BAUM BRIDGE

The causeway from Whalebone Junction to Roanoke Island connects Cedar Island and Pond Island en route to Roanoke Island by way of the high-rise Washington Baum Bridge. This 1990 bridge replaced a swing bridge that opened for boat traffic leaving Roanoke Sound. Crossing at night provides a view of the telltale flashing of the Bodie Island Lighthouse.

Washington Baum, the bridge's namesake, pushed for the construction of a bridge and causeway in the 1920s.

The causeway has become a little busier than just a mere passage. Marinas and boat ramps extend from the road into the estuary. Crabbing and fishing are permitted in traffic-safe locations along the route, including on the Melvin R. Daniels Bridge, east of the Washington Baum Bridge. There are also several fine restaurants along the passage, each of which offers its own soundside vista for dining.

ROANOKE ISLAND

Roanoke Island is between North Carolina's mainland and the peninsula resort beaches to the east. Croatan Sound, 3 miles wide, separates Roanoke Island from mainland North Carolina. The island is an 11-mile-long, 2-mile-wide complex of pine and hardwood forest, marsh and maritime shrubs, and two very different communities, Manteo and Wanchese. Though long populated—particularly after the Civil War—Roanoke Island has grown slowly and maintained its unpretentious rural and small-town character.

When Dare County was established in the late nineteenth century, Manteo on Roanoke Island became the county seat, and for nearly 30 years, until 1928, it was accessible only by boat. In 1928 a private toll bridge, the Baum Bridge, linked the island and the growing resort communities on the Outer Banks. The Wright Memorial Bridge carrying NC 158 to the Outer Banks in the 1930s accelerated growth at the resorts, but beginning in 1947 Roanoke Island was tied to the mainland by a private ferry operated by T. A. Baum, which ran from Manns Harbor to the north end of Roanoke Island. When the state purchased the business, this became the first official state ferry route in North Carolina.

Finally, in 1955–56, the William B. Umstead Bridge opened to carry US 64 to Roanoke Island. They built the bridge and people came. The additional access led to a "discovery" of Roanoke Island by mainland vacationers on their way to the Outer Banks. In 2002 the dedication of the four-lane Virginia Dare Memorial Bridge carrying US 64 Bypass to the middle of Roanoke Island completed its tethering to the mainland.

Vacation appeal spilled over to the island, especially on the Shallowbag Bay and Roanoke Sound waterfront. Both have burgeoned with houses, condominiums, and boat slips—Pirate's Cove is the large boat-based development perched on the edge of the marshes visible to the north of the Washington Baum Bridge.

Roanoke Island should be at the top of the list of day explorations on an Outer Banks vacation. The island attractions cut across a range of interests while being compelling for their people-friendly presentations and opportunities for engaging learning. In the past 75 years, archaeologists and historians working with federal state institutions have busily filled in the details on several compelling threads of the island's past. For example, during

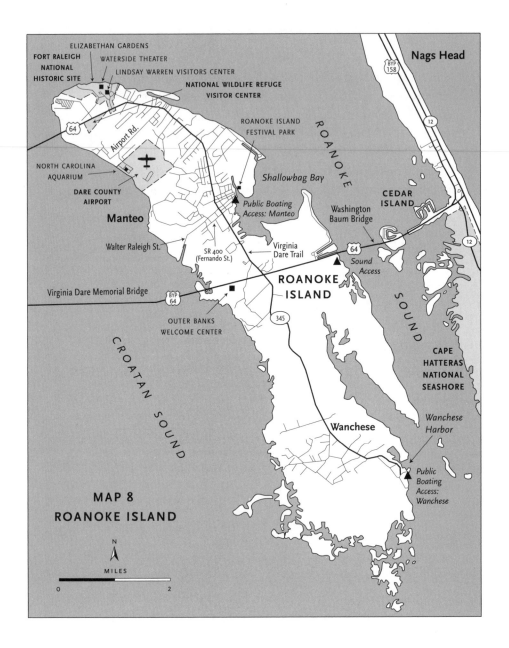

MAP 8
ROANOKE ISLAND

N

MILES

0   2

the Civil War, Union troops established the Freedmen's Colony of Roanoke Island, which grew into a village of more than 3,000 people and 600 homes. The colony was disbanded in 1866 after the federal government reversed a decision that had granted ownership of the houses to the freedmen. Many left the island, yet some remained to live and work here. An interpretive display at Weir Point, at the east end of the William B. Umstead Bridge, details this history.

The Sarah Owens Welcome Center at the east end of the Virginia Dare Memorial Bridge is a quick first stop to sort through the exploration options on Roanoke Island (and the rest of the Outer Banks). Pick up a welcome packet, which includes an "Outer Banks Vacation Guide" that provides an excellent listing of places and services. Enjoy the introductory video as well.

Options to choose among include the Roanoke Island Festival Park; the *Elizabeth II* State Historic Site; the restored, historic Island Farm; the North Carolina Aquarium; the Fort Raleigh National Historic Site; the Waterside Theatre; and the towns of Manteo and Wanchese, which present two very different sides of island living.

Search Roanoke Island or enter www.roanokeisland.com.

MANTEO

Here is a tip for visiting Manteo: any parking place will do. The town invites a strolling pace, with interesting shops, well-kept venues, and an easygoing atmosphere. Manteo rewards the time spent walking, window-shopping, and wandering, with or without a latte or ice cream cone.

The town of 1,500 residents has been the county seat since the legislature created Dare County in 1870. While government functions sustained the town, Manteo has moved into the mainstream of tourism. Shrewdly, the community and county have closely tied their appeal to both their local culture of watermen and the undisputed events of the sixteenth century. This all-American town hugging Shallowbag Bay wears and shares its past with understated style.

Street names matter here and set a respectful tone, resonating from the epoch of the First Colony beginning in 1584: Ananias Dare, Sir Walter Raleigh, Budleigh Street (Raleigh's English home), Devon (also in England), Croatan Avenue, and Queen Elizabeth Avenue.

The town architecture and signage is appropriate in style and scale. There is a cottage-like feel to streetscapes. Describing what makes a place charming is difficult, but it is easy to recognize, and Manteo has it by the blockful.

In 1984, the 400th anniversary of the first attempt by English-speaking people to colonize the New World, Manteo celebrated by opening a water-

Good Wood

Eighty years ago, a waterman's life was tied to the water like a boat to a dock—some fishing, some guiding, even traveling for supplies. Since there were no plastics or fiberglass, wood was very important: for boats, docks, and decoys; for siding, shingles, fences, and posts.

At that time there are no big-box house stores, and wood preservatives are not available—instead there are sawmills. A waterman with repairs needs wood: which wood is good wood?

Here are the desired attributes: it must be durable, able to withstand winter ice and torpid summer heat. It must not rot or at least must rot slowly enough to make it worthwhile for felling, hauling, barking, splitting, and shaping. Once fashioned, it will be in contact with water and air and the fungi and little animals that eat things of value. It will be tested.

It must be buoyant, lightweight, smooth-grained, and splinter-free; sandable, workable, and easily shaped; turned with the boatbuilder's tools and the carver's knife. It would be nice if it were aromatic—the shavings might sweeten the air.

It must be nearby and abundant, and it must be free or close to it.

Just such a tree was plentiful on the coast: Atlantic white cedar, known botanically as *Chamaecyparis thyoides*. (The local name was juniper, a misnomer derived from its resemblance to eastern red cedar, a *Juniperus* species.) It is a wetland species with a native range from Maine to Florida. The Great Dismal Swamp and the peninsula between Albemarle and Pamlico sounds once sheltered some of the largest stands of this soggy-ground evergreen within its range.

It became the waterman's tree and one of the most valuable commercial species in the East. Beginning in the late nineteenth century, railroad tracks and drainage ditches siphoned away the swamp's protective bogginess, giving access to pure stands of juniper for cutting. By the Great Depression, nearly all of the virgin stands had been cut over. How much timber was cut? At one time juniper stands may have covered some 62,000 to 112,000 acres within the Great Dismal Swamp alone. Today between 6,000 and 7,000 acres of juniper remain.

It may be that Atlantic white cedar now grows on only 10 percent of its original acreage in North Carolina. What is considered "old-growth" timber today is likely to be second-growth trees from natural reforestation in areas not previously drained.

In the mid-1970s, commercial timbering again boomed, removing the secondary growth. Ditching and road building altered groundwater characteristics that favor Atlantic white cedar—it prefers boggy ground. The yet-unanswered question is, Will Atlantic white cedar reseed and return?

Unlike with other commercially important trees, there is no large-scale replanting of Atlantic white cedar. The species needs assistance to recover from clear-cutting practices; seedlings must have direct sunlight. Planned burns to clear ground on the timbered area may help—the tree recovered somewhat from the initial cutting nearly 100 years ago. However, in those early days the swamp remained a swamp. Today the swamps are being drained.

The tree is not in danger of extinction, but the reduction in habitat jeopardizes other components of its unique environmental niche. An important element of maritime heritage is threatened along with the tree's reduction. Juniper skiffs, boats, and decoys *were* indispensable to the eastern North Carolina's waterman's story.

Fortunately, some handsome stands are now protected. The Emily and Richardson Preyer Buckridge Reserve, a 27,111-acre component of the North Carolina Coastal Reserve, protects extensive stands of Atlantic white cedar and bald cypress. A 30-year-old area of 4,000 acres represents the largest contiguous stand of the tree in the state. There are also Atlantic white cedar stands remaining in the Alligator River National Wildlife Refuge, and reforestation efforts are underway in the Great Dismal Swamp.

It's good wood—everything a waterman could ask for. Let's hope there's more in the future.

front renovation in time for the national commemoration. The still-spiffy mixed-use development along Queen Elizabeth Street became a new economic anchor downtown. There is a municipal boardwalk along the harbor, which has more than 50 boat slips.

The waterfront promenade offers a glimpse of the *Elizabeth II*, a full-scale reconstruction of a sixteenth-century sailing vessel, docked across the harbor at Roanoke Island Festival Park. (Shoaling of its channel to deep water trapped the *Elizabeth II* at dock. In 2018 funding for dredging was approved so the ship could journey to a shipyard for maintenance and preservation.) The park is a short walk over the Cora Mae Basnight Bridge. In summer the bridge is literally the jumping-off place for local kids who splash into the basin below.

The waterfront walk turns south onto Fernando Street, and perched in the harbor is a replica of the Roanoke Marsh Light. There is also a full-scale weather tower, of a type long used along the coast, fully flagged with the daily forecast. Next door, in the George Washington Creef Boathouse, is the Roanoke Island Maritime Museum, a working museum. It emphasizes the Roanoke Island boatbuilding tradition.

Take the time to wander side streets such as John Borden Street or Devon Street, moving through the residential areas of the town, working your way to head north on Wingina Street. It's a lovely walk with an evergreen ceiling provided by towering crowns of extremely large and lovely loblolly pines. In summer, private gardens abound in perennial and annual flowers. Manteo has a down-home look and feel.

At Collins Park, 622 Sir Walter Raleigh Street, is the Pea Island Cookhouse Museum, dedicated to the all–African American lifesaving crew that served under Richard Ethridge, the first African American U.S. Life-Saving Station keeper. The Pea Island Crew served with distinction in the face of institutional and societal racism. In 1996, on the 100th anniversary of their efforts to rescue the crew of the *E. S. Newman*, the station crew were honored posthumously with the Gold Lifesaving Medal.

A bronze statue of Keeper Ethridge, who was born into slavery and served with the Colored Troops of the Union Army, commands the traffic roundabout across from the Pea Island Cookhouse Museum.

Search Manteo NC or enter www.townofmanteo.com.

ROANOKE ISLAND MARITIME MUSEUM

The modest-sized weathered building at 104 Fernando Street is the restored boat shop of George Washington Creef Jr. It was a family affair: there has been a Creef family boat shop on this site since 1880. A fire in 1939 consumed the buildings on Manteo's waterfront, and the following year George Washington Creef Jr. built the present boathouse to ply his trade. The elder Creef is celebrated for developing the shad boat, a solid working boat particularly suited for the shallow waters of Roanoke and Croatan Sounds. Its utility was widespread, the design widely imitated. The shad boat has been designated the official boat of North Carolina.

This is a working museum; staff and volunteers ply the boatwright's trade and stay busy restoring and rebuilding wooden boats. Exhibits detail local boatbuilding history. On display are various small sailing skiffs and an 1883 Washington Creef shad boat. In addition to watching the boats-in-progress, visitors can watch a media presentation detailing the construction of the nearby *Elizabeth II*, which was built here.

Search Manteo NC or enter www.townofmanteo.com
and use the "Attractions" drop-down menu.

ROANOKE ISLAND FESTIVAL PARK

Here is a deft touch: the road crossing the Cora Mae Basnight Bridge to Roanoke Festival Park is part of the state's shortest designated highway route, NC 400, so named in celebration of the 400th anniversary of the 1584 colony attempts on Roanoke Island. The island's place in history and the personalities of the sixteenth century are interpreted creatively and in engaging detail in the multiple media venues of the park. Roanoke Island Festival Park is a full-fledged interpretive experience and one thoroughly enjoyed with a little advance planning.

Among the draws are a feature film, *The Legend of Two Path*; the interactive Roanoke Adventure Museum; and three distinct but obviously related living-history interpretive sites: the *Elizabeth II*, the Native American Town, and the European Settlement Site. The venues emphasize enjoyable learning; audience participation and engagement are welcome and rewarded.

A few suggestions: first view the docudrama *The Legend of Two Path*, an original story developed by the North Carolina School of the Arts. The film explores the relationships among Native Americans and the changes that the first European contacts brought. The fact that the *Elizabeth II* appears in the film is clue to the next stop.

The *Elizabeth II* is the full-scale reconstruction of a sixteenth-century sailing vessel manned by interpreters in Elizabethan dress. The 69-foot-long, 17-foot-wide ship, which was built in Manteo, is fully seaworthy by sail (with motorized backup). The seasonal interpreters are fully tourist-worthy too — take the time to chat with them and learn some Elizabethan English.

Interpreters also staff the nearby first settlement and the Native American Village.

The Roanoke Adventure Museum nicely finishes a visit by exploring the natural aspects of the island as well as cultural themes that are more recent historically. Take note of the sturdy, still-operable wooden shad boat built by Washington Creef that is on display.

The Outer Banks History Center is next to the park's visitor center. It's a treasure trove of information on the Outer Banks that is maintained by the North Carolina Division of Archives and History for historical research on topics concerning the Outer Banks.

The center includes nearly 35,000 photographs and a large collection of maps, some of which are more than 400 years old.

One planning tip: the park opens at 9 AM, and tickets are good for two consecutive days. Arrive early and pack a picnic lunch—restaurants in Manteo fill quickly, as do parking places—or come visit after lunch. Roanoke Island Festival Park can easily fill one-half day for a family.

There is an admission charge.

Search Roanoke Island Park or enter www.roanokeisland.com.

ISLAND FARM

Island Farm, 1140 US 64, Manteo, is a Roanoke Island living history site of the 1800s on the restored 1847 family farmstead of Adam Etheridge. A dozen buildings and exhibits frame island life in that time. Open April–November. Admission.

Search Island Farm or enter www.theislandfarm.com.

NORTH CAROLINA AQUARIUM, ROANOKE ISLAND

The North Carolina Aquarium on Roanoke Island offers a peek-below-the-surface coastal education with themes that illustrate the range of aquatic life inhabiting the rivers feeding the local sounds and extending to the nearshore. It showcases living vignettes of aquatic life from the brackish waters of the sound estuaries to the pulsing nearshore of the Graveyard of the Atlantic. It is always interesting to discover what might be near your bare foot or leg when in the water.

An exhibit re-creates a typical river environment that drains into the sounds, where river otters swim playfully and an alligator obligingly floats within touching distance. Coastal vegetation reaches overhead. The familiar turtles of the coastal plain—cooters and sliders—share space with bowfins and gars in the Coastal Freshwaters exhibit.

Shallow tanks allow visitors to choose their moment to touch a skate as it glides effortlessly across the wide pool. Hermit crabs and sea urchins are among the other creatures there.

Video narrations recount the experience of native islanders who lived through some of the most dramatic storms to strike the Outer Banks. The historical background is the memorable Ash Wednesday storm of 1962, which washed over and washed out Dare's resort communities.

Save your accolades for the silent swirl of sea creatures in the two-story, 285,000-gallon Graveyard of the Atlantic exhibit. Surrounding a one-third-scale model of the upended shipwreck of the USS *Monitor* are the finny stars that swim in stratified swaths throughout. A sand tiger shark moves through the water menacingly, and around it swim the game fish and the purely beautiful fish of the high-energy Outer Banks ocean.

Announcements of lectures and special programs resonate through the halls; the aquarium staff are constantly presenting various events of this type. The place fairly jumps with ecological educational offerings, including the opportunity to generate the voltage of an electric eel—it makes for quick study.

The aquarium is popular and always draws a crowd—do not save it for a rainy day. First thing in the morning through lunchtime and midafternoon typically find crowds waning.

An admission is charged. The facility is open 9–5 in summer, with shortened hours in the off-season.

Search Roanoke Aquarium or enter www.ncaquariums.com/roanoke-island.

NATIONAL WILDLIFE REFUGES VISITOR CENTER

Located on the north end of Roanoke Island, the Coastal North Carolina National Wildlife Refuges Gateway Visitor Center provides an introduction to the 12 national wildlife refuges of coastal North Carolina and southeastern Virginia as well as the Edenton Fish Hatchery. It's the best stop for an orientation to the variety of animals and habitats in these outstanding preserves.

In addition to brochures on the several refuges, the Gateway Center's dioramas detail the typical habitats and inhabitants one can expect to find. The dioramas provide a means of visualizing the refuges so that visitors

Roanoke Island's Freedmen's Colony

A historical marker on Airport Road near the aquarium hints at a significant event in Roanoke Island history. The marker reads:

> The first refugee slave community in N.C. Est. in 1863 by Union
> troops. It operated until 1867 on land nearby, extending S.

The marker shorthand abbreviates a complex story of liberation, military necessity, and opportunity that unfolded through several years beginning in 1861. This digest of events is drawn from online essays posted at the websites of both the National Park Service and the North Carolina Highway Historical Marker Program.

By February 1862, forces under Union General Ambrose Burnside defeated Roanoke Island's Confederate defenders and took control of the waterways serving northeastern North Carolina. This successful campaign also resulted in the liberation of the African American slaves who had constructed the Confederate fortifications. The Union forces labeled the slaves "Contraband of War" and emancipated them. As word of the conquest and favorable treatment spread, other enslaved African Americans fled inland plantations to the safe haven behind Union lines.

The Union commanders initially hired the refugee African Americans, paying them with rations, clothing, and an expected wage of eight dollars a month. They performed many tasks, including fort and bridge building; they served as shipwrights, woodcutters, longshoremen, teamsters, and carpenters. Some who were very courageous became spies and guides, since they knew the inland terrain and could travel safely behind Confederate lines.

By May 1863, Major General John G. Foster selected Chaplain Horace James to establish a colony for the growing number of emancipated people. At the time James was considered the "Superintendent of Blacks in North Carolina," and his specific charge was to "settle the colored people on the unoccupied lands and give them agricultural implements and mechanical tools."

James selected captured land on the north portion of Roanoke Island and surveyed streets and lots of nearly an acre. The freedmen constructed log homes and established gardens, building a community church. The American Missionary Association sent a schoolteacher. In addition, General Edward A. Wild began recruiting refugees to form North Carolina's first black regiment. (Richard Ethridge, originally born into slavery, was one of the men who enlisted. He would later gain fame as the captain of the Pea Island Life-Saving Station.)

The rapidly expanding colony outgrew the available resources—some laborers worked for a year without pay. An 1864 census reported that more than 2,212 black freedmen lived on the island. By the next year, the colony had a population of 3,901, and 561 houses had been built, along with a school.

At the end of the war, the government restored all confiscated lands to their original owners, denying the freedmen the rights to ownership they were promised. Reductions in promised rations forced colony residents to move away; between 1865 and 1866, the population dropped by half. Eventually only a few freedman remained on the island, forming the foundation of a black community still resident today.

know what to expect. The dioramas are particularly informative about the Red Wolf Recovery Program, which as of 2017 was ongoing at the Alligator River refuge.

One engaging interactive exhibit simulates a refuge flyover. Sitting in the mock cockpit of a retired wildlife aircraft, it is possible to select representative flyover film from several refuges.

There is a fascinating film and exhibit on long-ago Buffalo City, the logging town in the heart of the Dare County mainland that was the largest town in Dare County between 1885 and 1930. Nearly 1,500 people called now-abandoned Buffalo City home. Today the site is almost completely overgrown.

There are four walking trails through the 35-acre site that vary in length up to two-thirds of a mile.

The center also houses the offices of the Alligator River and Pea Island National Wildlife Refuges. There is an appropriately themed gift store as well.

The center is open 9–4 Monday–Friday, noon–4 on Sunday.

Search FWS NC Gateway or enter www.fws.gov/ncgatewayvc/.

Best phone number for more information: 252-473-1131.

FORT RALEIGH NATIONAL HISTORIC SITE

Beginnings are sometimes inauspicious, and Fort Raleigh National Historic Site celebrates an ambitious, speculative dream that landed here with great hope but was not realized. The event commemorated here is the first attempt of English-speaking people to colonize North America. While this effort failed, subsequent colonization attempts would succeed at Jamestown, Virginia. (The disappearance of the colonists is a mystery that in recent years has been partially unshrouded.)

Archaeologists have confirmed that English spades turned North American soil here, and blacksmiths worked metal on these grounds. In 1585 the members of the Ralph Lane colony dug a moat and constructed an earthwork fort for their protection. This disarmingly simple, accurately reconstructed earth enclosure is the heart of the historic site. The ramparts were reconstructed in 1950 by the National Park Service based on the remains of the original that archaeologists uncovered in 1936 and 1948 investigations.

The earthworks are spare, and the question unsaid is "Is that all there is to see?" No, there is more, but importantly, this is *the* place. Recovered artifacts, collateral research, and historical record combine to tell more about the settlement attempt than can be featured on the ground.

Programs by park staff expand the narrative of the earthworks. The orientation hints that the perceived threat was more from an overland attack by Native Americans than from an attack by sea from England's New World rival, Spain. These scheduled walks infuse the history with motives and personality, giving life to the people behind and involved in this attempt.

The Lindsay Warren Visitor Center offers a video introduction into the colonial history of the New World in the sixteenth century. Other exhibits include an Elizabethan-era reading room dismantled and reassembled here. It offers a glimpse of the lives of the backers of the colonization effort. Original artifacts uncovered at the site are also on display.

Outside, there is a monument commemorating the christening of Virginia Dare, the first child born to English-speaking people in the New World. The Thomas Hariot Nature Trail honoring the scientist who prepared reports on the New World winds through the woodlands punctuated by Hariot's words on display placards.

A short walk leads to the Waterside Theater, the site of the nation's first and longest-running outdoor drama, *The Lost Colony*, by North Carolina's own Paul Green. It is an opulent symphonic dramatization of the First Colony story. The script is tight, easily followed, and wonderfully enjoyable. Professional actors play the leads, but many locals have grown up through the ranks of the cast. In 2007 a fire claimed three buildings and the priceless collection of costumes accumulated since inception, but the show does go on. A note: it can be chilly, and the mosquitoes can be vicious; a sweater and repellent are a good idea, as is emergency rain gear.

In 1960 the Garden Club of North Carolina created the 10-acre Elizabethan Gardens a short walk from the historic site. These rival any formal gardens in the state for their design authenticity and the extensive collection of plant materials. True to form, it functions as a controlled retreat for strolling in the heart of the wilderness, a theme appropriate to the settlement of the New World. It is also accessible from a separate parking lot.

The park is free. Admission is charged for the Elizabethan Gardens and performances of *The Lost Colony*.

Search Fort Raleigh or enter www.nps.gov/fora.

Search Lost Colony or enter www.thelostcolony.org.

WANCHESE

Wanchese (locals pronounce it "*Won*-cheese"), at the southern end of Roanoke Island, is a fishing and boatbuilding village oriented to its commercial harbor. The North Carolina Seafood Industrial Park is the port of call for shrimp trawlers and flounder boats owned by residents. In addition to shipping their catch up and down the Eastern Seaboard, they also sell to local restaurants and to visitors who want to carry seafood home.

Like Manteo, it has a Native American namesake: Wanchese accompanied his chief on the 1584 return voyage to England of colonists Amadas and Barlowe.

Spreading west from the commercial harbor is a sleepy, tree-shaded village that it is much lower-key than Manteo, keeping the traditional rhythms of local work and life. The fishing and charter boats leave before sunrise, and the community is more private than tourism- and government-oriented Manteo.

The marsh and waterside setting and small-town feel impart the impression of decades past. This is a place to see and appreciate for its solid down-home character.

The first inkling of the Wanchese community is the white siding of Bethany Methodist Church at a fork on Old Wharf Road, which winds around and connects with other streets and eventually loops back to the main road. Take the left fork to reach the seafood packers quicker.

The boats bring in catches steadily and daily. Seafood vendors at Wanchese usually have low prices on fresh seafood, certainly worth the side trip to fill up a cooler before returning inland. No cooler or ice? They sell those too. The pungent breezes you would expect from fishing wharves scent the air.

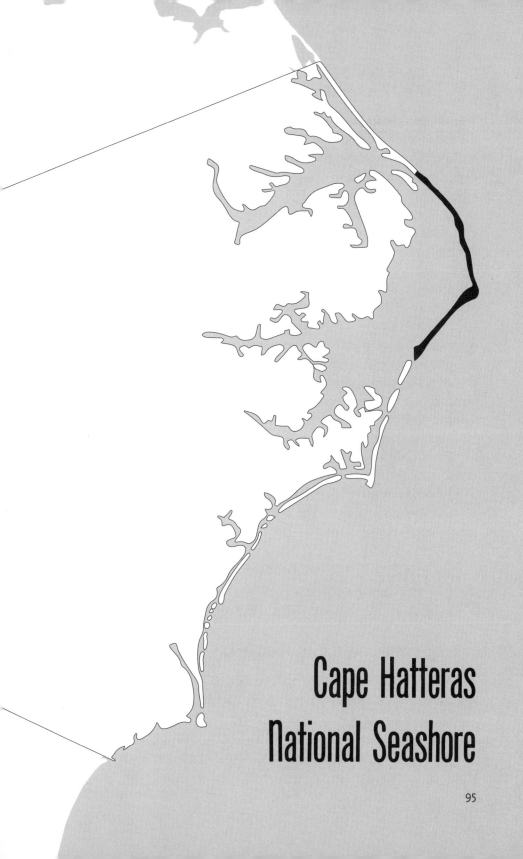

Cape Hatteras
National Seashore

CAPE HATTERAS NATIONAL SEASHORE/
OUTER BANKS NATIONAL SCENIC BYWAY

For southbound travelers, Whalebone Junction marks two beginnings: it is the nominative northern boundary of Cape Hatteras National Seashore, and it marks the start of travel along the Outer Banks National Scenic Byway, a designation recognizing the geographical, cultural, and historical elements unique to the Outer Banks.

In all respects, the 2009 byway designation by the U.S. Department of Transportation formalized what many travelers discovered individually: driving the Outer Banks is an unmatched passage through a magnificent coastal landscape blessed with and marked by a unique maritime heritage. The formal byway designation places a new frame around the well-known markers of maritime life accessible from NC 12 and US 70.

The route—a 163-mile passage over land and sea that requires two ferry crossings—is a joy to travel, in either direction. Two national seashores and two national wildlife refuges are along the byway, as are four remarkable, storied lighthouses, three of which are open for climbing. Historic structures abound, as do museums rich with interpretation of the Outer Banks culture. (Each of these places is mentioned in this text.)

There are places to swim, fish, kayak, windsurf, bird-watch, hike, and explore and, with the proper permit, drive on the sandy strand of the national seashore.

The links below provide specific information on the byway and are helpful in budgeting your time. The first site listed provides a downloadable printable map in PDF format.

Search Outerbanksbyway or enter www.outerbanksbyway.com.

Search Outer Banks Scenic or enter www.visitnc.com
/trip-idea/outer-banks-national-scenic-byway-1.

CAPE HATTERAS NATIONAL SEASHORE

As you drive south from Whalebone Junction on NC 12, the northern road routing the Outer Banks National Scenic Highway, the horizon becomes simpler and the windshield views more engaging. This is the beginning of a picturesque, contemplative trip: three islands, three lighthouses, two inlets, one wildlife refuge, two counties, eight communities, one ferry ride, and

Cape Hatteras National Seashore

nearly three centuries of settlement and culture. The 75-mile-long route through the 30,000-acre preserve is at once wild and tenuous, awesome and serene. A map or an app will show it to be about a 2.5-hour drive, but it can easily become a lifelong enchantment.

The dream of Cape Hatteras National Seashore began more than 80 years ago, and in 1937 the U.S. Congress authorized the park. It was officially dedicated as the first National Seashore in 1953 and formally dedicated five years later. Part of the original dream was to provide access to and preserve the extraordinary ecology of the Outer Banks.

While the seashore management has been broadly successful in fulfilling its dual and sometimes conflicting mandate to protect the resource and the wildlife native to it and to provide recreational access, it continuously encounters naturally occurring hiccups. Scientists, elected officials, and recreational personnel wrestle with the difficulties in setting any literal or figurative lines in the sand—whether roads, bridges, borders, or policies. The Outer Banks are a dynamic system—wind, water, and sand are in an unending, shifting natural equilibrium. These islands are naturally restless; they move around frequently and measurably.

"Permanent" (man-made) structures inevitably become benchmarks to chart the comings and goings of land. The 1963 Herbert C. Bonner Bridge crossing Oregon Inlet was replaced in the fall of 2018 because the channel beneath it continually shoaled and the elements pushed its concrete and steel to fatigue. NC 12 has been obliterated in several locations, repaired, and rebuilt with segments relocated and elevated; in 1999 the Cape Hatteras Lighthouse had to be moved; an entire campground at the north end of Pea Island was eroded; and in early summer 2017 an island appeared at Cape Point, igniting social media and generating Twittering excitement before shoaling welded it to Hatteras Island, extending the point. It may soon be gone; who knows? Visitors returning after a previous stay find the seashore is always different in small ways, and sometimes in large.

Today the road barely slips by the water in some locations. While the nearly 9 miles of Bodie Island have been comparatively stable, Hatteras and Ocracoke Islands have been breached or overwashed by storms many times. In the middle of September 2017 hurricanes forced the mandatory evacuation of Ocracoke.

It is an irony that place-names can linger longer than the geographical features they name does. Bodie Island and Pea Island are islands no more (for now); New Inlet, which once defined Pea Island, is filled but stirring again. (The pilings that once supported the crossing bridge are visible from the newly elevated road north of Rodanthe.) The names are reminders of mapable stability and inevitable change.

Along with this natural tumult, however, there are some constants, like the many villages, the deep green sward of Buxton Woods, and the lighthouses on Bodie Island, Cape Hatteras, and Ocracoke. In the 1930s the Civilian Conservation Corps constructed a dune line, and though it has been breached, battered, and whacked by storms, it remains intact for many seashore miles.

The waters offshore are known as the Graveyard of the Atlantic, and more than 400 oceangoing vessels have run aground on the ever-varying shoals to the east. Nearly 140 years ago, crews in the 12 stations of the U.S. Life-Saving Service, the forerunner of the U.S. Coast Guard, began to stand watch to save shipwrecked souls. One of those sunken vessels, the Civil War ironclad uss *Monitor*, has been partially salvaged. In World War II, German U-boats torpedoed thousands of tons of shipping, igniting oil fires offshore.

The restored Chicamacomico Life-Saving Station, the Little Kinnakeet Station, the Cape Hatteras Weather Station, the three lighthouses, and the Graveyard of the Atlantic Museum offer glimpses into those stormy years on the banks.

Cape Hatteras National Seashore encompasses a broad swath of nature, from foredunes to forest to salt marsh. The drive south from Whalebone Junction is a lovely, winding passage through a maritime shrub thicket that feathers to brackish marsh on the west. To the east are the rooftops of the private beach cottages of South Nags Head; to the south, the Bodie Island Lighthouse peeks from behind a slash pine forest bordering its entry drive.

The new bridge over Oregon Inlet has an expected 100-year life span, but its south terminal is on the battered and threatened eastern edge of Pea Island National Wildlife Refuge. There are hard choices ahead for highway construction to reach Rodanthe, where NC 12 swings inland to more stable footing. In 2018, construction was approved for the "jug-handle" bridge that routes NC 12 over Pamlico Sound, bypassing a frequently flooded portion of island north of Rodanthe.

Farther south, the road squeezes by Buxton and travels inland west of Buxton Woods. Beyond Frisco, the seashore again narrows precariously before flaring to make the wider base for Hatteras Village.

Southwest by ferry from Hatteras is the long, flat run to the village of

Ocracoke. The island is the charm on the sand bracelet, accessible by automobile and passenger-only ferry.

Here are some suggestions to burnish your visit:

- Bicycle trips here are best scheduled for fall or spring. Summer traffic is heavy, and NC 12 can be dangerous.
- Summer visitors should stop at the entrance kiosk at Whalebone Junction to ask for a copy of "In the Park," a National Park Service publication that lists scheduled events as well as user information about the seashore. It's indispensable.
- All anglers must have a NC Saltwater Fishing license.
- Beach driving is by permit only; permits are available in person at the three park visitor centers: Bodie Island Lighthouse and Visitor Center; Cape Hatteras Lighthouse and Visitor Center; and Ocracoke Visitor Center. Permits may be purchased online at the Cape Hatteras ORV site at www.recreation.gov. In 2018, fees were $50 for a 10-day pass and $120 for an annual pass.
- Make and/or confirm departing ferry reservations for the Ocracoke/Swan Quarter or Ocracoke/Cedar Island ferry crossings before going to the island. Call the Ocracoke reservation line, 800-293-3779, or visit ferry.ncdot.gov to make it online.
- Try the new (2019) passenger-only ferry from Hatteras to Ocracoke Village. Bicycles are welcome. The crossing takes about an hour and tickets are $15. A tram is available for village transport.
- Obey restricted area prohibitions. Shorebird nesting may close some beach areas; people, pets, and vehicles are forbidden entry.
- Swim at lifeguarded or populated beaches. Riptides are common.
- Evacuate as directed if a storm threatens.

For Your Bucket:

 Climb the Bodie Island Lighthouse
 Explore the north end of Pea Island
 Bird-watch at Pea Island NWR
 Visit Chicamacomico Lifesaving Station
 Beachcomb or fish between Salvo and Avon
 Take windsurfing lessons
 Climb the Cape Hatteras Lighthouse
 Drive or walk to Cape Point (if open)

Go deep-sea fishing from Hatteras Village

Drive a 4x4 to Hatteras Inlet

Access

While there are miles of seashore access, the park service may close areas temporarily to protect the nesting areas of shorebirds or sea turtles. The closed areas of beach will be clearly marked.

Park only at designated parking areas and use the designated ramps.

The park service maintains several locations with bathhouses and life-guards.

Reservations are recommended at the four designated campgrounds: Oregon Inlet, Cape Point, Frisco, and Ocracoke. There are bathhouses and restrooms at each campsite. Reservations may be made up to six months in advance and MUST be made at least three days in advance of arrival. Reserve campsites at www.recreation.gov. Enter the name of the campsite in the search bar. You can also make reservations by phone at 877-444-6777 or 252-473-2111.

Search Cape Hatteras Seashore or enter www.nps.gov/caha.

Best phone number for more information: 252-473-2111.

Best for campsite reservations: 877-444-6777.

Emergency numbers: life-threatening emergencies, 911.

WHALEBONE JUNCTION INFORMATION CENTER

The Whalebone Junction Information Center is a kiosk at a pullover on the west side of the highway at the entrance to Cape Hatteras National Seashore. Volunteers staff it during the summer and staffing may extend beyond the Memorial Day–to–Labor Day period. The park service produces "In the Park," an invaluable guide listing a schedule of activities and events. The volunteers will attempt to answer questions and advise on park alerts such as the closing of facilities.

It's a good place to confirm ferry schedules and wait times for departure to Ocracoke, accessible only by ferry. In a perfect world with light traffic and no stops the drive to the Ocracoke ferry dock is slightly more than one hour. Allow more time in summer.

There are restrooms at this pullover.

Cape Hatteras National Seashore

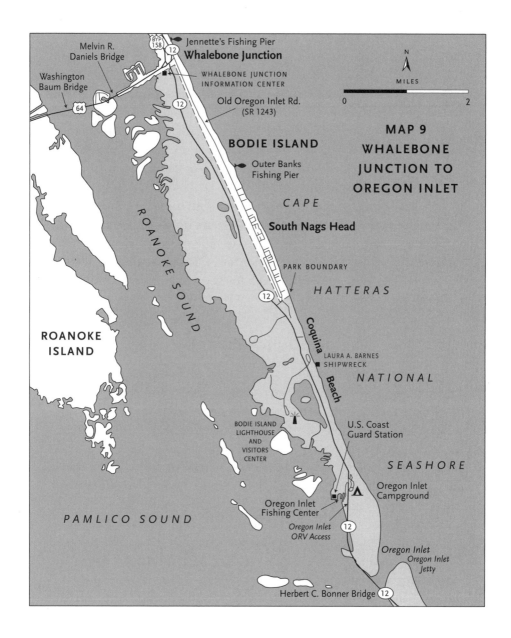

MAP 9
WHALEBONE
JUNCTION TO
OREGON INLET

Melvin R.
Daniels Bridge

Washington
Baum Bridge

Jennette's Fishing Pier
Whalebone Junction

WHALEBONE JUNCTION
INFORMATION CENTER

Old Oregon Inlet Rd.
(SR 1243)

BODIE ISLAND

Outer Banks
Fishing Pier

C A P E

South Nags Head

PARK BOUNDARY

H A T T E R A S

Coquina

LAURA A. BARNES
SHIPWRECK

Beach

N A T I O N A L

ROANOKE SOUND

ROANOKE
ISLAND

BODIE ISLAND
LIGHTHOUSE
AND
VISITORS
CENTER

U.S. Coast
Guard Station

S E A S H O R E

Oregon Inlet
Campground

Oregon Inlet
Fishing Center

PAMLICO SOUND

Oregon Inlet
ORV Access

Oregon Inlet
Oregon Inlet
Jetty

Herbert C. Bonner Bridge

N

MILES

0   2

BODIE ISLAND

The national seashore first traverses Bodie (pronounced the same as "body")
Island. The name persists from long ago. Roanoke Inlet, the island-defining
northern opening, shoaled in near present-day Nags Head. The name has
been recorded since 1770s, when its southern boundary was a more distant

inlet to the south. Bodie Island is presently framed at its southern end by Oregon Inlet, which opened in 1846. Today the name includes to the peninsula south of Whalebone Junction, excepting South Nags Head to the east.

Bodie Island is a serene introduction to the national seashore. The first 5 miles are a slightly elevated causeway that winds through wax myrtle thickets, by freshwater ponds, and beside the grassy meadows of the low-profile island. The drive is a study in summer greens, created by the jungle-dense vegetation crowding the road. In fall, wild grape vines thread yellow through the olive green of the wax myrtle, and sumac blazes vivid red.

The road winds so that it plays tricks on your mind. The Bodie Island Lighthouse, a stately landmark, appears to move from one side of the road to the other. There are several small, two-car pullovers with elevated observation platforms placed advantageously for bird-watching. Eventually the horizon widens as the maritime shrub thicket recedes and the lighthouse firmly plants itself to the west.

COQUINA BEACH

Coquina Beach is the first public beach access after entering the seashore. It is on the east side of NC 12 about 5.5 miles south of Whalebone Junction.

This is a great stop for day-trippers—a wide, nice beach with an impressive dune field. There are first-class facilities to serve visitor needs. In summer there are lifeguards. The beach width above the high-water mark varies between 75 and 100 yards of sand. Nevertheless, it is a vulnerable stretch and has been reconstructed several times to abate erosion loss and storm damage.

Coquina Beach's namesake is the brightly colored bivalve creature— the coquina clam—that digs into the sand with each return of the swash. Tidal pools, great for children, occur regularly here, particularly during the early summer, and the shelling is moderately good. The high wave energy of nearby Oregon Inlet damages shells quickly. Fishing is usually good as well.

Facilities include picnic shelters and a public bathhouse. Beachgoers should bring beach footwear: the soft sand after the dune crossing can become extremely hot on sunny summer days.

A longtime landmark here is the *Laura A. Barnes* shipwreck. The schooner ran aground in a sudden squall on June 1, 1921, and today part of the hull and keel is all that remains. Storms bury it, then unearth it.

An interpretive display once featured the *Laura A. Barnes* wreck in the median between two parking lots here. In the winter of 1992–93 storms knifed into this beach, shaved the sand away, and destroyed the picnic shelters and parking lots. The park service promptly retreated to build the current much-improved, fully accessible bathhouse. Today the *Laura A. Barnes* rests about 10 yards past the end of the boardwalk and is slowly being covered with sand once again. It comes and goes with the beach.

During the summer, park rangers may host a regular schedule of interpretive programs here.

Access

Coquina Beach is open during daylight hours only. Parking and picnic tables are on a first-come, first-served basis.

Off-road-vehicle access is periodically restricted, depending on the width of the beach.

Search Coquina Beach or enter www.nps.gov/caha.

BODIE ISLAND LIGHT STATION AND VISITOR CENTER

The entrance to the Bodie Island Light Station and Visitor Center is across NC 12 from the Coquina Beach entrance. A handsome, planted grove of slash pine trees shades the entry drive and bicycle path.

The horizontally striped Bodie Island Lighthouse has been in service at Oregon Inlet since 1872. Along with Currituck Beach, Cape Hatteras, and Cape Lookout, it is one of the four "great lighthouses" that signaled North Carolina's salient coast. All date from the nineteenth century and were considered "great" because each housed a first-order Fresnel lens to amplify the lamplight and project the beam as far as possible. From a focal plane height of 156 feet, the light projects 19 miles, blinking a repeating sequence of 2.5 seconds on, 2.5 seconds off, 2.5 seconds on, and 22.5 seconds off, with two cycles every minute.

In July 2000, the U.S. Coast Guard gave the lighthouse tower and oil house to the National Park Service as a private navigation aid. (The coast guard manages the lamp.) The park service uses the original keeper's quar-

The Bodie Island Light Station Keepers' Quarters now serves as
a visitor center. The Bodie Island Lighthouse is open for climbing.
(Photo by Bill Russ, courtesy of VisitNC.com)

ters as the Bodie Island Visitor Center. Its superb displays are a primer on
lighthouse operations, and it has a very good bookstore as well. There are
also public restrooms.

After nearly a decade of start-and-stop restoration, the park service
opened the tower for climbing, weather conditions permitting. The tower
is in excellent shape, but the engineers building it did not design the elegant interior wrought iron spiral stairway to carry an eager public 214 steps
to the exposed observation deck. The restoration efforts have now made it
secure, and the view of the diminishing spiral of the stairs before climbing is
a memorable way to remember the ascent. Note also the marble cornerstone
that gives the precise latitude and longitude of the beacon.

This lighthouse is the successful third effort to build a marker for this
stretch of coastline. The two previous lighthouses were built across Oregon
Inlet after it opened in 1846 much farther north than its present location.
The first lighthouse was destroyed because of poor construction and dete-
rioration, the second by the retreating Confederate army. The present site
was selected to avoid the inlet migration south. The inlet migration since
construction explains why the lighthouse is so distant from the inlet today.

Cape Hatteras National Seashore

Children descending the steps of the Bodie Island Lighthouse.
(Cape Hatteras National Park Service)

During the summer, the Bodie Island Visitor Center is the site for several interpretive programs and general information about activities in the seashore. The published summer schedule, "In the Park," will detail the planned programs.

Something to watch for is the Full Moon Climbs, a special program that permits climbing the lighthouse on nights with a full moon. Reservations are necessary.

Two trails begin at the visitor center: one leads to the sound. A 1.5-mile loop, the Dike Trail, details the history of the lighthouse property from when the Bodie Island Hunt Club created the impoundment near the tower for waterfowl hunting. In winter it is a superb location for waterfowl watching.

Access

The visitor center is open during daylight hours, 9–5 during summer months, with reduced hours in winter. Insect repellent is a good idea for the trails.

Best phone number for more information: 252-441-5711.

Search Bodie Island Center or enter www.nps.gov/caha
and use the "Plan Your Visit" drop-down menu.

OREGON INLET CAMPGROUND

The oceanside Oregon Inlet Campground is one of the most popular of the four national seashore campgrounds. It provides some of the best overall access to Oregon Inlet and the lengthy sand spit that has stretched south from the campground. This makes it a preferred location for anglers. Swimmers should be wary because inlet currents—though not immediate—can be strong and treacherous. Reservations are necessary at least three days before arrival for the 120 campsites. Prime vacation dates fill quickly, since they can be made six months in advance.

Better fishing, cooler temperatures, and reduced insects make spring and fall the prime camping times. The popularity of fall surf fishing causes a campground rush, so in October weekend sites are hard to come by. There are no utility hookups, but there are modern restrooms, cold showers, potable drinking water, picnic tables, and outdoor grills. Because of the sandy location, the park service recommends longer and wider tent stakes and mosquito repellent and netting during the warmer times of year.

Access

Campsites must be reserved a minimum of three days in advance and can be reserved as early as six months ahead of time. The campground opens at 7 AM. Campers with reservations may arrive as late as 11:30 PM.

Cape Hatteras National Seashore

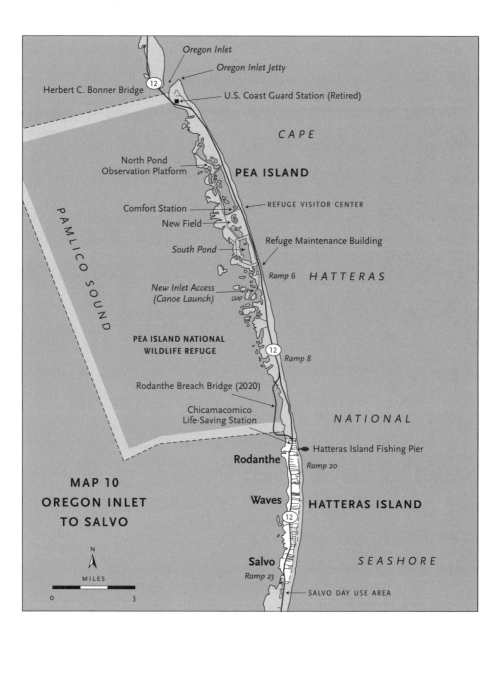

Oregon Inlet

Oregon Inlet Jetty

Herbert C. Bonner Bridge

U.S. Coast Guard Station (Retired)

CAPE

North Pond
Observation Platform

PEA ISLAND

REFUGE VISITOR CENTER

Comfort Station

New Field

Refuge Maintenance Building

South Pond

Ramp 6   HATTERAS

New Inlet Access
(Canoe Launch)

PEA ISLAND NATIONAL
WILDLIFE REFUGE

Ramp 8

Rodanthe Breach Bridge (2020)

Chicamacomico
Life-Saving Station

NATIONAL

Hatteras Island Fishing Pier

Rodanthe

Ramp 20

MAP 10

Waves   HATTERAS ISLAND

OREGON INLET

TO SALVO

N

SEASHORE

Salvo

MILES

Ramp 23

0   3

SALVO DAY USE AREA

PAMLICO SOUND

Best phone number for more information: 252-441-6246.

Search Oregon Inlet Camp or enter www.nps.gov/caha and use the "Plan Your Visit/Eating and Sleeping" drop-down menus.

Reservations: www.recreation.gov and search for Oregon Inlet.

RAMP 4: OREGON INLET OFF-ROAD-VEHICLE ACCESS

This clearly marked unpaved off-road-vehicle access ramp is on the east side of NC 12 nearly opposite the entrance to the Oregon Inlet Fishing Center. Only four-wheel-drive vehicles or vehicles modified to drive on soft sand should attempt to drive along the beach.

This is an excellent starting place for first-time beach drivers: the sand paths are plainly marked and heavily traveled, and when (not if) you get stuck, there is a high likelihood of someone to ease the embarrassment.

The park service may restrict travel north of the inlet depending on the width of the beach, the number of visitors in the Cape Hatteras National Seashore, or wildlife nesting seasons.

Access

All vehicles must be fully licensed and possess a valid National Park Service Off-Road Vehicle (ORV) permit. Permits may be obtained in person at any of the three visitor centers: Bodie Island, Cape Hatteras, and Ocracoke. Permits may be purchased for home printing at www.recreation.gov. Search Cape Hatteras ORV Permit. Allow 7–10 days for mail delivery of annual decals purchased online.

Search Cape Hatteras ORV or enter www.nps.gov/caha and use the "Plan Your Visit/Things To Do/Beach Activities/ORV FAQ" drop-down menus.

Access is year-round unless restrictions are posted.

OREGON INLET FISHING CENTER

The Oregon Inlet Fishing Center is a privately operated marina concession licensed by the National Park Service. The prime fishing waters of the Gulf Stream are only 35 miles to the east, and the center does a bustling charter fishing business. All necessary fishing gear, bait, and food supplies are available at the store, which also has a small eating area and grill that does heavy business during breakfast hours. Dioramas of mounted game fish of the type frequently caught in local waters fill several display cabinets. While visitors are not discouraged, this is a working marina centered around the charter fishing business.

There is also a public boat access with five ramps and adequate parking for vehicles with trailers.

Access

The center is on the west side of NC 12 immediately before the Herbert C. Bonner Bridge as you head south. The store and marina open very early and close around dusk.

Search Oregon Inlet Center or enter www.oregon-inlet.com.

Best phone number for more information: 800-272-5199.

U.S. COAST GUARD OREGON INLET STATION

The U.S. Coast Guard completed a new multimission station on land adjacent to the marina in 1991, and officers took command in March 1992. The station is the replacement for the retired station on the north end of Pea Island (still standing in 2018), rendered unserviceable by inlet shoaling. The new building's architecture draws strongly from the stylistic heritage of its precursor service, the U.S. Life-Saving Service, which constructed stations on the Outer Banks beginning in 1873.

Access

In the past, an innovative and cooperative program between the National Park Service and the U.S. Coast Guard sponsored public tours of the Oregon Inlet Station during the summer months. The tours occurred every Sunday and Wednesday afternoon June through August.

The summer publication "In the Park" will list any scheduled events.

Search Cape Hatteras Seashore or enter www.nps.gov/caha.

Best phone number for more information: 252-473-2111.

Where Does the Sand Go?

Nature incessantly shapes the beaches of the barrier islands, stealing sand here, dropping it off there. The waves running out on the sandy apron must recede, and, sliding seaward, they drag particles of beach with them. The sand is leaving; it always does. On the Outer Banks, erosion is the rule, not the exception.

Fixed objects such as dune crossover walkways serve as yardsticks of this continuing incremental change. One summer, the last step of the crossover perches high above the sand; two years later, that same step might be covered and young dunes may crowd the end of the deck. Winter wave action frequently pulls the sand away from where children make sandcastles and uses it to build an offshore sandbar. In summer this pattern slowly reverses, and the sandbar is gradually planed and returned to the foreshore. Tidal pools are a beach bonus from this process.

Wave action in the surf zone suspends loose sand in a churning slurry, and most of this sand moves parallel to the beach in a littoral current, a process known as the longshore transport of sand. Wave direction determines longshore currents. Most longshore transport along North Carolina's barrier beaches runs north-to-south.

The new Herbert C. Bonner Bridge crossing Oregon Inlet provides a terrific vantage point for gauging the effects of longshore transport and sand deposition. As you drive south over the bridge, note the braid of waterways and the superb sandy beach to the north and east. Early in this century, a sand pit curled under the bridge, fanning into the sound to the west. That tail of sand is gone, and the grand recreational beach that you see, sometimes covered with folks fishing, did not exist in this place in 1964, when the first Bonner Bridge opened. The beach arrived particle by particle via longshore transport from the resort beaches to the north. And it isn't going back.

While the south end of Bodie Island sprawls and spreads, the north end of Pea Island would have eroded rapidly as Oregon Inlet shifted south, but in 1991 contractors completed the terminal rock groin or jetty on Pea Island's north end. Now it cannot shift naturally, but if it could, it might eventually cost the south end of the new bridge

Regardless of design and cost, the new Herbert C. Bonner Bridge is likely to always be the bridge over troubling waters.

As the ocean shears sand from any headland, longshore currents move it parallel to the shoreline, depositing much of it farther south from its point of origin. On northern headlands, the loosened sand may be transported into the adjoining inlet, causing shoaling as is happening at Hatteras Inlet. On Pea Island much of this sand arrives unseen—ever—at Cape Point and in the treacherous fan of submerged sand known as Diamond Shoals, east of the Cape Hatteras Lighthouse. Deposition occurs where currents spread out or otherwise lose velocity and the particles drop to the bottom, at inlets and flattened bottom profiles like Cape Point.

In 2016, the deposition of this sand after storms resulted in a new island—dubbed Shelly Island—off Cape Point. In less than a year it was "automagically" absorbed into Cape Point. Easy come, easy go.

The vectors of wave and storm attack add to the woes of the beaches between Virginia and Cape Point. The waves strike obliquely, steadily eroding and transporting sand southward. Rarely does it reverse and return the sand. Between Cape Hatteras and Cape Lookout, waves take a smaller bite. Farther south, at Sunset Beach, North Carolina's southernmost barrier island, deposition from longshore transport and storms shoaled Mad Inlet, connecting to Bird Island and adding nearly an eighth of a mile of sand to the beach.

Longshore transport is just a part of the natural equilibrium of barrier islands. The sand must and will move. The same system that carries sand away from any given beach is likely to be bringing sand to the same location from elsewhere—so long as sand is available. When sand is dredged from a shipping channel and stored on an artificial island, it is removed from the sand transport system, depriving that system of natural replenishment. This was in fact the dredging practice at Beaufort Inlet for many years. Today dredge spoils from maintaining the shipping channel are sometimes deposited where prevailing longshore transport moves the sand along the face of Atlantic Beach and the rest of Bogue Banks.

Watch the sand in the surf someday when waves slant in on an angle. See if the foam and sand don't slide sideways when washing back. It is on the move to another length of beach, pausing now and again in its longshore journey. More than likely, replacement sand is on its way too.

In this way the ocean does give in this restless zone, but it also takes away, sometimes abruptly. That is life on the edge, and this has resort communities on the edge. Beach is their economic lifeblood; sand in place is their bulwark against demise. When the sand leaves naturally, it is replaced in a process known as beach nourishment: that is, it is pumped from offshore back onto the beach. This is happening with increasing frequency at increasing cost.

North Carolina has 326 miles of coast, 160 miles of which are developed. In 2017, 120 miles of the developed coast were scheduled to undergo or planning a beach nourishment program. And that sand, too, will inevitably go away.

THE OREGON INLET
(HERBERT C. BONNER) BRIDGE

The replacement for the original Herbert C. Bonner Bridge should open in the fall of 2019. This is a project with a lengthy genesis, and the new bridge will literally and figuratively span many of the dynamic issues that churn at this edge of the sea.

Since 1963, when the original bridge honoring the memory of North Carolina Congressman Herbert C. Bonner first opened, the bridge provided a magnificent crossing that closed the gap between the once-distant Outer Banks and the mainland. It became an essential and indispensable link to the Cape Hatteras National Seashore and eventually tied the private communities within the seashore to a modern tourism-based economy, supplanting the traditional livelihoods of the first half of the twentieth century. The bridge jump-started tremendous growth and change from Oregon Inlet south.

Bridges are built to stay in place, but dynamic environments such as inlets to the open ocean almost never do. Almost from the very start a natural tension developed between this stationary object and the movable environment around it. The inlet shifted and shoaled, with all the stability of Jockey's Ridge State Park. The land and water beneath the bridge has never looked the same from one year to the next—though people may not have noticed.

This degree of change is not surprising. Oregon Inlet has been a busy place since an 1846 hurricane blew it open; the first ship to pass through, the side-wheeler *Oregon*, was its namesake. Since 1964 the inlet has been migrating southward at the steady rate of 75–125 feet per year, independent of storm-powered alterations. (It originally opened approximately 3 miles north.)

The southbound inlet piled sand beneath the north portion of the original bridge as the ocean gnawed at the Pea Island headland. By the time serious replacement discussions began, much of the north end of this bridge was no longer "over troubled waters" but instead over the new sandy beach of Bodie Island, while the north end of Pea Island progressed southward. Eventually, to help secure the channel and partially to save the bridge, a contract was let to build a rock groin still visible today.

After nearly a decade of discussions, proposals, and cost analysis, the current bridge design — a higher, more stably constructed parallel span west of the original bridge — gained approval. Construction began in August 2011.

The loose end in this project is the north end of Pea Island — specifically, the 9-mile stretch of rapidly eroding island that is included in Pea Island National Wildlife Refuge. This is where the new bridge will land within arguably the most troubled miles of NC 12, miles constantly overwashed and even cut by ever-more-frequent storm impact. Since this is the only road serving the communities, it is constantly undergoing costly repairs, in the many millions of dollars since 1987. In August 2011, shortly after the replacement bridge construction began, Hurricane Irene breached Pea Island south of the freshwater ponds in the historical location of closed "New Inlet."

The replacement bridge is built to last 100 years. It will terminate on the north end of Pea Island, but what happens going forward (and heading south) on NC 12 is only as settled as the sands it must travel.

OREGON INLET JETTY

The shifting, fickle nature of Oregon Inlet has made the inlet precarious. In the 1980s the inlet movement and shoaling nearly strangled commercial fishing in Wanchese. Several fishing trawlers were lost, and the inlet was essentially abandoned in favor of more distant but more stable Hatteras Inlet to the south. The response to this crisis included a controversial proposal to construct a pair of jetties to secure the inlet.

After a furious debate, Congress funded a compromise proposal to build a 9-foot-tall, half-mile-long curving granite "terminal wall" on the north end of Pea Island, the south side of the inlet, for $13.5 million.

The North Carolina Department of Transportation completed the jetty in January 1991, and almost immediately sand began to accumulate on the

The U.S. Coast Guard Station at Oregon Inlet (retired).
(Photo by Bill Russ, courtesy of VisitNC.com)

landward side part of its original purpose. It certainly has resulted in significant sand accretion behind the wall. It also provided fine fishing for anglers, who parked at the old coast guard station nearby and lugged fishing gear nearly half a mile across soft sand to reach the jetty.

The Department of Transportation posted No Trespassing signs along the sandy approach to the jetty, warning that the area was dangerous: the rocks are slippery when wet. But enforcement of the restriction is not rigorous.

Access

There is no public access to the jetty.

OREGON INLET COAST GUARD STATION (RETIRED)

The weather-beaten U.S. Coast Guard station on the north end of Pea Island, the east side of NC 12, is still on the books, though it is officially retired.

All duties served by this station transferred to the new multimission station adjacent to the Oregon Inlet Fishing Center across the inlet. Con-

Cape Hatteras National Seashore

gress authorized this station and funded its construction in 1873. By 1888 it was decommissioned and moved 400 yards inland and south, to its present location, because of beach erosion and shoaling. Nearly a decade later it was destroyed by a storm, and a new station was constructed in 1897. Extensive renovation in 1933 gave the station its present form, and the U.S. Coast Guard served from this location until 1988, when erosion from the inlet's migration south threatened to destroy it. Inlet stabilization measures have since buffered and landlocked the location. The building, visible from the road and bridge, is on the National Register of Historic Places, but exposure to the elements is taking a toll.

Access

After crossing the Oregon Inlet Bridge, take the second left turn to reach the station. The station is closed, but the old road is used for access parking. Be careful of soft sand.

For information, call the Oregon Inlet Coast Guard Station at 252-987-2311.

PEA ISLAND, NORTH END

The north end of Pea Island is accessible from a parking area on the ocean side of NC 12. This area has portable toilets for visitors. The exact means of reaching this parking area from the replacement bridge and roadway is not clear at this writing, but it is very likely to be similar to the connections that were in place before the replacement bridge construction. Pea Island National Wildlife Refuge administers the north end of the island, and visitor access is part of their mission.

Both the oceanfront and the inlet are accessible from this parking lot, and well-delineated footpaths lead to both. There are quieter surf waters beyond the pull of the inlet currents well south of the end of the jetty.

Swimming is not advised except far south of the inlet currents. Shelling is only fair, partly because of the turbulence of the inlet waters. The beach widens and the dune line created by the Civilian Conservation Corps in the 1930s becomes more stable as the shore arcs south.

Areas may be closed periodically due to nesting wildlife, and such areas will be clearly signed.

Access

Parking is off the south end of the Herbert C. Bonner Bridge. There are trash receptacles and portable toilets.

PEA ISLAND NATIONAL WILDLIFE REFUGE

This refuge occupies the northern 13 miles of Hatteras Island south of Oregon Inlet; the bridge leaves the National Park Service lands of Bodie Island and ends in the U.S. Fish and Wildlife Service domain known as Pea Island National Wildlife Refuge. (The name Pea Island survives from when both New Inlet [1738–1945] and Oregon Inlet [1846–] were open.)

The narrow passage of NC 12 south from the bridge close to the steep banks of vegetation-free sand—not dunes—piled high beside the east side of NC 12 offers a dramatic introduction to the most tenuous boundary of this substantial preserve. The land and marsh visible to the west are the valued acreage at the core of the purpose. Pea Island National Wildlife Refuge includes 5,834 acres of upland and 25,700 acres of proclamation waters. To put it another way, all the land visible from the road is less than 20 percent of the protected, dedicated area.

Established in 1938, it is a jewel of a place to visit. The primary purpose is to provide nesting and wintering habitat for migratory waterfowl, wading birds, and shorebirds as well as critical habitat for endangered and threatened species such as migratory sea turtles. Importantly, the refuge purpose also includes opportunities for people to enjoy the wildlife riches that periodically populate the impoundments and waters.

Fall and winter are the best seasons for waterfowl. This when the tundra swans, Canada geese, greater snow geese, and many species of migratory waterfowl such as green-winged teal, American widgeon, pintails, mallards, black ducks, northern shoveler ducks, and ring-necked ducks visit the moist grounds and impoundments. Bald eagles, barred owls, herons, American egrets, and even ibises are present.

In summer, blue herons, great egrets, ands snowy egrets wade the waters in July and August. On the oceanfront, sea turtles come ashore to nest at night, a season that typically begins in April and can last into midsummer.

Before the refuge, commercial market hunters would relentlessly hunt the wintering waterfowl. The upland acreage was farmed and provided grazing for resident's livestock. The plight of the greater snow goose, hunted to near depletion, informed the decision to establish the refuge. The population has rebounded significantly from that early twentieth-century ebb.

To increase the benefits of the location, the Fish and Wildlife Service built a system of dikes and freshwater ponds to grow grasses and other plants favored by the migratory waterfowl. The dikes between impoundments are the best locations for viewing wildlife.

The refuge bird list includes more than 365 species, along with the 25 species of mammals and 24 species of reptiles that make the refuge their home. Endangered species recorded on the refuge include the peregrine falcon, the loggerhead turtle, and piping plover.

The refuge visitor center is about 4.5 miles south of Oregon Inlet. There is parking and a comfort station. The North Pond Trail begins at the south end of the parking area. It is 4 miles long and passes around the North Pond. Winter brings brisk wind chill to this walk, and in summer a long-sleeved shirt and pants, insect repellent, and bottled water are indispensable—and, of course, so are binoculars.

Across NC 12 from the visitor center, partially submerged just past the breaking waves, is the boiler of the federal steamer *Oriental*, a Civil War–era shipwreck.

Interpretive programs exist throughout the year, but the refuge bustles with the arrival of the waterfowl in fall. Every year in the first week of November, the refuge hosts the "Wings over Water" celebration of wildlife and habitats on the Outer Banks.

Access

Volunteers staff the refuge office between April and October.

There are several parking areas on NC 12 serving the refuge. There is a soundside parking area and canoe launch just south of the refuge office at New Inlet.

The beaches of Pea Island are open for swimming and fishing (permit required) year-round. Pea Island is open for daylight use only. The refuge closes some access areas during the nesting of certain shorebirds to prevent visitors from disturbing the birds.

Camping, campfires, hunting, guns, driving on the beach, and unleashed dogs are prohibited. Dogs are not allowed on the pond sides of NC 12.

The Plight of the Piping Plover

One creature's nursery may be another's playground, and sometimes the different uses cannot coexist. On one side is the piping plover; on the other, recreational anglers. Each needs a part of the beach most frequently during April and May, the time of big fish runs and the migratory shorebird's nesting season. Big tires, big feet, and small, easily overlooked eggs or chicks are not compatible.

After several years of what can only be characterized as a stormy and litigious conflict, the park service is managing a compromise between threatened species protection and recreational use on the national seashores.

The piping plover, a small shorebird that is nearly invisible against the dry sand of the dunes, is buying time against extinction on not-nearly-lonely-enough segments of the barrier beaches. Named for its "piping" song, the shorebird is one of several species that nest at the base of the dunes and the sandy dry flats of the beach, areas where people may walk or drive. In January 10, 1986, biologists placed it on the federal endangered species list primarily because of loss of habitat due to increased construction and more people playing where the bird prefers to nest. (It is considered a threatened population in North Carolina.) Fortunately, this small shorebird is finding refuge in the existing preserves along the Outer Banks. People could give this sand-nesting species a big boost simply by sticking to the trails and obeying notices closing areas to foot and vehicle traffic.

April and May are the critical times to temper your beach-driving ambitions on Cape Hatteras and Cape Lookout National Seashores. These months are when the nesting season begins for this plover, the least tern, the gull-billed tern, the common tern, and black skimmers, all of which leave their eggs in simple depressions in the warm sands.

Adult piping plovers will feign an injured wing to draw intruders away from an unseen nest. This behavior may be the only visible clue to carefully turn around. (Common terns, which nest in colonies, will attack and aggressively defend their nests.)

The plover and the least tern are the two species of most concern. By some counts, the population of the petite plover is close to 1,800 pairs along its Eastern Seaboard migratory range. The beaches of Pea Island, Cape Hatteras Bight, Ocracoke Island, and much of Cape Lookout are prime nesting habitat. The plovers and other birds could leave their camouflaged eggs in the open to hatch, threatened only by the pillaging of either raccoons or larger birds that steal chicks. Today human disruption, loss of suitable un-disturbed beach, and unleashed pets that disturb or destroy nests pose the biggest threats to nesting.

During nesting seasons, biologists walk the beach daily seeking evidence of nesting (and the crawl marks of nesting sea turtles). A find of either prompts park biologists to erect effective barriers to protect the nest. Sometimes—and here is the real rub—the beach is not wide enough to allow effective protection and so must be closed.

Cape Point, one of the most sought-after locations among recreational fishers, can also be a preferred nesting area. In most years Cape Point will be closed to vehicular traffic for about half of the summer. In 2016 it was open nearly all season long.

Helping these endangered birds recover is easy: stay out of flagged portions of the national wildlife refuges and national seashores. The eggs are extraordinarily difficult to see, and to hear the sound of eggs crushing underfoot is to realize too late.

The U.S. Fish and Wildlife Service is in charge of the protection program for the piping plover, but other National Park Service and state park personnel will relay any information about a suspected nest to them.

Search FWS Piping Plover or enter www.fws.gov
/northeast/pipingplover/overview.html.

Search Pea Island NWR or enter www.fws.gov/refuge/pea_island/.

Best phone number for more information: 252-987-2394 (visitor center).

Alternative Manteo office: 252-473-1131.

THE PEA ISLAND DRIVE

The drive through Pea Island National Wildlife Refuge is a memorable brush with the sea. NC 12 rides closely beside massive walls of sand. These are not relics of the great dune line the Civilian Conservation Corps constructed and planted in the 1930s. For the most part, these bulldozer-built sand barriers exist to protect one of the more threatened lengths of NC 12. North Carolina's Department of Transportation has been in a relentless war of attrition with the Atlantic Ocean that has repeatedly overwhelmed the dunes and made the highway impassable with sand. In some locations the road has been washed away. The road between the bridge and the visitor center has been covered repeatedly.

Believe that the ocean is really close beyond the sand hills. Don't park to climb and look: walking destabilizes dunes.

There is no parking east of the highway except at designated pull-offs, which are few. Crossing the dunes is off-limits except at the designated locations.

South of the Pea Island Visitor Center, NC 12 has been relocated west of its earlier routing because the protective dune line was destroyed approaching the New Inlet Access Area around milepost 7.5.

Approximately 2 miles south of the visitor center, NC 12 is elevated. This is the Captain Richard Etheridge Bridge, dedicated in February 2018 to honor a man born into slavery who became the captain of the nation's only all–African American U.S. Life-Saving Station, the Pea Island Station. In an otherwise segregated service, his crew served with heroic distinction, saving countless lives.

The views east and west from the bridge show why it is needed: this area was completely cut through in 2011 by Hurricane Irene. This "new" inlet cuts very close to the historical inlet known as New Inlet. This elevated length of highway provides convincing evidence of the tension between land, man-made structures, and the relentlessness of natural processes on a barrier island.

There is a pullover on the west side of the highway for the New Inlet boating access. The pilings visible to the west are the remains of the old New Inlet Bridge (the inlet closed in 1945). The interpretive displays east of NC 12 at New Inlet tell the story of the famed Pea Island Life-Saving Station, made famous by the heroism of its all-black crew. In 1995, after the persuasive arguments of four young historians who researched the Pea Island Station, the U.S. Coast Guard awarded the Gold Lifesaving Medal to members of the 1896 crew for their part in the rescue of all passengers and personnel of the schooner *E. S. Newman*. The foundation of the relocated station was once visible across NC 12 slightly north of the access area.

The drive south from the New Inlet Access site winds through an ever-narrowing island with stable dunes to the east and maritime shrub thicket spreading west toward the sound. Ironically, this section of the highway is deemed highly vulnerable to erosion. A 2.4-mile-long "jug-handle" bridge will arc NC 12 away from the coast and over Pamlico Sound, returning it to land in Rodanthe. The bridge is scheduled for completion in 2020.

RODANTHE

NC 12 curls through a wave-battered length island to enter Rodanthe (pronounced "Ro-*dan*-theh"), the first of the unincorporated older Outer Banks communities to be intentionally excluded from the national seashore. It is often referenced as part of a triplet with Waves and Salvo, the sequential communities to the south. It is the easternmost point in North Carolina.

The name Rodanthe, though arcane in origin, is somewhat easier to say and spell than Chicamacomico Banks, the original community name. It became Rodanthe with the 1874 arrival of the U.S. Post Office (the U.S. Life-Saving Service selected the original community name for its 1874 station). It is likely that federal postal officials rejected Chicamacomico because of its length: fitting it on a cancellation stamp would be a challenge.

Mysteriously, Rodanthe was substituted. It is possible that the name originated from botany: *Rhodanthe* is a genus name composed of two Greek words, *rhodon* (rose) and *anthos* (flower). That the species associated with the genus are several daisy-like flowers native to Australia compounds the mystery.

Rodanthe begins at a point where the island thins to the width of a sneeze. It looks tenuous, and it is: in 1878 this was Loggerhead Inlet, right at the northern edge of Rodanthe. By 2020 this section of NC 12 will be bypassed by a new bridge over the waters of Pamlico Sound.

The road veers sharply inland—it has to. It has been relocated several times because of increased oceanfront erosion. The accelerated rate of erosion here seems to correlate with the southward migration of an offshore ocean floor feature known as Wimble Shoals.

The oceanfront appeared solid in the 1980s when Mirlo Beach, a new gateway development, parked several large, handsome homes here seaward of Seagull Drive. The uniquely styled houses were 400 feet back from the breaking waves.

(The name Mirlo Beach is riveted in local history and honors the heroic rescue of crew of the *Mirlo*, a British vessel destroyed by either a German mine or a torpedo in 1918. The crew of the nearby Chicamacomico Life-Saving Station rescued most of the stricken sailors from the flaming vessel.)

A house in this eye-opening neighborhood of strongly themed architecture became the film setting for the 2008 movie *Nights at Rodanthe*. By then a series of storms launched by 1999's Hurricane Dennis had whittled the protective dunes to a minimal distance.

The coup de grâce for the development in general and the movie house in particular came in the form of a remnant storm of Hurricane Ida in November 1999, which buckled NC 12. Subsequently, the road was moved west and the house was sold and in January 2010 was relocated, refurbished to resemble the movie set, and opened as a bed-and-breakfast, the Inn at Rodanthe.

The fate of remaining homes at Mirlo Beach is still unresolved—several are more "oceanfront" than would seem to be comfortable.

Rodanthe is most likely built on the end of a prehistoric island that extended into the sea beyond the present-day oceanfront, similarly aligned as Pea Island. In 1611 the remnants of the island were charted as Cape Kendrick, east of present-day Salvo. Cape Kendrick disappeared sometime in the seventeenth or eighteenth century, and the remnants of the submerged spit are now known as Wimble Shoals.

The southerly compass alignment of Hatteras Island south of Rodanthe combined with Wimble Shoals offshore made for hazardous ocean navigation. The U.S. Life-Saving Service built Station Number 18 at Chicamacomico Banks in 1874. The station adopted the local name and became an anchor for the community.

Past Mirlo Beach, NC 12 meanders through the cedar tree–punctuated community in a lazy sequence of bends, passing the fully restored Chicamacomico Life-Saving Station on the east side soon after entering the community.

Rodanthe remains a place of slower pace in the vacation-charged summer traffic on NC 12—more like an eddy than a rapid. It offers a few quick-stop services, seasonal eateries, gas stations, restaurants, and resident campgrounds, and an amusement park geared to motorized entertainment. These businesses give a roadside impression that overrides the settled nature of Rodanthe, which is mostly residential, with some rental homes.

While tourism has taken hold in Rodanthe, it still has the salt-scoured veneer of a long-settled village. There is a boat basin still used by commercial anglers as a public harbor, even though the land around the basin is privately owned.

Rodanthe Pier Place at the end of Atlantic Drive commands the oceanfront as only a pier can do in a small town. It is surrounded by residences

Cape Hatteras National Seashore

and still holds a strong local appeal. Nights in Rodanthe might be spent well there.

Past the stock car amusement concession and the KOA Campground, NC 12 eases into the neighboring community of Waves.

By way of extreme local color, Rodanthe and surrounds still revere "Old Christmas," January 6 (Epiphany, or the Twelfth Day of Christmas), a vestige of the Julian calendar, replaced by the Gregorian calendar in the mid-eighteenth century.

Access

There is a regional access with 83 parking places, a bathhouse, and showers at 23731 NC 12, the second left turn south of the Chicamacomico Life-Saving Station.

Search Rodanthe for websites for rentals, real estate, and public advisory information or enter www.outerbanks.org, use the "Plan Your Trip/Towns & Villages" drop-down menus, and find /Rodanthe.

U.S. LIFE-SAVING STATION
CHICAMACOMICO HISTORIC SITE

As NC 12 enters Rodanthe, it arcs in a gentle curve toward Pamlico Sound. The road curves past an unpresupposing shingle building set back from the road that is easily overlooked, yet the grounds and the stories revealed here go straight to the historical heart of the Outer Banks.

The restored and preserved U.S. Life-Saving Station Chicamacomico is one of the most complete lifesaving stations in the nation. The buildings and the displays inside tell the story of the service that came to these shores in the late nineteenth century, bringing hope for stricken mariners and stability to the isolated existence of these island communities.

The Chicamacomico Life-Saving Station entered service in 1874, the first of the seven original stations of this type on the Outer Banks. It stayed active as a station until the U.S. Coast Guard closed it in 1954.

The station housed heroes in one era, and in another era heroes rescued the station. The volunteers of the Chicamacomico Historical Association, a private, nonprofit group, assumed maintenance of the neglected, disrepaired complex in the late 1970s; they turned it into a historical tour de force of the Outer Banks. In 1974 the indefatigable Carolista Baum, who had previously marshaled preservationists to save Jockey's Ridge in Nags Head, joined historian and author David Stick and artist Woodrow Edwards to spearhead the association's efforts.

Two stations, the 1874 boathouse (the original station) and the shingled sloped roof with simple look-out tower and porch 1911 building, are classic examples of the indigenous institutional architecture that the U.S. Life-Saving Service and its successor, the U.S. Coast Guard, adopted for their Outer Banks locations. The cottage-like complex was both office and home for the station keeper and crew. The buildings were all constructed for the single purpose of housing crews and equipment to save the lives of the shipwrecked.

The station's heyday was the decades between founding and World War II. Life was spartan and demanding for the crew, who stood at the ready to launch at the first sign of a ship in distress. The valor shown by the Chicamacomico crew became legendary even by the heroic standards of the actions of neighboring stations.

In August 1918 the crew members launched the boats from the same seaward 1874 boathouse to rescue the survivors of the British tanker *Mirlo*. The oil carrier had been ripped apart by either a German mine or a torpedo in the shipping lanes east of Rodanthe. Secondary explosions set the water on fire, and the British crew were scattered around the burning vessel. Most of the British sailors were saved. This feat was accomplished under the determined direction of J. A. Midgett, one of the many members of the local Midgett family who served in the U.S. Life-Saving Service.

The rescue gained international celebrity, and the British government was so moved and grateful that it created the King George Gold Medal for Valor and awarded the medal to each member of the surfboat crew. The heroic episode became known as the greatest rescue of World War I.

In 1930 the coast guard also recognized the heroism of the *Mirlo* rescue, awarding each member of the six-man crew the Grand Cross of the American Cross of Honor; five of those brave crew members were Midgetts.

The restored quarters are open to the public and showcase exhibits highlighting historic moments and rescues. There is a video introducing the U.S. Life-Saving Service and the history of the station. During the summer, volunteers hold mock lifesaving drills to demonstrate the rescue techniques that were standard among all the crews from Virginia Beach to Ocracoke.

The building is on the National Register of Historic Structures.

Access

The station is open Monday–Friday 10–5 summer through fall, closed November through Easter. There are scheduled events during the summer months. There is also a gift shop based around a "history of the Outer Banks" theme.

A separate paved bicycle/pedestrian path begins across NC 12 from the Chicamacomico site and extends through Rodanthe, Waves, and Salvo.

Search Chicamacomico or enter www.chicamacomico.org.

Best phone number for more information: 252-987-1552.

WAVES AND SALVO

Waves, the adjoining community south of Rodanthe, begins just past the KOA Cape Hatteras Campground on the east side of NC 12. The visual transition from one to the other is seamless. The highway continues through a residential setting. The roadside venues expand with lawns and contract with tree cover. In response to the growing number of summer visitors who either camp or rent homes, Waves has become a center for wind and water sports, as has adjoining Salvo.

This part of the island appears much different because large red cedar trees have grown sufficiently tall to give a nestled-in look. A few of the homes and churches may be glimpsed behind their evergreen cladding. Shelter from the salt spray facilitated growth, the first of any size to this point on Hatteras Island. NC 12 scoots through Waves and then curves back toward the center of the island, entering Salvo.

One informal marker that signals upcoming Salvo is the brick U.S. Post Office building just north of the Waves Market. Thalassa Avenue more or less marks the transition to Salvo. While the U.S. census has its own clear definition of Rodanthe, Waves, and Salvo, residents know where they live and seem less concerned about a public declaration of place.

The border between the two is not distinct—save for the Salvo sign (Waves signs tend to be stolen)—and the communities blend together. A resident expressed the local laissez-faire attitude about civic lines this way: "There's supposed to be a boundary here somewhere, but folks don't seem too sure about it."

Salvo has experienced a good deal of growth. New homes are filling the low grassy flats to the east of the highway, well behind a substantial dune line. The offshore configuration of Wimble Shoals that influences erosion in northern Rodanthe is having a different effect in Waves and Salvo. The beaches are stable, and the artificial Civilian Conservation Corps dune line, completely eroded in parts of Rodanthe, is expanding along the Waves/Salvo oceanfront. The reason is the steady accumulation of sand on the beach, which allows the dunes to rebuild naturally in summer months.

In spite of the growth, the island seems more stable through Salvo. The sky seems bigger and the horizon more expansive. The tree-buttressed road-side peels away, and the effect is not unlike leaving a low-walled canyon. The trees become less frequent—a few grow along the sound side—and then the road passes through a meadow and there are no more houses or streets. The island is wide open.

(Driving north to Salvo, the southern approach is one of the gentlest visual transitions along the entire Outer Banks. First there are the grassy flats, then some maritime shrubs, and slowly the punctuation of houses, churches, and trees appears, and then the community—sudden enclosure in an insular and enduring place.)

The name Salvo supposedly originates from an incident during the Civil War. After a Union naval officer commanded his sailors to "give it a salvo" or broadside of cannon fire, the name Salvo was entered into the logbook records and subsequently superseded the original name, Clarksville.

Salvo once famously maintained a small and portable post office, one of the smallest in the world. The little white building with blue trim was mounted on rails so that it could be easily moved when the postmaster changed. In 1992 arsonists torched it. The community moved quickly to rebuild but was rebuffed by the U.S. Post Office in Washington, DC, because the old post office failed to meet new disability standards. Nevertheless, the town rebuilt the old post office as a memorial, and mail now goes to a characterless brick structure that will never achieve the star qualities of its predecessor.

The National Park Service maintains Salvo Day Use Area, a site for picnics, cookouts, and open-space play with restrooms, showers, and access to the sound. It is immediately south of Salvo on the west side of NC 12. Drive through a road framed with young cedar trees to reach the day use loop drive, a serene setting. A historical marker informs about an early (if not the only) Civil War capture of a Union ship by a Confederate ship that occurred in Pamlico Sound. An old, private family cemetery adjoins the day use area and is closed to the public. It is possible to see the devastating effects of shoreline erosion from the sound on this particular part of the island here.

Access

The National Park Service operates a day use area south of Salvo that is designated for wind- and kitesurfing, but anyone is welcome. Also, this day use area is a good location to park to carefully cross NC 12 to the beaches beyond the dunes.

Ramp 23, providing all-wheel-drive vehicle access to the beach, is directly opposite the Salvo Day Use Area. Vehicles should be four-wheel drive and properly permitted to drive on the beach.

Search Waves or Salvo for websites for rentals, real estate, and public advisory information or enter www.outerbanks.org, use the "Plan Your Trip/Towns & Villages" drop-down menus, and find Waves or Salvo.

Search Salvo Day or enter www.nps.gov/caha/ and use the search feature for Salvo Day Use.

Best phone number for more information: 252-473-2111.

SALVO TO AVON

The thread of highway between Salvo and Avon is an elemental component of the Outer Banks National Scenic Byway. This is why the Outer Banks are unique among the many coastal islands of the United States. This length of highway is among the most evocative stretches of the Outer Banks. There are no distractions. The drive is elemental: land, sea, and sky. Except for the pavement and power poles, it offers a sense of what the Outer Banks were like many years ago.

The scenery is wondrously constant: a sinuous dune line, mounding masses of evergreen foliage, the slate green of the sound waters beyond the thickets of shrubbery, the hypnotic march of the utility poles, the cinema of the sky. Slow down and pull over into one of the parking areas to trek over the dunes and be alone on the beach.

The Little Kinnakeet Life-Saving Station stands amid this isolation

10 miles south of Salvo. Both the 1874 original station, now restored, and the 1904 expanded station are beside NC 12, partially screened by growing cedar trees. The station was originally on the ocean side of present-day NC 12, but in 1900 it was relocated to avoid destruction from erosion.

As in all of the original North Carolina stations, the crew, one keeper, and six surfmen lived here—the middle of nowhere—when on duty. The station was not staffed year-round until 1904. The job involved walking the beach in storms on the lookout for ships in distress and then risking their lives to rescue the stricken mariners.

The 1904 building, with its hipped roofs attached to a square tower, is one of the two architectural prototypes adapted for the lifesaving stations on the South Atlantic seaboard and is referred to as a "southern-pattern sta-tion." (The other architectural prototype is prominently preserved at U.S. Life-Saving Station Chicamacomico in Rodanthe.) The then-new building had a large room for the crew, an office for the keeper, and a kitchen/din-ing area.

The Little Kinnakeet Station remained in service until it was decom-missioned in June 1954. The U.S. Coast Guard delivered the 14.5-acre com-plex to the National Park Service as a historical component of the national seashore. Restoration efforts between 1976 and 1978 restored the 1874 boathouse to its authentic look from the 1885–1915 time period. The entire grouping is an excellent example of how buildings were added to the site as the mission evolved from the days of the U.S. Life-Saving Service through the site's service to the U.S. Coast Guard.

At Ramp 27 north of Avon, the schooner *G. A. Kohler*, which sank in August 1933, may be visible on the beach.

Access

There are several parking turnouts and off-road-vehicle access ramps be-tween Salvo and Avon. The ramps are numbered; 23, 28, and 30 have park-ing lots. Beach driving is available only to properly permitted four-wheel-drive vehicles.

There are also several off-road-vehicle trails on the west side of the high-way for water-sport access.

The buildings of Little Kinnakeet Station are not accessible; they are surrounded by chain-link fence.

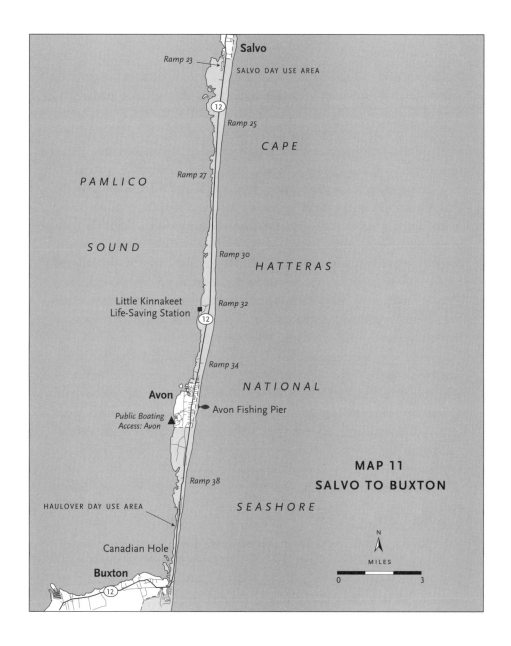

Ramp 23

Salvo

SALVO DAY USE AREA

⑫

Ramp 25

C A P E

P A M L I C O

Ramp 27

S O U N D

Ramp 30

H A T T E R A S

Little Kinnakeet
Life-Saving Station   Ramp 32

⑫

Ramp 34

N A T I O N A L

Avon

Avon Fishing Pier

*Public Boating
Access: Avon*

Ramp 38

**MAP 11
SALVO TO BUXTON**

HAULOVER DAY USE AREA   *S E A S H O R E*

N

Canadian Hole

MILES

Buxton

⑫

0   3

Search Salvo Day Use Area or enter www.nps.gov/caha/ and use the "Plan
Your Visit/Directions and Transportation/Maps" drop-down menus.

Search Little Kinnakeet or enter www.uslife-savingservice.org to
learn more about other stations of the U.S. Life-Saving Service.

AVON

Two miles south of the Little Kinnakeet U.S. Life-Saving Station, houses and commercial buildings signal the community of Avon, a traditional fishing village that is resurging with a tourism-based economy. Single-family vacation home development fills the land between NC 12 and the Atlantic Ocean and multiple new developments with sound access spreads to Pamlico Sound. Avon is a high-density, highly popular summer destination.

Compared with the resort cities north of Oregon Inlet, Avon lacks the multiple attractions that draw people to those locations. Its appeal is based in simple salt-water-based recreation because of its provident location in the national seashore—in an 18-mile length of sea-to-sound preserve. The extra driving time required to reach the community combines with the reduced entertainment opportunities to produce a more economical beach vacation. These simpler promises generated high demand for rental properties: since the 1980s, vacation development here has achieved a density surpassing that of any village south of Oregon Inlet.

Newer, very large homes, mostly on the west side of NC 12, set an elevated tone compared to the older weathered and shingled Avon homes on the ocean side. The earlier soundside community is a winding drive down appropriately named Harbor Road, SR 1224. It leads back to the original core of the community of more traditional livelihoods. Avon has a resort rhythm and appearance that is a sea change in character from its early days as Kinnakeet.

Commensurate commercial services have developed to meet the seasonal demand—groceries and a mix of dining venues and beach apparel are local. There are water recreation vendors as well.

The community remains a highly desirable destination for surf anglers because its beaches are consistently outstanding fishing locations for bluefish, red drum (channel bass), and mackerel (mostly from the Avon Pier). Pursuit of these game fish generates unbridled enthusiasm among anglers.

The annual fish runs of the spring and fall can change the pulse of the community. Local enterprises and anglers stay in constant radio and text contact with others similarly engaged to find out what is biting where. Game fish feeding furiously in the surf can generate a beach full of pole-wielding, all-wheel-drive enthusiasts eager to fill their coolers.

Avon has a private fishing pier, open to the public for a fee, with parking for the pier. This is a serious pier for serious pier fishing, somewhat renowned in the surf-fishing subculture for record catches of red drum, also known as channel bass. Red drum fishing is for the diehards; it may be best in the worst of weather because during the "shoulder season" red drum follow the migrations of bait fish such as menhaden. Avon is where a world-record 94-pound red drum was caught.

Access

Avon has no designated public access locations to the beach, but parking is comparatively easy. Once you leave town, you are back on the Cape Hatteras National Seashore, and the access ramps are spaced about every 3 miles.

Ramp 34, south of Avon, is a traditional fishing hot spot for bluefish or for red drum during their spring and fall runs. Ramp 38 provides access to the ocean and the sound. Ramp 41 provides beach access just north of the Buxton Village limits.

Search Avon NC for commercial websites offering real estate and travel reviews or enter www.outerbanks.org, use the "Plan Your Trip/Towns & Villages/" drop-down menus, and find Avon.

Best phone number for more information: 877-629-4386.

THE HAULOVER DAY USE AREA (CANADIAN HOLE)

The Haulover Day Use Area is approximately 1.5 miles south of Avon on the west side of NC 12. It has restrooms showers and angled parking for 100 vehicles that quickly fills in vacation season. The day use area provides access to Pamlico Sound for windsurfers, but there are several user-established dune crossovers across NC 12 that lead to the beach.

The name recalls a time when local residents would haul over their boats, nets, and caught fish from the sea to the sound or vice versa. The naturally narrow part of the island made this possible.

The island is also subject to storm overwash, and past overwash has widened the sound beach, making it easier to use as a windsurfing or kite-surfing launch.

While Pamlico Sound is generally shallow, dredging for replacement fill following a storm that blew out the dunes and road has deepened the waters offshore. The dredging made outstanding water conditions for windsurfing.

The word spread north to Canadian windsurfers in the 1980s, resulting in a steady influx of cars with Canada plates parked just off the road and windsurfers skimming the sound waters. The location quickly earned the moniker "Canadian Hole," and its reputation as one of the finest windsurfing locations on the East Coast is widespread.

The park service paved the first parking area in 1988 but then had to expand it and provide restrooms in 1990.

There are surf shops in Rodanthe, Avon, and Buxton that have windsurfing equipment for sale or rent. Windsurfing, kitesurfing, and "O Canada" are here to stay. C'est bon!

Access

Parking is on a first-come, first-served basis. Overnight stays are not permitted, so don't plan to camp in your car.

Search Haulover Day for multiple reviews or enter
www.nps.gov/caha and use the "Plan Your Visit/Directions
& Transportation/Maps" drop-down menus/.

BUXTON

Buxton is by no means the end of the road in Cape Hatteras National Seashore, yet it has a grand exclamation point of arrival: the Cape Hatteras Lighthouse. The famed barber-pole-striped beacon is one of the most exhilarating sights along the entire island chain. The approach from Avon frames the view: sand and dunes to the east, grassy flats feathering to the west, the great gray-blue pond of Pamlico Sound, and the distinctive beacon cutting sharply against the sky.

Before 1999, when the beacon was moved inland 2,500 feet to save it from immediate erosion, all visual lines—the edges of the road, the painted lane divider, and the procession of utility poles—converged on the striped tower as one drove south. The relocation eliminated this wonderful effect. Nevertheless, the lighthouse still draws visitors to it as though they were moths.

It is an assuring, transfixing spectacle, and nearly every car that comes to town makes the turn to the lighthouse before continuing on its journey.

For many visitors Buxton is the town synonymous with "Hatteras," al-

Wild Rides on the Sound Side

There is a widespread and growing use for the Wrights' stuff on the Outer Banks. The constant steady winds that brought the brothers and their lofty dreams here powers the recreational energy of windsurfers and wind kiters. These adventuresome athletes who harness wind for water play are cutting a wake in one of the breeziest sports around.

Dolphin-quick and butterfly-bright, these sailing surfers may have found a mecca on Hatteras Island. While the ocean here has long attracted surfers pursuing the wind-ginned waves, the slacker sound waters now have their sports-on-a-board as well. Fastening a sail to a surfboard—or a surfer to a kite, in the case of wind kiting—has brought new activity to the waters between Rodanthe and Buxton. Pamlico Sound is coming into its own as *the* place not to be bored with a board.

One particular confluence of steady wind and shallow smooth water has an international reputation—welcome to Canadian Hole. This proud nickname recognizes the pioneering windsurfers from our neighbor to the north who put this place on the windsurfing map. Stop at the Haulover Access north of Buxton. At one time, license plates sported a continental flair, especially in fall and early spring, when the water here is chilly but Canada is frozen.

Those who know rate Canadian Hole one of the best rides in the Southeast. Interest is booming; there are surf shops at Rodanthe, Avon, and Buxton that have the gear and the know-how for hire. While entry-level equipment can cost nearly $1,000, individual lessons can get you wet and hooked for much, much less. And what a ride!

Unlike a surfer, who is dependent on waves, a windsurfer fears only becalming. Soundside or surfside, windsurfers ride as long as the wind blows or until their arms tire, whichever comes first. Riders use their body weight to balance against the force of the wind on the sail; the stronger the wind, the greater the lean the rider needs to counterpoint that force. Steady, unvarying winds make for ideal long runs. As you might imagine, gusty winds present problems, as does a sudden becalming on the run out from shore.

Canadian Hole has no lock on ideal conditions. In fact, the prevalence of sound waters all along the North Carolina coast ensures that any location where sailors launch boats can be a hot spot for windsurfing. Duck and Corolla are busy hubs too. While wind and waves come together, there is usually more sailable wind than surfable waves, making windsurfing one of the faster-growing water sports.

Wind kiters, tethered to a parasail with a surfboard that is mounted much like a snowboard, reach all new heights of high-wire activism. The wind-driven kite that pulls wind kiters across the water gives them both power and loft. Unlike a windsurfer, who can tack like a sailboat, a wind kiter has a more problematic return trip.

Windsurfers are more than passengers. They join with board and sail, fused by the dream of flight before the wind and above the water. Advocates call it the ride of a lifetime; watching their brilliant-hued, buoyant-hulled fins flitter across the sound, it's easy to see why.

Search Canadian Hole for general reading.

though Hatteras village proper is several miles southwest. The casual confusion persists because of Buxton's proximity to Cape Hatteras and its vacillating tip of sand, Cape Point, nearly due south of the lighthouse.

An aerial or map view of Buxton/Cape Hatteras shows the sharp southwest alignment in the island at the Cape Point elbow. This new orientation changes the effects of prevailing winds and seas on the land in favor of depositing sand instead of simply streaming it parallel to the shoreline. The result is a series of dune ridges, and these, in turn, sheltered interdune spaces from salt winds, allowing vegetation to flourish. This process created an extensive maritime forest that is not easily perceived from a vehicle—it is on the south side of NC 12. The island width, wooded protection, fresh water, and high ground have sheltered a community here since the earliest days of European settlement. (Prior to that, Buxton was the site of a Native American village, a story told at the private Native American Museum in neighboring Frisco.)

The sharp curve inland of NC 12 as it enters Buxton from the north follows this higher (above sea level), historically stable island alignment. There's a softball field on the northern edge of town, and after that the road carries you into the surprisingly hilly and forested village center. Businesses and homes appear as commercial and residential notches in the thicket of the maritime forest.

Buxton has evolved along this winding rolling segment of NC 12 in a

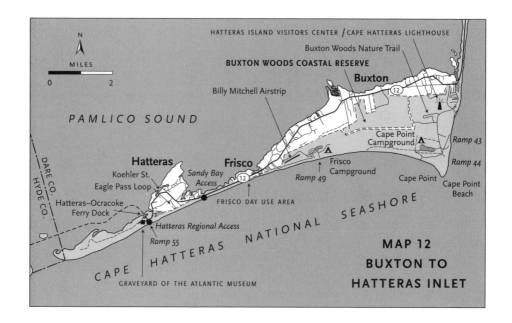

MAP 12
BUXTON TO
HATTERAS INLET

happenstance manner. Individual businesses exist beside older houses, and commercial enterprises tend to have their own frontage. There are a few commercial clusters primarily serving tourism, but those are exceptional. Most enterprises have a practical usefulness, since they serve a year-round population.

Although the community benefits from tourism, it does not look or feel like a beach resort community. Neither does it have much of that summer neon commercialism that seems ubiquitous at summer resorts. To guess at the reason, it is probably because this area was long settled before the tourism economy ramped into overdrive and because most visitors come for the fishing, water sports, national seashore attractions, and storied setting. These recreational preferences have a longer season that extends beyond the start of a school year.

There is never a dent in summer traffic, however; it can be heavy, distracting, and maddening for anyone in a hurry to catch a ferry at Hatteras. The visitor center at the Cape Hatteras Light Station generates a steady stream of summer visitors. And if going to the park complex is tough during midday in summer, leaving is completely vexing.

Tourists converge at this end of the village for good reason. Cape Point is the visible portion of shifting shoals and shallows that all north–south ocean travelers, fish or vessel, must pass. The subsurface shoals are a navigation hazard far out to sea and the reason a warning light was needed. Closer in, where Cape Point parts the waves, fish and the people who want to catch them converge.

This splashy, high-energy point has made Buxton the mecca of surf fishing. Spring and fall in coast migrations of game fish put a four-wheel-drive charge into the local tourism economy. When the fish are running, it's a grand time to visit. Buxton hosts the exclusive Outer Banks Invitational Fishing Tournament. The organizers have limited the numbers of teams because the event is so popular. Finding a place to stay during the tournament may be far more difficult than catching a fish. (The crowds here have been a boon to vacation rentals in nearby Avon.)

Surf anglers have a particular mind-set about their pursuit, and it informs the phrase "going to Hatteras." Those who are not willing to wait endlessly through inclement weather beside thundering surf for a fish that probably won't show, and still call it a good day, can't grasp the full import of the phrase. It is more of a shift in consciousness than it is a destination. A fish run at Cape Point looks like a utility vehicle dealership where shoulder-to-shoulder anglers stand playing the piscatorial lottery.

A beach nourishment plan completed in 2017 put 250 feet of beach back between Access Ramp 34 and the original site of the Cape Hatteras Lighthouse. This highly erodible length of beach needed help because erosion and storm seas were claiming sand and structures. Between 1958 and 1984 the U.S. Navy had a base adjacent to the original lighthouse location on Old Lighthouse Road. They transferred the property to the U.S. Coast Guard, which demolished the old base buildings, returned the land to the National Park Service, and built new housing on adjacent property between 1993 and 1995. These "Cottages at the Cape"—large duplexes—are now privately owned and available to rent.

Access

The motels and cottages at the north end of Buxton are the closest accommodations to the ocean.

The park service controls beach access and provides designated parking areas and off-road-vehicle ramps.

Search Buxton NC for commercial travel recommendations
or enter www.outerbanks.org, use the "Plan Your Trip/
Towns & Villages" drop-down menus, and find Buxton.

Best phone number for more information: 877-629-4386.

For park service information search Hatteras Light or
enter www.nps.gov/caha/planyourvisit/chls.htm.

CAPE HATTERAS LIGHT STATION AND HATTERAS ISLAND VISITOR CENTER

The National Park Service has made the Cape Hatteras Lighthouse the central feature of a reconfigured Hatteras Island Visitor Center. The complex of buildings is officially called the Cape Hatteras Lighthouse Historic District, a designation that both protects the buildings and recognizes the importance of this place to the national narrative of maritime history. As visitors soon learn, it is not *exactly* the place where a young nation built a towering landmark to aid mariners navigating the ever-variable Diamond Shoals. So many shipwrecks occurred offshore that the waters were known as the Graveyard of the Atlantic. In the early 1800s, when the first lighthouse (too short!) was built here, this lonely outpost was in the vanguard against maritime peril.

The 208-foot-tall present-day lighthouse, visible 19 miles out to sea, was first illuminated on December 1, 1870, and has the distinctive lighting pattern, or nightmark, of one flash every 7.5 seconds (eight flashes in a minute). In 1873 the Lighthouse Board assigned the famous barber-pole striping as its distinguishing daymark. At that time the lighthouse was 1,500 feet away from the edge of the sea. Sixty years later, the waves were less than 100 feet away. In 1935 the tower was transferred to the National Park Service (the U.S. Coast Guard maintains the light), and the lighting apparatus was transferred to a nearby steel tower; in the late 1930s the Civilian Conservation Corps constructed an artificial dune line. By 1950 the natural erosion had stopped and the light was returned to the brick tower. In 1953 the Cape Hatteras National Seashore was established and the light was open to the public, but wear and tear closed the tower, and by 1980 the shoreline was 50–75 feet away.

After many engineering feasibility studies and cost estimates, the park service endorsed a plan to move both the tower and the double lightkeeper's quarters. In February 1999 the contractors literally tunneled under the lighthouse, separated it from its foundation, jacked it up, placed a platform with rollers beneath it, put it on tracks, and snatched it from the edge of the sea, slowly, deliberately. The tracks led to the new foundation 2,899.57 feet to the southwest, 1,600 feet away from the Atlantic Ocean. On July 9, 1999, 23 days after the actual move began, the journey was over. By November 13, 1999, Cape Hatteras Lighthouse was relit in its new location. The path of relocation is clearly visible. The wider beach (of 2018) at the original site is a product of recent beach nourishment. The story is thoroughly documented on the park website.

The double lightkeeper's quarters was relocated and placed in the same relative position (to within a quarter inch) it previously had to the lighthouse. The building is a museum dedicated to the lighthouse network, the lives of lightkeepers, and the exploits of the U.S. Life-Saving Service. Interpretive programs are regularly scheduled during the summer.

Climbing the lighthouse is the big attraction; visitors can purchase a ticket and take a measured, orderly, and dizzying ascent to the catwalk at the top of the tower. It takes 257 steps to reach the top, and only one person at a time may be on a flight of steps.

In summer the lighthouse can be closed because of heat buildup in the tower—the heat index can exceed 100 degrees. On hot days the tower acts like a chimney. When it fills up with people, the heat increases.

Access is controlled by ticketing. Tickets may be purchased as early as 9 AM on the day of the climb. Tickets have the date and time of the permitted climb printed on them. Climbing begins at 9 AM. Only 30 people at a time may climb, and climbs begin every 10 minutes.

Access

There is a large parking lot at the visitor center. There are restrooms at the parking area.

Parking for the lifeguarded beach is located off the access road to the old lighthouse site. The park closes at dusk.

Search Cape Hatteras Lighthouse or enter www.nps.gov/caha and use the "Plan Your Visit/Lighthouse Climbs" drop-down menus.

BUXTON WOODS TRAIL

The park service maintains the Buxton Woods Nature Trail, a hiking/walking path that is a convenient way to experience a part of the extensive hardwood forest central to Buxton. Any aerial map overview of Buxton reveals the extent of the stable hardwood forest that is the heart of the community.

Only a small portion of this stable ecosystem is within the seashore boundaries, but it is contiguous to and representative of the 1,007-acre Buxton Woods Coastal Reserve, part of the North Carolina Coastal Reserve system. It's a no-stress stroll, readily accessible and easily hiked. The trail showcases the ecological community that develops when dune ridges shelter the swales between them from salt spray. This washboard-like ridge-and-swale topography allows vegetation to establish initially on the lee side of the dunes. Similar to Nags Head Woods 60 miles north, the protection enables the growth of a locally significant forest in the swales. As the pioneering vegetation grows taller, new plants fill in underneath and the forest grows in the number of species with an ever-taller canopy.

A three-quarter-mile compacted-sand loop trail begins at the picnic area on the way to Cape Point Campground. It leads through the varied canopy that thrives on the sequential ridges and swales parallel to the southwest-trending shoreline.

Interpretive markers highlight the ecological peculiarities of the woods and individual curiosities the trail passes. Large pines, hickories, oaks, and even beech trees grow in the interior. Inland residents will not find the hike memorable as a woodland experience, but this wooded acreage is old stuff, filled with familiar plants that may not seem extraordinary. The flowering dogwoods that grow here are a remarkable species on a sandy barrier island, as is the dwarf palmetto, common to South Carolina and pushing the northern limits of its historic range in Buxton Woods.

The trail also passes freshwater ponds that once held largemouth bass, the only known population to ever live on the Outer Banks. The presence of the water underscores the highly important role that these wooded acres play in replenishing the aquifer that provides local drinking water.

Another longer trail, the 4.5-mile (one way) Open Ponds Trail, connects the British Cemetery nearby to the Frisco campground.

Buxton Woods is much more to the island than a "chunk of rumply jungle" tangled with vines that provides wildlife habitat. A walk in these woods offers us a chance to sample a slice of long-ago island life that sustains the bustling life of today.

Access

From the Hatteras Island Visitor Center follow the signs to Cape Hatteras Campground. The trailhead and picnic area begin at a parking area on the right.

In summer, wear pants and a long-sleeved shirt, carry water, and use effective insect repellant. The trail can be a seasonal deerfly paradise.

Search Buxton Woods Trail for public information about the greater Buxton Woods. *Enter* www.nps.gov/caha and use the "Plan Your Visit/Things To Do/Hiking" drop-down menus.

CAPE POINT CAMPGROUND AND CAPE POINT BEACH

The Cape Point Campground is at the southern end of the main road serving the Cape Hatteras Light Station and Visitor Center. The campground is open from mid-April through the November, which picks up some very nice fishing times. Modern restrooms, cold showers, and a fish-cleaning station are provided at the campground. All the campsites are flat. Extra-long tent stakes and mosquito repellent are recommended for tent campers.

The walk east to the Cape Point Beach is lengthy. It is better to drive to that parking lot (although it is smaller by half) and bring everything you need for the length of stay. There is a slightly shorter walk south to the beach at Cape Hatteras Bight.

Access

Campsites must be reserved a minimum of three days in advance and can be reserved as early as six months ahead of time. The campground opens at 7 AM. Campers with reservations may arrive as late as 11:30 PM.

Search Cape Hatteras Camp or enter www.nps.gov/caha and use the "Plan Your Visit/Eating and Sleeping" drop-down menus.

Reservations: go to www.recreation.gov and search for Cape Hatteras.

Best phone number for reservations: 877-444-6777.

CAPE POINT BEACH

Drive past the visitor center entry to reach the campground. Continue on the main drive just past the turnoff to the campground. There is a ramp leading to Cape Point Beach, a large fish-cleaning station with running water and trash cans. North, past this station, is a large parking lot serving the curving spit of sand closest to Cape Point. Early arrivals in summer are more likely to get parking places.

CAPE POINT

Cape Point is the narrow salient of sand extending from the elbow of Hatteras Island. Waves batter and maul it, whipping it around like the tail of a skate. It changes randomly, seasonally, often. The colliding currents responsible for offshore Diamond Shoals also play havoc with the edge of the island. Cape Point is never exactly the same, and in early 2017 the currents wrought a wrinkle: Shelly Island, a sandbar that "surfaced" approximately 50 yards beyond the tip of Cape Point.

This was big news because the new "island" was more than a mile long and 500 yards wide. At one point during its existence, it was estimated to be nearly 30 acres in size. A channel of swift currents kept folks at bay and prompted multiple rescues. Locals who reached it named it Shelly Island because of the abundance of seashells.

Visitors to Cape Point soared during the summer, as did rescues, and then came September storms Irma and Jose, and by October the Cape Point gap was all buttoned up and the "island" was no more.

Most sandy comings and goings such as this occur underwater beyond Cape Point—the treacherous Diamond Shoals. Shelly Island played out in public.

All that water pushing all that sand around, creating troughs and channels, is one reason that Cape Point is the pinnacle of surf-fishing locations on the Outer Banks. The other is that migrating fish have to turn the corner close to shore. Anglers show where the fish have to go.

Red drum (or channel bass) and bluefish are two popular game species that circumnavigate Cape Point during their spring and fall migrations. Saltwater anglers are also predominately seasonal and teem on the shore as the fish are passing on their semiannual journey. Hundreds of people will stand shoulder-to-shoulder trying to fish the same spot.

Cape Point has always been southeast of the Cape Hatteras Lighthouse (even after the relocation of the tower), but the ocean decides the exact bearing. It changes almost daily. The landmark of the lighthouse relative to point confirms the movement.

Here the compass bearing of the Outer Banks makes a pronounced shift from a slightly west of south to a decidedly south of west orientation. Instead of the almost frontal assault that the ocean makes on beaches north of Cape Point, waves driven by northeast winds slice obliquely at the sands (and islands) south of the point. The waves and prevailing winds slide sand sideways along the face of the beach. And in general the barrier islands south of Cape Point have a characteristically long, low profile instead of the abrupt (and artificial) dune line to the north of the point, which prevailing winds have more or less sustained with nourishment help for nearly three-quarters of a century.

Cape Point is mesmerizing even without a fishing rod: charged waves, steered by currents from north and south, meet there. On a day with an onshore wind, waves will break from two directions simultaneously. This clash of waters occurs because waves, pushed by winds in the open ocean, refract or bend toward land until they curl to break nearly parallel to the shore. At Cape Point, a wave starts to "bend around" the submerged extension of the point beyond the visible beach. By the time it reaches breaking depth, it has nearly folded in half. The collision is explosive and underscores oceanographers' contention that the beach energy at Cape Hatteras is the highest on the East Coast.

Access

Cape Point is a long walk that can be reached from either Cape Point Beach parking area or the campground. The lengthy trek is often through soft sand and sometimes water-covered flats. Properly licensed and permitted four-wheel-drive vehicles can use Ramps 43 and 44 to reach the beach.

Search Cape Point Fishing for general reading.

Enter www.nps.gov/caha. Use the "Plan Your Visit/Things to Do/ Fishing" drop-down menus to see license and permit requirements.

BUXTON WOODS COASTAL RESERVE

The 1,007 acres of the Buxton Woods Coastal Reserve is part of the largest remaining maritime forest on the Outer Banks. The Cape Hatteras National Seashore forms the southern and eastern (seaward) borders of this preserve. NC 12 generally forms the extreme northern boundary (there is a parcel on the north side of NC 12). Although the actual property is crenelated with multiple outparcels and slot-shaped exclusions, the seashore surrounds the preserve on nearly three sides.

The highway frontage begins approximately halfway through Buxton when driving toward Frisco. A kiosk at Old Doctors Road on the south side of NC 12 is the first landmark when traveling in that direction.

The reserve is an extended forest of parallel dune ridges and swales, long made stable and forested by a mix of maritime evergreen trees and shrubs. There are also seasonally flooded and permanent freshwater marshes where cattails, sawgrass, wild rice, and various rushes thrive.

The forest provides important habitat for wildlife. More than 360 species of birds, including bald eagles and peregrine falcons, have been sighted within. Common mammals include gray fox, mink, river otter, and white-tailed deer. Two rare butterflies, the northern hairstreak and the giant swallowtail, have sustainable populations here.

The woods are an important source of water that recharges the local aquifer.

The protection of the Coastal Reserve system assures that a substantial portion of the Buxton-Frisco corridor of the island, in addition to the seashore, will remain in a natural state.

The state maintains the woods as a research preserve. It will remain undeveloped but not unexplored. The woods are open to the public for hiking year-round. Several trails thread the reserve and connect to Cape Hatteras National Seashore.

Access

Two perpendicular roads heading inland from NC 12, Old Doctors Road in Buxton and Water Association Road in Frisco, provide access to the woods. In Buxton, park at the kiosk at Old Doctors Road and NC 12 and hike into the woods. It is a sandy road, so only four-wheel-drive vehicles can drive deeper into the woods. At Water Association Road in Frisco, park at the turn where Great Ridge Road turns right.

Search NC Coastal Reserve or enter www.nccoastalreserve.net.

Use the "Reserve Sites" drop-down menu or click on the map at Buxton.

Best phone number for more information: 252-261-8891.

FRISCO

Frisco adjoins Buxton to the west, straddling NC 12 as it continues its winding course toward Hatteras. The unincorporated community includes a post office and a small village of enterprises serving the approximately 200 full-time residents and the surge of summer visitors.

Frisco is a traditional soundside village that started out as Trent or Trent Woods. The post office changed the name to avoid confusion with a mainland community. Some speculate that the first postmaster, a sailor who had frequented San Francisco but had had been shipwrecked at Cape Hatteras and settled here, suggested Francisco and subsequently shortened it.

Several marinas and private boat slips along NC 12 have restaurants, seafood retailers, and long, quiet creeks leading to open water. The oceanfront is miles away by car but just over the sand dunes and through the woods by crow. The oceanfront becomes immediate again at the west end of town, noted by the signs to the Frisco Campground at Park Road. This marks your reentry into Cape Hatteras National Seashore on the way to Hatteras.

At the extreme southern end of the community, NC 12 curls out of the forest to offer a view of the primary dunes, but up to this point the roadway from Buxton passes by a collection of independent buildings, businesses, and residences. These are somewhat sheltered by the pines and hardwoods of the Buxton Coastal Reserve oceanside and the trees between the highway and Pamlico Sound. The community is close to the water—the official elevation above sea level is barely 3 feet—but there is an illusion of greater height above the sound.

Explore Frisco by car or bicycle; it is linear and level and far less busy than neighboring Buxton. Commercial activity and traffic all but dissipates in Frisco.

The Frisco Native American Museum is a private, nonprofit venture established in 1987 that has developed a national reputation for the breadth and quality of its collections and displays. Anchored in the archaeological and historical record of Native American occupation of Hatteras, also known to the early English-speaking colonists, the museum has embraced nationwide Native American peoples in its exhibits and displays.

The 3,000-foot Billy Mitchell Airstrip and airport is approximately 1 mile west of Frisco center off of Park Road. In 1923 General Mitchell of the U.S. Army Air Corps took to the air from this field to change the face of naval warfare. He and his squadron bombed and sank a battleship, proving the capability of airborne attack against naval vessels.

The road to the airport passes some monumental dunes ending at the National Park Service campground. This campground is worth driving through to see the commanding view of the undulating grass-covered dune field and to experience the breezes. The campground is sequestered between parallel dune lines and adjacent to an extensive high-dune maritime forest. Cold showers and restrooms are provided. A splendid and isolated stretch of beach, lifeguarded during the summer, is available for campground users. It is one of the most serene spots on the seashore; the upper campsites offer a dramatic view of the ocean. The beach lies in the curve of the Cape Hatteras Bight, the protected bay south of Cape Point. It frequently has calmer water than the beachfront north of Cape Point. Parking is adequate, and the walk from the campground to the beach is no more than a quarter mile.

The Frisco Pier, locally loved and appreciated since 1962, once stood near the southern limits of town. Beginning in 2008 a series of storms over several years battered the pier substantially and repeatedly. For that reason, the National Park Service purchased the oft-photographed pier in 2013 and had it removed in 2017. Park service plans call for using the existing parking lot as a day use access and installing restrooms.

As you leave Frisco, between the last oceanfront houses and the Frisco Day Use Area is a distinctive stand-alone house. It is the restored 1878 Creed's Hill U.S. Life-Saving Station. The U.S. Coast Guard retired the station in 1947. It is now a private residence.

Access

Campsites must be reserved a minimum of three days in advance and can be reserved as early as six months ahead of time. The campground opens at 7 AM. Campers with reservations may arrive as late as 11:30 PM.

The park service provides several parking areas west of Frisco, including the campground. The campground is open from mid-April to the end of November.

Ramp 49 is near the campground; from there, a wonderful wandering trail leads across the interdune flats and then over the primary dunes to the beach. Shoes are recommended for this walk.

The Frisco and Sandy Bay Day Use Areas offer parking; the Frisco Day Use Area also has a bathhouse and restrooms. In 2003 Hurricane Isabel cut through the island and removed a parking area on the north side of NC 12.

Search Frisco Camp or enter www.nps.gov/caha and use the "Plan Your Visit/Eating and Sleeping" drop-down menus.

Reservations: enter www.recreation.gov and search for Frisco.

Best phone number for reservations: 877-444-6777.

FRISCO DAY USE AREA

On the ocean side, the day use area is west of the old Frisco Fishing Pier site. This site is plainly visible just after the road curves back behind the primary dunes along one of the narrowest lengths of Hatteras Island. The access site is reserved for daytime use and enables one to reach the sheltered waters of the Cape Hatteras Bight.

Access

The Frisco Day Use Area has paved parking, full restrooms, cold showers, and a dune crossover ramp. There is additional parking at the Sandy Bay Oceanside Access.

SANDY BAY DAY USE AREA

This access area, about 1 mile south from the Frisco Day Use Area, is on the north side of NC 12. It is day use parking that provides access to Sandy Bay and the Atlantic Ocean by means of a dune crossover. A crosswalk on NC 12 leads to the obvious crossover to the comparatively calm waters of Cape Hatteras Bight.

DIAMOND SHOALS

The turbulent waters of Diamond Shoals, southeast from Cape Hatteras, have shaped the history of these islands and made the passage around Cape Hatteras a mariner's nightmare.

The malleable shoals reach approximately 12 miles from willy-nilly Cape Point. Shallow waters of varying depth cover the shoals. The existential terror of the place is that the waters are both shallow and wildly unpredictable. Oceangoing ships with deep drafts such as fully laden freighters or tankers navigate the shoals at great risk. Disclaimers and danger signs cover navigation charts of the shoals.

This expansive, ever-changing area is a great mixing bowl where the warm waters of the Gulf Stream collide with the cooler, slow-moving, closer-to-land remnants of the Labrador Current flowing south. The mixing becomes turbulent, forming dangerous subsurface bars of sand.

Three distinct shoals—the innermost is Hatteras Shoals, followed by Inner Diamond Shoals and then Outer Diamond Shoals—comprise the full subsurface topography. Channels pass between the three—Hatteras Slough separates Hatteras and Inner Diamond Shoals, and Diamond Slough separates Inner and Outer Diamond Shoals. Unfortunately, these are not like the lanes of traffic on a highway; they move around a lot, so the exact locations are not stable. Mariners needed help, and lights became the answer. In addition to the Cape Hatteras light, the Diamond Shoals light tower stands at the extreme eastern edge of the hazard. When the tower was erected in 1967, it replaced a lightship that had been on duty for more than 50 years.

This extensive and extreme navigation hazard has claimed countless commercial and pleasure craft. According to one estimate, 1,500 vessels have been lost in the passage from Cape Henry, Virginia, to Cape Fear south of Wilmington. The waters have been aptly declared the Graveyard of the Atlantic.

In the days of sail, north or southbound maritime traffic would try to skirt the coast as closely as possible, which frequently came to a tragic end.

During World War II, the shoals provided a natural pinching point exploited by predatory German submarine commanders. The U-boats waited offshore for the commercial transport ships to sail around Diamond Shoals and then attacked. The tactics sank more than 80 vessels in and around Cape Hatteras, resulting in the terrifying nickname "Torpedo Junction." It's a chapter of Diamond Shoals history that fades with every passing year.

Not all of the results of this mixing of currents are bad. This mingling of nutrient-rich waters that originated in such disparate locations creates a rich breeding ground for fish at all levels of the ocean food chain. The species that migrate in the nearshore ocean are the reason Cape Point is a magnet for saltwater anglers.

HATTERAS

The village of Hatteras anchors the southwest end of its namesake island, a few miles beyond Frisco. The road squeezes between marsh and dunes along a narrow, vulnerable pinch of the island. NC 12 arcs in a gentle curve away from the oceanfront to serve as the village's "Main Street."

Hatteras is an informal patchwork of businesses and dwellings: year-round enterprises and seasonal tourism shops, vacation homes and permanent homes (less than 600 people are permanent residents). At the entrance to town is a real estate office across from seasonal houses and the multistory Durant Station, an oceanside condominium building with the architecturally distinctive, restored nineteenth-century namesake U.S. Life-Saving Station on its grounds. It's a visual hint of how traditional and new coexist in Hatteras.

The business of Hatteras has shifted from commercial fishing to tourism and sport fishing. Commercial fishing still has a place, particularly in pursuit of bluefin tuna, but is stepping back in acknowledgment of the increasing numbers of vacationers since the 1970s.

That's when Hatteras became a desirable spot for second-home construction, which began filling in the vacant lots. The village and its vendors have adapted to the tastes of the changing clientele. New merchants and less utilitarian merchandise are deftly weaving themselves into the town without displacing its essential small-town character.

NC 12 crosses a tidal creek called "the Slash" as it swings to the northwest side of the island. A slight right on Kohler Road swings past the Burrus Red and White grocery, a Hatteras institution dating from 1866, and just beyond it is another, the restored Hatteras Weather Station, reputed to be the first official building constructed by the U.S. Weather Bureau. Now owned by the national seashore, the National Register of Historic Places building serves as an Outer Banks Visitors Bureau office.

Kohler Street is a peaceful residential street that threads higher ground on the west side of the village. The houses are unpresupposing and comfort-

Cape Hatteras National Seashore

able. This is a side trip that unveils the village. The island architecture tells a pragmatic story: there are bungalows, traditional frame farmhouses, and chimney-buttressed houses that radiate durability. A few homes date from the nineteenth century. A printable village walking tour available on the town website (www.hatterasonmymind.com) is a delightful guide.

The working harbor is along the northwest side of the highway, now buoyant with a mix of shopping and dining enterprises on the basin. Spring through fall, there's a bustle around sport fishing—charter and head-boat fishing trips for recreational anglers throttle out of the harbor. All types of sound, open-water, and half- and full-day fishing trips are available. The deep water accessible from Hatteras is one of the great fall and winter aggregation points for game fish. Front and center, surprisingly, are giant bluefin tuna, adding a real bounce to the charter fishing season.

NC 12 leads to the ferry dock serving neighboring Ocracoke Island. Summer traffic through the village pulses with the arrival and loading of the Ocracoke ferries and can be tedious. Eagle Pass Loop, a left turn off of NC 12 before you cross "the Slash," winds through a residential section of the village intersecting with NC 12 short of the ferry loading lanes. It also passes the delightful Hatteras Village Park. This little side trip is a good place to get a slice of the natural ecology of the island.

Hatteras has had its share of nature's wrath. On September 18, 2003, Hurricane Isabel slammed the village, then blew through NC 12 in the narrow section just to the north. It left a 300-yard gash in the barrier beach, and, surprise!—the storm uncovered pilings from a long-ago bridge that spanned an earlier gap in nearly the same place. Road crews quickly filled the breach and repaired the gap.

In the fall of 2016, Hurricane Matthew, a massive rainmaker, swamped the village with wind-driven floodwaters that overwashed the town from Pamlico Sound. It was the worst flood damage in memory, but the town dried out, repaired the damage, and got back to work. That's what they've always done.

Access

There is an access location just past the Ocracoke ferry terminal on Coast Guard Road/Museum Drive. A 100-yard wooden ramp leads over the primary dune line to the wide beach. The same road leads to the soundside access road and the dune crossover for driving on the south end of the island.

Search Hatteras Village or enter www.hatterasonmymind.com.

Best phone number for more information: 252-986-2203 (Outer
Banks Visitors Bureau in Hatteras, staffed March–November).

GRAVEYARD OF THE ATLANTIC MUSEUM

The unique architecture of the Graveyard of the Atlantic Museum evokes
the shipwrecks that storms occasionally reveal on the beaches of the Outer
Banks. One of three North Carolina Maritime Museums (the other two are
at Beaufort and Southport), the facility is dedicated to interpreting and por-
traying the tumultuous maritime history of the Outer Banks. The collections and displays focus on the occasionally tragic consequence of navigation
along the Outer Banks. The safer navigation of today allows the museum to
focus on North Carolina's undersea heritage; recreational and archaeological diving are bringing more artifacts and stories to the surface and to the
museum's displays.

Hatteras is a prominent dive center, providing access to numerous shipwrecks and the theme for one of the museum's permanent displays, "The
Evolution of Diving."

Another exhibit frames the story of the sinking and recovery of the
Union ironclad uss *Monitor*. Following the historic sea battle with the css
Virginia (originally named the css *Merrimac* in Hampton Roads, Virginia),
the *Monitor* was swamped and sunk in a storm nearly due east from this
point of land. (The wreck was located upside down in 230 feet of water 16
miles offshore. The rotating gun turret was salvaged in August 2000.)

There is a desk and Bible from the *G. A. Kohler*, wrecked on August
23, 1933 (and sometimes visible from Ramp 24 north of Avon), as well as a
charming exhibit of local interest on the mail boat *Aleta*, which was the only
means of reaching Ocracoke until the mid-1950s. There are numerous artifacts that have been recovered from many shipwrecks; many were passed
down among islanders, as salvage was a way of life and a means of obtaining
building supplies in the nineteenth century.

One of the most fascinating displays is the original radio message received at United Wireless Station "HA," the 1901 Weather Bureau. It is a
message from the *Titanic* dispatched cqd—"Come Quick Distress." What
happened next is one of the museum's best stories.

The museum is 100 yards south of the Ocracoke Ferry Terminal. Traffic signs indicate the proper lane for the museum. It is open from 10 AM to 4 PM all year, remaining open an hour later in summer.

Search Graveyard Atlantic Museum or enter
www.graveyardoftheatlantic.com.

Best phone number for more information: 252-986-0720.

FORT HATTERAS

Approximately 2 miles south from the Ocracoke ferry dock were the remnants of two earthwork Confederate forts, Fort Hatteras and Fort Clark, constructed to harass Union traffic through the inlets and defend this port of entry. In 1861 the Confederate soldiers were driven out as the Union seized the sea lanes and blockaded the inlets to cut off those supply routes.

Most of the original earthworks have been claimed by island migration and subsequent erosion.

HATTERAS FERRY

The free ferry from Hatteras to Ocracoke is the most popular ferry ride in the state. It's a delightful passage, worth the inevitable wait, which varies greatly depending on the season, day, and time of intended departure. The early vehicles get the first berths. From mid-May until October 1, the schedule bustles with departures; there are at least six departures before 10 AM and approximately every 25 minutes after 3 PM. The ferry is free.

The North Carolina Department of Transportation offers the following useful information: "Motorists who arrive at Hatteras before 10 AM or after 3 PM will generally avoid the daily crowds."

Returning to Hatteras from Ocracoke also has a lower volume in the evening. According the Ferry Division, the busiest summer days on the Hatteras Inlet route are Tuesday, Wednesday, and Thursday.

There is no shade at either terminal, and on Ocracoke there are no commercial services at the ferry dock—but there is a lot of readily accessible sand and ocean.

Crossing Hatteras Inlet is as engaging as it is circuitous. Gulls and terns follow the ferry looking for an easy feed and may be fed according to ferry protocols. Feed from the back of the ferry.

The route wanders the inlet as a curious dolphin might: shoaling pushes the route close into Hatteras Island, then swings it way to the north into the sound before bending back toward the Ocracoke dock. The new routing has increased the length and time of the passage, though as of publication the crossing time still hovered slightly more than an hour.

That storms and natural erosion have beat up the inlet is plainly visible as the ferry docks at Ocracoke: the pilings from two previous ferry docks are visible at the edge of the island's north end.

Waiting at the Hatteras dock gives you time to explore the nearby shops or the Graveyard of the Atlantic Museum, but do not abandon your car.

In 2019 the Ferry Division began a new passenger-only ferry service from Hatteras to Ocracoke Harbor. Park your car on Hatteras and ride along until the ferry docks in Silver Lake. The fee is $15 round trip. Bicycles, a great way to explore Ocracoke, are permitted on the ferry. A golf cart concession is available on the island for those who do not wish to explore by foot. There is also a shuttle, the Island Tram, that circulates between the ferry dock and the beach access location north of Ocracoke Village.

Search NC Ferry or enter www.ncdot.gov/divisions/ferry/.
The left menu has the full ferry schedule.

HATTERAS INLET

The same hurricane that plowed open Oregon Inlet in 1846 also severed the island south of Hatteras, creating a primary passage between Pamlico Sound and the Atlantic Ocean. Maps prior to 1760–70 show an inlet closer to Ocracoke Village, the higher, more stable portions of the island and the site of that community.

Hatteras Inlet has been a stable, navigable channel since it opened, although storms have moved the channel. Hurricane Isabel (2003) initiated shoaling that created sandbars visible at low tide where none had been visible before.

Despite such sudden alterations, Hatteras Inlet has been more reliable for a number of years than Oregon Inlet, the preferred choice of the Wanchese-based commercial fishing fleet. Hatteras is a long haul for commercial boats from Wanchese, and uneconomical because of the time lost and fuel costs. In early 2018 Hatteras Inlet needed emergency dredging, as it had shoaled to treacherously shallow depths.

Cape Hatteras National Seashore

The Houses of Heroes

Outer Banks homes sporting wide dormers, hipped-roof towers, shingled siding, and Carpenter Gothic ornamentation pay homage to the building traditions of the U.S. Life-Saving Service. One of the forerunners of the U.S. Coast Guard, the Life-Saving Service is a legendary institution on the North Carolina coast. Beginning in 1874 with seven stations, the service eventually grew to 29 barrier island locations.

The federal lifesaving service was modeled after the all-volunteer system of the Massachusetts Humane Society. It initially struggled for more than two decades, overwhelmed by need and plagued by inconsistency, floundering until 1871, when Sumner Increase Kimball, a Maine lawyer, took charge as chief of the Treasury Department's Revenue Marine Division.

Politically connected and blessed with excellent organizational abilities, Kimball completely remade the service. He built new stations and established the standard six-man boat crew led by a keeper or captain (who had to be able to read and write). Kimball standardized equipment and rescue techniques and established station routines. By 1874, North Carolina had its first outposts up, manned, and in service.

The treacherous waters nicknamed "Graveyard of the Atlantic" were the necessity for the stations. The service provided steady employment and reliable paychecks for six crew members at $120 a year, and $200 a year for the station keeper. These were dangerous but coveted jobs, and the crew families became the nucleus of towns; the buildings became community landmarks. Some were often the only building visible along the lonely, empty, sand-swept shoreline.

The business of the U.S. Life-Saving Service was heroism. The job description was simple; the demands incredible: walk the beach every night for eight months a year, and if a ship wrecks near the station, rescue everyone they can, regardless—regardless of sea conditions, regardless of their own safety.

The North Carolina stations made their contribution to the lore of the service and the legends of the Outer Banks. Best known, perhaps, is the Chicamacomico Station at Rodanthe and its crew's rescue of the survivors of the tanker *Mirlo* in World War I, a story well documented at the restored station today.

Keeper Patrick Ethridge of the Creed's Hill Station (the restored station is a private residence south of Frisco) is representative of the dedication expected of crew members. When a crew member reported a ship stranded on Diamond Shoals off Cape Hatteras in a terrible storm, Ethridge commanded the lifeboat out. One of the crew shouted that they might get there but might not make it back. Ethridge looked at him and said, "The Blue Book says we've got to go out and it doesn't say a damn thing about having to come back."

The zenith of the service was the years between 1871 and 1915. These are the statistics: "28,121 vessels and 178,141 persons became involved with its services." Only 1,465 were lost during rescue and recovery operations. Particularly heroic efforts, like that of Rasmus Midgett, were recognized with the Gold Lifesaving Medal.

At 3 AM on August 18, 1899, Surfman Rasmus Midgett of the Gull Shoals Station (south of Salvo) on North Carolina's Outer Banks came upon the *Barkentine Priscilla* shipwrecked 100 yards offshore. He heard cries for help, but his station was three round-trip hours away—time the shipwrecked crew did not have. Midgett followed a receding wave toward the ship and yelled for the crew to jump overboard one at a time and he would help them. He did this seven times, leaving three incapacitated men on board. Undeterred, Midgett struggled to the wreck and brought each one back. He single-handedly saved 10 men.

The first stations were simple boathouses (visible in Corolla, at Chicamacomico, and at Little Kinnakeet) where some of the crew bunked upstairs. The boathouse was a single large room like a garage, usually with three bays for the high-prow surfboats. The quarters were sometimes over the boathouse. Some stations had distinctive watchtowers capping the main building.

All were wood, and many, particularly the Currituck Beach Lightkeeper's quarters, were prefabricated and shipped to their locations. The siding and roof were cedar shakes. An extensive guttering system carried rainwater to a cistern for storage. The stations were constructed with a Victorian Carpenter Gothic flair, and their decorative brackets adorning end gables and their use of paneling as trim have been creatively adapted for use in new houses.

In 1915 the U.S. Life-Saving Service merged with the U.S. Revenue Cutter Service to become the U.S. Coast Guard, a change that meant little in the day-to-day operation of the lonely Outer Banks stations. But by the 1930s, the need for the stations had declined, and the coast guard began to decommission them, only to reactivate them during World War II. Following the war, the stations were decommissioned and sold. The last on active duty, at Ocracoke, has been retired and given to the State of North Carolina.

The remainder are neither gone nor forgotten. Many now wear different hats, and if you know what to look for, you can spot them and enjoy these treasures of a bygone era. By far and away, Chicamacomico Historic Life-Saving Station in Rodanthe is the single best place to see both generations of stations fully restored and open for visitors. Here are a few more to look for.

The retired Wash Woods Station is now a real estate office within the boundaries of the Currituck National Wildlife Refuge north of Corolla.

Twiddy and Company maintain offices in the restored 1896 Kill Devil Hills station, which Twiddy moved to Corolla. Visitors are welcome.

The Sanderling Restaurant and Bar in Sanderling is the former Caffey's Inlet Life-Saving Station, which is on the National Register of Historic Places. The original sign is at Owens' Restaurant at Whalebone Junction in Nags Head, which is modeled after that station.

The Black Pelican restaurant at milepost 4.5 on Beach Road (NC 12) in Kitty Hawk survives from 1874, although it has been moved back from the oceanfront. This is one of the more ornate Gothic structures. Slightly south and on the west side of Beach Road stands the old Kitty Hawk Coast Guard Station, now privately owned.

Owens' Restaurant echoes many of the architectural traits of the former station at Whalebone Junction. The bar is appropriately called the Station Keeper's Lounge.

On the north end of Pea Island, the weathered Oregon Inlet station is barely holding on. A new multimission station has been constructed next to the Oregon Inlet Fishing Center.

At the Pea Island National Wildlife Refuge maintenance building at the south end of the refuge are the foundations of the old Pea Island station. This was the only all-black life-saving station in the history of the service.

Chicamacomico at Rodanthe is on the National Register of Historic Places and is currently operated by the private Chicamacomico Historical Association. This is the station made famous by the Midgett family, six of whom lived and served here. Seven Midgetts have won the Coast Guard Gold Medal and three the silver, an accomplishment unmatched by any other family. It is restored and open for visitation and interpretive programs.

South of Avon is Little Kinnakeet Station, one of the original life-saving stations constructed along the Outer Banks. Its isolated location best captures the severity of being in the service. The National Park Service began restoration work in the summer of 1991; it is still ongoing.

Hurricane Isabel struck Hatteras Village and destroyed the historic Durant Station, which had been converted to serve as part of a hotel. The building has been restored and is visible in front of the Durant Station condominiums.

The Portsmouth Island Station was also damaged by Hurricane Isabel, but will be restored as funding becomes available.

The Cape Lookout Station is used as a headquarters for ecology tours by the North Carolina Maritime Museum.

Even in their new uses, the buildings have a distinctive look. Today that distinction is a part of the architectural vernacular of the Outer Banks.

The inlet stability is relative: Hatteras Inlet is on the move, churning south. In 1954 a storm and subsequent erosion claimed an abandoned U.S. Coast Guard station at the north end of Ocracoke. Pilings from older docks long since rendered unusable are visible at the north end extending into the inlet today.

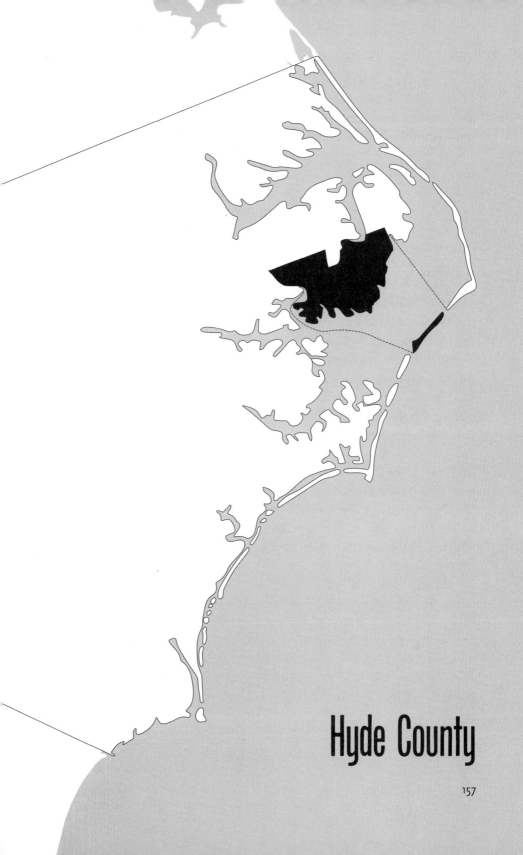

Hyde County

AT SOME WATERY POINT on its now-wandering route to Ocracoke Island the Hatteras ferry exits Dare County and crosses into Hyde County. The common border was delineated in 1870 when Dare County was cobbled together from Currituck, Tyrrell, and Hyde Counties and most likely split Hatteras Inlet, which opened in 1846. The exact location of the line is a moot point—the inlet has shifted south, and both headlands are in Cape Hatteras National Seashore.

The county question does matter down-island in the community of Ocracoke, which joined Hyde County in 1845 from Carteret County, south and west. The village is not in the national seashore, and it is probably the most widely recognized component of Hyde County, while the rural mainland geography is not well known. The Hyde County seat, Swan Quarter, is approximately 2 hours northwest by a toll ferry. This separation is more than a matter of miles and water.

Mainland Hyde County will be a sight unseen for most North Carolina beach travelers because it is not on a primary route to the Outer Banks. Although it includes some of the state's most magnificent and accessible coastal plain features, Hyde County remains as underappreciated as it is underpopulated: it has fewer than 6,000 residents. US 264, the primary east–west highway through the county, arcs along Pamlico Sound, curling under Mattamuskeet National Wildlife Refuge, the state's largest natural lake (40,000 acres). The lake is barely 6 feet deep at some points and has long been prime waterfowl habitat. It is a traditional waterfowl hunting location but was once drained for agriculture, and a pump house built to keep the lake drained and now owned by the state is listed on the National Register of Historic Places. NC 94, a north–south highway, spans the lake, and improved roads circumnavigate it, affording access to boat docks and the permitted hunting blinds.

Pocosin Lakes National Wildlife Refuge—consisting of Alligator or New Lake, a 6-foot-deep, 6,000-acre lake, and the adjoining wetlands and fields—lies north and west of Lake Mattamuskeet. A refuge for whistling swans, it is a remote location better known to permitted hunters and bird-watchers than to vacation travelers. Still, the cypress-rimmed lakes bordered by incredibly wild woodlands and cultivated fields make for interesting travel. Hyde County has big places with vast horizons that take city residents by surprise.

A substantial portion of the mainland, not drained for agriculture, is high swamp or pocosin, a term that literally means "swamp on a hill." Don't conflate this term with high ground. The county seat, itself on the perimeter of Swan Quarter National Wildlife Refuge, is barely 10 feet above sea level. Hurricane Isabel slam-dunked Swan Quarter and the Hyde County mainland when it pushed across Pamlico Sound in 2003. Hyde County was one of the hardest-hit areas in the state. Four feet of water filled the county courthouse, and many, many homeowners lost everything. The damage was not widely reported because the area is isolated and lightly populated. In the aftermath, many mainland houses were elevated, and a protective dike was built to thwart future storm surge. In 2016 it worked as planned to thwart Hurricane Matthew.

The life and lifestyles on the mainland center on the straightforward and traditional means of making a living from the earth or from the seas and sounds. Agriculture, including huge timber plantations, is the economic base of the mainland. This is large-scale agriculture; the farms and plantings are vast, horizon-to-horizon big, and flat. It is no exaggeration to say that some of the homes along US 264 south of Lake Mattamuskeet have backyard "gardens"—tilled and planted with cash crops—that are one-quarter to one-half mile in length, stretching from the back door to the pocosin swamp beyond. A tour de force of the county's history is captured in the Lake Landing National Register Historic District, so designated for its archetypical settlement patterns of family farms, churches, and commercial buildings. It comprises 13,400 acres and 25 buildings.

Traditional fishing villages rim the Pamlico Sound waters, and commercial fishing—particularly commercial crabbing—is an industry with a lot of small practitioners. While Ocracoke's crabbing operations are obvious, the crab fisheries of the Hyde County mainland at Stumpy Point, Engelhard, and Swan Quarter are more substantial.

The Intracoastal Waterway skews across the county from a neck of the Alligator River in a southwest line north of Lake Mattamuskeet until it reaches the waters of the Pungo River. The passage is 20 miles long, the longest inland traverse of the waterway.

Tourism, mostly in the form of hunting and fishing, plays an increasing role in the mainland economy. It struggles somewhat because the opportunities and resources—local historic sites and four magnificent wildlife refuges—are not widely known. Also, accommodations are limited because the county is not on a heavily trafficked route and population centers are village-sized communities.

Ocracoke Island is another story entirely. Consider this: there are 634 square miles of land in Hyde County; Ocracoke may have 10 of those square miles. Ocracoke is both outnumbered (the population is around 950) and out of the way, but not out of mind. Ocracoke Village is one of the largest permanent communities in the county and accounts for nearly all of the county's tourism revenues.

Ocracoke, certainly unique, has more in common with the northern resort communities than it does with its parent mainland county. The village is the natural and cultural culmination of the Outer Banks. After all, it is an emblematic endpoint for NC 12, and many travelers have come to view it, rightly, as the exclamation point at the end of their Outer Banks outings.

These fundamental differences between the island and mainland can be a source of civic strain. Ocracoke islanders have expressed a wish to leave Hyde County for Dare County; it is physically closer to Dare County, and the two have much more in common economically. In fact, Ocracoke already receives marketing assistance from Dare County—a recognition of commonalities and the simple reality that Dare County tourists perceive Ocracoke as an extension of the same tourism experience.

Access

The National Park Service provides access on Ocracoke Island.

Search Hyde County NC or enter www.hydecountync.gov
for mainland attractions; search Mattamuskeet or
enter www.fws.gov/refuge/mattamuskeet/.

Search Ocracoke or enter www.visitocracokenc.com.

Best island phone number for more information: 252-928-6711.

OCRACOKE ISLAND

The attraction of Ocracoke is its people, a resilient and self-reliant population (approximately 950 in 2017) whose lifestyle is quaintly anachronistic when compared with that of the mainland visitors who arrive each summer. (Some visitors' cars may have more technology than there is in some residents' homes.) The island makes no apologies; it is a fundamentally simple place deeply infused with a unique culture.

There is more than a nod to tourism, because the summer crush of visi-

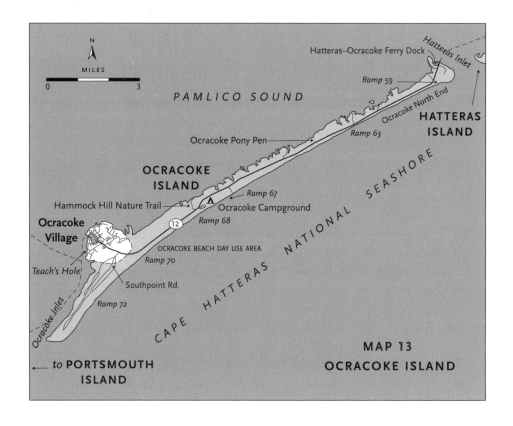

MAP 13
OCRACOKE ISLAND

tors brings many dollars here. Yet Ocracoke remains true to an inherently honorable code of conduct that echoes a passing era. It's not a resort; it is a small town on an awkwardly accessible island that people visit because it remains just that. The community smartly and politely opens the doors to guests in season, then gently closes its doors and windows for winter.

Yes, there are T-shirts for sale and internet access and an enterprising golf cart rental start-up to help visitors without bicycles motor around. There are many places to eat and multiple options for rooms, but some merchants still take out-of-town checks, and as sure as the sun comes up, the one service station suddenly is out of gas or the power goes out. This is not frequent, but not a total surprise either. All these things are a fact of island living. Everything that comes to Ocracoke arrives by ferry, weather permitting. And when the weather doesn't permit, when a storm threatens high wind and storm surge from the sound, everyone who is not a resident must evacuate. This, too, is a part of island life.

If islanders hope for anything from visitors (they will never ask outright; island natives are extremely circumspect and polite), it is civility and courtesy, because these are the indispensable traits that enable coexistence in a small place. Everybody here knows everybody here and may be distantly related. For the long haul it's best to get along.

Ocracokers' easygoing, tolerant personality is infectious. While the island presents a charming first impression, longer stays sharpen the focus on the local quirks such as goods or services assumed but not available, the idiosyncratic power supply, and isolation from the world beyond the inlets. These things contribute to the island's tone and personality. Life on Ocracoke is different from everywhere else.

Years ago a visitor said, "It's like being at summer camp with lots of free time. All the pressure comes off when you're here." Yes, what is necessity?

Summer camp memories can have such a fierce hold on feelings about a place that when Ocracoke, like the barrier island itself, changes and adapts in order to survive, the changes are not always well received. There will always be people who lament the inevitable alteration in the Ocracoke of their memory. They decry the improved access, new hotels, discovery, and tourism. There are more specific complaints about nontraditional new buildings, commercial enterprises catering to tourism, and traffic. The heart of the matter is edginess about the homogenization of Ocracoke Island, the sanding of its distinguishing elements to make it work a little better and more convenient for those who live there.

It will never become too smooth. The power will still go out arbitrarily, and it is possible to walk everywhere and to allow children to ride their bikes all over the island.

The village is an appealing counterpoint to the northern and southern resort communities, but the sheer numbers of tourists creates tension. (A passenger-only ferry from Hatteras to Silver Lake Harbor—an effort to reduce car traffic—began running in 2019.)

The island includes 775 acres of private land surrounded by the Cape Hatteras National Seashore. The condemnation of land for the seashore was not popular, yet it is probably the central reason the island's character has remained intact.

The lack of private land makes the island exclusive. The inability to provide fresh water and dispose of waste is limiting, so it is likely to remain small. Housing is increasingly expensive, and that's an issue for younger island residents who want to live here. While Ocracoke will always be distinctive, the population may steadily grow, and as it does, the village will slowly relinquish some of the insular characteristics that flavor life today.

First-time visitors should arrive with only two things: hotel reservations and a laid-back and receptive attitude. Then they should let the island reveal itself slowly.

The island includes wide prairie-like grassland where the famed ponies once ran freely, expansive beaches with a characteristic low dune field, gnarly live oak trees, and Teach's Hole, where Blackbeard died. There is Springer's Point and its engaging walk of commemorative offerings, the Ocracoke Lighthouse, the U.S. Coast Guard station (retired), the British Sailors' Cemetery, the new Ocracoke trolley, and the iconic Community Store. There are Scotch bonnet seashells on the north end and mullet in the sound. There is Howard Street, a place to walk the dirt lane of bygone days. Note the wonderfully tended family cemeteries that snuggle in among the houses along residential streets. There are few streetlights; the night skies are an awakening.

Walk, look, and listen. Allow yourself to live on "island time," a temporal measure without hurry.

The oceanfront is glorious; in 2004 it was ranked as one of the best beaches in the nation. The park service provides parking and lifeguards; the island provides the rest. The beach offers only the sky, dunes, and sea. There are no houses behind the dunes, no motels with seaside swimming pools, no streetlights. The beach is the beach, and except for the lifeguards, no one makes a living directly on the oceanfront.

An off-road-vehicle beach with an astonishingly orderly crowd of beachgoers will frequently spread south from the town toward Ocracoke Inlet when not seasonally closed for wildlife protection.

The village, in the wooded soundside portion of the island, is where people live and work. The separation emphasizes that Ocracoke is an island of simple pleasures, mingled, to some extent, with history and a colorful personality.

Note: It is not wise to visit Ocracoke in the summer without a ferry departure or room reservation. If you are day-tripping from Hatteras, note the ferry schedules and allow yourself plenty of time to line up for the return crossing. Remember also that the departure line may be a half mile long and you'll be in full sun while you wait. If you arrive too late, well, the ferry dock is not the coolest place to sleep in summer . . .

For Your Bucket:

    Go shelling at the North End

    Stop at the Pony Pen

    Stargaze on the beach

    Walk to the Ocracoke Lighthouse

    Breakfast at the Pony Island Inn

    Walk Howard Street

    Stop at Annabelle's Florist and Antiques; chat
        with Chester Lynn, Ocracoke historian

    Visit Springer's Point

    Hike to Ocracoke Inlet

    Photograph an Ocracoke cat

Access

The National Park Service maintains several beach access locations on Ocracoke. Ramps 59, 68, 70, and 72 provide vehicle access for the beach.

Ramp 70 adjoins the Ocracoke airstrip. From this ramp, it is about a 4.5-mile walk to the south end of the island and Ocracoke Inlet. Park only at designated parking spots or on a paved or hardened surface.

> *Search* Hatteras Seashore or *enter* www.nps.gov/caha and use the "Plan Your Visit/Directions & Transportation/ Maps/" drop-down menus to see ramp locations.
>
> *Search* Ocracoke or enter www.visitocracokenc.com or visit www.ocracokenavigator.com.
>
> Best Ocracoke phone number for more information: 252-928-6711.
>
> *Search* NC Ferry or enter www.ncdot.gov/divisions/ferry/.

OCRACOKE NORTH END

Because it is so distant from the village and close to the inlet, the north end of Ocracoke is a shelling hot spot. High seas from storms other than hurricanes push shells higher on the beach. Finding a safe place to park is probably harder than finding shells (there is parking at the ferry dock). Walking the north end holds the potential of excellent beachcombing. Ramp 59, an access area slightly south of the ferry dock, gives access to this end of the island, which is also a good location for fishing and bird-watching.

This end of the island stays wide, low, and flat. In stormy weather, the waves surge over the sandy spit and deposit shells scoured from offshore and the intertidal zone. This is a place for many different species of mollusks that may be different from those found on Hatteras Island beaches. Angel wings, turkey wings, razor clams, and even some helmet-shell species (native to warmer waters) turn up more frequently here. The state shell, the Scotch bonnet, begins to appear in profusion along Ocracoke's strand.

Mollusk species native to warmer water wash up here because of the island's latitude, orientation, and proximity to the Gulf Stream. The low-energy nature of the wave action, generally gentle surf, does not grind the shells as the ocean north of Cape Point on Hatteras Island does. People who wake up early and walk the beach immediately following storms get the first pick of shells. Winter is an excellent time for shelling because there are fewer visitors competing for the same treasures.

Be sure to respect any roped-off areas set aside for shorebird nesting.

Access

Parking is available at the ferry docks, or you may park along the side of the road about 200 yards south of the ferry dock—the place is obvious.

OCRACOKE PONY PEN

The Ocracoke ponies live in a 188-acre fenced pasture that prevents them from wandering across the highway. This necessity became law in 1959, two years after NC 12 was paved. The penning eliminated car/horse collisions. In 2017 the enclosure housed 16 of the distinctive Banker ponies.

The National Park Service feeds them daily and provides a veterinarian as needed, which was impossible when the animals roamed freely.

The ponies are direct descendants of Spanish mustangs and are anatomically distinct—they have a different number of vertebrae—from horses that came from English-speaking countries. Given the turbulent nature of the Outer Banks ocean passage, it seems likely that a shipwreck brought the first ponies to the island, but it is not known when this occurred. The ponies were first noted in 1730, when the island was settled.

The ponies thrived. At one time there were several hundred roaming free on the island, and each year there was a pony penning and auction.

Islanders put the ponies to practical use. The U.S. Life-Saving Service

Seashell Serendipity

Shelling is beyond control: it is joyous serendipity—half-buried treasure. That's the hook, and that's why everybody does it. Shelling is without a doubt one of the few free, money-back-guaranteed things to do that only requires showing up.

Shelling has a special twist between Cape Hatteras and Cape Lookout for two reasons: first, a confluence of currents brings together a large number of different shell fauna (the animals that live inside) that normally live in different waters; and second, there's more beach and fewer people.

On the first reason: the cold waters of the Labrador Current slink down the Eastern Seaboard. As they do, they bring a drift of cold-water fauna such as the surf clam; the quahog; the knobbed whelk and its left-handed look-alike, the lightning whelk; and their smooth cousin, the channel whelk. People find these regularly between the Virginia border and Cape Hatteras.

Hop the ferry to Ocracoke and the beaches are likely to reveal some southern fauna such as the angel wings, the giant murex, the heavily armored helmet shell, the giant tun, and of course the Scotch bonnet, North Carolina's official seashell. These shells are rarely found farther north.

The shell-fauna mixing bowl is the North Carolina Capes. Colliding currents originating in different latitudes bring their resident seafloor life with them. The Labrador currents bring seafloor "snowbirds" south, while the Gulf Stream ushers semitropical-water shells north. Everybody meets and mixes at the salient of Cape Hatteras. If you think it is a tough corner for ships, try it underwater at a snail's pace, so to speak. Hatteras is where shelling fortunes, not shells, make the turn.

The North Carolina Aquariums at Roanoke Island, Pine Knoll Shores, and Fort Fisher have representative shells (both occupied and empty) on display.

The Cape Point hot spot became a 2016 internet viral sensation with the rapid formation of Shelly Island a stone's throw offshore from Cape Point in Buxton. The massive detached sandbar became an instant shelling mecca before welding onto Cape Point—a summer sheller's *Brigadoon*.

Nearly 1,300 species of mollusk have left their calling cards along the Outer Banks. Almost any foray on the beach, particularly in winter, is going to bring an unusual discovery.

Why winter? Mainly because the typically stormy seas deposit more shells higher on the beach. Also, fewer people visit to walk the beach and collect shells (surf anglers don't divide their time with shelling). If you pick an isolated stretch of beach following a February storm, shelling can be phenomenal and solo.

Summer tactics have to be different except for the timing. A post-storm beach is improved even further by a location with fewer people or comparatively difficult access. Ocracoke's north end is probably the most accessible, bountiful location year in and year out, particularly for a mix of shells from north and south.

The same is true for the island south of Hatteras—a long walk or ride that not many visitors make.

If the surf's edge is barren, glean the sand-blown overwash flats landward of the surf zone. Strong waves can easily drop shells well beyond the high-tide line.

Adventuresome shellers can reap rich rewards. A trip to Portsmouth Island from Ocracoke early in the year can be bountiful. This lightly visited beach that is part of Cape Lookout National Seashore receives a lot of flotsam and shells with comparatively fewer collectors. Farther south, Core and Shackleford Banks, also part of Cape Lookout, have outstanding potential because the beaches can be reached only by private boat or park service ferry.

Other locations rewarding off-season shelling ambition are Hammocks Beach State Park near Swansboro, Masonboro Island south of Wrightsville Beach, and Fort Fisher State Recreation Area south of Kure Beach. The possibility of finding the delicate sand dollars, sea biscuits, and keyhole urchins increases with proximity to Cape Fear because of the comparatively gentle slope of the beach and the generally lower wave energy, which allows these fragile shells to wash up intact.

So hit the beach and give it a shot. Remember, the perfect sand dollar or pristine Scotch bonnet appears when it is time for it to be found, and not before.

trained them to haul boats on the beach, and some ponies were harnessed to buggies. In the 1950s there was a mounted Boy Scout troop on the island that lassoed, trained, and cared for their horses.

Small, lithe, and durable, the ponies roam free within the confines of their enclosure, which secures several miles of rich grassland and freshwater sources. A marker at the pen, which is located on the west side of NC 12, details what is known about their origin and distinguishing physiology.

Access

There is parking at the pen. The horses are fed daily at approximately 8:30 AM and 6 PM.

Search Ocracoke Ponies or enter www.nps.gov/caha
and use the "Learn about the Park/History & Culture/
Stories/Ocracoke Ponies" drop-down menus.

OCRACOKE CAMPGROUND

Ocracoke Campground is on the east side of NC 12, 3 miles north of the village of Ocracoke. Campsites must be reserved as in other locations. There is a $28 fee per night per campsite, and the campgrounds are open mid-spring to mid-fall. There are 136 tent and trailer spaces, but no utility hookups. The campground has a bathhouse with cold showers, restrooms, drinking water, and a dumping station. The campsites are windy and bare, and there is no shade. Long tent stakes are advised, since Ocracoke can be the windiest of the campgrounds.

The campground offers ample access to the wide sandy beaches of the island. In the past the beach had a lifeguard, but now lifeguards are on duty during the summer only at the beach at Ramp 70 farther south. Ramp 68 provides access to the beach here, but the beach south from this ramp is closed to vehicular traffic from Memorial Day to Labor Day. There is also a self-guided nature trail that leads through an ecological cross section of the island.

Access

Campsites must be reserved a minimum of three days in advance and can be reserved as early as six months ahead of time. The campground opens at 7 AM. Campers with reservations may arrive as late as 11:30 PM. Check-out time is noon.

Search Oregon Inlet Camp or enter www.nps.gov/caha and use the "Plan Your Visit/Eating & Sleeping/Campgrounds" drop-down menus.

Reservations: go to www.recreation.gov and search for Ocracoke.

Phone number for reservations: 877-444-6777.

Phone number for information and late arrival: 252-928-6671.

OCRACOKE BEACH DAY USE AREA

This Ocracoke beach is the primary public beach maintained by the National Park Service. The paved parking area is on the ocean side of NC 12, plainly signed as you approach the outskirts of the village.

This is tip-top beach, with a beautiful sand berm and a gently sloping gradient into the water. It is also lengthy. From the parking area the walk southwest to Ocracoke Inlet is approximately 5 miles; Hatteras Inlet is about 10 miles to the northeast. Beachgoers willing to hike will always find plenty of room and few people. This is separation and isolation as opposed to privacy, since the dune field is 100 yards from the surf line.

Arrive early or arrange to take the Island Tram shuttle. In summer the parking lot fills quickly.

On hot summer days the clean fine sand can be extremely hot, so bring shoes or beach sandals.

There is a bathhouse and showers. The National Park Service provides lifeguards during the summer. The parking lot is closed at night.

Beach rules are posted at the parking area, but here's a reminder of the most important: no fires on the beach; pets must be kept on leashes; and stay out of the areas clearly marked for shorebird nesting.

RAMP 70 ACCESS AREA

Ramp 70 is also known as the Airport Ramp, since the road serves the Ocracoke Island Airport. The road is in the middle of the NC 12 curve slightly north of the village. The windsock is a good landmark. It is open year-round and is a convenient access road for exploring southwest to Ocracoke Inlet. The inlet is 5 miles south of the ramp, accessible by foot or four-wheel-drive vehicle.

The beachfront to the south is typically empty, and bathers and shell seekers seldom visit. Keep your clothes on, though. The south beach has a well-deserved reputation for nude sunbathing—it's common knowledge, accepted by residents of this live-and-let-live island—and the park service used to look the other way, so to speak. But enforcement priorities have changed, and nude sunbathers could get burned in more ways than one.

The south beaches sometimes hold nesting sites of pelagic turtles and of certain bird species that lay their eggs in shallow depressions in the sand, such as the piping plover and the least tern. During such times the beach is posted and you must confine your vehicle to the wet sand beach. There is often excellent fishing on the spit of sand that curls into Ocracoke Inlet at the south end.

Access

Vehicles must have a valid National Park Service ORV permit. It is best to have four-wheel drive.

Search Cape Hatteras ORV or enter
www.recreation.gov and search Cape Hatteras ORV.

SOUTHPOINT ROAD

South of the turn for the Ocracoke airstrip and nearly opposite Howard's Pub and Raw Bar is Southpoint Road, the sand road leading to the southern point of the island. Also known as Ramp 72, this 3-mile route is suitable only for four-wheel-drive vehicles.

The southern point at Ocracoke Inlet is a terrific location for shelling and fishing, and there are usually fewer people there. Pack a cooler and picnic lunch and go explore wildest, remotest Ocracoke.

Access

Vehicles must have a valid National Park Service ORV permit. It is best to have four-wheel drive.

Search Cape Hatteras ORV or enter
www.recreation.gov and search Cape Hatteras ORV.

OCRACOKE VILLAGE

A bend in the highway, the flag of the post office, a half mile of restaurants, a grocery, a gas station, and an inn announce Ocracoke Village. The speed limit slows to 25 miles per hour at the outskirts of town; the landmark to look for is the sheriff's office and post office on the left side of the highway. This busy stretch of road is filled with pedestrians, bicyclists, golf carts, and indecisive or bewildered drivers. It's a good place to slow down and begin the island chill.

This commercial spillover from the original harborside village has been inevitable and welcome. The businesses bustle to serve the many, many visitors to the island (there were 300,000 ferry crossings in 2017). Several of these outlying establishments—True Value Hardware, Ocracoke Variety Store, Jason's Restaurant, and Howard's Pub—keep nearly a year-round schedule. Ocracoke Village is on the sound side of the island, the highest location above sea level, and it rims the basin locals know as "the Creek," aka Silver Lake. (It was a naturally shallow basin until dredging that took place around 1938. During World War II the navy established an antisubmarine base in the location of the ferry dock and park visitor center.)

Although the village is on "high" ground, it quickly becomes apparent that this is a relative term. One telling feature of permanent residency is that very few buildings are on ground level. The restaurants and hotels on the outskirts of town are at least 3 feet or more above grade. Yes, the village is subject to flooding, typically from wind-driven waters from Pamlico Sound. (On threatening occasions, visitors are subject to mandatory evacuation with or without their cars.)

The village is not large and the streets are narrow—an apt description is that it is "bicycle perfect." The mostly residential streets wind and have some tree shading; the grade is flat, and except on the Irving Garrish Highway (NC 12), traffic is accommodating. The bicycle pace is an outstanding way to explore, but not mandatory: the village is easily walked, and lovely from a walker's perspective. Yes, you can walk it completely in just over one-half day, but why would you? Drop the mainland attitude; get on island time. Do some today and the rest tomorrow or whenever . . .

Bicycles and walking shoes also take out of play the frustrating pursuit of a parking place in summer. It is an inside joke of frequent visitors that many people travel from Hatteras only to U-turn in town and go back to the north ferry dock.

In 2019 North Carolina launched a passenger-only (bicycles/strollers welcome) ferry service from Hatteras. The crossing is about an hour. Once passengers disembark, they may use the Island Tram shuttle or rent bicycles or golf carts to get around.

The village transforms at dusk in summer; pedestrians and pedalers take to the streets in the cooler air to watch the sunset over Pamlico Sound, strolling/riding around the lake or to the lighthouse and then back to their hotel. It's far more enjoyable to be on foot to observe the "Dingbatters," a traditional Ocracoke term (long before the 1970s sitcom *All in the Family*) for those who are sublimely oblivious — say, cyclists who ride in the middle of the highway as traffic clots behind them.

The side streets are more like winding paths that thread past homes, small stores, and family cemeteries intermixed. Cedar trees, live oaks, yaupon, and grape-tangled young pines crowd the roads in places, partially screening the modest homes behind their evergreen drapery. The salt spray shears the tops from the few large trees on the island — the largest live oaks seem to be on Howard Street — and the gnarled and wild limbs seem to press the houses down into the soft gray sand with an effect both mysterious and enchanting. In summer the houses are bright with flowers. The side streets lead to places like Albert Styron's General Store on Lighthouse Drive, a building disassembled and moved here. It is now on the National Register of Historic Places and still has the atmosphere of a 1920s general store. Across the island is Ocracoke Coffee Company on Back Road, the place for starting your day with a pastry and a cup of wake-up. Ocracoke Coffee is in the new wave of ventures that is meeting a need in the independent spirit of Ocracoke.

NC 12 loops at the dock where ferries serve Swan Quarter and Cedar Island and the new passenger ferry from Hatteras. In the center of the large loop of pavement is the National Park Service Office and Interpretive Center for the Cape Hatteras National Seashore, a small picnic area in a lovely grove of cedar trees, and an old family cemetery. Adjacent to the ferry dock is the retired U.S. Coast Guard station, which was constructed in 1934 and is now used as its eastern campus by the North Carolina Center for the Advancement of Teaching. The building is on the National Register of Historic Places.

The pulse of the Cedar Island and Swan Quarter ferries' loading and discharging (nine combined departures and arrivals in summer) spreads ripples at predictable intervals around Silver Lake. Suddenly the roads are filled with bumper-to-bumper traffic that nearly as suddenly rinses away. This is the innate rhythm of island life, since everything and everybody must arrive and leave by ferry.

In early spring and fall, when the fish runs commence and the beaches are open, the mainland ferries will be crammed with custom all-wheel-drive vehicles outfitted for surf fishing. These are vehicles with purpose: bristling with fishing rods, laden with coolers, on a mission.

The road to the ferry dock passes the Community Store (1918) on Silver Lake. This was the island's original year-round bread-and-butter grocery/ home goods store. The Ocracoke Foundation (www.ocracokefoundation .org) purchased the store and established the Community Square Revitalization Project to preserve it and important adjoining buildings as an island heritage site. Elsewhere, Ocracoke shows a healthy commercial balance between stores and restaurants serving tourism and/or the local economy.

Ocracoke has a lengthy story. Settlers first arrived in the early eighteenth century, when Silver Lake was indeed a creek. Ocracoke Inlet to the south has been continuously open since recorded history, the longest of any state inlet. The town's early commerce swelled with the maritime, mercantile economy using the inlet to reach mainland ports. Shallow Pamlico Sound thwarted deep-draft sailing ships, so these would anchor offshore and unload their cargo to shallow-draft ships to continue to mainland ports, a process called "lightering" (making the vessel lighter). Ocracoke began its steady mercantile-based growth when it received designation as a port with a permanent harbor pilots in the nineteenth century. (The town was originally called Pilot Town.) Not all pilots lived here, however; some lived in Hatteras. Outer Banks historian David Stick noted they would walk to work (perhaps some rode ponies?). This was before Hatteras Inlet opened in 1846.

The Ocracoke Lighthouse is the visible reminder of this mercantile era, and its longevity matches that of the inlet. It has been in continuous use longer than any other lighthouse on the coast. The U.S. Life-Saving Service arrived in the late nineteenth century, followed by the U.S. Coast Guard. During World War II, the navy dredged the creek deeper and created the ferry dock and transportation system. In the 1950s, following the military's departure, the park service became the largest island landholder.

Much of this history is presented at the Ocracoke Preservation Society

The Ocracoke Lighthouse, the familiar
landmark of this delightful destination.
(Photo by Bill Russ, courtesy of VisitNC.com)

house near the ferry dock. In 1956 author Carl Goerch penned *Ocracoke*, a
descriptive and delightfully anecdotal book considered a classic depiction of
the island early in the tourism era. *Ocracokers*, by Alton Ballance, uninten-
tionally reads as a follow-up volume, bringing the somewhat dated story by
Goerch into contemporary times. The two books provide a rich feel for the
place and the people who live here—on island time.

Access

The closest beach access is the Ocracoke Beach Day Use Area, north of town.

The park service maintains Silver Lake Marina and 400 feet of dock space at the park service headquarters. The overnight fees are reasonable; senior pass discounts are provided.

Search Ocracoke or enter www.visitocracokenc.com
or www.ocracokenavigator.com.

Best Ocracoke phone number for more information: 252-928-6711.

Search NC Ferry or enter www.ncdot.gov/divisions/ferry/.

OCRACOKE LIGHT STATION

The walk to the lighthouse ("Light Station" refers to all the buildings on the site) is almost a mandatory stroll on the island: turn south off of NC 12 onto Lighthouse Road at the site of the 1901 Odd Fellows Lodge restoration project, once part of the Island Inn. Continue on Lighthouse Road for one-quarter mile, until you see the picket fence. Take the photograph; everybody does.

The squat white tower is modest by the standards of the other lighthouses on the Outer Banks: a mere 75 feet tall, with 5-foot-thick walls. The focal plane of the light is at 65 feet. Its steady white beacon is visible 14 miles at sea, signaling safe harbor. It was one of four lighthouses authorized by Congress in the late eighteenth century, along with Cape Hatteras, Cape Lookout, and the Baldhead light at the mouth of the Cape Fear River. It has been in operation since 1823, making it the oldest continually operating lighthouse in North Carolina and, after the Sandy Hook Lighthouse in New Jersey, the second oldest in the United States.

The purchase for the original 1-acre lot was voided because the construction did not begin before 1801, as specified in the contract of sale. The existing 2-acre site was purchased in 1822 for $50 from Jacob Gaskill, a member of a family still prominent on the island today, and this time construction proceeded immediately.

The light guided mariners to the only reliable inlet north of Cape Lookout. The reach of Diamond Shoals at Hatteras made the Ocracoke light doubly important. A ship sailing north around the Outer Banks that could see the light at Ocracoke would know it was on a collision course with the shoals. It could then tack to the east, riding the Gulf Stream current north as it makes its natural curl around Cape Hatteras.

The lightkeeper's quarters, constructed at the same time as the light, is currently in use as the residence of a National Park Service ranger.

Access

The lighthouse is not open to the public, but the grounds are.

SILVER LAKE

Silver Lake is the tidal basin and harbor of Ocracoke, the central body of water that serves the town. Natives refer to it as "the Creek." If you're arriving from Cedar Island or Swan Quarter, the ferry powers past the retired U.S. Coast Guard station on the north side of the entrance, a shrubby spoils area, and some private residences on the south. It's a scenic arrival of boats, buildings, and Silver Lake. The Ocracoke Lighthouse peeks above the trees to the southeast.

Travelers arriving by car from Hatteras first see Silver Lake through a framing of small dock houses, trees, and private homes on the southwest horizon. Try and time this approach for sunset . . .

The dredged and bulwarked entrance to the basin, the only way in and out, is deep enough to serve the ferries and coast guard vessels. Before World War II the Creek was a very shallow tidal basin, according to some accounts about the same size but not more than 4–5 feet deep. The navy, which had an extensive base on the island to monitor German submarine activity in nearby "Torpedo Junction," dredged the basin during World War II to serve their vessels. The bulwarks were added because the larger vessels that use the Creek create a wake that causes erosion.

If you stroll around the basin early, before the sun rises high, or at sunset, you will see gulls on pilings, mullet and menhaden skipping over the water, and the low-gunnel, high-prow wooden fishing boats designed to ride the sound waters safely while their captains work—photographs waiting to be taken against the backdrop of waterside buildings.

There are several marinas here; private docks are plainly marked.

BRITISH SAILORS' CEMETERY

The British Sailors' Cemetery is owned neither by private citizens nor by the Cape Hatteras National Seashore. It is considered the property of the United Kingdom, a legacy of the death and devastation wreaked offshore during World War II.

In 1942 German submarines preyed freely on shipping offshore from the Outer Banks. By the end of April their captains had torpedoed and sunk 66 vessels rounding the point at Cape Hatteras. The passage earned the ominous nickname "Torpedo Junction." The United States was wholly unprepared to combat submarines and suffered tremendous losses as the U-boats maneuvered without resistance or threat.

The United Kingdom responded by sending experienced crews and antisubmarine vessels to the Outer Banks. One of the ships was the HMS *Bedfordshire*, a 170-foot-long converted commercial fishing vessel. The *Bedfordshire* reported at Ocracoke with 4 officers and 33 crew members and began patrolling east of the island.

On May 11, 1942, in the ship's second full month of patrol, the *Bedfordshire* was torpedoed, and all of the crew members were lost. Within three days, two bodies washed ashore and were identified by islanders as British sailors Thomas Cunningham and Stanly Craig. The Williams family donated the land adjacent to their family cemetery as a burial site for the two men. A week later, two more bodies, dressed in similar clothes but not identifiable, came ashore and were placed in the same cemetery.

The small cemetery lies beside British Cemetery Road about one block beyond the west end of Howard Street. Back Road also intersects with British Cemetery Road. The cemetery is always open for visitation. The British War Graves Commission and the U.S. Coast Guard maintain the graves. The flag of the United Kingdom, the Union Jack, flies above the graves. The British government sends a new flag each year. Every spring a memorial service is held to commemorate the loss of these and other sailors during World War II.

A plaque on the cemetery fence quotes lines from Rupert Brooke's poem "The Soldier": "If I should die, think only this of me: / That there's some corner of a foreign field / That is for ever England."

A repeating broadcast detailing the history of the events leading up to the interment and the cemetery may be heard by tuning an AM radio to frequency 1590.

Search Ocracoke British Cemetery for additional information.

SPRINGER'S POINT PRESERVE
AND TEACH'S HOLE

The woodland on Ocracoke Island's east side is the 122-acre Springer's Point Preserve, a rare combination of maritime forest, red cedar tidal forest, grassland, wetlands, and beach on Pamlico Sound. This is Ocracoke's wilder side and one of the lesser-known but highly rewarding ventures on the island. It is recognized as one of North Carolina's Significant Natural Heritage sites because of the unique maritime forest and its importance as a rookery for colonizing waterfowl. It has some history, too: known locally as "Teach's Plantation," it was reputedly the preferred haunt of Edward Teach, aka the pirate Blackbeard.

In 2002, 31 acres of what was the last undeveloped land on Ocracoke was purchased to thwart development. The remaining 91 acres was purchased in 2006 with grants from the Clean Water Management Trust Fund. The purchase forever preserved a unique parcel of Ocracoke's environment and history.

Beyond the gnarled live oaks and the thick yaupon is a gentle embayment in the sound and navigable channel known as Teach's Hole, the snug eighteenth-century harbor of Blackbeard.

Virginia's royal governor, Alexander Spotswood, perceiving Blackbeard and his fellow pirates as a threat, sent Lieutenant Robert Maynard and two sloops south to trap Teach in Ocracoke, his port of call at that time. They found Teach in this place, and Maynard's boarding party beheaded Teach in hand-to-hand combat. Several of Maynard's men were killed in the costly fight, but all of the pirate's band were killed or captured and later hanged. Legend has it that Teach's body circled his grounded ship seven times before it sank. Teach's head made one last sailing trip, mounted on the bowsprit of Maynard's sloop, as it returned to the mainland. Apparently the secret of Teach's buried plunder died with him. It is allegedly still on the island.

In a great underwater archaeological coup, the wreck of Edward Teach's flagship, *Queen Anne's Revenge*, has been discovered and confirmed just out-

Springer's Point, home of this impressive oak tree, is believed by locals to have been one of Blackbeard's favorite hideouts when he visited the area. (Courtesy of VisitNC.com)

side Beaufort Inlet. The ship was sailed there following Blackbeard's death. The Beaufort branch of the North Carolina Maritime Museums exhibits several artifacts from the ship.

A kiosk with a map showing the preserve greets visitors at Springer's Point trailhead. From the kiosk, a self-evident path leads to trails within the preserve.

Access

Access only by foot or bike. There is no parking at the entry to Springer's Point Nature Preserve, which is located off of Loop Road. Walk or bike to the end of Lighthouse Road and turn left. The entry is straight ahead and plainly marked.

Running shoes, insect repellent, a camera, and water will greatly improve the experience.

Search Springer's Point for multiple references/reviews.

OCRACOKE ISLAND VISITOR CENTER

The Ocracoke Island Visitor Center is opposite the toll ferry dock and provides information about the Cape Hatteras National Seashore and the village of Ocracoke. During the summer season, the center bustles with activity. If you disembark the ferry with little or no idea of what to do, then go to the center. The helpful staff will give you information about attractions and locations on the island or elsewhere in the seashore.

Most important, the visitor center and its small outdoor amphitheater are the hub for many of the interpretive programs about Ocracoke. A full schedule of events is posted for these activities, which usually begin in mid-June and continue until Labor Day. Programs target various ages, and children usually find most of them enjoyable. In past years, the programs have included morning bird walks, cast-net fishing demonstrations, exhibitions on pirates, and historical presentations on Ocracoke. Participants in certain limited programs such as snorkeling are chosen by drawing names out of a hat.

The center also provides maps and various materials on both Cape Hatteras and Cape Lookout National Seashore. Information on the availability of campsites is also provided on request. There are restrooms at the center.

Access

The center is open all year (except Christmas) from 9 to 5.

Search Ocracoke Visitor Center for several listings or enter www.nps.gov/caha and use the "Plan Your Visit/ Places to Go/Visitor Centers" drop-down menus.

Best phone number for more information: 252-473-2111.

OCRACOKE PRESERVATION SOCIETY MUSEUM

For an intimate look on the island, visit the Ocracoke Preservation Society Museum next to the ferry dock parking lot. The renovated house of U.S. Coast Guard captain David Williams, circa 1900, houses the museum. The building itself is a preservation case in point, having been moved from its original site, where the Anchorage Inn now stands.

The museum seeks to preserve elements of Ocracoke's traditional way of life, including the remarkable "Ocracoke brogue" reminiscent of dialects spoken 300 years ago in the south and west of England. By far and away, one of the more enjoyable and entertaining exhibits is a repeating video titled *The Ocracoke Brogue*, the outgrowth of a 10-year-long linguistics study involving nearly 100 island residents from ages 10 to 91. It is a joy to watch and probably one of the best chances to hear one of the island's treasures, which is its manner of speech. "O'cokers," as residents call themselves, are more inclined to free and easy traditional speech between each other than in front of guests. The video captures some delightful exchanges that need a careful listening to understand. Some of the takeaways from the video include "Dingbatter," generally a nonnative who is oblivious or lacking in common sense; "quamish," meaning sick to the stomach; and "meehonkey," a form of hide-and-seek.

There is a research library upstairs with donated materials particular to Ocracoke life and accessible by appointment. Outside exhibits include an early twentieth-century ship's rudder found at South Point and a renovated high-prow, round-stern fishing vessel, *The Blanche*.

Access

The museum is open from mid-March through early December. Summer hours are 10–5 Monday–Friday, 11–4 Saturday and Sunday.

Search Ocracoke Museum or enter www.ocracokepreservation.org.

For more information, contact the Ocracoke Preservation Society, 49 Water Plant Road, Ocracoke Island, NC 27960, 252-928-7375.

OCRACOKE TO PORTSMOUTH ISLAND

Portsmouth Island is the island across Ocracoke Inlet. The name persists from an earlier era; the beach and low, frequently flooded flats extend south connecting with North Core Banks, a barrier island in Cape Lookout National Seashore. Ocracoke is the closest point of departure to visit what is rightfully called "the only ghost town on the East Coast," the historic, restored village of Portsmouth (see Portsmouth Island in the next chapter).

Visiting Portsmouth is a unique outing because it offers the most accurate re-creation of life on the Outer Banks before the modern era. It is an unmatchable day trip, not necessarily one of creature comfort because the environment—heat, humidity, and insects—can be absolutely daunting, nearly hostile. Yet this is the way people lived on Portsmouth.

The National Park Service licenses individuals and businesses to operate ferry services to the island. The Ocracoke Island Visitor Center will have information on the options for making the trip to Portsmouth, as the list sometimes changes. One local option offers a slice of Outer Banks life. For many years the Austin family has ferried visitors to Portsmouth in their sturdy boats, dropped them off for several hours of exploration, and returned them across the inlet. As of 2018, Captain Rudy Austin and brother Donald, a retired ferry captain, carry on the tradition, running daily round-trips in the summer and by appointment in the off-season. The Austins have family ties to Portsmouth; their great-grandfather served in the U.S. Life-Saving Service there in the early 1900s.

Call at least one day in advance for reservations: 252-928-4361 or 252-928-5431.

Remember to take insect repellent, sunscreen, and something to drink. Good walking shoes that can get wet are also recommended.

Access

Best from Ocracoke Village. Check the park's visitor center for approved concessionaires; the Austins are the go-to service. Call at least one day in advance for reservations: 252-928-4361 or 252-928-5431.

Other transport is available from Atlantic, North Carolina.

Search Visit Portsmouth Village or enter www.nps.gov/calo and use the "Plan Your Visit/Places to Go/Portsmouth Village" drop-down menus.

OCRACOKE TOLL FERRY

The North Carolina Department of Transportation operates two ferry routes that carry passengers and vehicles from Ocracoke Island to the mainland. One crosses northwest to Swan Quarter, the Hyde County seat. The other crosses Pamlico Sound southwest to Cedar Island in Carteret County, the continuation of the Outer Banks Scenic Highway. The ferries are comfortable, the crossings easy: approximately 2 hours 15 minutes to Cedar Island, 2 hours 30 minutes to Swan Quarter.

The Ocracoke–Swan Quarter ferry primarily serves traffic to the seat of county government and the schedule increases to meet summer needs. From May 22 to September 24, there are four daily departures; the first is at 7 AM, the last at 3:45 PM.

The Cedar Island ferry, a popular route that is included in the Outer Banks National Scenic Byway, increases its tempo of departures on the same dates. Between May 25 and September 27 there are five scheduled departures daily from Ocracoke: the first is at 7:30 AM, the last at 9 PM.

The name of the driver and the license plate number of the vehicle making the crossing must be given when making reservations. Reservations must be claimed at least 30 minutes prior to departure and are not transferable. It is strongly advised to be on time for all departures. The cost is $15 for a passenger car under 20 feet long, $30 for larger vehicles or combinations, $3 for bicyclists, and $1 for pedestrians.

Reservations are easily made online. Be sure to provide a phone number where you can be reached: the Ferry Division is proactive in alerting travelers to schedule interruptions and the possible need to reschedule.

Search NC Ferry or enter www.ncdot.gov/divisions/ferry/.

SWAN QUARTER

Swan Quarter is the seat of Hyde County, just inland from Swan Quarter Bay, a branch of Pamlico Sound. Swan Quarter was first settled in early 1836, when it became the county seat. It is believed that the town is named for Samuel Swann and was originally called Swann's Quarter, where "quarter" referred to a division of land. It was incorporated in 1903 but repealed the charter in 1929.

This traditional commercial fishing hub sits on the edge of Swan Quarter National Wildlife Refuge and only a short drive from the magnificent Mattamuskeet National Wildlife Refuge. The ferry dock on Oyster Creek Road is in a forested setting south and east of town and skirts farmland before passing the county courthouse and the volunteer fire department and entering modest downtown Swan Quarter. A south (left) turn onto Landing Street leads over the reinforced dike that protects the town from flood-

A Slice of Island Life

North Carolina's barrier islands are neither a single environment nor uniformly alike. Any island is likely to have several different mixes of soil, water, sunlight, and wind, and each combination becomes home for its own group of dwellers. Every island does not have all the possible barrier island environments or have them in the same proportion of the total island area as a neighboring island.

A stroll from sea to sound on an undeveloped barrier island such as Bear Island in Hammocks Beach State Park would pass through several of the distinct ecological niches described below. Here is a walk through the wild sides found on a barrier island.

BEACH Surprise! There are two parts to a beach: the foreshore, which the typical tides cover daily, and the backshore, beyond the tides but just short of the dunes. Spread a towel on the backshore, build sandcastles in the foreshore.

The foreshore is a high-energy environment (for animals and children) where waves and the tides rearrange the sand daily. Wave action makes for a challenging environment, so only a few creatures are regular residents. They have a consistent survival strategy: they stick their heads in the soft wet sand of the backwash. The two most common creatures are the brightly colored coquina clam and the mole crab. Look quick!

The brightly, individually marked coquina lives in large colonies. It spends much of the time being exposed by wave, then upending and rapidly burying into the sand as the revealing wave recedes. A simultaneously burying colony looks synchronized.

Mole crabs are the adorable, streamlined, retro-looking crustaceans that tunnel backward into the sand as waves recede, leaving antennae waving above their hidey-hole. Some anglers will seek them out because they can be used as bait for red drum and other surf-feeding game fish.

In summer the backshore sand is unrelentingly hot; few plants grow there and few creatures choose to live there. The nocturnal, sideways-stalking ghost crab is the most common resident. These swift-moving creatures tunnel deeply into the sands to remain cool, scooting out only to feed and wet their gills in order to breathe. They emerge mostly in the evening.

The nesting of the great pelagic turtles—the loggerhead, green, Kemp's ridley, and leatherback—elevates the backshore to essential, indispensable seasonal habitat. Each turtle species (the loggerhead is the most prevalent) comes ashore in early summer to crawl to the backshore, excavate a cavity in the sand, lay eggs, cover the cavity, and leave. The eggs hatch and young turtles crawl back to the sea in slightly more than two months. The turtles crawl at night, and the nests are easily recognized the next day by crawl marks above the high-water mark across the backshore.

DUNES Dunes develop where the wind can pile sand into mounds and vegetation is able to root, anchoring the sand. Dunes serve as the island's shock absorber during storms. The dunes closest to the ocean are known as frontal or primary dunes. This is a harsh environment, battered by ocean storm surge and whipped by salt-filled wind.

In the 1930s, the Civilian Conservation Corps created an artificial dune line along most of the Outer Banks. This dune line still exists to varying degrees. Dunes build and stabilize when seasonal prevailing winds blow onshore and offshore. Dunes have a lower profile when prevailing winds blow sand parallel to the shore. This is the case on Ocracoke, the Cape Lookout National Seashore islands, Portsmouth, and North and South Core Banks.

It takes a tough, salt-tolerant plant to live on and anchor a dune. Sea oats, easily recognized by their tall "flags" of seeds in late summer, are the most elegant (and photographed) of all beach plants and are well adapted to dune life. So, too, is the tender fleshy sea elder, a plant with succulent-like leaves that also can tolerate this hot environment, living closer to the ocean than any other woody plant species.

A primary dune field can deflect salt-laden spray upward, creating an environment where less salt-tolerant plants can grow. In undisturbed locations, there can be parallel dune ridges separated by a trough. On the lee side of the secondary or back dunes, the conditions may favor the growth of woody shrubs. While tolerant of the arid conditions, these plants are frequently salt-sculpted, sheared at the height of the dunes that shelter them. The most prevalent are the southern wax myrtle and the red cedar tree.

Few creatures live in the dunes, but several species of shorebirds, including the endangered least tern and piping plover, along with royal terns, nest in shallow depressions or flats at the base of the dunes.

MEDAÑOS If wind piles sand high enough and it can remain free of vegetation, it becomes a medaño, a sand dune on the move. Such dunes are active and naturally wig and wag with the push of the wind. If these move over adjoining maritime thickets and forests, as is happening on the southwest side of Jockey's Ridge State Park, it will engulf and suffocate the plants. Jockey's Ridge is the best-known medaño, but there are others too, including nearby Run Hill and the now-stabilized Big Kill Devil Hill.

BARRIER FLATS Behind some dunes there are flat, grass-covered areas where water may stand. These meadows usually are found behind a relatively low dune line such as those at Ocracoke, Portsmouth, and North and South Core Banks. The plants that thrive are grasses that are able to survive periodic inundation. The flats were traditional grazing acreage for livestock and wild ponies. Currituck National Wildlife Refuge, Salvo Day Use Area, Ocracoke and Portsmouth Islands, and Shackleford Banks have grassy flats. When grazing stops and wind protection increases, shrubby growth can take root and begin ecological succession.

SHRUB THICKETS The maritime shrub thicket takes root in the shelter of dunes. It can be thick with tough pioneering shrubs and vines. It develops naturally where oceanic influence is minimized by a combination of distance and dune height. The woody plants of this pioneering zone—southern wax myrtle, yaupon, bayberry, and red cedar—are sturdy. As they mature, they reach for height and become glorious sculptural mounds, rounded and leaning due to prevailing winds. Examples exist on nearly every barrier island in undeveloped areas. Folks avoid them and don't give them a thought. The North Carolina Coastal Reserves, Fort Macon State Park, and Fort Fisher State Recreation Area have easily accessible examples of shrub thickets.

Thickets are a sign of stability, harboring many creatures including rabbits, raccoons, opossums, mice, and sometimes snakes. Mockingbirds and catbirds also seem to thrive in the thickets among the berry-producing trees and shrubs.

MARITIME FOREST Thickets are the ecological leading edge of a maritime forest, the species of which need shelter and/or distance from salt-laden wind to thrive. Mature maritime forests like Kitty Hawk, Nags Head, and Buxton Woods are nearly indistinguishable from inland forests. Forests grow on the highest and most protected part of a barrier island and provide shelter and food for wildlife and people. This is the location of the traditional barrier island villages.

Pine trees are a pioneering species providing a layer of shelter that allows hardwoods like American and yaupon holly, red maple, and sweet-gum to grow. The live oak is a climax hardwood tree in the maritime forest. It is at the limit of its natural range on the northern islands and grows into a gnarled and weathered form on the Outer Banks. By the time live oaks grow to develop a spreading canopy, the pioneering shrubbery of the thickets wanes in the shade and the woods becomes comparatively open. Springer's Point on Ocracoke is a good example of this. In Nags Head Woods Ecological Preserve, the mix of species, which includes hickories and American beech, is normally found far west on the mainland, making it extraordinary for a barrier island and indicator of both great age and protection.

The Outer Banks maritime forests support populations of coyote, fox, and white-tailed deer in addition to the mammals of the maritime thickets.

SALT MARSH Invariably, you step out of the forest and into the muck, sinking ankle-deep or more into the salt marsh. This is the soggy, grassy habitat influenced by tidal waters on the island's sound side. The forest and thicket shrubbery, hard-pressed to withstand a salty environment, fade, and black needlerush occupies the highest marshy ground, terrain that is intermittently flooded and characteristically above the normal tide line.

The more pervasive the tidal influence, the more abundant is salt marsh cordgrass or spartina. Spartina forms the shimmering expanses of marsh that sweep across the horizon, growing in soil that is inundated daily. Without a doubt, this is the most productive habitat of the many that you can find along the coast. It is abundantly evident at Mackay Island, Currituck, Pea Island, and Cedar Island National Wildlife Refuges as well as the north end of Bodie Island. It is the nursery for many species of animals and fish that inhabit the waters adjacent to the barrier islands. The decaying spartina provides the nutrients at the base of the food web radiating from the salt marsh.

ing (the town is less than 2 feet above sea level) and to the working landing, where the shrimping and crabbing fleets dock. Yes, seafood is for sale and anyone may buy.

Oyster Creek Street leads into Swan Quarter sideways. The town is small and dignified, and residents have struggled since the 2003 assault of Hurricane Isabel. At the corner of NC 45 and SR 1129, the main street of the small town, stands the Hyde County Courthouse, listed in the National Register of Historic Places. Handsome, modest homes line the streets of this residential community, many of them elevated dramatically since Isabel's visit.

Several churches front SR 1129, including Providence United Methodist Church, located at the corner of Main and Church Streets. Known locally as the "church moved by the hand of God," this church is the subject of an intriguing legend. As the story goes, the congregation's offer to purchase a building site was refused by a landowner, so they built a wood-frame church on brick piers elsewhere. On the day of the building's dedication, a terrible flood struck Swan Quarter. The floodwaters lifted the church from its piers and floated it down the street and around a corner, dropping it in the middle of the lot previously refused for sale. The once-reluctant, now newly enlightened owner deeded the land to the congregation.

Search Swan Quarter for additional reading and enter www.hydecountync.gov for the county website.

Search NC Ferry or enter www.ncdot.gov/divisions/ferry/.

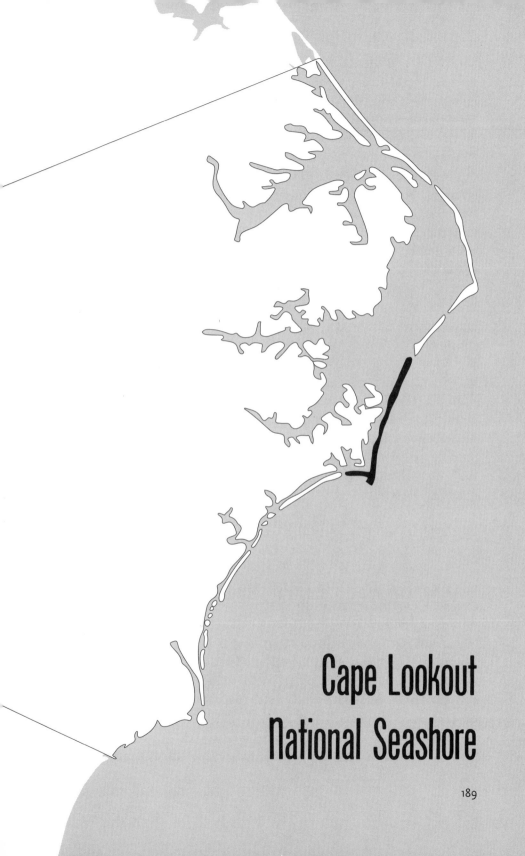

Cape Lookout
National Seashore

SOUTH OF OCRACOKE INLET is Portsmouth Island, the historic northern part of the lengthy two-island barrier, Core Banks, and the first element in the 56-mile-long chain that comprises Cape Lookout National Seashore. Authorized in 1966, Cape Lookout is the younger, wilder sibling of the Cape Hatteras National Seashore. The major difference between the two is evident immediately: there are no bridges to the islands of Cape Lookout.

The best lens through which to look at Cape Lookout is this: it is a living laboratory, protected and preserved so that barrier islands in their natural state may be studied and enjoyed. In May 1986 it was designated a North Carolina Natural Heritage Site, and the following month it was included in the UNESCO Carolinian–South Atlantic Biosphere Reserve, an outgrowth of the Biosphere Program established by the United Nations in 1971. In its capacity as Cape Lookout National Seashore South Atlantic Biosphere Reserve, the seashore serves as a research "constant," managed for conservation purposes. The islands, offshore locations, and water and air around and above them are all included in the reserve. The seashore's participation in the Biosphere Program strongly influences the management plans of the National Park Service and decreases the likelihood of human encroachment. There is not a single road or widely available sources of potable water on the Cape Lookout barrier islands. Except for park service volunteers, there are no residents. What the seashore does have is miles of beach and marsh, singularly outstanding fishing, terrific bird-watching, and some of the finest shelling in North Carolina. It is also home to a unique population of historically wild horses.

Cape Lookout is as serene as Hatteras is invigorating, as solitary as Hatteras is social, and it is powerfully, desolately beautiful. It is cherished for being "the edge of the sea," in the words of one of the most insightful observers of this coastline, Rachel Carson. With modest exceptions, what naturally happens at Cape Lookout tends to be observed and recorded rather than bemoaned and remediated. Cape Lookout is a laboratory of acceptance.

History notes that several islands have been dunked and overwashed by hurricanes. In 2003 reversed winds from Isabel slapped a storm surge around the Cape Lookout Lighthouse but spared the lightkeeper's quarters (which today houses a museum). The storm surge was 8 feet on North Core Banks and 6 feet on South Core Banks. Portsmouth village flooded again—one more entry in a long list that cannot be tallied.

The storm surge took sand from the meager oceanside dunes and dispersed it over the soundside marshes, "rolling" the islands imperceptibly toward the mainland. Afterward the National Park Service and their cabin-owning concessionaires tidied up, repaired, reset, and carried on.

The islands in Cape Lookout National Seashore have figured prominently in local and regional history, less so for national impact or recognition. The village of Portsmouth (abandoned in 1971) was North Carolina's most important port in the eighteenth century; Diamond City (destroyed by a hurricane in the 1890s) once prospered on Shackleford Banks as a fishing and whaling center, and Cape Lookout Village, settled in the 1890s, thrived until slowly waning in the middle of last century. Only buildings at Cape Lookout and Portsmouth Village Historic District mark settlement's footprints on these sandy banks. History records that a sturdy few endured as residents, but many have come and gone, using the islands primarily for fishing, hunting, and grazing livestock.

North to south from Ocracoke Inlet to Cape Lookout, the component islands are known by the single name Core Banks. This is the longest barrier complex in the seashore. The artificial opening of New Drum Inlet in 1971, east of Atlantic and south of where sand had filled in an old inlet long ago, thwarted the natural process, creating a single barrier island. The new inlet divides the lengthy stretch into North and South Core Banks.

In a "you can't fool Mother Nature" series of weather events, the new inlet between the two islands shoaled and closed, and a storm opened up another one at the location of the original (1899) Drum Inlet. That also shoaled, and in September 2005 Hurricane Ophelia opened a new inlet south of the 1971 Drum Inlet. This inlet is stable so far and, with a "what's in a name?" insouciance, is called both Drum Inlet and Ophelia Inlet. Although there is now (in 2018) another, smaller breach of North Core Banks to the north, Ophelia Inlet is still the more easily navigable passage between Core Sound and the Atlantic Ocean in 2018. This could change suddenly and probably will.

These two islands align northeast–southwest, shielding the mainland and creating Core Sound. The prevailing winds have the same compass orientation, and the result is a low, nearly flat island profile void of any significant dunes. Core Banks is a narrow, thinly vegetated barrier (the trees near the Cape Lookout Light Station were planted in the middle of the twentieth century). Core Banks is similar in appearance to the north end of Ocracoke or the narrow beach between Avon and Buxton without its artificial dunes. The wind will not let the sand lie, streaming it along the beachfront in stinging ankle-high sheets. There is hardly a dune for shelter of any kind for any creature, and the shrubby growth of the mid-island flats is uninviting. Extensive marshes fringe the sound side, creating rich, productive fisheries.

At Cape Lookout, the coast dramatically shifts alignment to east and west. Shackleford Banks marks that shift and is part of the national seashore. Shackleford Banks is vastly different in appearance; the wind has built dunes, and the island has developed a maritime forest that once supported the village of Diamond City. Today more than 100 wild horses call the 9-mile-long island home.

Although people have lived on Cape Lookout, beyond building shelter they have not altered the islands' natural state. The park service notes three significant intrusions: the artificial opening of Drum Inlet between North and South Core Banks, the jetty at the Cape Lookout Hook, and the state-mandated opening of Barden Inlet between Cape Lookout and the east end of Shackleford. None of the buildings within the seashore interfere with the natural processes of the island; all are subject to the whim of nature.

The islands once were seasonal outposts for hunting and fishing, activities still allowed within the boundaries in accordance with state and federal regulations. Before the park service acquired the land through condemnation in 1966, there were several private hunting and fishing clubs—some quite comfortable—on Core Banks. The clubs were granted leases after purchase, and when the leases expired, most of the clubs were razed. Shackleford Banks had horses, sheep, and swine living on the island.

Cape Lookout National Seashore is undeveloped, nearly pristine, with limited visitor accommodations. It is easy and delightful to explore on a day trip to Portsmouth Village, Cape Lookout Light Station, or Shackleford Banks. Each location has particular logistical challenges, none of which are onerous. There is little if any shade. Summer day visitors should wear lightweight, protective clothing (loose-fitting long sleeves and running or watersport shoes are best), a hat, and sunglasses and carry water, sunscreen, insect repellent, food or snacks, and a plastic bag to carry out all trash.

Overnight visits (camping or in cabins) reward more intrepid travelers, and these visits are restricted in location and require heady planning. In general, overnight visitors need to bring the items listed above and everything else needed for an overnight stay. Potable water is available at some locations, but not all. Confirm the need to carry water before departure. Camping is permitted on all islands, with some restrictions on proximity to existing buildings and wildlife. Campfires are permitted, but only on the beach below the high-tide line.

The one guarantee is 56 miles of plenty of sun, wild, broad beach, and enough room for all comers.

The Cape Lookout National Seashore Visitor Center, located at Shell Point on Harkers Island on a gorgeous, windswept site at the end of the island's main road, is easily reached by car. The Cape Lookout Lighthouse and the tree line of Shackleford Banks are visible from Shell Point.

Search Cape Lookout Seashore or enter www.nps.gov/calo.

Best phone number for more information: 252-728-2250.

For Your Bucket:

Visit Portsmouth Village
Go shelling on Portsmouth Beach
Rent a rustic cabin on Core Banks
Climb Cape Lookout Lighthouse during a full moon
Go shelling on Cape Lookout Bight
See the Shackleford Banks wild horses

Visiting the Seashore

Access to all islands of Cape Lookout is by authorized ferry or private boat or watercraft. Park maps indicate the 10 locations on the sound side of the islands where personal watercraft may dock. Fishing requires a valid North Carolina Coastal Recreational Fishing License and adherence to all the North Carolina size and catch regulations. The license may be purchased online or at the Long Cabin and Great Island Visitor Centers.

Here's a rundown of recreation opportunities for the several islands and how to go to each.

PORTSMOUTH ISLAND

Portsmouth Island lies at the northern end of North Core Banks in Cape Lookout National Seashore. It is the southern headland of Ocracoke Inlet, most easily reached by passenger ferry or private boat from Ocracoke.

Swash Inlet, an intermittently flooding breach where wind tides may flood the flats behind the dune line, separates Portsmouth Island from the rest of North Core Banks. While the flooded flats are common on Ports-

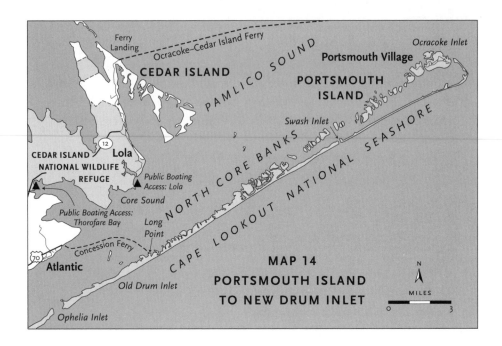

mouth, the island is one of the few historic locations far enough above sea level to support permanent settlement. The North Carolina General Assembly established the village of Portsmouth in 1753. It prospered well into the middle of the nineteenth century and then slowly, very slowly faded.

There are no permanent residents in Portsmouth today. The 21 surviving structures of the village, including a church, a coast guard (originally a lifesaving) station, and the island's schoolhouse, still stand proudly (though beaten up) on the highest ground available, which is not always high enough. The freshly painted yellow houses and the blue and white Methodist church are the centerpieces in a 250-acre historic district that is on the National Register of Historic Places. The Dixon/Salter House serves as a visitor center, and the church is also open to the public. Visiting the island turns back the clock to a rugged way of life pursued by a village of resilient residents.

During its heyday in the eighteenth century, Portsmouth was a major port of call for all shipping into North Carolina; it eventually became the state's busiest seaport. Oceangoing vessels would put in at Portsmouth to transfer their cargo to smaller craft for the continuation of the journey across shallow Pamlico Sound to Bath or Washington, a practice known as "lightering." Portsmouth was sufficiently important to North Carolina's economy that British troops seized and occupied the port, along with the port of Ocracoke, during the War of 1812. Portsmouth thrived until a storm carved Hatteras and Oregon Inlets in 1846, after which Ocracoke Inlet soon shoaled, ending Portsmouth's commercial days.

One of the more poignant stories of Portsmouth is that of Henry Pigott, an African American who was the last male to live in the village. Henry Pigott was born May 5, 1896, of descendants of slaves who were brought to the island and decided to stay after emancipation. As the economy waned in Portsmouth, he continued to fish to support himself. In 1967 he sold his house on Doctor's Creek to the State of North Carolina and retained a life estate to the house. He fell ill and died on January 5, 1971, and is buried in the cemetery near the Methodist Church. Shortly after his death, Elma Dixon and Marion Babb, the remaining two inhabitants of Portsmouth, moved to the mainland, and the community that was known as Portsmouth ceased to exist.

That doesn't stop reunions of descendants, however. Every even-numbered year in April, the island is the site of Portsmouth Homecoming, a gathering of descendants of the island residents to celebrate history and community. Anyone who wishes to attend is cordially invited.

On Portsmouth Island there are several private holdings, some leases authorized by the park service, and cemeteries still visited and tended by descendants. The park service requests that visitors to the island respect private property.

It is a rewarding place to visit, but it is not for those expecting a cushy getaway. In summer, Portsmouth can be searing. There is little shade, and the beaches are about a mile from the village beyond often-flooded flats. The flats of the island are substantial—wide areas of sand, sometimes dry and sometimes covered with nearly 2 feet of water. Winds from the north can pile the water onto the island and create a moat between the village and the beach.

A strong suggestion: be prepared to walk. Wear lightweight, protective clothing (loose-fitting long sleeves and running or water-sport shoes are best), a hat, sunglasses, binoculars, camera, sunscreen, insect repellent (the mosquitoes can defy description!), water (two quarts per person), food or snacks, and a plastic bag to carry out all trash. There are composting toilets a short walk from the ferry dock and near the U.S. Life-Saving Station.

En route from Ocracoke, it is possible to see remnants of Beacon Island and Shell Castle Island north and west of Ocracoke Inlet. Beacon Island was named for two beacons used by pilots to navigate Ocracoke Channel. The south end was fortified in 1794–95 by an act of Congress because of the importance of the shipping channel. Shell Castle Island is where John Gray Blount and John Wallace launched a speculative venture to expand the island in order to make a more favorable "lightering dock" for oceangoing vessels. In the 1800s Shell Castle supported a lumberyard, tavern, dwelling house, and notary public's office, but hurricanes sweeping through the inlet sealed the fate of both islands.

Access

Portsmouth Village: Trips to Portsmouth Village depart from Ocracoke. The Austin family provides transportation, and they request at least a one-day advance notice for reservations: 252-928-4361 or 252-928-5431. For additional operators during the summer months, call the Ocracoke Island Visitor Center at 252-928-4531.

> *Search* Visit Portsmouth Village or enter www.nps.gov/calo and use the "Plan Your Visit/Places to Go/Portsmouth Village" drop-down menus.

PORTSMOUTH VILLAGE

The "ghost" village of Portsmouth , once the largest community on the Outer Banks, was a busy port for nearly 100 years beginning in 1753. The last residents left the island in 1971. The village is on the National Register of Historic Places. There is a seasonally staffed visitor center in the Theodore and Anne Salter House, a short walk from the ferry dock. Programs are offered in the village from June through September. Exhibits about the village may be viewed at the school, the general store, the U.S. Post Office, and the U.S. Life-Saving Station. Links to downloadable audio tours may be found at www.nps.gov/calo/planyourvisit/visit-portsmouth.htm.

The village is of haunting historical interest, and the beach east of the village can be a superb location for finding seashells.

There are restrooms in the visitor center and composting toilets on the road to the lifesaving station. Caution: Mosquitoes can defy description when there is no breeze. Insect repellant is a must; lightweight pants and long-sleeved shirts, comfortable walking shoes, a hat, sunscreen, and drink-

Cape Lookout National Seashore

ing water are also essential. A daypack can be very useful for shellers, as the beach is about a half mile from the village.

Access is by passenger ferry or private boat from Ocracoke. Check the park visitor center for approved concessionaires. The Austins are the go-to service. Call at least one day in advance for reservations: 252-928-4361 or 252-928-5431.

LONG POINT CABIN AREA– NORTH CORE BANKS

Long Point, which lies about 5 miles north of Ophelia Inlet, is the vehicle access location for the 22 miles of North Core Banks and Portsmouth Island. This is a wild, undeveloped island for swimming, shelling, fishing, and exploring. There are permitting requirements and driving restrictions, including long-term parking permits necessary for parking at the overnight lots at the cabin area. See www.nps.gov/calo/planyourvisit/orv.htm and additional information below.

The 10 duplex cabins available for short-term rental have electricity, shared unscreened porches, showers, baths, bunk beds, and kitchen table and chairs; propane stoves are also available. Six cabins have air-conditioning. Rental season is from mid-March to the end of November. This encampment and its companion facility at Great Island on South Core Banks are in high demand during the spring and fall fish runs. Cabin reservations may be made at www.recreation.gov beginning in early January each year.

Long Point is served by car ferry from Atlantic, North Carolina, requiring a separate reservation. Confirm ferry concessionaires and schedule at www.nps.gov/calo/planyourvisit/ferry.htm.

All cars must be transported to Cape Lookout by National Park Service–licensed ferry concessions. Applicable state vehicle registration, insurance, inspection, and licensing requirements apply to all vehicles. Cape Lookout requires those who drive on the beach to obtain an ORV Education Certificate at no charge. The certificate may be obtained in advance online; it is also available at the offices of the licensed auto ferry operators and at the island's visitor center. Transportation fees are separate.

GREAT ISLAND CABIN AREA-
SOUTH CORE BANKS

Great Island Cabin Area is about 6 miles south of Ophelia Inlet and 10 miles north of the Cape Lookout Light Station Visitor Center. This location provides access to miles of wild beach for fishing, swimming, sunbathing, bird-watching, shelling, and exploring. There are also many miles of sound waters for crabbing, fishing, and swimming.

As with Long Point Cabin Area, vehicle access does come with permitting requirements and driving restrictions, including long-term parking permits necessary for parking at the overnight lots at the cabin area.

See www.nps.gov/calo/planyourvisit/orv.htm and additional information below.

There are 25 rustic individual cabins at Great Island. Each cabin has a screen porch, bunk beds, kitchen table and chairs, hot water heater, shower, and propane stove and propane. The cabins are wired for electricity but renters must supply their own generator. One cabin is handicapped accessible, but there are no paved walkways.

Great Island is served by car ferry from Davis, North Carolina, requiring a separate reservation. Confirm ferry concessionaires at www.nps.gov/calo/planyourvisit/ferry.htm.

All cars must be transported to Cape Lookout by National Park Service–licensed ferry concessions. Applicable state vehicle registration, insurance, inspection, and licensing requirements apply to all vehicles. Cape Lookout requires those who drive on the beach to obtain an ORV Education Certificate at no charge. The certificate may be obtained in advance online; it is also available at the offices of the licensed auto ferry operators and at the island's visitor center. Transportation fees are separate.

CAPE LOOKOUT LIGHT STATION

This precise name includes the magnificent lighthouse and the supporting buildings such as the keeper's quarters (open seasonally as a museum). The lighthouse began service in 1859 but did not receive its distinctive diagonal-checker or "diamond" daymark until 1873. The pattern is not arbitrary: the dark diamonds are aligned north–south, the white diamonds east–west, resulting in a different appearance from different vantage points. It is the only lighthouse in the state with this effect.

In 2017 a ribbon-cutting at the lighthouse celebrated that it had turned "green," completing a conversion to solar power. An LED array replaced the twin airport beacons that rotated every 30 seconds. The array pulses to replicate the recognized 15-second pattern. A five-day battery backup is in turn backed up by a diesel generator, providing redundancy to the solar power (the solar panels are visible near the lighthouse). The previous electrical supply came from the mainland by underwater cable. The solar conversion eliminates the loss of the navigational aid due to any mainland power failure.

The lighthouse is open for climbing Wednesday through Sunday, mid-May through mid-September. The climbs begin at 9:45 AM and end at 4:15 PM. There are 207 steps spiraling to the focal plane catwalk—the equivalent of climbing a 12-story building. The lighthouse was built with double walls, and the outside wall is 9 feet thick at ground level, tapering to 1 foot thick at the top. The inside wall, which contains the stairs, is a much smaller diameter, and the cast-iron stairs spiral tightly up to the observation deck. Tickets may be purchased at the visitor center on Harkers Island and are stamped for the date and time of the permitted climb. Do not be late.

Swimming, sunbathing, shelling, and exploring can fill a day easily. The oceanfront is less than a quarter mile from the dock, and the adjoining sound waters are shallow and calm. Shuttles are available to carry folks the several miles south to Cape Lookout Village and the "hook" of Cape Lookout Bight, 1.5 miles from the visitor center, where the shelling can be fantastic after rougher seas.

Camping is primitive, since there are no developed campsites. Insect repellent and long tent stakes are advised. Mosquito netting helps tremendously for a good night's sleep. Bring plenty of water for cooking and drinking.

There are restrooms in the visitor center and limited concessions. Visitors should wear lightweight, protective clothing (loose-fitting long sleeves and running or water-sport shoes are best), a hat, sunglasses, sunscreen, and insect repellent and bring water (two quarts per person), food or snacks, and a plastic bag to carry out all trash.

Ferry transportation is a separate fee and is available online or at the dock in Beaufort or the Harkers Island Park Headquarters. Tickets for the lighthouse climb may be purchased at the park headquarters or the auxiliary office in Beaufort across from the ferry dock.

SHACKLEFORD BANKS

This offshore island is fundamentally different from the remainder of the Cape Lookout islands in two ways: it bows in a gentle arc from east to west, and it is home to a remarkable group of wild horses. This combination is a magnet for visitors, and summer can bring herds of day-tripping horse-watchers to this splendid, unfettered island. There are approximately 120 horses on Shackleford Banks. Historical records and blood typing indicate that the horses are descended from Spanish horses that arrived here more than 400 years ago. The horses on Shackleford Banks are a unique group observed and watched over by the National Park Service.

A ride to the island does not guarantee a horse sighting; the animals roam freely, and the 9-mile-long island can swallow the entire population. Then again, they sometimes meet the ferry. Here is a key: come prepared to walk. Wear lightweight, protective clothing (loose-fitting long sleeves and running or water-sport shoes are best), a hat, sunglasses, binoculars, camera, sunscreen, and insect repellent, and bring water (two quarts per person), food or snacks, and a plastic bag to carry out all trash. There are composting toilets at the west end of the island near the ferry dock.

Campers need to bring EVERYTHING (including water) for an overnight stay and carry back EVERYTHING they bring. This is primitive camping. Campfires are permitted, but only on the beach below the high-tide line.

Any trip to Shackleford Banks guarantees an experience of an island maintained as though it were a national wilderness area. Shackleford was nominated for the wilderness system in the 1970s but is not yet included. The island's guiding management is status quo until a final determination.

The east end of the island is tucked behind Cape Lookout Bight; the west end is the headland of Beaufort Inlet. Prevailing winds strike the face of the island and have created impressive dunes, maritime shrub thickets, and patches of maritime hardwood forest. The island profile is quite different from Core Banks and Portsmouth Island.

It's a great place to spend a half day or more. The waters of Back Sound are superb for swimming; the oceanfront is as well. (There are no lifeguards.) Successful shelling and wildlife watching (including the horses) can correlate to time spent walking to explore more distant reaches of the island.

The maritime forest at the east end has remnants of Diamond City— fences and foundations from a whaling community destroyed by a hurri-

The Coastal Constant Is Change

Coastal geologists describe the relationship of natural forces such as wind and sea level to barrier islands as a system having "dynamic equilibrium." A simple explanation is that the system has a moving balance, like a person riding a unicycle. The rider stays upright so long as there are no restrictions on movement.

The dynamic equilibrium of the coast is analogous but more complex. To survive as islands, barrier beaches must be able to shift and reshape freely when shoved about by wind and waves. Each individual island is part of a system that includes other islands. Restrictions on a single island's ability to respond naturally to wind and wave introduce a wild card that may play havoc elsewhere—perhaps on an adjacent island. There's no certainty about when or where or even whether this will happen.

The system is not unlike an unbreakable balloon filled with water—any force exerted on it will bulge in an unexpected place. Similarly, trying to restrict part of an island (usually sand) from moving where natural forces direct it (by constructing a jetty to trap sand) robs the replenishment material naturally going to beaches elsewhere. Erosion is not stopped, it's just directed elsewhere.

There's a lot to be learned from unrestricted barrier islands such as those of Cape Lookout National Seashore. The islands constantly shift and reshape, responding to wind and wave action throughout the system. In fact, the whole system stays fairly constant; coastal geologists have established that the total amount of sand in the system changes little, but how and where the sand is piled changes constantly. When Hurricane Isabel rolled over Core Banks, it didn't destroy the sand that formed the dunes or the beach, it just moved that sand inland.

You could characterize the response of barrier islands to wind and waves as a form of coastal aikido—they literally roll and rearrange with the punches. The islands are malleable; they do not actively resist the forces, and in this way the system "survives" intact.

Back to an earlier point: islands retain the total mass of sand within the barrier island chain. In some places the beach is eroding; at others it's accreting, or growing. Some inlets are more or less stable; others are on the move. Within the big overall picture, the sand remains constant.

The greatest force at work on North Carolina's barrier islands is the rising sea. It is elevating at a rate of 1 foot per century. It is widely accepted that barrier islands respond to this chronic pressure (as opposed to the acute attack of storms) by deliberate, strategic retreat, moving landward, uphill on the coastal plain shelf, at the press of the ocean. This is an orderly retreat with a sequence of steps.

First, sand fills the marsh behind the island and vegetation secures this new sand. Then, the entire vegetation and land pattern of the island shifts toward the mainland. The stable ground of the island inches steadily away from the ocean.

"Wash Woods" in Currituck, where tree stumps emerge from the wet sand beach, provides vivid evidence of this landward island march.

The rate of retreat—how far an island will move each year—is determined by the slope of the offshore bottom (which is not constant along the coast) and can be calculated. The ballpark range is that for every inch in sea-level rise, the coastline retreats somewhere between 10 feet and 100 feet. (In 2004, Duke University researchers estimated that a 1-foot rise in sea level could flood 770 square miles of coastal North Carolina.)

If the coastal system is moving (geologically speaking), then permanent structures are at an inherent risk. The operative question about artificial structures on nearly every barrier island is *when* they will be threatened, not *if* they will be threatened (although the time period could be quite lengthy—Ocracoke and Portsmouth Village have been around for more than 200 years).

It is difficult for us to think this way, but storms do not threaten the islands themselves—the island is not permanent but a movable part of a system that is permanent. Storms threaten humans and their "permanent" possessions. To put it another way, you do not own land on the barrier islands—you rent it. Some leases are longer than others, depending primarily on the location and elevation above sea level.

The changes along our coast are severe enough to be noticed from season to season because there are many benchmarks—homes and businesses, mostly—marking the sea's advance. Some of these may not survive, but there will always be an island.

cane in 1899. The storm effectively ended a community that had been active since the eighteenth century.

Access

Shackleford is accessible by private boat or park service–approved ferry. Reservations are necessary, and service departs from Beaufort and Harkers Island. Confirm available ferry concessionaires at www.nps.gov/calo/planyourvisit/ferry.htm.

Search Shackleford Horses or enter
www.nps.gov/calo/learn/nature/horses.htm.

Carteret County

IF DARE COUNTY flings the Outer Banks to its seaward salient, Carteret County gradually reels the island necklace back in. The county claims 81 miles of barrier islands, and except for distant, lonely Portsmouth Island, the beaches of the other four islands are less than 4 miles from the mainland: not "outer," but banks nonetheless.

Carteret County's barrier beaches are every bit as marvelous as their counterparts in the northern tier of barrier islands, but there are distinguishing differences from the Outer Banks. The 56 miles of barrier islands of the Cape Lookout National Seashore are undeveloped and minimally visited by comparison with the islands of Cape Hatteras National Seashore. The resort communities of Bogue Banks form a seamless stream of residential subdivisions, developed from a local affinity beginning in the middle of the last century as travel destinations. The longtime appeal builds on simple pleasures—owning or renting a place near the water to stay and play.

In total, the county has approximately 83 miles of oceanfront guarding the mainland. Beaufort Inlet, serving its namesake community and Morehead City, is a recreational dividing line. East of Beaufort Inlet, Cape Lookout National Seashore is accessible only by boat. One bridge from Morehead City and another from Cape Carteret serve the 25 miles of tourist-friendly Bogue Banks communities across Bogue Sound.

Cape Lookout in southeast Carteret County is where the previously southwest-oriented string of barrier beaches alters direction to a nearly compass-perfect run due west. West of Cape Lookout, the barrier islands align end to end in a great concave arc sweeping inland to a midpoint on Topsail Island before bending back again to the promontory of Cape Fear. Capes Lookout and Fear frame a great area of water known as Onslow Bay. This crescentic pattern is more or less repeated in Raleigh Bay, the less well-known name of the area between Capes Hatteras and Lookout. But this similar large-scale pattern of embraced bays and arcing islands does not produce similarity in the character of the included islands. Instead, the prevailing winds make a big difference.

Portsmouth Island and Core Banks, Carteret County's eastern barrier islands, align with the northeast–southwest orientation of the prevailing winds. This means there is no landward breeze to continually pile sand higher behind the wet sand beach. Instead, the wind more frequently streams sand along the beachfront, parallel to the line of the water.

There is little shelter for plants or people because the dunes are few, distant, low, and well away from the beach. (Some similarly aligned portions of Cape Hatteras National Seashore benefited from a Civilian Conservation Corps dune-building effort in the 1930s.)

The island alignment and prevailing winds explains the low, flat profile and minimal foredunes north of Cape Lookout. There is little shelter to encourage shrubs and trees to grow: salt-spray shears vegetation, and the elements keep it diminished and stressed. The absence of dunes means these islands may easily flood due to storms. Hurricanes—Isabel in 2003 comes to mind—roll right over the islands, dissipating some of the damaging force of the storm surge before it reaches the mainland. The island responds naturally, and "damage" is limited to the minimal visitor accommodations and historic structures on the island. Rinse and repeat.

Shackleford Banks and Bogue Banks, stretching east to west from Cape Lookout, offer a marked contrast to Portsmouth Island and Core Banks. The former arc inland from Cape Lookout, and their beaches face south.

Onshore winds and waves and a steady supply of sand grace these islands with relatively stable dunes. On both islands the dunes—some are quite large—deflect salt spray upward, allowing vegetation to thrive inland. Shackleford Banks features one of the few remnant stands of maritime forest in this particular section of coastline; residential development fills the substantial corresponding forest that covers large tracts of the widened, western end of Bogue Banks.

Because of a generally flattened nearshore profile, Carteret County beaches tend to have gentle surf. The average wave action is not as energized as it is north of Cape Hatteras. On Bogue Banks, the primary recreational island, the waves laze and plop across the sands but will break enough to appeal to surfers. There are red-flag days of high surf and strong, threatening rip currents often prompted by distant weather fronts, but by far and away the summer waters are benign. For nearly two decades the Carteret County Shore Protection Office has monitored and directed timely beach management strategies, including proposing and effecting beach nourishment to offset storm damage and minimize incremental beach erosion. An attractive, usable beach is the economy of the island communities, and carefully monitoring the economic line in the sand has so far proven effective and more cost efficient than a reactive program that responds only to acute storm damage. It is a model program that has yet to be adopted elsewhere along the coast. This proactive approach absorbed the impact of Hurricane Florence in September 2018, thwarting storm surge damage to the beach and oceanfront homes.

Many features of statewide and regional interest draw folks to the Crystal Coast, the marketing umbrella that covers the area. In 1964 the 12,000 acres of the northeastern tip of the county, a region of tidal marsh and low grassland and some upland, were preserved as the Cedar Island National Wildlife Refuge. Harkers Island is host to the Cape Lookout National Seashore headquarters, and a quick ferry ride from Harkers enables day trips to the Cape Lookout Light Station or Shackleford Banks.

The Rachel Carson component of the National Estuarine Research Reserve program, comprising Horse Island and Bird Shoal across Taylor Creek from historic Beaufort, completes the conservation packet that is close to the oceanfront.

The western part of Carteret County, between US 70 and NC 58, is part of the 160,000-acre Croatan National Forest. These coastal acres have several ecological zones. Native longleaf pine is present in many of them, and 30,000 acres in northwestern Carteret County are wild enough to qualify as four federal wilderness areas—Catfish Lake South, Pocosin, Pond Pine, and Sheep Ridge.

In Beaufort, home to the North Carolina Maritime Museum, a National Register Historic District guards the remnants of the state's third oldest town—the town is old, but it is lively. Morehead City bustles as a dining, fishing, and scuba-diving center. Fort Macon State Park, a reconstructed brick fortification, dominates the eastern end of Bogue Banks. At Pine Knoll Shores, mid-island, is one of North Carolina's three state aquariums.

The villages east of Beaufort are referred to as "Downeast," and their inhabitants are "Downeasters." The traditional means of making a living here—farming, fishing, and maritime-related commerce such as boatbuilding and waterfowl hunting—are still the primary livelihoods. The uniqueness of the individual communities is intricately differentiated at both the Core Banks Waterfowl Museum and Heritage Center on Harkers Island and in Beaufort's North Carolina Maritime Museum.

Downeast remains rural. US 70, part of the route of the Outer Banks National Scenic Byway, crosses or passes tidal water, marsh, farms, and residual upland forests. It passes through local crossroads, skirts some of the larger communities in the south, and winds through both Sea Level and Atlantic at the northern end of the county.

Harkers Island, home to Cape Lookout National Seashore headquarters and several concessionaires who cater to seashore visitors, is moving more directly to serve a tourism economy. The communities of Marshallberg, Sea

Level, Davis, and Atlantic remain traditional maritime and fishing villages protected behind the open ocean barrier islands of North and South Core Banks.

In 2003 aforementioned Hurricane Isabel gave residents and eager second-home property seekers reason to pause because it shattered the illusion of protection. Still, it is likely that Downeast and the traditional farms and forests will gradually yield to increasing numbers of vacation homes.

The primary routes to Carteret County, US 70 on the northeast and routes NC 58 and 24 on the west and south, funnel most traffic to the two high-rise bridges crossing Bogue Sound at Morehead City and Cape Carteret. Except for five-lane NC 24 between Jacksonville and Morehead City and bustling US 70, the routes serving the coast in Carteret County are two-lane and rural in character.

US 70 parallels the North Carolina Railroad line to Morehead City. That railroad—the project of nineteenth-century governor John Motley Morehead, a Greensboro resident—is the reason for the city.

Morehead pushed for the development of another deepwater harbor in North Carolina (the Cape Fear River is the only dependable natural deepwater port) linked by rail to the industrial Piedmont. The railroad made the oceanfront more accessible, and as leisure time became more common during the early twentieth century, Morehead City's evolution as a vacation destination gained momentum even as it grew modestly as a commercial deepwater port. The port retains its commercial importance, but tourism is what really drives the local economy.

For Your Bucket:
> Kayak or canoe Cedar Island NWR in the fall
> Visit the Core Sound Waterfowl Museum & Heritage Center
> Spend a day in Beaufort
> Take boatbuilding lessons at the Watercraft Center in Beaufort
> Take a guided tour of Rachel Carson Estuarine Reserve
> Take an interpretive tour of Fort Macon
> See the Salter Path Regional Access
> Buy fresh seafood in Salter Path
> Ride the Emerald Isle bicycle trails
> Walk the point at Emerald Isle

Access

The individual municipalities and management agencies in Carteret County provide beach access locations.

Renting a cottage or staying in a motel is the best avenue for access on Bogue Banks.

Search NC Beach Access; click the NC DEQ Beach and Waterfront Access Map link; at the bottom of the second column, click "Go to Beach Access Locator."

Search Crystal Coast NC or enter www.crystalcoastnc.org.

Best phone number for tourism information: 252-726-8148.

CEDAR ISLAND

The passenger ferry to Ocracoke docks at the slice of land named Cedar Island. Ferry riders approaching the dock see an island in miniature—some small dunes, a layer of shrubs, and trees sheared by salt spray. Occasionally one can see livestock ranging into the waters east of the jetties that protect the ferry dock. Cedar Island is small, but it has a post office, a restaurant, and, near the ferry facilities, a small motel. There are also several homes on the sandy island beach west of the ferry dock.

The community spreads along NC 12 under the shelter of salt-twisted red cedar and pine trees. There is a church, a sundries store, and a community graveyard. This area is remote, and if you are departing the ferry, NC 12 moves into the forested "high ground" of the island as it follows the western bank of Cedar Island Bay. It is a surprising passage, a winding, unhurried route through the marshes of Cedar Island National Wildlife Refuge. Drivers heading north will see a few enticing and disorienting glimpses of water, and then NC 12 comes to an abrupt end at the ferry dock.

Access

There is a large parking lot at the ferry dock where you may leave your car if you're taking the ferry to Ocracoke. A small motel, restaurant, and campground offers food and accommodations of all kinds here. Call 252-225-4861.

Advance reservations for the ferry are a must. See ferry.ncdot.gov to make reservations online, or call 800-293-3779.

The Ocracoke ferry operates a seasonal schedule, which varies yearly.

Between May 22 and September 24, there are five daily departures each from Ocracoke and Cedar Island, beginning at 7 AM and ending at 6:30 PM from Cedar Island. There are three daily departures each way the remainder of the year, beginning at 7:30 AM. The crossing takes 2 hours 15 minutes.

CEDAR ISLAND NATIONAL WILDLIFE REFUGE

At the eastern end of Carteret County, 40 miles north of Beaufort, NC 12 knifes through the middle of the 14,494-acre Cedar Island National Wildlife Refuge. The U.S. Fish and Wildlife Service describes the refuge as 11,000 acres of irregularly flooded brackish marsh and 3,494 acres of forested wetlands. The classic marsh, dense with shimmering needlerush and cordgrass in summer, encloses the view from NC 12 as the grasses mature with the season's growth. The passage through the Cedar Island Marsh rivals the exquisite winding of Princess Anne Road onto Knotts Island in Currituck County and is one of the finest such drives anywhere.

Established in 1964, Cedar Island offers a rare crossing often shimmering in the warmer light of the lower-angled sun of a waning year when the grasses waver bleached against the horizon. High ground—the forested wetlands are hummocks supporting loblolly, longleaf, and pond pines, wax myrtle and gallberry, and even the occasional live oak—punctuate the plains of pale threads. Without question, what makes the lasting impression is the expanse of marsh, mostly black needlerush, spreading endlessly to either side.

Nearly 270 species of birds can be seen here each year. December and January are the peak season for waterfowl, and the predominant species are redhead ducks, lesser scaup, and a few black ducks. During the summer season, even on a quick drive-through you will likely see some of the permanent populations of wading shorebirds.

As an undeveloped wildlife refuge, Cedar Island offers little access to vehicles, and there are few public facilities. Hunting and fishing are permitted. The road crosses a high-rise bridge over the 40-foot-wide slough linking Thorofare Bay on the east side of Cedar Island to West Thorofare Bay on the west side of NC 12. Drive slowly if you can: the elevation of the bridge provides one of the best changes in perspective for viewing the marsh. All lands west of NC 12 are in the refuge; the land on the southeast side of the slough is not. This location has a boat-launching ramp frequently used by anglers and hunters.

Access

Cedar Island National Wildlife Refuge is open during daylight hours all year.

There is an improved boat-launching ramp at the refuge headquarters on Lewis Creek south of Lola and a boat-launching ramp on the southwest side of NC 12 at the Thorofare Bay Bridge.

The refuge is administered as a satellite refuge of Lake Mattamuskeet in Swan Quarter.

For information, contact Cedar Island National Wildlife Refuge, c/o Mattamuskeet National Wildlife Refuge, 38 Mattamuskeet Road, Swan Quarter, NC 27885, 252-926-4021.

Search Cedar Island NWR or enter www.fws.gov/refuge/cedar_island.

ATLANTIC

Surprisingly, Atlantic is home to nearly 600 people, but many more know it as the departure point for one of the concessionaires providing automobile-ferry service and cabin rentals service to North Core Banks in Cape Lookout National Seashore. This is also the eastern terminus of US 70, which tails out just beyond its intersection with Salter Drive. Salter Drive connects to SR 1378, Morris Marina Road, which connects to Old Cedar Island Road (NC 1387) and leads back to NC 12. This convoluted trek loops around a retired but guarded Marine Corps airfield, MCOLF (Marine Corps Outlying Field) Atlantic. This connects to NC 12 a few miles north of town. Coming from Cedar Island, SR 1387 is a lovely winding approach to the community arriving at an intersection with Morris Marina Road (NC 1378). Turn east to go to the marina; turn west to go toward town.

Atlantic is a traditional Downeast fishing village; the houses are as tight and neat as a coil of rope. The street names—Morris, Willis, Fulcher, and Bullock, among others—are a telltale collection of long-present Downeast surnames. Follow that with School Road, Core Sound Road, and Air Base Road. Folks in Atlantic make it easy to know where you are or where you are going.

It is a handsome, tidy town, and tied to the sea, as evidenced by the trawlers and fishing boats tied at their moorings. Many living here still depend on the ocean for their living.

A key to their economy is the somewhat reliable passage to the ocean, currently known as Ophelia Inlet, shifted as it was by that namesake storm from the prior New Drum Inlet location.

The closing of the first Drum Inlet sometime during the eighteenth century made the passage to the ocean arduous. A new inlet was dynamited in the early 1970s nearly due east of Atlantic. Already the inlet shoals heavily, and from Core Banks, Drum Inlet almost seems to be a crossing that could be made on foot at low tide. Along came Ophelia in 2005 and realigned access for the time being.

The Morris family, which once owned nearly 1,000 acres of land on Core Banks, operates the ferry concession, Morris Marina, Kabin Kamps, and a ferry service. The ferry is equipped to carry four four-wheel-drive vehicles and disembarks passengers at a dock on North Core Banks, north of Drum Inlet.

Search Cape Lookout or enter www.nps.gov/calo and use the "Plan Your Visit/Eating and Sleeping/Lodging/Long Point Rates" drop-down menus.

Search Cape Lookout Ferries or enter www.nps.gov/calo and use the "Plan Your Visit/Directions & Transportation/ List of Authorized Ferry Services" drop-down menus.

See the Cape Lookout section for additional detail.

DAVIS

This small community—smaller than Atlantic—sits where US 70 makes a right-angle turn. Travelers from the east turn left to continue to Cedar Island; travelers from the north turn west to continue to Beaufort. The rest of Davis strings along US 70 west of the turn and sleeps out of sight down several small side roads. From this community, two concessionaires operate ferry service to South Core Banks.

Davis is a favored launching point for folks crossing to Core Banks to hunt and fish. There is a small campground here. Cape Lookout Cabins & Camps Ferry Service has a dock due east of the right-angle turn in the highway. It transports automobiles and campers to Great Island Cabins.

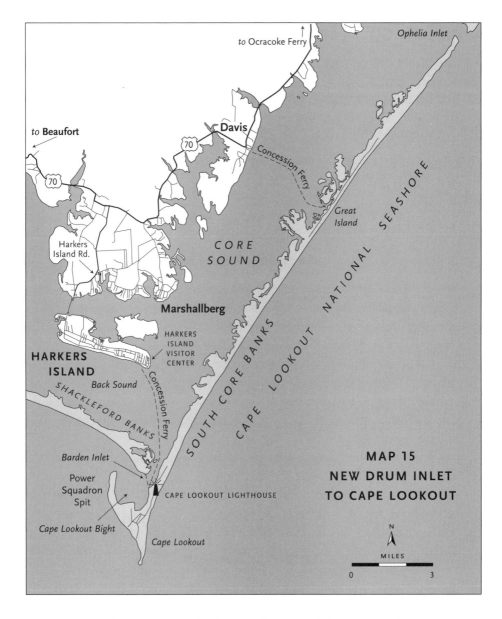

Davis Shore Ferry Service is located at 148 Willis Road, one block south of the US 70 turn. It also transports automobiles and campers to Great Island Cabins.

Visitors using either ferry crossing and looking northeast may catch a glance of a building known as the Core Banks Club, a private hunting and fishing club built in 1902 under another name. The building and land were purchased for the seashore in 1976; the building was intended for park use, but with budget restrictions, it is slipping into disrepair.

Access

Search Cape Lookout or enter www.nps.gov/calo and use the "Plan Your Visit/Eating and Sleeping/Lodging/Great Island Rates" drop-down menus.

Search Cape Lookout Ferries or enter www.nps.gov/calo and use the "Plan Your Visit/Directions & Transportation/ List of Authorized Ferry Services" drop-down menus.

See the Cape Lookout section for additional detail.

HARKERS ISLAND

The elbow of Cape Lookout and the east end of Shackleford Banks shield Harkers Island from the open ocean. It is sequestered between these islands and the mainland on the waters of Back Sound. A coastal map reveals the island to be a brief boat ride due east from Beaufort across the waters of the Rachel Carson National Estuarine Research Reserve. The land route is more indirect: Harkers Island is a sharp turn south off US 70, the Outer Banks National Scenic Byway, onto Harkers Island Road, which is nearly 11 miles east of Beaufort. Drivers heading south should look for the turn 2 miles west of the village of Smyrna.

The route to the island crosses by a causeway and two bridges, one of which is a low, fixed-span bridge and the other a swing bridge over local waters known as "the Straits," a name also given to the mainland community. A single-span replacement bridge with 45 feet of navigational clearance is scheduled to be built to the east of the present crossing starting in 2020. The crossing connects the forested mainland area known as the Straits to the wind-sheared low island, a difference you see almost immediately. A local dock filled with stout working boats beside the road as you reach the island signals the strong working-waterman presence.

Harkers feathers into the shallow, greenish sound waters with ruffles of marsh and armies of pilings, legions of piers and docks, old boats, boats under construction, salt-sheared cedar trees, modest homes, a school, and limited services. The main street is not so much lined as framed by the live oaks of adjoining yards. It has the feeling of a neighborhood street.

The island is a part of "Downeast." It would be out of the ordinary vacation traffic pattern except that the headquarters for Cape Lookout National Seashore is at Shell Point, the end of the road on Harkers Island. This headquarters is the primary jump-off location for ferry service to the Cape Lookout Light Station and the opportunity to climb the Cape Lookout Lighthouse. The 25-minute drive there from Beaufort is an opportunity to see and appreciate Harkers Island's out-of-the-mainstream offerings in addition to the national seashore.

The island has a tradition of building sturdy wooden working boats and still has artisans who can look at a stack of lumber and envision how to rearrange it to make a boat. It's not unusual to glimpse a boat in progress beneath the shade of one of the island's sculpted cedar trees. The traditional boat style here had a flared bow and was crafted to facilitate heavy work in shallow sound waters.

While boatbuilding has waned somewhat, water sports such as fishing, sailing, kayaking, canoeing, and windsurfing on Back Sound have become more popular. Harkers Island has the appeal of both terrific access and reduced traffic. Recent decades have brought increased construction of vacation and permanent homes on the island. The newer houses are obvious and may signal the beginning of a wholesale change in island life.

Today, because of the excellent docking facilities and the proximity of two popular portions of the Cape Lookout National Seashore—Cape Lookout and Shackleford Banks—the island is a launching point for day-tripping and camping at the edge of the sea, on the islands visible at the horizon.

The art of decoy carving flourished on Harkers Island and other Downeast communities as a means for supplemental income or for personal use. The recognition of this practical skill and the preservation of the traditional ways of life in eastern Carteret County led to the establishment and construction of the Core Sound Waterfowl Museum & Heritage Center here. It is next door to the Cape Lookout headquarters, a handsome building with echoes of traditional coastal architecture.

The museum depicts a marvelous, gritty history of life and communities—far beyond the stunning collection of traditional decoys and artisan competitively carved decoys. Then there are the rest of the engaging stories embracing the range of traditional water-related working arts peculiar to Down East, including with decoy carving, boatbuilding, storytelling, and hunting and fishing practices.

Accommodations are limited to one motel next to one of two marinas on the island.

At Shell Point, at the end of SR 1335, you might see at least one or two cars drive to the dead end and turn around. This is a tradition, noted in an island cookbook: if you're a true islander, you have to drive down to Shell Point at least once a day.

It's easy to see why—just to catch a glimpse of the lighthouse, if for no other reason.

Search Cape Lookout Seashore or enter www.nps.gov/calo.

Search Crystal Coast NC or enter www.crystalcoastnc.org.

Best phone number for tourism information: 252-726-8148.

Access

The Cape Lookout National Seashore Visitor Center has a large parking lot and picnic area at Shell Point, the end of SR 1335. You may inquire about ferry schedules and operators to reach Cape Lookout National Seashore at this location.

On the east side of the fixed bridge to the island, Carteret County has constructed a small T-shaped wooden access way for fishing or crabbing near the north bridge. There is ample parking.

SHACKLEFORD BANKS

Shackleford Banks remains under review as a possible wilderness area, a curious, ironic legacy of a late nineteenth-century hurricane that cleaned the island of most structures and all residents. (In the nineteenth century as many as 600 people lived and fished from here.) While it is not likely to become a part of the federal wilderness system, the 9-mile-long, 2,500-acre barrier is managed as though it might be. This means no development, minimal artificial structures, and no roads.

Two thriving whaling communities sailed from Shackleford: Diamond City at the east end and Wade's Shore on the west. A series of hurricanes that pummeled the island beginning in the 1890s destroyed the maritime forest and the houses in it.

The survivors abandoned what had been a village of at least 500 people at Diamond City, leaving only grave markers and some livestock behind to move to Harkers Island, Salter Path on Bogue Banks, and a section of More-

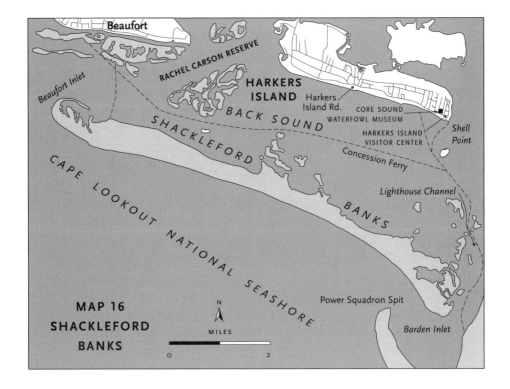

MAP 16
SHACKLEFORD
BANKS

head City colloquially known as "the Promise Land." Until the 1970s, only feral animals populated Shackleford Banks, and with no fences, the animals were free to roam the island. The National Park Service removed the pigs and sheep; the horses were permitted to stay.

The horses are one of the great attractions of Shackleford Banks. The animals descend from noteworthy stock—genetic markers link their ancestry to Spanish animals arriving here more than 400 years ago. (The peculiar genetic marker also appears in the Paso Fino horses of Puerto Rico and the Prior Mountain mustangs of Montana.)

The exact timing and origins are uncertain. The animals are small and lithe, averaging 12 hands in height (a "hand" equals 4 inches) at the withers. The herd today numbers about 120 and is organized into multiple harems and several bachelor bands. Dominant "alpha" stallions guard the harems.

Daniel I. Rubenstein, a professor of zoology, ecology, and evolutionary biology at Princeton University, studied the horses for nearly two decades and has documented a territorial behavior by the stallions that does not usually occur in wild horse populations.

The wild horses of Shackleford Banks are descended from Spanish horses perhaps shipwrecked offshore more than 400 years ago. (Photo by Bill Russ, courtesy of VisitNC.com)

The National Park Service leaves well enough alone with the herd, intervening to maintain genetic diversity by using immune-contraception selectively and periodically removing horses from the herd for private adoption. These efforts sustain both a healthy herd and a healthy island.

Horse-watching is the big draw for day-tripping to the island. A boat ride there is no guarantee that passengers will see the horses. Then again, they may be standing beside the ferry dock.

The maritime forest is still recovering from the damage of hurricanes and generations of occupancy. Most of the rejuvenating forest is along the western third of the island, behind the extensive dune ridge that in some locations is more than 40 feet above sea level. The eastern end of the island, the one closest to Cape Lookout, is low and flat and resembles neighboring Core Banks in physical appearance.

Shackleford is perhaps the least known of the barrier islands, but increased ferry access in recent years has made it popular for day trips.

Wear lightweight, protective clothing (loose-fitting long sleeves and running or water-sport shoes are best), a hat, sunglasses, binoculars, camera, sunscreen, and insect repellent, and bring water (two quarts per person), food or snacks, and a plastic bag to carry out all trash. There are composting toilets at the west end of the island near the ferry dock.

The park service mandates the following restrictions to protect the island's resources:

- All wildlife is protected.
- All vegetation is protected and should not be disturbed.
- Fires are allowed only below the high-water mark.
- Visitors must walk only at the lowest part of the dunes.
- Shelling is limited to two gallons of uninhabited shells per person per day.
- Metal detectors are prohibited.
- Visitors must carry their trash off the island.

Access

Shackleford is accessible by private boat or park service–approved ferry. Service departs from Beaufort and Harkers Island made by reservation with the service. Confirm available ferry concessionaires at www.nps.gov/calo /planyourvisit/ferry.htm.

Search Shackleford Horses or enter
www.nps.gov/calo/learn/nature/horses.htm.

BEAUFORT

Beaufort (pronounced *Boe*-furt) is one of the most enjoyable small towns on the coast. If it has a rival in things to do and visual appeal, that rival is Manteo. Both are small enough to easily walk and good places to become lost in time. Figure a long half-day to a full day for a visit that might include a museum tour, a quick boat ride to nearby islands, lunch on the waterfront, and a self-guided tour of the historic district. The town is chock-full of pleasures for the unhurried and curious.

Beaufort balances a dapper appearance true to its colonial roots while still appealing to the here and now of present-day tourism. Residents decided (discovered?) little necessity in becoming anything other than what it is—a three-century-old waterfront town. It once served industry, but now

The Shapes of Islands

All southeastern states have barrier islands, but they differ in form and alignment. The difference is the result of the response of sand to the particular coastal influences from one state to another. Where islands look alike, the coastal environments are much alike.

North Carolina's barrier islands are long and narrow, typical of barrier islands shaped by wind, wind-generated waves, and strong currents. Texas has similar islands; Padre Island National Seashore is virtually a mirror image of North Carolina's barrier preserves (but closer to the mainland).

Along coasts where tidal forces predominate and the source of new material are inland rivers, such as South Carolina and Georgia, barrier islands tend to be short and wide, more like a turkey drumstick.

Island configuration varies greatly within North Carolina although not so much in shape as in cross section. It is most evident at Cape Lookout National Seashore. The Cape Lookout Lighthouse is on South Core Banks, the southernmost lengthy northeast-to-southwest-trending island of the seashore. Next to it, across Bardon Inlet, is Shackleford Banks, the first of the islands on the east and west arc of Onslow Bay.

What a contrast! Core is low with sparse vegetation and barely any dunes; Shackleford has extensive dunes and, behind them, thickly forested sections. Accounting for their difference is their response to the prevailing winds that seasonally come from the northeast or southwest. On Core Banks, the wind moves sand in stinging, wispy streams along the beach, parallel to the ocean. This makes dune formation difficult and makes a dry windy day on Core Banks an endurance test. That same wind, though, moves sand perpendicular to the long axis of Shackleford Banks. Over time, this results in the widening of the island and the piling of sand into higher dunes.

This pattern of dune formation repeats periodically along the coast as the orientation of the barrier islands shifts between north–south and east–west. At three locations—Cape Hatteras, Cape Lookout, and Cape Fear—the compass orientation of the islands shifts abruptly. Each increasingly westward bend of the islands changes the effects prevailing winds have on the sand available for the beaches. While in theory it might seem that *all* islands trending east–west would typically have higher dunes, sheltered forests, and higher elevations, that is not exactly so. Too many other factors come into play—such as sand supply and the underlying geological history, to mention two. As each island responds individually to the forces of nature, the chain of islands adapts collectively to the same. What wind, water, and tides do to one island changes the way it affects an adjacent island. These effects are readily observed at inlets between islands. The general north-to-south movement of sand typically has the northeast headland of an inlet accreting while the southwest headland erodes. As sand comes and goes, so do islands, in ways that make it difficult to cover all beaches with a blanket declaration.

serves hospitality, history, good food, and a real easy attitude. It's a lovely old place with a lively new purpose.

But Beaufort comes by a lot of character honestly. Amazingly, it remains far nicer than many other places so close to salt water for so long. The wonderfully cockeyed village reveals itself readily at a walking pace. Looking closely, building by building, many details seem slightly askew, and the cants and tilts of age are in fact proudly worn badges, confirmed by the plaques that proclaim the date of construction.

The soul of the town is the National Register Historic District, which reaches from Broad Street south to Taylor Creek, the waterfront. Live Oak Street bounds the east, and the Beaufort Channel is the western boundary. Though there are more than 100 restored eighteenth- and nineteenth-century buildings, the age per se does not flavor the district. Instead, it is the proportion and scale of house and lot, trees and street that make the district so attractive to stroll. Truly, these blocks are made for walking.

To reach Front Street, the town's bustling main street and waterfront, visitors must pass through the eighteenth-century portals of the historic district. Coming from the west, turn south off of Cedar Street (old US 70) at the light signaling Turner Street. The Beaufort Bypass (US 70) has a Turner Street exit as well. Turner Street leads directly to Front Street. Folks arriving from the east should consider following old US 70 (Live Oak Street) instead of the newer Beaufort Bypass. This local route goes directly to Front Street.

On the east side of Turner Street is the distinctive redbrick Carteret County Courthouse. The residential district begins shortly after crossing Broad Street—picket fences, broad columned porches, tall cedar and magnolia trees. There are apartments and churches—it's obviously a lived-in place.

There are several parking lots on Turner Street. Unless it is very early on summer days, park opportunistically—Front Street will be less than two

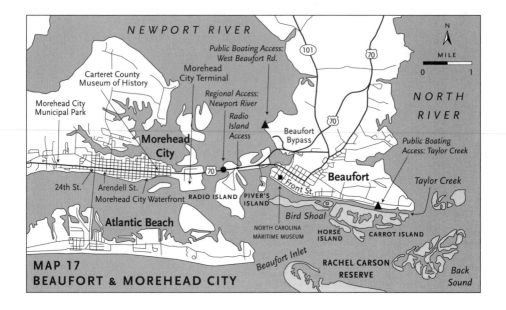

NEWPORT RIVER

Public Boating Access:
West Beaufort Rd.

Morehead
City Terminal

Carteret County
Museum of History

Morehead City
Municipal Park

Regional Access:
Newport River

NORTH
RIVER

Radio
Island
Access

**Morehead
City**

Beaufort
Bypass

Public Boating
Access: Taylor Creek

24th St.   Arendell St.
Morehead City Waterfront   RADIO ISLAND   PIVER'S
ISLAND

Beaufort

Taylor Creek

Atlantic Beach

Bird Shoal

NORTH CAROLINA
MARITIME MUSEUM   HORSE
ISLAND   CARROT ISLAND

Beaufort Inlet

RACHEL CARSON
RESERVE

Back
Sound

N
MILE
0   1

MAP 17
BEAUFORT & MOREHEAD CITY

blocks away. Beaufort is easily walked, and walking is quicker and more efficient than trying to wait out vacation traffic.

The Beaufort Historical Association's Robert W. and Elva Faison Safrit
Welcome Center, 130 Turner Street, is a great first stop. The association
offers several tours for a fee. Docents in period dress guide the Historic
Buildings Tour and the Old Burying Ground Tour. The former is given twice
daily, Monday–Saturday, year-round; the latter on Tuesday, Wednesday, and
Thursday at 2:30.

A 1967 London double-decker bus is the star vehicle in the Historic District Double-Decker Bus Tour, offered twice daily on Monday, Wednesday,
Friday, and Saturday.

Front Street shows how well Beaufort is trading on its past to build a
future. In the late 1970s Beaufort completed an ambitious waterfront restoration right in the middle of this seafaring town. Though it was a gamble at
the time, the venture jump-started an economic shift by making the waterfront attractive and usable to travelers on the Intracoastal Waterway. As they
sailed up and down the Eastern Seaboard, they spread the word about this
newly hospitable community.

The restoration created a two-sided downtown, appealing from both
water and land. It removed some older buildings—one resident remem-
bers them as "fish houses" serving local trade—that blocked the view. The

renovation made Taylor Creek the feature, glimpsed between renovated, usable buildings. The harbormaster's office sits like a control tower centrally located between two parking lots—and it also houses a restaurant. It overlooks the waterfront promenade adjacent to the Beaufort Docks, the name for the boat slips. A summertime walk along the docks makes clear that Beaufort no longer hauls in lowly menhaden; rather, it attracts "big fish" that hang around for a few days.

The backdrop to Taylor Creek is Carrot Island, part of the Rachel Carson component of the National Estuarine Research Reserve system. At dusk the setting sun casts golden light across the marsh grasses and myrtles on the island and warms the waterfront with a sunset glow. The small herd of feral horses that roam Carrot Island will occasionally slip into view. Take a seat and watch the world sail by; here, have another.

A small commercial cluster, Somerset Square, is almost directly at the end of Turner Street. Several restaurants line the 300 block of Front Street. The Harvey W. Smith Watercraft Center, a boatbuilding warehouse on Taylor Creek, is an adjunct of the North Carolina Maritime Museum across Front Street.

The west extension of Front Street is residential, and the homes look toward the waterfront. The five adjacent houses in the 100 block have both first- and second-story porches that seem to have been built to a single chalk line. As you look along the length of Front Street, the porches nicely frame the view of Piver's Island and the Duke University Marine Laboratories.

Welcome to Beaufort. Park the car and walk around.

Access

There is off-street and on-street parking near the waterfront. There is a public access off of Turner Street at the Beaufort Bypass and north of the Beaufort Bypass.

Search NC Beach Access; click the NC DEQ Beach and Waterfront Access Map link; at the bottom of the second column, click "Go to Beach Access Locator."

Search Beaufort NC or enter www.beaufortnc.org.

Search Beaufort Historical or enter www.beauforthistoricsite.org.

For tourism information, enter www.crystalcoastnc.org/Beaufort.

Best phone number for more information: 252-726-8148.

NORTH CAROLINA MARITIME MUSEUM

Each of the regional locations of the North Carolina Maritime Museum emphasizes the flavor of the local maritime tradition. The North Carolina Maritime Museum on Front Street follows that interpretive pattern. And because it is the first of the three maritime museums, the exhibits here comprise a story with greater reach. The Beaufort branch of the museum showcases the coastal life of North Carolina from traditional sailing vessels to motorboats, from boatbuilding to commercial fishing, and from lighthouses to the heroics of the U.S. Life-Saving Service. It is impressively concise and surrounds visitors with the exploits of watermen and the creatures and events they encountered. The museum bolsters its expansive static exhibits with seasonally relevant programming scheduled throughout the year.

The building itself is a good neighbor to historic Beaufort and fits in nicely. The nearly 18,000-square-foot structure is complimentary to the scale and feeling of the town. It tips its architectural hat to both the styling of the U.S. Life-Saving Service stations and the Beaufort vernacular. The interior is comfy and jammed with information, unfolding much as a well-organized and displayed nautical attic might. Eye-catching exhibits of mounted ocean fish—a great white shark is especially evocative, as is a suspended whale skeleton—provide an imaginative ornamentation to the several story lines about fishes, boats, and those who sailed them.

The museum is the official repository of the artifacts recovered from an eighteenth-century sailing ship, *Queen Anne's Revenge*, that wrecked off Beaufort Inlet. Yes, this was the flagship of the pirate Blackbeard (aka Edward Teach), who was killed off Ocracoke in 1718. Following the grounding, the ship remained lost until discovered by a private company, Intersal, Inc., in November 1996. Recovery and restoration began (13 cannons have been recovered!), and visitors may see the ship's bell, cannons, cannonballs, pewter plates, belt buckles, navigation instruments, and wine bottles. Additional displays detail the other daily items a pirate needed to be successful ... and remain alive.

Exhibits plunge into North Carolina nautical traditions, with particular attention to regional boatbuilding styles that evolved to make serviceable boats for men who made their livelihood by fishing the shallow sound waters.

In support of this theme are several wooden boats made by area boat-builders, along with exquisite replicas of the reliable vessels preferred by local watermen. There are detailed scale models of famous vessels. There is a glimpse into the saga of waterfowl hunting, decoy carving, and the hunting tradition of Downeast communities. Among the most moving exhibits are the stories of the lighthouses and the crews of the U.S. Life-Saving Service. A poignant vignette is about the Gold Lifesaving Medal awarded to Rasmus S. Midgett for single-handedly saving 10 members of the barkentine *Priscilla* on August 18, 1899, from the Gull Shoal station near present-day Salvo on Hatteras Island.

Across the street in the Harvey Smith Watercraft Center, artisans work on a variety of wooden boats. The workers repair and restore some and craft others from the keel up. The watercraft center grew from the museum's effort to preserve both North Carolina's sailing and working boats and the woodworking artisanship necessary to build these indigenous watercraft.

Throughout the year, the museum sponsors programs in-house and out. It uses field trips to introduce participants to the local cultural and eco-logical history. Programs are frequently held at the Rachel Carson compo-nent of the North Carolina National Estuarine Research Reserve, directly across Taylor Creek from Beaufort.

Access

The museum is open seven days a week: 9–5 weekdays, 10–5 Saturday, and 1–5 Sunday.

Search NC Maritime Museum or enter
www.ncmaritimemuseumbeaufort.com.

Best phone number for more information: 252-504-7740.

For more on the *Queen Anne's Revenge*, enter www.qaronline.org.

RACHEL CARSON NATIONAL
ESTUARINE RESEARCH RESERVE

Beaufort's waterfront is Taylor Creek. Beyond Taylor Creek are Carrot Island and Bird Shoal. These two tracts of high ground along with Town Marsh, Horse Island, and Middle Marsh form the 2,375-acre Rachel Carson component of the North Carolina National Estuarine Research Reserve. The view across Taylor Creek is the permanent view from the Beaufort waterfront.

Carrot Island, Town Marsh, Bird Shoal, and Horse Island form the part of the reserve directly opposite Beaufort; this section is 3 miles long but less than 1 mile wide. Middle Marsh, nearly 2 miles long and 650 acres, forms the eastern segment of the reserve, across the North River channel to the east.

While there are dredge spoil depositions from Taylor Creek, these islands and the marshy flats are unspoiled sanctuaries supporting a diversity of wildlife in many varied habitats. The reserve provides excellent refuge for wildlife, especially birds—there are more than 200 species here, including 23 bird species that are endangered, threatened, or decreasing in number. The site is an important feeding ground for Wilson's plover in summer and the piping plover in winter.

Historically, residents have used these islands for recreation and for horse pasturage. The horses there now are feral animals descended from horses released on the island in the 1940s, when it was common practice to allow livestock to graze on these islands. The present herd of 48 animals is the optimal number for the reserve and will be kept constant and actively monitored for their health and for any damage to the ecology of the islands.

These isolated hammocks almost became condominiums. In 1977 the proposal was thwarted and the North Carolina Nature Conservancy purchased 474 acres of Carrot Island, the principal high ground. Since that time the remainder of the marsh, tidal flats, and barriers have been secured, protecting both the charm of the Beaufort waterfront and the integrity of the sites.

Reserve personnel conduct guided walks typically on Tuesdays and Thursdays during the summer months. There is no charge, and the tours depart from the North Carolina Research Reserve Office at Duke Marine Lab on Piver's Island. There is a schedule of summer tours on the website below. Reservations must be made through the website. Directions to the starting point are provided at the same web location.

DUKE UNIVERSITY MARINE LABORATORIES

Easily visible from the west end of Beaufort's front street, Piver's Island has the village-like campus of the Duke Marine Lab, a unit of Duke University's Nicholas School of Environment. Rachel Carson worked here when she wrote part of her superb seashore-ecology book, *The Sea Around Us*. Carson drew heavily on her visits to nearby Bird Shoal and Carrot Island and is the namesake of the Rachel Carson component of the North Carolina National Estuarine Research Reserve. The offices of the reserve are here, and tours of the reserve assemble at the offices in the NOAA building.

The property is not closed, but as an academic facility it is generally not set up for public visitation.

Search Rachel Carson Reserve or enter
www.nccoastalreserve.net. Use the Reserve Sites menu.

RADIO ISLAND

Radio Island sits in the thick of the port action, within easy bait-casting distance of the Beaufort channel. It is also blessed with protected waters for swimming and an informal beach. It has traditionally been a local access area.

Carteret County provides an access location for daylight use only off of Olde Town Yacht Club Drive, reached by turning onto Marine Road from Old Causeway Drive.

The state maintains a large access area with boat ramps and restrooms on North Radio Island, sometimes referred to as the Newport River Pier and Ramp. Turn north off of Arendell Street to reach the access location. See below.

Access

To reach Radio Island, turn south off of Old Causeway Drive or Arendell Street (US 70) at the first median break east of the high-rise bridge over the Newport River. Turn onto the island, travel for several hundred feet, and turn left on the paved road.

Search NC Beach Access; click the NC DEQ Beach and
Waterfront Access Map link; at the bottom of the second
column, click "Go to Beach Access Locator."

NEWPORT RIVER REGIONAL ACCESS AREA

This is a fully developed regional facility, with restrooms, a boardwalk, pic-nic tables, a dune crossover, and trails leading to riverfront fishing sites. The site provides excellent opportunities for fishing and crabbing along the Intracoastal Waterway, which follows the Newport River here.

The boardwalk has a surreal view of the state port terminal at Morehead City, where many domed storage buildings are interlaced with catwalks and conveyor-belt delivery tracks. A dune ridge trail leads among plantings of seaside goldenrod and other pioneering plants to views of the north side of the basin and the Newport Marsh.

Search NC Beach Access; click the NC DEQ Beach and Waterfront Access Map link; at the bottom of the second column, click "Go to Beach Access Locator."

MOREHEAD CITY

People flock to Morehead City in summer. It has an allure rooted in tradi-tion and habit: it is where Raleigh-Durham residents have gone and will go. The preference started more than 100 years ago, when this coastal town crackled into statewide consciousness with the rise of railroads and its port.

The gathering point has always been the east end of this water-hugging community of nearly 9,000. Most visitors arrive driving US 70 from the west. The highway wades through a heavily commercial area before skirting tree-lined streets and residential neighborhoods adjoining Bogue Sound.

The railroad tracks appearing between the opposing lanes of highway are conspicuous. The pattern continues through downtown, a present-day reminder of the railroad's importance to city history. These are active tracks carrying freight, gleaming metal proof that the mid-nineteenth-century vision of its founder was spot on.

Slightly east of where the railroad slips into the median of Arendell Street, just past the North Carolina Fisheries Building, is the Visitor and Information Center of the Crystal Coast Tourism Authority. The building echoes the classic U.S. Life-Saving Station architecture, featuring a "watch-tower" and hipped roofs shading porches. It is a first stop for information on programs, facilities, and current events throughout the Carteret County communities marketed as the Crystal Coast.

The municipal park behind the center has a soundside setting with large live oaks to shade its picnic areas. There is a free boat ramp. The memorial obelisk behind the center honors Josiah Bogue, namesake of Bogue Sound, who deeded to his daughter land known as Shepherd's Point, which became the site of Morehead City.

The park is off 34th Street, and the numbered streets descend numerically approaching downtown, framing blocks of small homes that have access to the sound. The ramp to the Atlantic Beach Bridge is just before South 24th Street; South 23rd Street is the exit from the Atlantic Beach Bridge. The mainland bulges two more blocks to the southeast of 23rd Street, where Shepard Street leads to the commercial district. Shackleford Street, the waterfront road, runs parallel to Arendell Street, Morehead City's main thoroughfare.

The commercial center of town lines both sides of the tracks in the median of Arendell Street. The History Museum of Carteret County, once known as the History Place, at 11th Street, is close to the center of the business district. Businesses on this main street sit close to the road, with street parking in front.

Shepard Street and Evans Street join at Seventh Street. This is where the pace of the community picks up with the beginning of the waterfront. A duck crossing sign is a reference marker letting drivers know they are entering Morehead City's thriving waterfront and tourism district. The waterfront extends slightly beyond Fourth Street.

Morehead City's boardwalk is squeaky clean for a working charter center. This is the port for one of the largest sport fishing, commercial fishing, and diving fleets on the East Coast. On offer are Gulf Stream outings or head-boat trips for bottom-fishing excursions.

The waterfront hums: kiosks are covered with local information; diners wander about after their restaurant meals; charter crews tend to their boats. A major draw is the Big Rock Blue Marlin Tournament, which leaves these docks every June with anglers in pursuit of a blue marlin that could be worth a half million dollars. Every October the waterfront hosts the North Carolina Seafood Festival. It's a hopping waterfront that stays dressed up—a remarkable combination.

The high ground of cedar-covered Sugarloaf Island is the backdrop to the moorings. It is visible between the facades of buildings and from some of the restaurants. Across the street are shops and restaurants that can help fill an afternoon before eating dinner.

Parking is tight, so it makes some sense to consider parking on Arendell Street, the main commercial street, and walking the short distance to the waterfront.

The waterfront today is the outgrowth of the vision of John Motley Morehead, who served as governor from 1841 to 1845. He literally made tracks in North Carolina as a rail baron but started by buying land to create a deepwater port.

He purchased 600 acres in this area in 1853. Served by the railway, Morehead City grew into a fashionable Victorian resort; much later, when the state pitched in to dredge the channel and improve docking facilities, it became a major port.

In 1883 the Atlantic Hotel opened and became a celebrity destination, a place of gala ballroom dancing. In that golden age of railroads, Morehead City attracted the barons of incredible industrial wealth through the 1920s.

On April 15, 1933, the lights went up in a blaze when the Atlantic Hotel caught fire. (Photographs of the hotel and the fire can be seen at the History Museum of Carteret County.) The fire and the Depression dramatically altered the role Morehead City would play in the social life of the East Coast. (Condominiums at Fourth Street and Terminal Road stand on the site.) The Atlantic Hotel was served by the railroad, and the Morehead City Train Depot stood slightly west, at the block of Sixth and Arendell Streets. In 2004 the terminal went for a ride to the park at 10th and Arendell, across the street from the History Museum of Carteret County and closer to the center of the present commercial district.

Morehead City has miles of waterfront on Bogue Sound to the south and the tributaries feeding Calico Bay to the northwest. Visitors rarely see these areas, but they are popular for those who prefer a safe anchorage and reasonably convenient water access with a channel to the open ocean. Bogue Sound and Calico Bay attract more permanent residents than vacationers.

To see a slice of vintage Morehead City, turn in to the municipal park at the Crystal Coast Visitor Center and drive east on Evans Street. This quickly becomes a neighborhood of bungalow cottages and permanent homes, many of which are holdovers from the first wave of second-home construction and the continual resettling of Morehead City as a retirement community.

The homes on Sunset Drive, a bulge into the sound, are larger but have a weathered presence that evokes vacation places such as Martha's Vineyard.

The Atlantic Beach Bridge has smoothed crossings for cars above and boats below, clearing away a memorable aggravation: the opening and closing of the previous bridge. Still, traffic can be dicey at night in Morehead City because the trains do much switching and use the middle of town—the limits of the switching yard end at just about Sixth Street—to align cars onto the proper spur. They can block the intersection of US 70 and the bridge road.

The Morehead City Terminal, which is open to the public for tours during weekdays, serves ocean-crossing vessels from all seafaring nations. It is also a major shipping port of call for the U.S. Marine Corps from nearby Camp Lejeune.

Heading east, you cross the tracks and vault over the Newport River Bridge to Beaufort. Here you can sometimes see an immense pile of an indistinguishable material. The product is hardwood chips from the North Carolina coastal plain forest, destined for Asia to make fine papers. A tremendous covered building on the north side of US 70 is a shelter for phosphate, mined near Aurora.

Access

Morehead City has no beach access and only limited locations for public access to sound waters. Swimming is not recommended in these locations.

Search Morehead City NC or enter www.moreheadcitync.org.

For tourism information, enter http://www .crystalcoastnc.org/region/morehead-city.

Best phone number for more information: 252-726-8148.

THE HISTORY PLACE: THE HISTORY MUSEUM OF CARTERET COUNTY

While it is not possible to portray all the historical influences that shape a county in one location, a composite portrait of the richness of Downeast life is certainly possible. This is exactly what the Carteret County Historical Society accomplishes at 1008 Arendell Street, between 10th and 11th Streets. It is a museum, a research center, and an archive of the people and events of this extraordinary coastal county.

Fueled by citizen donations and volunteer work, the Carteret County

Historical Society has assembled a delightful cross-cultural portrait. It had won state awards for historic preservation before its move to this new location, and that enthusiasm and commitment continue here. The museum building is a renovated store of the former Colonial Grocery brand, once a fixture across the South and the only grocery in town for many years. The museum honors that story by displaying promotional items once used here.

The museum captures the flavor of earlier Morehead City by means of multiple vignettes of earlier eras—a Victorian parlor, a doctor's office, and an old general store. The span of exhibits reaches back to precolonial times, including the indigenous Tuscarora Indians, and showcases Native American artifacts. The museum also contains an extraordinary local reference and genealogical library of more than 10,000 books relevant to Carteret County and its families.

Morehead City relocated the original Morehead City Train Depot across Arendell Street on the southwest corner of 10th Street, in Morehead City Depot Park. The renovated depot is highlighted in a working circa nineteenth-century model train circulating in the gallery of the museum's exhibit space.

In a historical footnote, the museum was originally located in the original school of the World War I army encampment, Camp Glenn, west of downtown.

Search History Place Morehead or enter www.carterethistory.org.

Best phone number for more information: 252-247-7533.

BOGUE BANKS

Bogue Banks, nearly 25 miles long, is the second-longest island southwest of Cape Lookout (Topsail Island is 26 miles long). Since bridge and highway access improved in the mid-1970s, it has become one of the most popular and completely developed beach destinations in the state. A 2018 *USA Today* survey declared it the best beach in North Carolina. This is where folks agree to disagree. Regardless of any personal preference, Bogue Banks beaches do merit a high ranking.

There are four incorporated communities. They are, east to west, Atlantic Beach, Pine Knoll Shores, Indian Beach, and Emerald Isle—plus one stubbornly independent settlement, Salter Path, within the limits of Indian

Beach. "Salter Pathers" adhere to traditional fishing ways as a means of making a living, and their attitudes about fishing follow suit. Salter Path, one of the oldest settlement areas, is on comparatively high ground mid-island.

This is one island with several characters—from minimalist through worn and weathered to extravagant and plush. The towns, sections within towns, reveal different expressions and means to the vacation home aspiration. There are cushy second and permanent home subdivisions; affordable houses on gridded blocks; trailer parks that have been there forever; and high-rise condominiums. There are mom-and-pop private campgrounds, hotels, and motels. This island has a lot of options for staying and playing.

Atlantic Beach evolved as an entertainment center across Bogue Sound from Morehead City and was *the* place for oceanfront gathering from the 1920s until the island opened for development in the late 1950s.

Pine Knoll Shores opened as an exclusive, initially private subdivision, carefully designed and sensitive to the maritime forest of its location. The several oceanfront neighborhoods are sequestered behind the natural forest.

Indian Beach incorporated in 1973 and adjoins Salter Path. The oceanfront has large condominium blocks, and the sound side has recreational vehicle and prefabricated home sites. Indian Beach settled and developed freely; the mix of land uses reinforces that impression.

Emerald Isle neighborhoods grid the former dune flats and the maritime forest east of the NC 50 bridge from Cape Carteret. Newer subdivisions to the west of the bridge have larger homes with a more relaxed road layout.

One awkward truth of the island is that it developed quickly at a time when public access was not considered a necessity. Oceanfront homes always have access; homes on the second row (and farther back) need to be a short walk from a dedicated access path to easily access the beach, and not every Emerald Isle vacation rental home has that luxury.

There are compelling reasons for the island's popularity: Bogue Banks is the most easily reached beach between Ocracoke and Topsail Island. The island tends to have a wide beach, and the typical wave action can support a surfer and still not be a hazard to small children. Much of the island is covered with a stable forest, and the dune ridges are high and have been stable for a long time.

Bogue Banks is a beach ridge barrier island, meaning there is a spine of high ground along its length. The prevailing north–south seasonal winds that strike Bogue Banks at right angles to the line of the beach tend to push wave-loosened sand into dunes. Those dune fields sheltered the interior from damaging salt winds, and this, combined with higher elevation, set the right conditions for a maritime forest to evolve. By contrast, at the low-profile Core Banks of Cape Lookout National Seashore the prevailing winds blow parallel to the beach and are thus unfavorable to dune development. There is variation along the Bogue Banks oceanfront: in some locations, dunes soar 15 to 20 feet above the tide line; elsewhere, the dunes are flat as beaten biscuits.

Bogue Banks naturally has superb elements for undergirding a barrier island tourism economy. The island showcases every barrier environment, from low, narrow, treeless lengths, windswept and unsheltered, to salt-pruned and sculpted forests of live oak and yaupon. There are tall, grassed dunes and expanses of low plains of American beach grass.

Sand doesn't stay put, however, and Bogue Banks wrestles with the situational tandem of beach erosion and beach nourishment. Carteret County has been proactive in maintaining a healthy shoreline. The county established a Shore Protection Office in the late 1990s. Its purpose to systematically monitor the county beach profiles from behind the dune lines to several thousand feet offshore. The data are used to continually update the "state of the beach." This baseline information provides guidance for supplemental nourishment projects and storm response as needed. Shore Protection Manager Greg Rudolph has developed an exemplary program that is advisory and, to the extent it can be, anticipatory. The office also helps the island communities comply with federal requirements to provide public access and public parking in exchange for beach nourishment funding. The upshot is a generally stable beach and dune line with improved public access. The nourishment program certainly helped minimize erosion and structural damage to homes when Hurricane Florence hit the beach in September 2018.

The settlement history of Bogue Banks has some interesting twists. The island was first named for settler Josiah Bogue—he sold the land that eventually became Morehead City. Its history begins with the quiet livelihood of small fishing communities on the sound side of the island and roars through a second-home explosion after the 1971 opening of the west-end bridge from Cape Carteret. A bridge between Morehead City and Bogue Banks led to the creation of the playground of Atlantic Beach in the late 1920s. However, most of the remainder of the island, from Atlantic Beach

The Nitty, Gritty Beach Sand

Carteret County Shore Protection Officer Greg Rudolph maintains a database of shoreline erosion/replenishment for Bogue Banks. Here is a summation of the comings and goings of the beaches of Bogue from the 2017 "State of the Beach" report.

The report looks at an "18-year window" of data collected by shore surveys that extend from the dunes well beyond the surf zone.

Here's a quote:

> Also, 2017 marks the eighteenth anniversary of Hurricane Floyd and since 1999 Bogue Banks has gained roughly 8.75 million cy [cubic yard: a unit of volume 3 feet high, wide, and long] of sand, which again is mostly attributed to the many beach nourishment projects that have been constructed along the island beginning in 2001. A total of approximately 14.5 million cy of sand have been placed on Bogue Banks as a result of beach nourishment, meaning 5.8 million cy have since eroded off the beach (14.5 million cy placed on the beach minus 8.75 million cy remaining). If we average the volume loss (−5.75 million cy) across the entire 128,393 feet (24.3 miles) of Bogue Banks oceanfront, the island has lost sand at a rate of 2.5 cy/ft/yr since 1999 (an 18-year window). Our average volumetric change for the previous year (1999–2016) was −2.7 cy/ft/yr.

The good news for Bogue Banks is that there is more sand than after Hurricane Floyd and the beaches actually gained sand in 2016, dropping the average loss rate for the 18-year window.

The negative factors were not hurricanes but winter storms with unusually high waves.

west, belonged to two people, Alice Green Hoffman and Henry Fort. They and their respective heirs controlled the island up until the 1950s.

Alice Hoffman became the most colorful, notorious, and ironically beneficent owner of land here. Her domain, and she treated it as such, extended from Atlantic Beach to Salter Path. She constructed a large estate with elaborate gardens on the sound side of the island in what is now Pine

Knoll Shores. (The estate was razed long ago.) Her disagreements with local fishermen (she sued for trespass and lost) led to the legal establishment of Salter Path.

At her death, she willed the land to her niece, Mrs. Theodore Roosevelt Jr. The Roosevelt heirs sold most of the land, which was subsequently developed, but they dedicated 290 acres to the state for the Theodore Roosevelt State Natural Area. In other words, though Hoffman had sued to protect this property, she indirectly returned a portion of it to the people of North Carolina for their enjoyment.

Hoffman's next-door neighbor in an insular sort of way was Henry Fort, an entrepreneur from Pennsylvania who planned to build a tremendous resort on his property, which encompassed a great deal of the island west of Hoffman's estate. He needed a bridge to serve his development but was never able to get permission from the state for construction. His plans summarily died with the Great Depression.

The development of Atlantic Beach began with the economic boom following the Second World War. But even though the island was accessible by bridge, very few people owned cars. The concept of extended vacations seems to have grown both as an idea and reality with the steady climb of the postwar industrial economy. The few folks who could drive to the island did not travel much farther than Atlantic Beach or the points east of there. The only road to the west, continuing to Salter Path, was not paved, and not many travelers wanted to go to Salter Path anyway.

By the early 1950s, the demand for land was rising, but the island was essentially unavailable. This changed in the mid-1950s when the heirs to the Fort property sold the western half of the island and Alice Hoffman died, leaving her property to the Roosevelt family, who also began selling their lands. In effect, all of Bogue Banks west of Atlantic Beach was placed on the market at a time when the economy had cycled high.

Within 30 years it was a done deal, and access was becoming a problem because of the great numbers of people visiting each summer and because providing access to the beach was an afterthought. As one Emerald Isle town official commented, "A few simple things a long time ago would have made a difference. If we had extended the right-of-way of the north–south streets to the water, we would have had plenty of access."

Efforts to enhance beach access by the state and federal requirements attached to the use of federal money for beach nourishment have greatly improved the situation. There are multiple large access areas, and each community on the island provides additional neighborhood access.

Reaching Bogue Banks is not a problem. The two high-rise bridges—from Morehead City and Cape Carteret—loop NC 58 over the sound, along the spine of the island, and back to the mainland. It is a very leisurely loop—the speed limit on NC 58 is 45 miles per hour and closely enforced, particularly in Indian Beach, where it drops to 35 miles per hour.

On the rental changeover days in summer, the line of traffic crossing to Emerald Isle from Cape Carteret frequently backs up on the mainland. It is similar at the Morehead City Bridge. That's understandable and widely known, and beachgoers adjust arrival times to minimize the wait. Bogue Banks has superb beaches and a range of accommodations, and a lot of people want to vacation there.

Access

The new access ways at Pine Knoll Shores, marvelous boardwalks through the maritime forest, are outstanding walks in their own right.

Fort Macon State Park, the largest and one of the most popular access locations on the island, serves Beaufort Inlet and the beaches at the east end of the island.

Atlantic Beach maintains two regional access sites, the Les and Sally Moore Regional Access at New Bern Street and the new West Atlantic Boulevard Regional Access just west of the "circle."

One of the most widely used facility is at Salter Path, featuring 65 parking spaces on 22 acres with a bathhouse and dune crossover.

Emerald Isle Regional Access, west of 25th Street, is adjacent to the site of the Emerald Isle Fishing Pier. A plaque commemorates this island landmark's story.

As a public service, the Shore Protection Office maintains a website at www.protectthebeach.com that has an excellent sequence of Bogue Banks maps showing all of the public access areas. The link is easy to follow and the maps are outstanding.

Search Carteret Beach Access or enter
www.carteretcountync.gov/296/Beach-Access.

Search Crystal Coast or enter www.crystalcoastnc.org.

FORT MACON STATE PARK

This is the state's second-oldest park and the most visited annually because it includes nearly all the east end of Bogue Banks adjacent to Beaufort Inlet. Within its borders are 1.5 miles of beach; a total of 424 acres of beach, dunes, and maritime forest; and one carefully restored and maintained nineteenth-century coastal fortification, the namesake Fort Macon.

To take full measure of the experiences, be sure to attend one of the interpretive talks, especially if it includes a period weapon demonstration. The park staff can shake the 4.5-foot-thick walls of this five-sided fortification.

In the mid-nineteenth century the fort commanded the approach to Beaufort Inlet, dominating the east end of Bogue Banks. A brick road reinforced with stone wheel track installed to bear the weight of caissons and cannon carriages descends into the fort's interior from the heights of the earth ramparts. It crosses a moat, and inside the citadel the bricked facades of vaulted casemates, the underground barracks, rim a geometrical parade ground. Three staircases ascend to the top of the citadel. On a summer day, the interior bakes.

The most surprising view atop the covert way is a view of the entrance road. The fort engineers sited and constructed the fort so skillfully that the citadel isn't seen on the approach drive. The widened field of fire controlled by the location is evident from the gun emplacements.

The army built the fort between 1826 and 1834. While designed to secure the inlet militarily, the armaments were useless against erosion by the sea. During the 1840s a young West Point graduate by the name of Robert E. Lee designed and supervised the construction of the jetty, stabilizing the inlet, protecting the fort, and providing great recreation for today.

During the Civil War, Confederate troops quickly seized Fort Macon. On April 25, 1862, the Union took it back after an 11-hour siege. Following the war, the fort served as a penitentiary. The jail cells are under the outer ramparts.

In 1924 Congress permitted North Carolina to take possession of Fort Macon for use as the state's second state park. But the facility languished until the Civilian Conservation Corps restored it during the mid-1930s; it officially opened in 1936. While the fort is the centerpiece of the park, there are 389 acres in the entire preserve, encompassing the eastern end of Bogue Banks. There is a great deal of beautiful beach here.

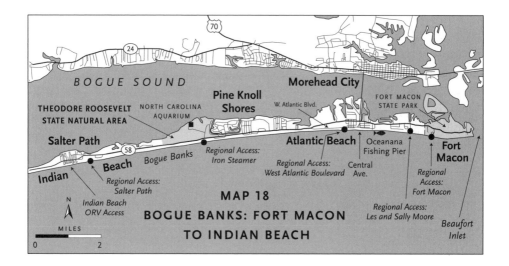

MAP 18

BOGUE BANKS: FORT MACON

TO INDIAN BEACH

Exhibits inside detail typical Civil War artillery, most of which was found on the grounds, and a furnished officer's quarters. There is a reconstructed barracks from World War II, when the fort garrisoned a coastal artillery defense troop. Touring the inside takes about an hour.

The Elliot Coues Nature Trail is a 3.2-mile round-trip trek through the salt marsh and maritime forest to the swim beach at the regional access. The trail can be accessed from either parking lot.

The Yarrows Loop Trail, a self-guided walk through a maritime shrub thicket, leads up to higher ground that is the beginning of a maritime forest. After leading you through this emerging forest with varying ecological niches, the trail reaches the high dune ridge and beach overlooking the inlet, then it returns to the parking lot at the fort. The stroll takes about 45 minutes.

The park's big draw is the beachfront on Beaufort Inlet and the regional beach access facility with lifeguards on duty in summer. Fishing is permitted in the park, and the inlet provides both choice beach and choice angling. Lee's jetty caps the east end, arresting erosion and creating some shallower, calmer waters The fort parking lot is close to the jetty, but a longer walk to the open ocean beach. Shackleford Banks of Cape Lookout National Seashore is across the inlet.

The park encompasses a U.S. Coast Guard station that is not closed to the public but offers no public services.

Access

There is a major regional access site with showers, bathrooms, and parking for 300 cars. Arrive early to secure a parking place. Lifeguards are on duty in June, July, and August.

In addition, there is a smaller parking area at the fort, but it's a good hike to the beach from this parking area.

Search Fort Macon Park or enter www.ncparks.gov
and use the search feature for a park link.

ATLANTIC BEACH

For decades the core of Atlantic Beach, the waterfront directly south of the Morehead City Bridge, served as the hub of coconut-oiled vacation energy along this arc of the coast. Right through the middle of last century, it was *the* spot on Bogue Banks, beckoning people seaside to mix, splash, and cavort in the grand tradition sparked in Morehead City much earlier. The center of action was "the circle"—a closed arc of roads that looped through and around amusements, eateries, and beach-themed commerce. A neat grid of small lots for vacation homes spanned east and west, creating a compact village that is humble and classic by the resort home standards of today.

The neighborhood of settled, modest cottages still thrives. But while time hasn't quite passed the circle by, it is a-changin'. The generations who built their summer soirees around this loop of youthful movement don't dance so much anymore. Atlantic Beach serves a different time and era today—the super kid-friendly Atlantic Beach Skate Park/Town Park a quarter mile west points to the shift. Moms, strollers, kids, and skateboards aggregate in lieu of teens cruising old haunts. The beach is still fabulous, access has improved, and the beach is wide and well maintained, but the circle seems to be biding time for a reinvention.

The residential streets to either side, built long ago and honoring the natural dune line, perch above the circle in many ways. There is a steadiness and settled quality about the houses that has been missing from the circle since the old-style pavilions and rides disappeared.

Expansion of the early village was accomplished under protest and perhaps pique. The original developer of Money Island, trying to avoid incorporation, intentionally skewed Tryon, Dobbs, and Caswell Streets so they

Sea Turtles' Sandy Crawl Home

May begins one of nature's most marvelous, mysterious homecomings on North Carolina's coast: the return of female sea turtles to nest. The mystery? How they find their way back to the beach of their birth after surviving in the open sea for 20 to 30 years to reach reproductive maturity.

The 326-mile coast with its gently sloping, sandy, unobstructed beaches has been a turtle nursery for eons. Up until recent decades, scientists only knew this certainty in the life cycle of pelagic turtles: they come ashore to nest. By tagging young and nesting adult turtles, the scientists have concluded that the female turtles return to the beach of their hatching.

Here's a general sequence of these events. Between May and October, the females come ashore on the nighttime rising tide. If undisturbed, they will crawl to the soft sand at the base of dune and, using their back flippers, excavate a nest; deposit their clutch of 80–120 eggs; cover the nest; and crawl back to the sea. A single female may nest as many as three times or more a season. The males? Well, they are like Charlie on the MTA—they never return.

Five different species—the leatherback, green, loggerhead, Kemp's ridley, and hawksbill—will visit North Carolina waters, but only the leatherback, green, and loggerhead turtles nest here. The loggerhead is far and away the most common.

The eggs incubate the sand between 50 and 60 days, and the average temperature of the sand determines the sex of the brood: if the sand is warmer than 87 degrees, the clutch will be all female; if it's less than 81 degrees, the clutch will be all male. Sand temperatures that vary between these extremes produce a mixed-sex brood.

Almost all of the eggs hatch within minutes of each other, and the hatchlings dig out nearly simultaneously, "boiling" out of the sand and rushing to the ocean. The sprint means avoiding ghost crabs, birds, and then large fish as they swim to seaweed rafts and the Sargasso Sea. The odds are not good: it is estimated that only 1 in 1,000 hatchlings survive their first year.

Nesting turtles and new hatchlings are guided by the difference in ambient light between the ocean and the beach. Activity on the beach and the lights of oceanfront homes can disorient both. Beach activity can repulse a turtle seeking to nest, and brightly lit oceanfront homes can confuse the emergent turtles, causing them to fatally head inland instead of to the sea.

The National Park Service monitors the beaches of both national sea shores daily during nesting season. (Cape Hatteras National Seashore reported 260 nests in 2017.) Nests are identified and marked off, and a countdown begins to the estimated hatch dates. Nesting can result in a beach being closed to ORV traffic.

A few days before hatching, park service biologists will put down a corridor that leads the hatchlings to the surf.

Similarly, most oceanfront communities have volunteers who patrol the beach during nesting season to identify nests and begin preparations for the hatchlings to emerge and start their journey to adulthood.

How to help sea turtles:

· Turn off outdoor lights during nesting season
· Direct floodlights down
· Use amber or red bulbs
· Close interior blinds at night
· Fill in all beach holes and flatten all sandcastles daily
· Walk quietly on the beach at night
· Do not approach a crawling turtle
· Honor all beach closures and driving restrictions

For additional information:

The North Carolina information site, www.seaturtle.org.

The original sea turtle conservancy, www.conserveturtles.org.

The Karen Beasley Sea Turtle Rescue and Rehabilitation
Center, www.seaturtlehospital.org.

To report a beached whale or other marine mammal contact the Cape Hatteras National Seashore Sea Turtle and Marine Mammal Stranding hotline at 252-216-6892.

would not align with the corresponding streets in Atlantic Beach. The result is that on the east side of the older village, not all the streets parallel to the ocean align. This reduces through traffic but can be confounding to newcomers.

The town grew in such a way that Atlantic Beach has the greatest number of hotel rooms on Bogue Banks and attracts people nearly year-round through convention and business gatherings. The hotels are interspersed with other land uses—multifamily and commercial sites generally are east and west of the original community.

This softens the beachfront appearance—there is great access in the circle—and keeps a cottage feel in the center. National hotels are to the west. The town has a lively condominium/apartment rental market, and smaller, family-owned motel businesses are on the east, toward Fort Macon. Newer, midrise oceanfront condominium properties set back from the road occupy much of the oceanfront on the way to Fort Macon.

Second-home construction has prospered since the 1960s, and the city and island have benefited from approaches that are more sensitive with regard to building at the beach. Many housing units have been added, but there is a great deal of open space because newer units are clustered. Some locations, such as the private property of the Dunes Club, visible from the Les and Sally Moore Regional Access Area, give you an idea of unaltered Bogue Banks.

Time and storms have been hard on fishing piers. In the 1990s there were three: the Triple-S, the Sportsman, and the Oceanana. Only the latter stands today. The other properties have become multifamily residential developments.

The state built the first bridge from Morehead City in 1928. Captain John Newsome Willis III, the first person to be born in the town of Atlantic Beach (his father was the first mayor), provides a detailed history of the community on the town website, www.atlanticbeach-nc.com. The history and period photos are terrific. Here is a brief recap.

Ironically, the bridge and the simultaneous opening of a complex of bath and dance pavilion spelled the economic end of two earlier beach-bathing pavilions farther east. Both had been served by ferry lines from Morehead City. These earlier developments, dating from the turn of the twentieth century, were for the patrons of the Atlantic Hotel in Morehead City. One was at Money Island Beach (a city street name) where the Sportsman's Pier once stood.

In 1922, during the time of segregation, Asbury Beach developed around the construction of another bathing pavilion and ballroom by a gentleman named Asbury just east of Henderson Boulevard where the Triple-S Pier stood.

A fire and the Depression took out the original development and bankrupted the owners, but in 1930 a new owner built two new bathhouses and dance hall called the Casino, and the beach was open for business. (The road alignment in the circle dates from this era—it never was a real circle.)

The final, formative chapter of Atlantic Beach came in this era when the land adjacent to the circle was subdivided for cottages. The street plan, from Durham Street in the west to Wilson Street in the east, is evident today.

As soon as that first bridge opened, Atlantic Beach became the "center" of dance and band music.

In the 1950s NC 58 opened the length of Bogue Banks and the community spread out. The building boom of the 1970s spilled north into Bogue Sound on either side of the Atlantic Beach Causeway. Developers dredged channels and filled marsh to create residential and commercial building sites. The five-lane causeway is a healthy clue to the mood and rhythm of the town: it screams a commercial welcome. You can rent a sailboard, charter a fishing trip, dine on fresh seafood, or buy a T-shirt. From the central intersection of NC 58, the town reaches east to Fort Macon State Park and west to its residential neighbor, Pine Knoll Shores.

Access

Atlantic Beach has multiple access locations. Here is how to find them:

Enter www.carteretcountync.gov/295/Shore-Protection.
The heading Beach Access leads to excellent PDF
maps showing access points for Bogue Banks.

Search NC Beach Access; click the NC DEQ Beach and
Waterfront Access Map link; at the bottom of the second
column, click "Go to Beach Access Locator."

For tourism:

Search Atlantic Beach NC or enter www.atlanticbeach-nc.com.

Search Crystal Coast or enter www.crystalcoastnc.org.
Under Communities find Atlantic Beach.

Cones, Coils, and Columns

It's a seashelling rite of passage to hear the sounds of the ocean in a whelk shell. What a mystery that a hand-sized item could contain the very sea! Whelks, conchs, tulips: each of them is an example of one of nature's most exquisite blind alleys known only to nimble hermit crabs and, of course, the creatures that made them.

The coiling class of Mollusca, known as gastropods or snails, is fascinating, exquisite, and outright amazing. Their names don't do justice to their artistry. In a fantastic diversity of variation on a successful concept, nature took a simple form, the cone, and applied a simple formula, the coil, and then gave it a decorative twist. The living quarters of snails are some of the finest houses you will ever find. The Greeks knew it—they transcribed the spiral of a snail to become the volute or curved decorative capital appearing on the Ionic column.

The Greeks noticed that the coil of the whelk enlarged in an elegant manner. It seems proportional; indeed, it is, as the French mathematical genius René Descartes deftly discovered. He analyzed the graceful curve of snail shells, naming the mathematical function that describes it the "equiangular spiral." Each successive coil of a snail's shell enlarges from the previous coil by a fixed proportion. A baby channel whelk is mathematically identical to a mature channel whelk: the proportions of the shells are the same—one is merely smaller than the other.

If you have ever opened the egg case of a whelk—the canvas-colored strings of rounded "pocketbooks" looking something like vertebrae—and found juvenile snails inside, then you have observed this mathematical precision. The spiral growth of the shell is logarithmic and numerically graphical (as if the snails cut from a digitized pattern).

To this self-regulating, enlarging shape, nature added curious ornaments, such as the knobs of the whelk, the flared lip of the queen conch, or the irregular mouth of the helmet shell—embellishments on the theme of cone and coil. Color and pattern adorn the snail further, but the greatest variation comes from the experimentation with the basic formula—the twisting, tapered tube.

If you can imagine that a cone is stretched out before you (or try one with modeling clay) and that you are the molluscan artist, first coil the cone in one plane, flat on the table, like the fiddlehead of a fern. This is the shell of the nautilus, native to gift shops on the coast. Next, coil the cone to the left. This is a sinistral shell (like that of the left-handed lightning whelk). Reverse the coil, and you have a dextral shell. The "handedness" of a shell is determined by whichever hand—right or left—cups behind the mouth of the shell when the thumb points in the same direction as the top of the shell. This is important: you want to collect the correct snail for cooking left-handed whelk chowder.

If the cone is fat and curls in a cushion, it is the full, round coil familiar as the moon shell. Stretch the coil out for a great length in few revolutions, and it makes the great horse conch. Coil the cone tightly in a narrow taper, and it is the sharp pointed shape of an auger.

Each snail species has its own rules for coiling and color pattern. Among individuals of a given species, color and patterning vary sufficiently to strike a note of individuality, but the coiled shape remains constant and telltale, as does the basic patterning of coloration.

PINE KNOLL SHORES

Pine Knoll Shores begins at milepost 4 (Atlantic Beach Causeway is approximately milepost 2) and is developed on some of the highest land and in the most mature maritime forests on Bogue Banks. Except for a town sign, the entry into the community from the east is imperceptible. There are several hotels and motels along the oceanfront side of NC 58. These are about the only commercial buildings within the city limits (there's also at least one bank). This is key to the character of Pine Knoll Shores: it is an incorporated residential island on an island. From its incorporation in 1973, it has exerted strong controls over land use through zoning and, until early this century, through restricting beach access to members of local homeowners' associations and their guests. The city limit signs are the only key that you are not among several subdivisions of Atlantic Beach.

Pine Knoll Shores occupies some gorgeous forest, but it is difficult to appreciate the richness because the native evergreen vegetation of yaupon trees, live oaks, and wax myrtle shrubs bounding NC 58 is densely thick. The highway seems to bore through the forest, revealing a wild, natural beauty. Intermittently, driveways wander into the forest, offering a glimpse of the roll in the land and the deep shade of the interior woods. Rarely can you see a home.

North of the highway, the tree mix of the forest becomes more diverse. Pine trees, youthful hardwoods, and understory trees appear—full canopy and subcanopy layers. The town hall, off Pine Knoll Boulevard, is in a beautiful maritime woods. The remarkable mature woods of the Theodore Roosevelt State Natural Area sprawl nearly next door to the town hall. North Carolina has sited the Pine Knoll Shores Aquarium in these woods. Hiking trails thread through the forest from the aquarium.

Pine Knoll Shores suffered increased chronic beach erosion at the turn of the century in addition to catastrophic beach loss from severe storms. This forced the town to join public efforts to pump sand and replenish their beaches after an unsuccessful private effort failed. As a condition for using public funds for beach nourishment, Pine Knoll Shores (and any other private association) must provide public beach access. This was a first for Pine Knoll Shores, and the access locations are quite nice, though parking is sometimes distant from the dune crossover.

Access

Pine Knoll Shores is tricky to spot; most parking is north of NC 58, so you have to cross the highway to reach the beach.

There is a regional access with 60 parking places and restrooms at approximately milepost 6.5.

> *Enter* www.carteretcountync.gov/295/Shore-Protection.
> The heading Beach Access leads to excellent PDF
> maps showing access points for Bogue Banks.
>
> *Search* NC Beach Access; click the NC DEQ Beach and
> Waterfront Access Map link; at the bottom of the second
> column, click "Go to Beach Access Locator."
>
> *Search* Pine Knoll Shores NC or enter www.townofpks.com.
>
> *Search* Crystal Coast or enter www.crystalcoastnc.org.
> Under Communities, find Atlantic Beach.

IRON STEAMER PIER ACCESS AREA

For nearly six decades the Iron Steamer Pier jutted into the ocean at the western limits of Pine Knoll Shores. In 2006, after being rebuilt two years earlier, time ran out on this venerable institution. Today part of the property is a 60-car public access site with a bathhouse. The name honors the wreck of the *M. V. Prevensy*, a side-wheel steamer and blockade-runner that ran aground and wrecked here on June 9, 1864.

Enter www.carteretcountync.gov/295/Shore-Protection.
The heading Beach Access leads to excellent PDF
maps showing access points for Bogue Banks.

THEODORE ROOSEVELT STATE NATURAL AREA

The Theodore Roosevelt State Natural Area is the only location showcasing the full natural richness of undeveloped Bogue Banks. The Roosevelt descendants inherited the 265-acre preserve from its litigious former owner, Alice Green Hoffman. Her lawsuit against the owners of cows that destroyed one of her gardens led to the legal establishment of Salter Path. When Hoffman died, she willed the land to her niece, Mrs. Teddy Roosevelt Jr. The family, in turn, dedicated it to the state as a natural area in memory of President Theodore Roosevelt.

The preserve is a coastal ecological laboratory under the administration of the staff of Fort Macon. As with all state natural areas, part of the management scheme is to leave it alone; the public has only limited access.

The North Carolina Aquarium at Pine Knoll Shores is within its borders, sited at the edge of a small tidal creek and marsh; the woods of the preserve wall it off from the rest of the island. The natural area preserves many of the ecological niches found on an undeveloped barrier island, including maritime forest, freshwater bogs, salt marsh, and the sound. Trails lead through the full range of island vegetation, home to rare inhabitants such as ospreys and alligators.

A self-guided nature trail starts at the northeast corner of the parking lot, passes through the woods, and eventually reaches the marsh. It is a good introduction of the thick forested island habitat.

Insect repellent or long-sleeved shirts and long pants are recommended.

Access

The gate at the entrance of Roosevelt Drive off of Pine Knoll Boulevard usually opens by 8 AM and closes at 5 PM. Parking for the natural area is at the North Carolina Aquarium.

For additional reading from nongovernmental travel websites, search Theodore Roosevelt State Natural Area.

NORTH CAROLINA AQUARIUM, PINE KNOLL SHORES

The Pine Knoll Shores aquarium showcases — eventually — the unique ocean life that touches Carteret County. Visitors will see aquariums that portray the complexities, but only after going to the mountains and following the long journey of native streams as cascading waterfalls and winding rivers make their way to the coast. The exhibits in this aquarium start high and finish deep. A weave through the exhibits is a refresher course in the state's ecological niches, the plants and the creatures to be found from the mountains to the sea.

The aquarium journey brings visitors eye to eye with mountain trout and hellbenders, the giant salamander native to the mountains. In the Piedmont section are screech owls and river otters, and as the exhibits level out to the coastal plain you will find a cypress swamp, pond turtles, and alligators.

In the Tidal Waters Gallery children can touch rays, watch seahorses, and learn about the journey of the loggerhead and other great sea turtles that sometimes nest on Bogue Banks.

Offshore Carteret County is a great mixing bowl of the cold currents that originate near Labrador and the warmer Gulf Stream that flows north from the Caribbean. The currents and everything that rides them mix around Cape Lookout. This creates a remarkable diversity of fishes, crustaceans, and other sea life.

This mix of sea creatures is featured in two magnificent displays. The first is the *Queen Anne's Revenge*, Blackbeard's flagship offshore from Beaufort Inlet. The second is a huge 306,000-gallon ocean tank featuring a partial replica of a 1942 German U-boat sunk offshore during World War II. The stars of the show are the sharks, turtles, and schools of fish typical of the Carteret County coast.

The aquarium conducts multiple outings and summer school pro-

How to Behave on a Pier

Maybe this should be "How *Not* to Behave on a Pier." The first thing to understand is that pier anglers are territorial. They don't just fish from a pier, they stake a claim on a spot; first come, first served.

Several years ago, a grizzled, red-eyed, foul-weather-loving, mackerel-slaying veteran of the fabled Kure Beach Fishing Pier groused about how pier fishing was going all to hell. To paraphrase his colorful words, nobody knows how to fish well with others. He got no respect (perhaps another matter) and less room to land a fish—a real problem. If the fishing gods smiled and he hooked a real "rod bender," other anglers rushed to his place on the pier to fish in the same place. (Fish travel in schools, don't they?) He didn't need neighbors, he needed company, and he needed real estate to land the fish. It was a Homer Simpson moment when the lines got tangled.

It is funny in retrospect, but only because it tramples over all the tenets of pier behavior. (Think of a stranger spreading a blanket between you and the water when it's open beach as far as you can see. *Grrrr.*) Such actions are a sharp elbow to sociability in a sport well known for its solitary and contemplative waiting luckily punctuated with bursts of activity. On a pier, a linear, two-sided world, a little courtesy goes a long way.

The fraternity of pier anglers has informal rules of etiquette, perhaps better described as pier protocol. It is self-policing way of ordering the hoped-for bursts of adrenalin when fish begin biting.

Regulars know the truth about pier fishing: some days fish bite; some days they don't. It takes time either way, and it's not personal. The angler 30 feet away catching everything is probably not fishing any differently. Patience and persistence increase the possibility of success. In fact, fishing makes real the rewards of patience and the arbitrariness of luck—great life lessons. Meanwhile, keep these things in mind:

- Buy something—a soda, cheese crackers, bait—from the pier owner. It lubricates conversation and they might share a good tip.
- Some piers offer rental gear for first-timers who want to give it a splash without buying the gear.
- The first angler to arrive at a given length of pier has seniority. Ask this angler for permission before setting up shop immediately next to them.

- Unoccupied coolers, rods, and chairs stake claims for anglers who are temporarily absent.
- Allow plenty of elbow room when setting up.
- Don't intentionally cast across another angler's line.
- After *accidentally* casting across another line, apologize and then move around the afflicted to reel in.
- If it happens again, move or leave.
- If someone hooks a fish that really runs, reel in and give way to play the fish. Large fish will have to be walked to the beach.
- Got questions? Ask. If people don't want to talk, be quiet. A crowded pier is where some people go to be alone.
- Use headphones on portable radios or other music players, and keep cell phone calls to a minimum.
- Do not walk behind someone casting. Similarly, before casting, look behind.
- Don't litter.
- If you are a spectator, don't stand behind anglers casting.
- After a backlash or throwing the rig off, just turn red and get on with it. Everybody has done it, but they will laugh anyway.
- After landing a big fish, be gracious. It is like winning the lottery; everybody will share your joy and stifle their envy. If you crow about it, the pier gets chilly quick.

Search www.fishing-nc.com for a list of current piers.

grams for children, and its offerings increase with the swelling summer population.

Access

The turn for the aquarium is marked on NC 58 at the western end of Pine Knoll Shores. The aquarium is open 9 AM to 5 PM Monday through Saturday, 1 PM to 5 PM on Sunday. Admission charged.

Search NC Aquarium Pine or enter
www.ncaquariums.com and select Pine Knoll Shores.

A family takes in the beautiful marine life at the North Carolina Aquarium at Pine Knoll Shores. (Photo by Chip Henderson, courtesy of VisitNC.com)

INDIAN BEACH (EAST)

The eastern portion of Indian Beach is adjacent to Pine Knoll Shores. Unincorporated Salter Path is bookended by Indian Beach and separates the community into two segments. The remainder is on the west side of Salter Path.

Here, just west of Pine Knoll Shores, Bogue Banks begins to narrow, imperceptibly because of the dense vegetation along the road. As you drive west from Pine Knoll Shores, the first section of Indian Beach is just under a mile in length. Suddenly you are in Salter Path. There are no public access facilities in this portion of the community.

Search Indian Beach or enter www.indianbeach.org.

SALTER PATH

As you drive west on Salter Path Road from Indian Beach, a small sign greets you: "Welcome to Salter Path." Beneath it is another that reads, "The Oldest Community on Bogue Banks Circa 1890." Across the street is Hoffman Beach Road, a hint at the historical entanglement that resulted in this wonderfully steady community of very independent fishing families and local small businesses.

Carteret County

The laissez-faire land use along this curving length of NC 58 and a fabulous regional beach access facility introduces Salter Path.

Salter Path never joined the spit-and-polish builder boom that crushed the island after the 1971 opening of the high-rise bridge from Cape Carteret. That's because these folks were here and well settled. This is and always has been a fisherman's village, populated by folks who in many respects sail against the tide of change around them. Catching and selling seafood is the prime livelihood—the village shouts it from nearly every roadside sign. The good news is that the fish for sale in Salter Path—or by Salter Pathers at roadside stands elsewhere—is as fresh as can be bought.

The settling of Salter Path rivals that of any coastal community. In 1880 Riley Salter just wanted to fish and be left alone when he set up a household on Bogue Banks. He certainly didn't intend to start a movement. Salter and his neighbors had sailed their goods, their dismantled homes, and their families to this yaupon- and live oak–sheltered cove. They moved onto the island and stayed busy fishing and living, even though they didn't have a deed or permission from the landowners.

Their pace of life always picked up in the fall, when great schools of mullet migrated close to the beach. The villagers mobilized, set nets, and hauled in fabulous catches. The women of the village cleaned and gutted the fish, salting the catch in great barrels that they would leave on the beach until they could transport them to the sound side of the island. The path they wore through the island to the sound went by Riley Salter's house, hence it was called Salter Path.

Many of the families who moved here at the dawn of the previous century had been dislocated elsewhere by hurricanes or shifting sand dunes. They set themselves apart by illegally building homes on the property of Bostonian John A. Royall. They were squatters. The land passed from Royall to Alice Green Hoffman, who built an estate in present-day Pine Knoll Shores. Hoffman sued the residents of Salter Path in 1923 because their cows wandered onto her estate and destroyed a garden.

Well, the cows indeed came home: the court settlement, known locally as "the Judgment," decreed that the residents of Salter Path could remain, but their cows could not graze on the Hoffman estate. The village was restricted to the 81 acres the squatters occupied at the time, and direct ownership of the beachfront was granted not to any single person but to the village to use collectively, since they fished it that way. The ruling further maintained that only the current residents and their descendants could occupy the property. It did not, however, give them title.

In 1973 the residents of Salter Path withdrew from the petition by citizens to incorporate as Indian Beach. The 81-acre plot was removed from the petition, and Indian Beach incorporated on either side of Salter Path.

The villagers lived in a legal nether world until 1979, when Carteret County conducted a tax assessment. The court again stepped in and sorted through the entangled ownership web, which included the residents of Salter Path and the heirs of President Theodore Roosevelt, who had inherited the land from Alice Hoffman. The upshot was that Salter Pathers could now hold title to their property—and be taxed for it—which, believe it or not, was something new. Salter Path, which had been on the map for so long, was now on the books as well. So far the residents have shown no desire to incorporate.

Access

Salter Path has a 22-acre access area that is possibly one of the most beautiful access areas in the state. Clearly marked from the highway, the parking area is fronted by a picket fence and shaded by huge live oak trees. The access area includes 75 parking spaces, restrooms, a bathhouse, a deck, and a dune crossover walkway. The walkway to the beach is simply wonderful.

Not surprisingly, the area stays full from dawn to dusk during the summer season, since it carries the burden of access demands for the central part of Bogue Banks, so arrive early.

Enter www.carteretcountync.gov/295/Shore-Protection
and select beach access.

Enter www.crystalcoastnc.org and select communities.

For information, contact Crystal Coast Tourism Authority, 3409
Arendell Street, Morehead City, NC 28557, 800-SUNNYNC;
www.nccoastalmanagement.net/Access/sites.htm.

INDIAN BEACH

The largest portion of Indian Beach is west of Salter Path. The town hall is on the north side of NC 58, a small building on at the edge of Paradise

Bay. When the finger canals of Paradise Bay were excavated, the contractor uncovered a Native American encampment. This became the community's namesake.

Indian Beach most likely has the highest density of trailers and camp-sites on the island. There is a small cluster of businesses tuned to serving year-round needs rather than summer traffic. The most noticeable development is a beautifully crafted and large oceanfront retreat named Summer Winds. It dwarfs the Ocean Front Trailer Court, its immediate neighbor.

Heading west past Summer Winds, the island landscape changes from the wooded acreage of the Ocean Club Condos. The tree line recedes, then disappears as the island narrows. The road passes through the grassed dune fields of the pinched island. The Indian Shores trailer development marks the site of the Indian Beach Fishing Pier removed by storms in the late 1990s. Green signs just farther on note the Emerald Isle city limits.

Access

Indian Beach has the only off-road-vehicle access location in the middle of the island, with limited parking as well. The access ramp is at the end of SR 1192, the only paved road heading south. You must have a permit from the town before taking your vehicle on the beach, and you'd best have a four-wheel-drive.

Enter www.carteretcountync.gov/295/Shore-Protection
and select Beach Access.

Search Indian Beach or enter www.indianbeach.org.

Search Crystal Coast NC or enter www.crystalcoastnc.org.

EMERALD ISLE

The western end of Bogue Banks—12 miles of beach and expansive maritime forest—is the town of Emerald Isle. In 2018 the *USA Today* Reader's Choice Awards selected Emerald Isle as the Best North Carolina Beach. Even setting aside this popular sentiment, this community has a lot going for it—exquisite, carefully maintained and patrolled beach, expansive maritime forests, a network of bike trails, and a smorgasbord of homes, cottages, and resort communities available for vacation rentals. The drive from Piedmont

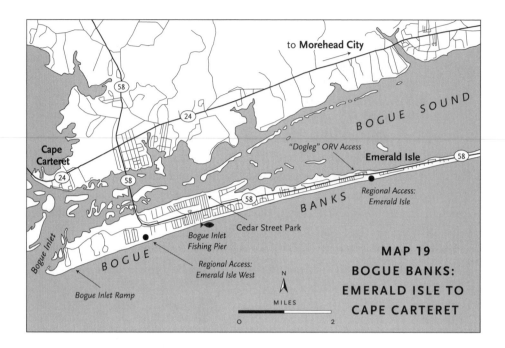

to **Morehead City**

BOGUE SOUND

Cape Carteret

"Dogleg" ORV Access

Emerald Isle

Regional Access: Emerald Isle

BANKS

Cedar Street Park

Bogue Inlet Fishing Pier

Regional Access: Emerald Isle West

BOGUE

Bogue Inlet

Bogue Inlet Ramp

N

MILES

0   2

MAP 19

BOGUE BANKS:

EMERALD ISLE TO

CAPE CARTERET

population centers is easy: 2.5 hours from Raleigh. It is an easy and easily doable destination for a week at the beach, but the community's attributes, relative proximity, and popularity can create some traffic aggravation.

While 3,700 people live here year-round, 50,000 crowd the beach in summer. Real estate/beach tourism drives the economy and the tax base. Emerald Isle, an aggregation of second-home neighborhoods, is a vacation beach community where vacationers rent homes by the week.

A little planning—arriving before 3 PM on summer Fridays and Saturdays—can minimize the bridge crossover crush. Traffic queues for a half mile on the mainland waiting for the traffic light at Cape Carteret. No worries, really, because slow-crawling the bridge provides time to study the exquisite marshes of Bogue Sound. Use the time to count the egrets and herons.

Emerald Isle meets expectation with a pleasant, low-key island attitude. It is neutral as a town; it doesn't grab you, grab at you, or push you away. Activity and entertainment opportunities are salted throughout the community; there are amusements, but no amusement park center. Waterslide, miniature golf, yes; these activities are vacation add-ons, not necessities. There is a commercial aggregation around the intersection of NC 58 and Bogue Inlet Drive, the road that leads to the Bogue Inlet Fishing Pier. Emerald Isle is vacation homes marching out of the forest across the back dunes and toward the beach.

The town serves as an everyone-entertain-themselves backdrop to the beach. People play in the ocean—all day. They bring wagons full of chairs, sand buckets, coolers, umbrellas, and other beach stuff, set up camp above the high-tide line, and hang out. They take "field trips" to Cape Lookout, Beaufort, and Fort Macon. The big draw is the high quality of the beach for small children (which is generally true for all of Bogue Banks).

Beginning at the Indian Beach limits, the eastern end of town includes 3 miles of the narrowest part of Bogue Banks. The first paved road after the town sign is First Street, and the streets number consecutively through 19th Street. The houses here are perched in a dune field. One block south, Ocean Drive runs parallel to NC 58 in the trough between houses on the parallel peaks of the dune field, a passage that ends at the wooded section of the island.

The road moves out of the open-sky dune fields to a forested mid-rib, several blocks farther from the beach. Occasionally, glimpses of ocean blink as a bright flash at the end of one of the wooded side streets.

NC 58 passes a shopping center and makes a slow arc south to cross the bridge leading to Cape Carteret. There are nearly 2 miles of island west of that curve. Turning west on Coast Guard Road, at milepost 21, an easy drive—often with bicyclists and runners—passes through a towering pine forest marked by salt-wind damage, the most stable part of the island. This is filled with newer subdivisions and houses that are distinctly upscale. The road leaves the tall woods and eases back into the dunes. This open western end of the community is filled with summer second homes. There is a ramp providing pedestrian access to the island's expansive sandbar and west end. (Sadly, parking is limited.)

Emerald Isle incorporated in 1957, and a small commercial interlude along NC 58 at Bogue Inlet Drive has seniority and still seems to be the figurative center of the community. Turn east on Bogue Inlet Drive to go to the Bogue Inlet Pier and several small motels. A turn west leads to the sound.

Stores and services are few, modest, and practical—places such as groceries, hardware stores, and gas stations. Newer shopping areas have been added 1 mile west of Bogue Inlet Drive, but "beach boutique" doesn't thrive in Emerald Isle. Given the size, age, and tourism base, the reduced commercialism sets it apart from the rest of the island.

The community tends to remain the same. Changes are few, and that sort of predictability is a solid trait for a vacation community. It is stable and beautiful-beach ordinary, with more than enough to help unplug the Wi-Fi generation.

Ironically, while it is the first place you come to from the western bridge, it does not easily accommodate day travelers or overnight guests. Motel/hotel space is limited, and adequate parking for beach access is confined to larger regional access sites spread throughout the town.

Access

Before renting a non-oceanfront home in Emerald Isle, ask the real estate company or owner the exact location of the nearest access. Plan to walk to the access area from your rental; parking at access locations is limited.

Emerald Isle has a tremendous number of pedestrian access locations but a horrible parking shortfall. Access is constantly improving, but a wagon to haul beach gear is a good idea for second- or third-row homes without clear neighborhood access.

You must obtain a permit from the town to drive on the beach, and driving on the beach is not permitted between Memorial Day and Labor Day.

Enter www.carteretcountync.gov/295/Shore-Protection
and select Beach Access.

Search Emerald Isle NC or enter www.emeraldisle-nc.org.

Search Crystal Coast NC or enter www.crystalcoastnc.org.

CAPE CARTERET TO CEDAR POINT

NC 24 intersects with NC 58 at Cape Carteret, a commercial center for many Bogue Banks visitors and residents. Morehead City lies to the east, an easy drive that is much less tedious than driving Bogue Banks in summer. This road is named the Freedom Way, in honor of the Camp Lejeune marines who served in operation Desert Storm.

West (and south) on NC 24 leads to Swansboro through the hamlet known as Cedar Point. A sign claims that Cedar Point was established in the early 1700s, but there is not much visible from the roadway that evokes that era.

Hook, Line, and Rulebook

North Carolina requires all anglers 16 years of age and older to have a North Carolina Coastal Recreational Fishing License to fish in the oceans and sounds.

- The license is required for ANY type of recreational fishing activity: fishing, crabbing, clamming, or collecting oysters.
- The license covers personal use only; the catch may not be sold.
- The fee is $15 per year; for $5 one can purchase a 10-day license instead.
- The license may not be transferred or assigned.
- Children under 16 and in school do not need a license.
- Lifetime licenses are available. The fees are:
    Residents and nonresidents to age 1: $100.
    Residents and nonresidents age 1 through 11: $150.
    Residents age 12 through 64: $250 ($500 for nonresidents).
    Residents age 65 and older: $15 ($500 for nonresidents).
- Anglers using this license will be held to the state's Recreational Size and Possession Limits governing the legal numbers and sizes of any catch. **Note: these limits change frequently.**
- The license covers fishing in Coastal Fishing Waters, which includes the sounds, the coastal rivers, and their tributaries out to 3 miles. Recreational anglers who catch fish in the Exclusive Economic Zone (3–200 miles offshore) will be required to possess this license to land fish in state waters.
- This license is required in addition to the Wildlife Resources Commission Lifetime Fishing License that an individual might already have.

Three different agencies govern fishing on North Carolina's coast: the North Carolina Wildlife Resources Commission governs inland creeks, bays, and rivers; the Division of Marine Fisheries governs coastal creeks, bays, rivers, sounds, and the ocean out to 3 miles; both of these agencies govern joint creeks, bays, and rivers; and, finally, the National Marine Fisheries Service governs ocean fishing beyond the 3-mile limit.

People over 16 and going fishing in a boat—or riding in a boat with a fishing rod—should buy the license. In areas jointly administered by the

Wildlife Resources Commission, called Joint Waters, both licenses will be required.

Although the entrance to restricted waters will be posted, it is prudent to know the intended location and the intended gamefish before leaving the dock. Check with local marinas or tackle shops for any restrictions that might affect the outing.

Size, limit, and closed water restrictions will change frequently. It is the angler's responsibility to abide by these regulations. Break the rules and get caught, and the price can be steep in dollars and/or forfeited equipment.

CRABS The new license is required for crabbing or "chicken-necking" for crabs off of a dock or pier. Crabs must meet a 5-inch minimum (tip-to-tip across the shell). You may catch 50 a day and may not exceed 100 crabs per vessel per day.

OYSTERS The new license is required. The oyster season is usually in the fall. Because of pollution-decimated populations, some waters may be closed. It is advised that you check with the North Carolina Division of Marine Fisheries to determine the areas in which oyster harvesting is permitted.

Oysters must be a minimum of 3 inches in length, and the limit is one bushel a day, not to exceed two bushels per vessel per day.

CLAMS The new license is required. Clam season is open year-round. The limit is 100 per day per person or 200 per day per vessel without a license. The clams must have a minimum thickness of 1 inch.

SHRIMP Cast-net only. The license is required. Cast-netting is permitted in closed or open shrimping waters. In closed shrimping waters, the limit is 4 quarts per person per day with heads on, or 2.5 quarts with heads off. The limit in open shrimping waters is 48 and 30 quarts, respectively.

FISH Fishing limits are based on the species. Three popular game fish—striped bass, red drum, and southern flounder—could be expensive catches if you exceed the regulations. These are closely regulated because of declining numbers.

Striped bass is zealously regulated, with different seasons in different waters and different limits in each. Check with Marine Fisheries before you go.

Season: October through April, statewide. Albemarle Sound Management Area: contact Division of Marine Fisheries for seasons, areas, or other limits. Atlantic Ocean year-round: 1 per person per day at 28 inches total length. Other Coastal Fishing Waters: 2 per person per day at 18 inches total length, EXCEPT unlawful to possess between 22 and 27 inches total length in Joint Fishing Waters.

Red drum migrate through the surf zone in fall and spring. Limit 1 per day 18–27 inches total length. The maximum size is 27 inches. In addition, you cannot gig, spear, or gaff red drum.

Both red drum and striped bass are illegal to possess beyond the 3-mile limit (Exclusive Economic Zone, 3–200 miles) regardless of where they are caught. Do not transport either of these fish into these waters. If it's caught in federal waters, release it.

North Carolina is the southernmost range for summer flounder and the northernmost range for southern flounder, so it has to manage both. Summer flounder, a popular fish for recreational fishing that is typically caught in the ocean, has been overfished in recent years, and recovery is dependent on adhering to limits. The best way to be safe is to return any flounder caught in the ocean that is less than 14 inches in length. You may keep 4 fish per day that are larger than 15 inches total length.

Bluefish have no minimum length restriction. You can take 15 fish per day, but no more no more than 5 longer than 24 inches per day.

It's a good idea to be able to identify fish. Any doubts about the legality or the identity of a caught fish should prompt a quick inquiry or a release of the fish.

Piers, tackle shops, and marinas can offer advice on any restrictions, but knowing the regulations is the only way to be certain.

There is a mobile app that helps with fish identification and regulations details: Search NC Fish Rules or enter fishrulesapp.com.

Search NC Marine Fisheries or enter portal.ncdenr.org/web/mf.

For license information, call 800-682-2632 (NC only).

During the summer, produce stands along this highway do a bustling business.

A road widening claimed some handsome old red cedar trees. These windswept, sculptured evergreens stamped the name Cedar Point into memory.

The White Oak River separates Carteret and Onslow Counties.

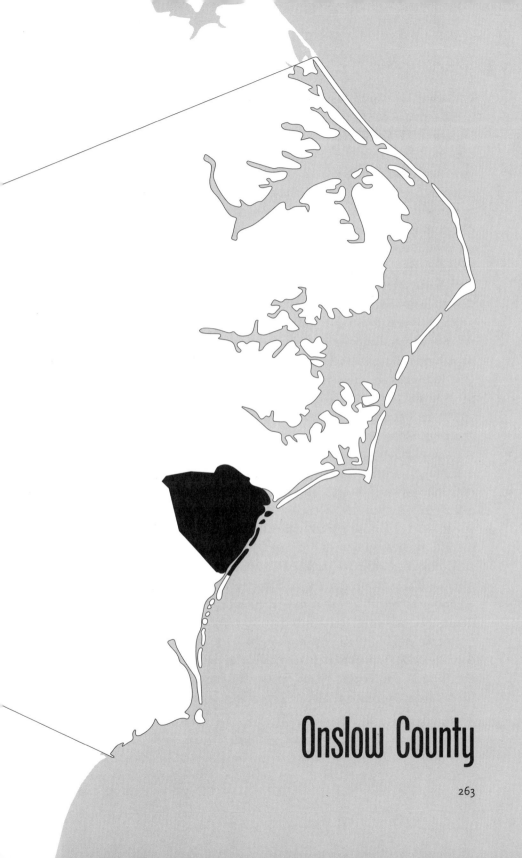

Onslow County

THE PUBLICLY ACCESSIBLE BEACHES of Onslow County, Bear Island of Hammocks Beach State Park and North Topsail Beach on Topsail Island, are two barrier islands that derived different benefits from the historically awkward access of Onslow County. Access, by means of roads, bridges, and interest, jump-started only in the middle decades of the last century. Since those years the two have evolved in distinctly contrasting ways: Bear Island is completely undeveloped except for minimal, environmentally friendly visitor accommodations, while North Topsail Beach has surged with single- and multifamily home development.

Coastal geography isolated Onslow County from the flow of state commerce in the nineteenth century. Present-day Jacksonville developed as a secondary port on the New River trading in naval stores. The low, sometimes wet, densely vegetated interiors of the county and neighboring Pender County inhibited commerce inland or north and south along the coast until much later than areas north and south.

The deepwater ports of Wilmington and Morehead City, connected by rail to inland centers, became magnets attracting visitors from inland. Onslow County remained mostly agricultural and sparsely populated. Even the dredging of the Intracoastal Waterway in the 1930s failed to stimulate growth on the islands. Jacksonville's population in the 1930s was around 700 people (it is over 70,000 today!).

While widely scattered building began on Topsail Island in the mid- to late 1930s, Onslow County's oceanfront acreage remained sleepily rural until the 1940s and World War II. The isolated, sequestered oceanfront was discovered then and quickly employed in the national war effort.

In short order, the military purchased Topsail Island to set up a secret rocket testing program code named Operation Bumblebee. Holly Ridge, southwest of Jacksonville, received Camp Davis: 45,000-plus acres, an artillery and antiaircraft training base with two paved runways, and nearly 20,000 personnel. The initial construction began on what would become Camp Lejeune.

At the end of the war, the military pretty much folded its tents (abandoned and sold Topsail Island), removed nearly all of the 3,000 buildings at Camp Davis, and vacated except for ever-burgeoning Camp Lejeune, now the headquarters of the II Marine Expeditionary Force. The base absorbed two of Onslow County's four barrier islands, Onslow Beach and Browns Island (aka Shacklefoot Island), for its purposes. The military remains the biggest player in the county; it is the primary reason that Jacksonville has soared in population and has the youngest average age of any North Carolina city.

Bear Island of Hammocks Beach State Park is one of the crown jewels of the entire state park system. Visible beyond Bogue Inlet from the Emerald Isle sand spit, it is accessible only by ferry and private boat. It is the one island in the entire state that, in the view of coastal scientists, most closely approximates an island still in an unaltered natural condition. Unlike many islands along the southern third of the coast, it is blessed with an ample sand supply and a favorable orientation to wind. Though subject to the typical "nibblings" of inlet migration and occasional smackdowns by storms, it historically featured tremendous primary and secondary dune fields, a wooded interior, and an enviously flat and gentle beach.

Topsail Island, south of New River Inlet, is 26 miles long, making it the longest barrier island in the south-central coast. One half of the island, the community of North Topsail Beach, is in Onslow County; the remainder is in adjoining Pender County. North Topsail Beach and Surf City (Pender County) are neighbors, but the city limits of the latter encompass some Onslow County properties.

Topsail Island has always been more easily reached and in the last two decades has become a hot beach for home and condominium construction. In fact, in North Topsail Beach building has accelerated, a frenzy blissfully forgetful of 1996, when Topsail Island took a one-two hurricane punch in an eight-week period.

Bertha, an 85-mile-per-hour Category 1 storm that eroded a stressed dune line on July 12, 1996, was a harbinger for Hurricane Fran, which followed on September 6. A Category 3 behemoth, it made landfall in Brunswick County, but the powerful northeast quadrant crushed Topsail Island, temporarily severing it in two locations, removing the dunes and destroying 80 percent of the buildings. The island had been bypassed by severe storms since 1954, when Hurricane Hazel erased 210 of the 230 homes on the island.

The last storms were more than two decades ago—time enough to forget. There is no evident reluctance to build on the island today. North from Surf City on NC 210, nearly all the oceanfront lots have houses, many reflecting a newer influence of fashion and size. Building is responding to the prerequisites for an easy, gentle-beach lifestyle here. By all appearances,

North Topsail Beach has recaptured the island's somnolent charm. The southeastern-facing beach casts a bewitching spell. It is wide, with a flattened profile and typically gentle waves.

North of the NC 210 turn off-island to Sneads Ferry, single-family homes on the ocean begin to yield to large multifamily apartment/condominium developments. The northern end of North Topsail Beach is being undermined by the instability of New River Inlet. Erosion is severe, and multiple homes and a condominium development are sandbagged against the sea. In 2018 North Topsail Beach wrestled with the cost of a terminal groin to arrest erosion on the south headland.

Solving this chronic oceanfront erosion is complicated, because 6 miles of the north end of North Topsail are in a federal Coastal Barrier Resources Act or CoBRA zone. This designation makes those properties ineligible for federal flood insurance and beach nourishment.

Two fast-growing areas of the county are on the mainland around Sneads Ferry and south and west of Swansboro, around Queens Creek and approaching the Atlantic Intracoastal Waterway. Sneads Ferry began as a small mainland community south of Camp Lejeune and is now sprouting resorts and second homes, somewhat supplanting its traditional fishing and agricultural base. Boating access through the New River Inlet is a tremendous attraction.

The same is true around Queen's Creek: inexpensive forest and agricultural lands are being converted to homes, some of which have boating access to the open ocean over tidal waters and through Bogue Inlet. Similarly, Fulcher Landing and Swan Point, historic areas within Sneads Ferry, have taken on more bustle with the influx of newcomers.

For Your Bucket:

Take the walking tour of historic Swansboro
Kayak the marshes of Hammocks Beach State Park
Spend a day on Bear Island
Visit the point at North Topsail Beach
Beachcomb for shark's teeth

Access

Onslow County Parks and Recreation has four regional access sites in North Topsail Beach.

Onslow Beach Access Site Number 1 is slightly south of the Topsail Dunes development, on the north side of New River Inlet Road.

Access Site Number 2 is 4 miles south of the NC 210 bridge. There are concession areas, showers, restrooms, and parking for 250 cars.

Access Site Number 3 is farther north, at the end of the private road at the mouth of the New River north of the St. Regis Resort. Pay to park by phone. There is 4x4 access, but a permit is required and may be purchased on-site.

Onslow Beach Access Site Number 4 is approximately 1 mile north of NC 210 on New River Inlet Road. It has restrooms, showers, a concession area, and 100 parking spaces.

Search NC Beach Access; click the NC DEQ Beach and Waterfront Access Map link; at the bottom of the second column, click "Go to Beach Access Locator."

Search Onslow County Tourism or enter www.onlyinonslow.com.

Search North Topsail Beach or enter www.ntbnc.org.

SWANSBORO

Swansboro perches on the west bank of the White Oak River, the first community greeting southbound travelers entering Onslow County on the pulsing five-lane of NC 24 en route to Jacksonville, North Carolina. The small town of less than 2,000 people has a valuable asset that has contributed greatly to its longevity: elevation. Swansboro sits on a hill, and the high point is more than 30 feet above sea level, four blocks away from the White Oak River.

This helps to explain why Swansboro has a walking tour featuring many clapboard homes from the eighteenth and nineteenth centuries. Swansboro is a handsome, charming destination that is walkable and wonderful. The outside of the shops and restaurants is as delicious (in a different way) as what's inside.

The widening of NC 24 to five lanes around Swansboro squeezed the waterfront edges of this small community but it also made visiting easier. Swansboro embraced its increased tourism interest shrewdly, by highlighting its two finest assets—water and historical character.

It's easy to take to the water here, whether in a kayak or at a water-view

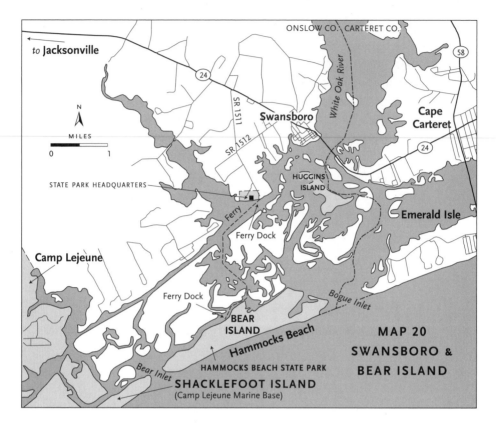

To Jacksonville

N

MILES

0   1

STATE PARK HEADQUARTERS

Camp Lejeune

Ferry Dock

BEAR
ISLAND

Bear Inlet

Hammocks Beach

HAMMOCKS BEACH STATE PARK

SHACKLEFOOT ISLAND
(Camp Lejeune Marine Base)

ONSLOW CO. CARTERET CO.

White Oak River

Swansboro

HUGGINS
ISLAND

Ferry

Ferry Dock

Bogue Inlet

Cape
Carteret

Emerald Isle

MAP 20
SWANSBORO &
BEAR ISLAND

or waterside table for dining. Swansboro began as a port for shipbuilding, sawmills, naval stores, and fishing. Those industries waned, but the foundational engagement with the water never faded. From its perch on the hill, Swansboro still looks to the sea, less for work and more for play.

Small clapboard houses march down the hill to the banks of the White Oak River, which opens to the sea through Bogue Inlet. The open water begins at the end of a wandering passage through channels threading salt marsh islands. The inlet has been open and navigable since the first settlers arrived in the mid-eighteenth century. The community grew around a local plantation known as the Wharf and thrived in its early years as a port. By the Revolutionary War, it was the only town on the coast between Beaufort and Wilmington.

The General Assembly passed articles of incorporation for the community in 1783 and formally named the town Swannsborough (shortened in 1877), honoring Samuel Swann, a former Speaker of the House from Onslow County. Shipping and shipbuilding dominated the economy following incorporation. In Bicentennial Park, on the north side of NC 24, a statue honors Captain Otway Burns, a daring privateer during the War of 1812 who was born nearby. Swansboro is where Burns in 1818 built the *Prometheus*, one of the first steam-powered vessels constructed in the state. Burns is better known in Beaufort, where he is buried in the historic cemetery, the Old Burying Ground; he is also honored in the naming of Otway in Carteret County and Burnsville in Yancey County.

Many of the older buildings in Swansboro are marching toward their third century renovated for reuse. The town itself unfolds with enduring, sensible architectural discoveries as you stroll outward from the center.

The Swansboro Visitor Center at 203 West Church Street has a printed walking tour of the town in addition to other information on shops, restaurants, and activities.

Search Swansboro NC or enter www.visitswansboro.org.

Search Historic Swansboro or enter www.swansborohistoricsite.org.

HAMMOCKS BEACH STATE PARK

Bear Island, the central feature of Hammocks Beach State Park, is one of North Carolina's outstanding environmental treasures. It is 2 miles off the Onslow County mainland, sequestered behind a bewildering salt marsh maze, and is only accessible by private boat or state park toll ferry from the mainland park headquarters. The ferry ride is a simple pleasure, although sometimes subject to routing changes and temporary closures brought about by shoaling in the ferry channel. The passage proceeds through a beautiful expanse of salt marsh, frequented by wading birds and an occasional sea turtle. The boat-only access does not hinder attendance.

In 1999, 200-acre Huggins Island in the mouth of the White Oak River became part of the park following its purchase from citizens who wanted it preserved. The island has an amazing range of habitats, including a rare freshwater seep and sizable live oak trees. Abandoned furrows from long-ago farming are still visible. The island will be maintained as a preserve, and ecological and archaeological inventories are scheduled in the near future. There is a kayak loop trail around the island.

Visitation to the park was close to 200,000 people in 2017, and the park manages the number intelligently. They restrict the total number of daily

The concession cabanas and picnic shelters on Bear Island, Hammocks Beach State Park, greet visitors to this essentially unaltered barrier island. Hurricane Florence carved the dune line after this photo was taken. (Author photo)

visitors to a number that they can safely transport back to the mainland by park closure. Early arrivals are more likely to get their place in the sun, with this reminder: bring everything you need, including shade.

Visitor facilities on Bear Island are minimal: the marsh-side ferry dock; a paved walkway to a behind-the-dunes cluster of restrooms, showers, indoor cookstoves for campers, and a small concession stand; a dune crossover walkway; and a swimming area with lifeguards in season.

This cluster of facilities is barely a footprint or intrusion. Bear Island is as wild and wonderful as the North Carolina coast has ever been and about as empty as a beach can be.

Bear Island is 3.5 miles long and 1 mile wide, with approximately 900 acres of varied habitat, including salt-tolerant trees and shrubs along the marsh side. The island had possibly the largest intact natural dune field along the North Carolina coast with some dunes approaching 25 feet tall. The primary dunes were all but obliterated by Hurricane Florence in September 2018, taking the impact of the storm surge and protecting the island's

The ferry ride to Bear Island from the Hammocks Beach State Park
mainland visitors center passes through this pristine salt marsh.
(Photo by Chip Henderson, courtesy of VisitNC.com)

interior and most park facilities. Returning visitors will recognize that their
beach of memory has been greatly altered. While there are no restrictions
on walking amid the dunes, not too many visitors linger there during summer, according to park rangers: the heat can be stifling, and the dunes block
any breeze. Biting insects can also be an issue away from the oceanfront.

The beach is very flat; at low tide, it is about 80 yards wide to the generally gentle surf. There are tidal flats and pools at the island ends, but the
only way to explore these areas is to walk from the central concession area.

As of 2016, master planning for an additional 289 acres adjoining the
mainland visitor center was completed to expand recreational and education opportunities. The following is part of the story to be told in the new
facilities.

William Sharpe, a New York neurosurgeon, owned Bear Island, its marshes, and considerable acreage on the mainland as a recreational hunting and fishing area in the early twentieth century. John Hurst, a black hunting guide who lived in Onslow County, originally directed Sharpe to the property and became his preferred guide. Sharpe wanted to will the property to Hurst and his wife, Gertrude, in 1949, but at her request he left Bear Island and marsh holdings to the North Carolina Black Schoolteachers' Association. In 1961, during the era of segregation, the association gave the land to the state for a park for black citizens, who had few beach vacation locations available to them.

Begin the exploration of the park at the handsome headquarters and interpretive center and ferry dock overlooking the extensive marsh and labyrinth of channels. Exhibits in the headquarters provide a glimpse of the type of environments that can be experienced in the park.

Summer is incredibly busy, but this is not to say that the island stays full. Still, mind the time and return to the ferry dock before the last departure, or prepare to pay a fine for camping without a permit—the next day.

Prior to Hurricane Florence, Bear Island had 14 designated family campsites on the island, 11 of which were behind the destroyed frontal dune and 3 that were accessible only by private boat or kayak. There are 3 group campsites. Expect the location and possibly the number of campsites to have changed. Campsites must be reserved in advance as far ahead as 11 months or same day subject to availability. Getting a campsite for weekdays is not nearly as competitive. The park is a favored nesting site for the loggerhead sea turtle. During the three-day full moon period of the nesting season in the months of June, July, and August, the park restricts camping.

All visitors should wear comfortable walking shoes and bring plenty of water, sunblock, insect repellant, sunglasses, and a hat. There is very little shade on the island and none at the campsites and the beach. Although camping is primitive, there is potable water on the island from mid-March to mid-November.

Search Hammocks Beach Park or enter www.ncparks.gov and use the search window or scroll down the "Go to Park" menu.

Reservations may be made through www.ncparks.gov.

Reservations phone number: 877-722-6762.

Best phone number for park personnel: 910-326-4881.

CAMP LEJEUNE

A city of more than 30,000 covering more than 153,000 acres (including 26,000 acres of water), Camp Lejeune is a major training base for the U.S. Marine Corps Expeditionary Force and the individual commands that comprise this force. It is here because of the islands offshore, which are necessary for an amphibious training ground. The base wraps the southern boundary of Jacksonville from east to west, and straddles the New River, including the north bank and the northern headland of New River Inlet. The base expands north and west from Sneads Ferry across US 17 and continues until it reaches NC 50.

Brown's Island and Onslow Beach, the barrier islands that comprise the middle third of Onslow County's oceanfront, were a prime reason that Camp Lejeune came to Onslow County in 1941. Several other reasons contributed: the stable New River Inlet to the Atlantic Ocean, access to the deep-water ports Morehead City and Wilmington, available land, and comparative isolation. Onslow County was rural, agricultural, and unpopulated.

The islands have been very important to amphibious landing training. Brown's Island is backed by extensive salt marsh along the Intracoastal Waterway. Brown's Inlet separates this island from 7.5-mile-long Onslow Beach, which is an island in that the Intracoastal Waterway separated it from the mainland. Since the 1970s Onslow Beach has been monitored as a Sea Turtle Sanctuary. Personnel from the Environmental Management Unit of Camp Lejeune monitor and protect sea turtle nests on Onslow Beach and are also responsible for stranded turtles.

The Beirut Memorial stands along the Jacksonville-Lejeune Boulevard (NC 24), paying tribute to the 268 marines and sailors from Camp Lejeune who died in the 1983 barracks bombing in Beirut, Lebanon. The granite memorial wall, set in a grove of oak trees and dogwoods, lists the names of the casualties of the bombing, along with those of three servicemen who died on Grenada. The memorial is always open.

NC 172, Sneads Ferry Road, which forms the eastern boundary of the base before routing through the southern portion to a bridge over the New River, is no longer open to the public.

Access

Visitors must check in the Lejeune Visitor Center (Building 812) near the main gate off of Highway 24 in Jacksonville. Call for information: 910-451-7735.

Search Camp Lejeune or enter www.lejeune.marines.mil.

SNEADS FERRY

Sneads Ferry is one of the oldest settlements in the county and is a single name applied to an aggregation of small crossroad neighborhoods between NC 210 and NC 172 and the New River. The older part of Sneads Ferry is a modest-sized village off of NC 172 with a cluster of small stores, a community center, fairgrounds, and a few churches well away from the New River.

The nearest marinas are southeast of Sneads Ferry. Nearby Fulcher Landing and Hatch Point on the New River are the principal commercial fishing docks in the area, with several seafood companies and a restaurant. Swan Point is a commercial and recreational boating center downriver from Fulcher Landing, taking advantage of the Intracoastal Waterway leading to the New River Inlet.

The first licensed ferry operator here, Edmund Ennett, started the passenger business in 1725. Robert W. Snead arrived in 1760, took over the ferry, and opened a tavern. His name stuck to the vicinity, even after the bridge over the New River was built in 1939 upriver from the ferry landing.

The town sprawls freely amid fields and coastal forests, and in the first decades of the twenty-first century has grown to become the second-largest census area in Onslow County, after Jacksonville. The growth has happened quickly as forest and field have converted to housing.

While Sneads Ferry has a significant shrimp fishery, home development and construction is becoming more important to the local economy. Golf course living and waterside homes have rapidly developed and expanded. The new locations have a Sneads Ferry address and are visible from NC 210 and the Intracoastal Waterway, but the original community is south and east, toward the New River Inlet. Every August the town hosts the Sneads Ferry Shrimp Festival on the grounds of the Sneads Ferry Community Center.

Search Sneads Ferry Shrimp or enter www.sneadsferryshrimpfestival.org.

TOPSAIL ISLAND

Topsail Island has the beach for Onslow and Pender Counties. It is a 26-mile-long island, slightly longer than Bogue Banks (nearly 25 miles) on this part of the coast. Because the island aligns northeast–southwest, the beach faces mostly south, so it's superb for sunning.

From Jacksonville, the direct route is NC 210, which sails over a high-rise crossing of the Intracoastal Waterway to North Topsail Beach, several miles south of the island's north end. From the south and west, most visitors arrive by way of combined NC 50/NC 210. These highways cross to Topsail Island into the heart of Surf City (see Pender County). The crossing over the Intracoastal Waterway is accommodated by a new fixed bridge that replaced one of the few remaining swing bridges left in North Carolina. (The new bridge opened well ahead of schedule in December 2018.)

Topsail Island is the midpoint of the westward crescentic arch that begins at Cape Lookout and ends with Cape Fear. This coastal segment is named Onslow Bay, and the deepest part of the arc is approximately Topsail Beach. There is plenty of recreational water here, and also plenty of crabs, shrimp, and fish, bringing folks who want to catch them. Boating accesses— marinas and ramps—cluster at the ends of the island, closer to the inlets. The configuration of New River Inlet and its marshlands makes for a lengthy and indirect access by means of the Intracoastal Waterway.

Topsail Island stretches through two counties—Onslow and Pender— and three incorporated communities: North Topsail Beach, in Onslow County; Surf City, in Onslow and Pender Counties; and Topsail Beach, in Pender County. The multijurisdiction confusion sometimes comes up during vacationers' calls for emergency services.

North Topsail Beach is at the northeast end of the island, Surf City is in the middle, and Topsail Beach is at the southwest end. Surf City is the largest community, with about 2,500 citizens. The increased building of recent years has filled in the oceanfront for nearly the length of the island, but its narrowness in places and the size of lots contributes to a roomy feeling. In season, slow traffic on the lengthy two-lane road serving Topsail can make the island seem much more crowded than it is.

Geologically, Topsail Island is nearly welded to the mainland; the sound waters to the north are narrow and marshy. (In fact, north of the New River, only the channel of the Intracoastal Waterway maintains Onslow Beach as

The beaches of Topsail Island are one location where visitors can see the release of sea turtles rehabilitated at the Karen Beasley Sea Turtle Rescue and Rehabilitation Center in Surf City. (Courtesy of VisitNC.com)

an island.) The marsh indicates that the sound is beginning to silt in, and peat deposits on the beach reveal that the island has indeed migrated inland over ancient sounds.

The island once had a single natural dune line, not a dune field, which stretched most of the length of the island. Severely damaged by the 1996 hurricanes and subsequent storms, it is recovering, but Hurricane Florence in 2018 created an abrupt escarpment rising from the back of the beach and drastically cut the dune line. Before Florence struck, the dune line of North Topsail Beach north of the NC 210 bridge grew beach grass on the crest and inland side, but the face was steep and bare down to dry sand above the normal tide line. Florence whacked these dunes, and forward of the dune line, the foreshore was planed flatter. It will likely restore to its generally wide, flat profile that has gentle wave action. This makes it a good location to find sand dollars and other fragile shells intact. The island is also a shelling hot spot for the more durable ancient shark's teeth.

Loggerhead turtles frequently lumber ashore on Topsail. The popular work of the Karen Beasley Sea Turtle Rescue and Rehabilitation Center, which began at Topsail Beach, has done much to educate residents and visitors about how to enjoy the beach and share it with these nocturnal nesters. At the turn of the century, as many as 100 nests have been confirmed on the island, but nest numbers vary widely (and inexplicably) over the course of a decade or more.

These seagoing reptiles come ashore to dig nests at the high tide between April and May. The comparatively undeveloped beach provides a darkened skyline for the turtles, a key they use to judge the safety of a potential nesting site. It is customary when renting on the oceanfront on Topsail Island to turn off all oceanside house lights at night as a simple act of assistance to the turtles. The nesting is monitored by local volunteers and is one of the celebrated natural summer rituals of the island. Eggs usually hatch in August.

The island has a great curiosity: abandoned reinforced concrete towers along the length of the island, beginning with the initial tower in Topsail Beach. The U.S. Navy built these monumental structures in the 1940s as observation platforms for Operation Bumblebee, the nation's nascent rocket-testing program headquartered at Topsail Beach. Seven towers still stand and probably will forever. The first tower at Topsail Beach is a private residence; another was once incorporated into the structure of the Ocean City Fishing Pier. The pier has been destroyed.

Because they were used to document the flight of early rockets, the towers were precisely located in relation to each other, and the precise longitude and latitude of their location was recorded. In fact, the U.S. Coast and Geodetic Survey used the first tower as a sea-level monitoring station.

In many comforting ways, visiting Topsail Island is a trip into earlier decades. This is an island of predominantly modest single-family cottages, and the focus of activity is the beach. Some resort-style accommodations and some much more substantial "cottages" have found their way to Topsail Island, particularly at North Topsail Beach. Larger, amenity-filled dwellings for the rental market are changing the face of some parts of the island, but not its tone. The big beach buildup of other places has lagged on Topsail Island, so it appeals to those who want to spend time at a low-key place by the sea.

Lines out, low tide, and time to spare. Topsail Island is a favorite location for surf fishing. (Photo by Chip Henderson, courtesy of VisitNC.com)

Access

Search NC Beach Access; click the NC DEQ Beach and Waterfront Access Map link; at the bottom of the second column, click "Go to Beach Access Locator."

Search Onslow County Tourism or enter www.onlyinonslow.com.

Search North Topsail Beach or enter www.ntbnc.org.

Search Surf City NC or enter www.surfcitync.gov.

Search Topsail Beach or enter www.topsailbeach.org.

Search Visit Pender or enter www.visitpender.com.

NORTH TOPSAIL BEACH

North Topsail Beach formed on January 1, 1990, and officially became the lengthiest community on Topsail Island, extending from the New River Inlet to the city limits of Surf City, a distance of slightly more than 12 miles. Building trends at the previous North Topsail Shores, the portion of the island north of the NC 210 bridge, spurred the incorporation. This portion of North Topsail Beach is one of the most threatened locations on the North Carolina coast.

To look back with some detail: on September 6, 1996, Hurricane Fran confirmed the worst fears of coastal geologists and wiped the sands of North Topsail Beach clean. It is difficult to describe the destruction, except to say it was practically total. The island was breached in two places, and 80 percent of the structures were damaged or destroyed. The dune line disappeared, and the ocean served notice to the large multifamily units and single-family homes within a half mile of New River Inlet. Waves sloshed underneath many of them. Emergency "temporary" sandbags were put in place, and that is the status quo as of summer 2017.

What is remarkable is the recovery of the community since Fran's visit. People rebuilt destroyed homes, or new buyers purchased the lots and built new homes. Conditions, banking, and weather have been favorable to construction, and many newcomers have joined the community, which has a population of fewer than 900. The recovery has proceeded even though 6 miles of the community, nearly 70 percent of the land, is included in a 2005 reauthorization of the 1982 CoBRA (Coastal Barrier Resources Act) zone, making these properties ineligible for federal flood insurance or beach nourishment funds. (North Topsail Beach is working with its congressional delegation to have the decision revisited based on town data not previously considered.)

Most of the large building development along New River Inlet Road north of the NC 210 Bridge had been approved prior to the community's incorporation. This is a community of residential and rental properties. There is no commercial center; most folks drive north to the growing commercial center at the intersection of NC 172 and NC 210 (nicknamed "Four Corners") to do their shopping.

The beach here is certainly appealing, with a beguilingly flat profile: the waves tend to be low. North Topsail Beach has some of the cleanest, least

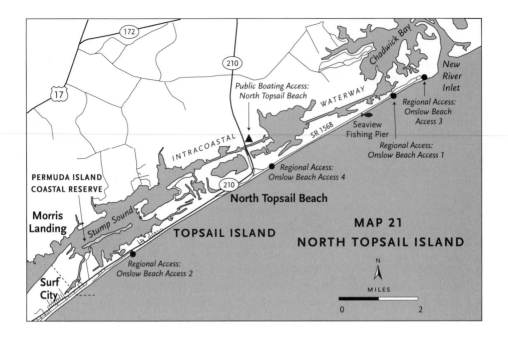

commercial beaches on the coast. The recent building push has brought ornate beach architecture to the shores; the new homes have been engineered to withstand hurricane-force pounding as per strengthened building codes. Nearly all of the oceanfront lots have houses with dune crossovers that drop off from the top of dune line on multiple steps to the wide flat beach. In 2018 Hurricane Florence shortened these crossovers and removed the dunes from beneath them.

Closer to New River Inlet, North Topsail Beach homeowners are facing the prospects of substantial expense to protect the structures by effectively stabilizing the beach. The issue continue to be lateral erosion across the face of the beach caused by the flood tide entering New River Inlet. It is possible that a costly terminal groin on the North Topsail Beach headland could arrest the erosion. As of this writing, North Topsail Beach is evaluating repair and proper replacement of the existing sandbag support.

Access

All of the streets perpendicular to NC 210 provide pedestrian access to the beach. A few of these areas include parking spaces.

There are four major public access areas in North Topsail Beach. There

       Onslow County

is a 4x4 access pay kiosk at the north end of North Topsail Beach. All vehicles driving on the beach must display a proper permit, which can be purchased at the kiosk.

Search NC Beach Access; click the NC DEQ Beach and Waterfront Access Map link; at the bottom of the second column, click "Go to Beach Access Locator."

Search Onslow County Tourism or enter www.onlyinonslow.com.

Search North Topsail Beach or enter www.ntbnc.org.

PERMUDA ISLAND COASTAL RESERVE

Permuda Island is a marshy island that rises slightly above sea level in Stump Sound west of North Topsail Beach. The island is about 1.5 miles long, its center nearly due west of the Onslow Beach Access Site Number 2. In 1987 the state acquired the 63 acres of marsh, subtidal flats, and shrub thicket upland for the North Carolina Coastal Reserve system.

The island is a mix of habitats, including stunted trees such as red cedar, live oak, and yaupon and abandoned agricultural fields that are reverting to woodland. The island's marsh and mudflats provide habitat for willets, American oystercatchers, egrets, herons, black skimmers, and sandpipers. It is also known that early Native Americans used the island as a seasonal fishing and shellfish-gathering enclave.

The island narrowly escaped modernization in 1983, when a proposal to develop it met tremendous, prolonged opposition. Development, opponents argued, would irreparably damage the shellfish harvest in Stump Sound. In January 1985 the North Carolina Coastal Resources Commission officially designated Permuda Island as an Area of Environmental Concern because of the significant archaeological features on the island, including a centuries-old Native American living site where thick deposits of shell refuse date occupation to as early as 300 B.C.E.

The Nature Conservancy eventually purchased the island for $1.7 million. In January 1987 the state purchased half of the island from the Nature Conservancy, completing the purchase the following September. There are no plans to change the traditional use of Permuda Island for fishing or wildlife habitat.

The best way to take in the island is to kayak or canoe around it. You may

Plane Speaking

Military jets leave their roar far behind, and the reflex to look up when that unmistakable sound sweeps through the air is nearly universal and frequently too late: the plane is long gone. The skies of the North Carolina coast and coastal plain can be filled with such amplitude. The air force, navy, and marines sometimes conduct training flights over this geography, and this makes for a different kind of bird-watching. Here are some field guide keys for plane-watchers.

The two most important keys to identifying planes are tail configuration and wing shape.

TWIN-TAIL PLANES There are four twin-tail jets actively deployed here: the F-15E Strike Eagle (U.S. Air Force), the F/A-18 (U.S. Navy and U.S. Marine Corps), the F-22 Raptor (U.S. Air Force—unusual, here), and the F-35 Lightning II, Joint Strike Fighter (U.S. Air Force and U.S. Marines).

F-15E. The F-15 is easily distinguished because the twin vertical stabilizers are extremely tall in proportion to the body, one with an obvious light. The plane profile is sleek and flat, with a high-domed two-seater canopy and typically two fliers. Wings rigid, their tips angled back. The small ailerons at the rear extend past the tail, forming a "notch." This is a large, very agile plane that is unmistakable because of the high tail. Location: Coastal plain near Goldsboro.

F/A-18. The twin tails are canted at an angle much as if holding up two fingers and are in front of the rear wings and ailerons—an immediate giveaway. It does not appear "big." The twin engines' exhaust extends far past the vertical tails. The wings are fixed, their tips parallel to the body, and the plane has a long nose extending in front of the single-seat cockpit. It appears waspish and lithe. Location: Northern Banks (Navy), rarely; Bogue Banks, Topsail Island more frequently.

F-22 Raptor and F-35 Lightning II. These planes look very much alike. The F-22, rare in North Carolina, has twin tails canted at angle and set above the rear edge of the stubby triangular wings and also forward of the large, boxy rear wings. The rear wings form a deep notch for the twin engine exhausts.

The F-35 Lightning II, Joint Strike Fighter, is being made in three versions, one of which is capable of near-vertical takeoff for the Marine Corps. The F-35 is a single-engine jet with a smaller, less boxy body. The canted twin tails are at the end of the body, after the trailing edge of the wing. The rear wings are nearly triangular, with the notch between them for the single exhaust. The plane is likely to have a camouflage paint scheme.

SINGLE-TAIL PLANES The single-tail planes you're most likely to see are the F-5 (U.S. Navy) and the AV-8 (U.S. Marine Corps).

F-5. One seat. Recognized by its stiletto profile and short wings extending straight from the middle of the plane. Looks like a dart. There are twin intakes and twin exhausts. This is a small, lithe flier. The navy uses it as a trainer (two seats) and to simulate enemy tactics. General aspect: swift, darting flier. Location: Northern Banks.

AV-8. Single seat. This is the Harrier, a vertical-takeoff jet. It is heavy through the middle, with variable-angle thrust deflectors under the wings. The wings have distinctive ribbing. Although "chunky," it is still streamlined, with some speed in the lines of the plane. Camouflage coloring is a good tip-off. The jets frequently practice takeoffs at night at the Bogue auxiliary field near Morehead City. The AV-8 is an efficient, deliberate flier.

glide alongside wildlife, but the shrub thickets are just that, close to impenetrable, and there are snakes on the island.

Access

The closest marina is at Morris Landing in Bethea, at the end of SR 1538.

Search Permuda Island Coastal Reserve or enter
www.nccoastalreserve.net and click the Reserve Sites heading.

Pender County

THE BEACHES OF PENDER COUNTY, Surf City and Topsail Beach, are on Topsail Island, a narrow barrier that fronts on Onslow Bay, a great arc of the coast between Cape Lookout and Cape Fear. As the gull flies, the island's central access—the iconic swing bridge over the Intracoastal Waterway to Surf City (a fixed bridge replacement is scheduled to open in 2020)— is about halfway between the storied resort of Wrightsville Beach to the south and undeveloped Hammocks Beach State Park to the north.

There's a parallel in island appearance and character: Topsail Island is a pleasant medium between the closely packed urban density of Wrightsville and the bring-your-own-shade of undeveloped Bear Island, the signature feature of the Hammocks Beach State Park. Topsail Island is snuggled along the coast, growing slowly as a laid-back place-by-the-sea, more an oceanfront getaway than a resort. While Surf City has a quicker pulse than Topsail Beach, both are low-key. The island has benefited from the awkward access from major population centers, which is a blessing but makes for a full-time travel challenge in Pender County.

Interstate 40, the main route from the Piedmont cities to Wilmington, divides Pender County. To the west are well-tended fields; to the east, tangled, impenetrable woods. Burgaw, the county seat, is west of I-40; satellite photos show it surrounded by rowed and groomed fields. Move the cursor across the interstate or pick up a highway map to confirm the sizable road-free areas lying between Topsail Beach and the rest of the state. There is wild country in this county.

East of I-40, the Northeast Cape Fear River runs from north to south, bisecting the county, a winding, braided passage feathering to wetlands on either side of its channel. The interstate rides atop gently sloping ridges that drain east to the floodplain of this river and crosses it near Castle Hayne, North Carolina. The Black River winds on the county's western border. Between these two small raft-size rivers and their broad wetlands stretch the prime farmlands of Pender County, some of the finest in the state.

Much of Pender County's roadless areas are included in two vast evergreen shrub bogs managed as game lands by the North Carolina Wildlife Resources Commission. These two tracts—Angola Bay and Holly Shelter— present different management challenges to wildlife officials. Angola Bay, in the northeast, is the wilder of the two, covering 24,483 acres in forbidding wetland with no roads and few fire lanes. By contrast, Holly Shelter, in the east-central part of the county, has 64,743 acres actively managed for big game and waterfowl hunting. It too is a wild, generally poorly drained area, but there is better access to the interior than in Angola Bay. Both are rich in fragrant flowering shrubbery and rare herbaceous plants.

These nearly impenetrable wild tracts shaped the settlement of the county by thwarting commerce and easy transportation. Fortunately, there is a high and drier ridge that parallels the coast southeast of the Holly Shelter Game Land. This serviceable route became the old post road known as King's Highway, and eventually the route of US 17. Southeast of US 17, the land drains into the sounds behind the barrier beaches of Topsail, Lea-Hutaff, and No-Name Islands.

The Pender County coast, like that of adjoining Onslow County, has been below beach development radar until recent decades. North to south, Surf City and Topsail Beach comprise slightly less than half of Topsail Island. Surf City is the central, most populous community attracting a lot of building, while Topsail Beach, at the southeast end, is more established and slightly sleepy.

NC 50 and NC 210 cross the Atlantic Intracoastal Waterway at Surf City. At the Surf City stoplight—not so long ago the sole island stoplight—the roads part ways. NC 210 turns northeast and NC 50 heads southwest. A new bridge and traffic circle speeds island traffic along.

People have summered Topsail Island since before the 1930s, but the awkwardness of reaching the island has made its real estate more "accessible"—that is, affordable—than many other locations for second homes. Mobile home and camper parks still carve out a niche, but since 2008 the slow uptick in building has increased, along with the size of the homes being built.

The island profile is wider in Surf City than in Topsail Beach. It is also the portion of the island with the largest frontal dunes that served the island well when Hurricane Florence made landfall in 2018, but the island profile is still comparatively low.

While Hurricane Florence was a trial, it was the summer of 1996 (Hurricanes Bertha and Fran) that shattered the 42-year nap Topsail Island had enjoyed beside a benevolent ocean (in 1954 Hurricane Hazel destroyed 210 of the island's 230 homes). Bertha (July) and Fran (September) took a shovel-cut out of the dunes, giving the still-gentle beach a steep, sharp incline. The 6 miles between Surf City and Topsail Beach were spared the worst of those storms. Topsail Beach, which then had far fewer houses than Surf City, seemed to be no worse for wear, except for the oceanfront, where nearly all homes were highly damaged and many had the supporting sand beneath them washed away. Fran breached the island in two locations.

That tumultuous year is long forgotten; the gentle beach that spurred storm victims to rebuild has lured newcomers who also built. The beaches again are ample, flat, and washed with soft, easy wave action with a dune line rebuilding from Hurricane Florence.

The towns have twinned appeal, offering a different expression of the understated beach character that is the hallmark of Topsail Island. Topsail Beach is always less crowded than Surf City, and it has easy access to New Topsail Inlet.

There once were two islands remaining in southern Pender County: Lea Island, closest to Topsail, and Hutaff Island, south of Lea. Both are southwest from Topsail Island and were privately owned by namesake families. The islands are sandy, low-profile beaches backed by extensive marsh. Old Topsail Inlet previously separated the two, but hurricanes closed the inlet completely in 1998, making 4-mile-long Lea-Hutaff Island. Rich Inlet flows between Lea-Hutaff and Figure Eight Island in New Hanover County to the south. New Topsail Inlet is the stable inlet between Topsail Beach and the hyphenated island.

Back on the mainland, the land between Holly Ridge and Hampstead east of US 17 has gone to golf and limited subdivisions that offer boating access to the Atlantic Intracoastal Waterway. This has meant increased traffic on US 17. The resort real estate market in Pender County is becoming an increasingly important player in the local economy, which will no doubt result in changes along the coastline.

A new high-rise bridge over the Intracoastal Waterway to Surf City is scheduled for completion in November 2020, retiring the last remaining swing bridge in the state.

For Your Bucket:
    Visit the Karen Beasley Sea Turtle Rescue and Rehabilitation Center
    Attend a scheduled release of sea turtles
    Learn Topsail's World War II history at the Topsail Historical Museum
    Walk the west end for shark's teeth
    Visit Lea-Hutaff Island Preserve

Access

Search NC Beach Access; click the NC DEQ Beach and Waterfront Access Map link; at the bottom of the second column, click "Go to Beach Access Locator."

Search Surf City NC or enter www.surfcitync.gov.

Search Topsail Beach or enter www.topsailbeach.org.

Search Visit Pender or enter www.visitpender.com.

Best phone number for tourism information: 910-259-1278.

KAREN BEASLEY SEA TURTLE RESCUE AND REHABILITATION CENTER

Originally founded in 1997 in Topsail Beach, the Karen Beasley Sea Turtle Rescue and Rehabilitation Center is one of the East Coast's finest dedicated treatment centers for injured pelagic turtles. The mission of the center is simple: rehabilitate injured sea turtles of all species and return them to the wild. It was the dream of namesake and founder Karen Beasley, who died at the age of 29 in 1991.

In 2013, three years after ground was broken, the new 13,000-square-foot hospital and rehabilitation center opened its doors off of Tortuga Drive on the mainland in Surf Center. The facility is now large enough receive visitors and hold classes. Volunteers staff the center, which bustles with visitors during the summer.

Admission is charged; the funds are used to help the center operate. The center opens for tours on Thursdays and Saturdays beginning in April. Check the calendar for scheduled events such as releases of rehabilitated turtles.

Access

The hospital is located on the mainland of Surf City at 302 Tortuga Lane. Turn south on Charlie Medlin Drive off of NC 50/210. Use Shipwreck Mini-golf as the landmark for the turn. Continue through the rotary. The center is on the left.

Search Sea Turtle Hospital or enter www.seaturtlehospital.org.

Hunkered Down: Storms and the Coast

Since forever, nature has collided with the halcyon illusion of living on North Carolina's islands. Every mile of the 326-mile long coast has been (or will be) savaged by a hurricane or northeaster—some places more than others, some places more than once. The historical record speaks to a simple truth: be ready to hunker down; it's only a matter of time.

The following is a brief bit of meteorology.

HURRICANES Hurricanes are tropical cyclones (counterclockwise rotation of winds around a center) that brew in the heated waters off of Africa, most frequently between July and October. A storm is designated a hurricane if its sustained wind speeds exceed 74 miles per hour. (The Saffir-Simpson hurricane scale ranks hurricanes into five categories based on wind speed: Category 1 is 74–95 mph; Category 2, 96–110 mph; Category 3, 111–30 mph; Category 4, 131–55 mph; Category 5, 156+ mph.)

As they migrate west, hurricanes frequently gain strength from the seasonally heated waters of the Caribbean. Upper-atmosphere winds and weather fronts vary the speed and direction of a hurricane's movement over water or land. Fast-moving hurricanes strike and move on; slow-moving storms can produce catastrophic damage from flooding. The northeast quadrant of the storm packs the biggest wallop. It has the strongest winds and pushes the most water before it.

Hurricanes can have a multidirectional effect. As they approach landfall, the winds push water in a storm surge onto shore and drive water through inlets into the sounds behind the islands. When the storm crosses the islands, the winds that piled water ahead of the storm now circulate around the eye to reverse direction relative to the landfall point. The winds blow the water out of the sounds against the dune-free side of the islands, causing flooding. Hurricanes wreak havoc coming and going.

NORTHEASTERS Northeasters take their name from the wind direction as the storm impacts the mid-Atlantic and northeastern coastlines. North-easters are extratropical cyclones, forming in the latitudes between Georgia and New Jersey, usually between November and April. The difference in air temperatures (warmer air at sea coming up from the Gulf of Mexico and cold polar air from the jet stream) initiates and fuels these storms. While these storms also rotate counterclockwise, northeasters rarely attain hurricane wind speed, are large systems, and move slowly. Northeasters can blow hard, steady, and long, piling water against the beach through several tide cycles. The wind makes the high tides surge higher and prevents the low tides from ebbing completely. The water piles up against the shore. Stalled northeasters pile increasing amounts through successive tidal cycles and simply overwhelm an island's natural defenses. Northeasters give little warning and don't have the cinematic attraction or buildup of hurricanes.

The Ash Wednesday storm of March 6–8, 1962, remains one of the most destructive storms ever to strike the Outer Banks. The storm lasted through five tidal cycles, and its 60 mph winds piled water past the dunes and into houses and flooded NC 12 in multiple places.

A SHORT LIST OF NORTH CAROLINA STORMS

September 7, 1846. A slow-moving hurricane blew open Hatteras and Oregon Inlets.

August 18, 1899. The San Ciriaco Hurricane covered Hatteras in 4 feet of water and destroyed all the buildings of Diamond City on Shackleford Banks.

September 16, 1933. The Outer Banks Hurricane pushed water inland and flooded New Bern, leaving 1,000 people homeless.

October 15, 1954. Hurricane Hazel (Category 4) came ashore near Calabash. Nearly every waterfront building in Brunswick County was destroyed. It prompted the establishment of the National Hurricane Center.

March 6–8, 1962. The Ash Wednesday storm flooded the Dare County resort communities and NC 12 and 550 more miles of the mid-Atlantic coast.

August 31, 1993. Hurricane Emily flooded Hatteras Island from Avon south, with floodwater depths ranging from 4 to 8 feet, and 168 homes were completely destroyed.

July 12, 1996. Hurricane Bertha made landfall north of Wrightsville Beach and slammed an 8- to 10-foot storm surge into Topsail Island. Two piers went missing.

September 6, 1996. Hurricane Fran delivered a 12-foot storm surge to Topsail Island, cutting the island in two places and washing away a temporary police station (a legacy of Bertha) housed in a double-wide trailer.

September 16, 1999. Rainfall from Hurricane Floyd brought 500-year flooding inland along with a 10-foot storm surge at the Cape Fear coast. Flooding closed I-95 for several days.

September 18, 2003. Hurricane Isabel cut a 2,000-foot inlet (Isabel Inlet) between Hatteras and Frisco, destroying all utilities and isolating Hatteras Village. It caused massive destructive storm-surge flooding of Swan Quarter and inland Hyde County.

August 26–27, 2011. Hurricane Irene cut an inlet north of Rodanthe and made Pea Island an island again. NC 12 was overwashed and buried under sand in multiple locations.

October 8, 2016. Hurricane Matthew produced massive inland flooding and erased dunes throughout Brunswick County.

September 14–16, 2018. Rainfall from Hurricane Florence causes widespread, devastating inland flooding that isolated Wilmington, drowned Lumberton, and closed I-40 and I-95.

SURF CITY

In the family beach vacation of an earlier time, the swing bridge always opens two cars ahead, stopping beach-bound traffic 200 feet short of arrival as a single small boat putters past—the slowest boat in the world . . .

Surf City had the swing bridge (it was replaced in late December 2018), and it also has an appeal drawing from a nostalgic undercurrent. Founded in 1949, this 6-mile-long ocean-to-waterway community has all the beachy elements. There's a pier nearly in the middle of town, small eateries abound, and there are ice cream shops, real estate offices, a grocery store, beach gear, and T-shirts. This compressed commercial area is quite walkable, spanning between Kinston Avenue to the south and Goldsboro Avenue to the north—three double blocks. Shore Drive is behind the dunes, New River Drive is closest to the sound, and Topsail Drive is in between.

This community of some 2,500 people (20,000+ in summer) evokes those memories of youthful summer romance. There are just enough amusements and hangouts, and not so many as to crowd out laid-back charm. There's enough parking to keep things moving on summer nights—which means not quite enough—and the town seems made for cruising and maybe stirring up the evening, as teenagers and 20-somethings are wont to do. Then again, two blocks north or south of the Surf City Pier, folks can sit on an oceanfront porch and listen to the surf.

Private oceanfront homes perch behind the dunes not two blocks from the pier and ripple north and south from there. The focus here is on the water and the sand. Surf City still echoes that small-town summer-at-the-beach of the mid-twentieth century.

The town tourism motto, "Discover the Magic," invites guests to find their individual enchantment. Surf City has its priorities straight, and "chillaxing" is obviously high on the list. It promises to speed up in late 2020 with the opening of the new Topsail Island bridge, 1,100 feet south of the swing bridge. The new bridge will accommodate pedestrians and bicycles and connect with Topsail Drive by means of a roundabout. When that circle is complete, island tourism will swirl freely.

Surf City is the most populated of Topsail Island's three communities and is compressed around the junction of NC 210 and NC 50; the latter continues southwest through the wide and most heavily developed portion of Topsail Island to Topsail Beach. The northern city limits of Surf City actually extend over the Pender County line at Broadway Avenue into Onslow County just past West Ninth Street—a pair of beachy restaurants across NC 210 from each other and a North Topsail Beach sign mark the city limit. Surf City shares its southwest border with Topsail Beach.

South of the main road there is a handsome soundside park with a band shell, picnic shelters, and a walkway along the water. Marinas cluster the shores.

The intimate grid of streets has much to do with the projection of a small-town atmosphere. The community is not wide from surf to sound, the roads are two-lane, and buildings are close. Generic commercial beach stores seem too large for the place. Surf City's charm revolves around the idiosyncratic individualism of restaurants, stores, houses, and motor inns that embody the era in which they were built. This better reflects the individualism that brought and kept people here initially.

On September 5, 1996, the strongest winds and highest storm surge of Hurricane Fran piled into Surf City, destroying most oceanfront buildings, including the four fishing piers. The Surf City Pier rebuilt, but Barnacle Bill's, the Scotch Bonnet, and Ocean City passed into history.

So far, Surf City redux is not wandering too far from its sunny origins. More individual homes showcase that "I've arrived" heft, but that is not the usual way here. Topsail Island's general popularity is hitting close to this easygoing home for many. Turnover of humble houses to bigger and bolder is beginning to cross over the bridge.

Access

The city has 35 public access locations. Two are regional: Broadway Street has a bathhouse, showers, and parking for 50 cars; New Bern Avenue has expanded parking, restrooms, and a gazebo.

Search NC Beach Access; click the NC DEQ Beach and Waterfront Access Map link; at the bottom of the second column, click "Go to Beach Access Locator."

Search Surf City NC or enter www.surfcitync.gov.

Search Visit Pender or enter www.visitpender.com.

Best phone number for tourism information: 910-259-1278.

TOPSAIL BEACH

The drive to Topsail Beach from Surf City is best enjoyed with windows down and an arm outside, a lazy tour along Shore Drive (NC 50). It is a surprisingly lengthy, unhurried cruise through an oceanfront subdivision; there are no stores, no hotels, and no amusements, just a pleasant passage through 3 miles of Surf City homes before you enter the Topsail Beach city limits.

Just before the city limits is an oceanside landmark: a battered, weathered three-story concrete tower. This is one of the historic tracking stations that monitored a top-secret testing program for rocket development during World War II. Yes, sleepy, remote Topsail Beach was once a hot spot for top-secret military research.

Topsail Beach has extensive wind-sculpted vegetation, and in several locations the residential cross streets seem to tunnel into the maritime forest, boring a path to the sound and creating an illusion of great height. At the town limits, the road rides a crest of the back frontal dunes and there are glimpses of the wide beach.

Shore Drive becomes North Anderson Boulevard at the town limits and changes name again, to South Anderson Boulevard, at Banks Channel Court, opposite an obvious cove where the island narrows. At this point a

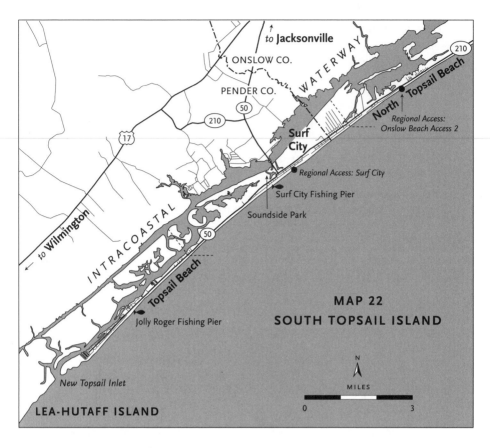

to Jacksonville

ONSLOW CO.

PENDER CO.

WATERWAY

210

North ↑ Topsail Beach

*Regional Access:
Onslow Beach Access 2*

**Surf
City**

Regional Access: Surf City

Surf City Fishing Pier

Soundside Park

to Wilmington

INTRACOASTAL

Topsail Beach

Jolly Roger Fishing Pier

New Topsail Inlet

LEA-HUTAFF ISLAND

MAP 22

SOUTH TOPSAIL ISLAND

N

MILES

0   3

bike path on the west side of the highway parallels the road into the community's center. South Anderson continues until it enters the modest village parallel to Ocean Boulevard, a frontal street that runs directly behind the front row of buildings several miles to the end of the island.

The community's center is tight and tidy. There is a children's playground at the corner of Davis Drive and South Anderson Boulevard, and the Jolly Roger Pier and Motel and a novelty golf course provide a sense of arrival. The motel's patio is on the site of the launching pad of rocket tests conducted here by the navy in the 1940s, named Operation Bumblebee. The motel's original building dates from that era.

The top-secret phase of Topsail History is told in the Topsail Island Museum: Missiles and More, located in the large rocket assembly building on the west side of the community, known as the Arsenal Center.

Between 1946 and 1948 Topsail Beach was a center for rocket scien-

.

tists. In fact, the principle of the ram jet engine, the mainstay of supersonic flight today, was developed and proved on Topsail.

The reinforced concrete observation towers along the island were used to track the flight of the missiles. When the military abandoned Topsail, it returned the island and sold the buildings to the former owners, and the resort era began. It has grown to a whopping 500 or so year-round residents.

Ocean Boulevard, with its beachfront houses, continues south until the buildable oceanfront land disappears after the road jags around the Sea Vista Motel.

The oceanfront past the Sea Vista has been a source of contention over building rights. After this strand was badly damaged by storms, the town passed and then modified a dune protection ordinance. Beach nourishment at this end widened the beach sufficiently that the lots once deemed unbuildable might now be legal for oceanfront construction. Owners of the homes on the finger canals directly west of the oceanfront contend that new construction will eliminate the protection afforded by the replenished dunes and widened beach. Nature and/or the courts will decide.

New Topsail Inlet is moving south, and the end of the island is gaining ground. At the end of Ocean Boulevard, a left turn onto Inlet Avenue leads to public parking and inlet access.

The south end of the island is arguably the best beach in town, with fewer visitors. Sit down in an expanse of "sea hash," as the multicolored debris of shell fragments is known, and carefully sift through it with an eye for sharp, triangular shapes—shark's teeth. Topsail is a hot spot for tiny ancient shark's teeth, and a practiced eye can turn some time on the beaches here into a pocketful of treasures.

Access

Each street that is perpendicular to the oceanfront terminates in a dune crossover.

Search NC Beach Access; click the NC DEQ Beach and Waterfront Access Map link; at the bottom of the second column, click "Go to Beach Access Locator."

Search Topsail Beach NC or enter www.topsailchamber.org and click the Topsail Area Guide link.

LEA-HUTAFF ISLAND

Lea-Hutaff Island, the next island in the sequence along the Pender coast, is generally small and low, but it does have some upland. Nearly 40 lots were platted on the island as recently as the 1980s. The recent history notes that despite its low profile, some homes were built, the last one in 1990. That particular vacation outpost was destroyed by a storm in 2015.

A coalition of conservation groups, led by Audubon North Carolina and including the North Carolina Coastal Land Trust, the State of North Carolina, and the U.S. Fish and Wildlife Service have purchased most of the islands and marsh. This became the Lea Island State Natural Area in 2003. Audubon North Carolina is managing this coastal complex for the benefit of the wildlife that uses its unspoiled beaches and marshes for nesting and habitat. In total, Lea-Hutaff Island is 5,641 essentially pristine acres of sand and marsh and is thus a haven for birds.

The complex supports nesting loggerhead sea turtles and hundreds of nesting terns, skimmers, and shorebirds. In season, thousands of migrant shorebirds stop off to feed and rest during their long flights. The island has never had any severe disturbance by people and is considered one of the last and best undeveloped barrier islands on the Carolina coast.

Old Topsail Inlet more or less split the mass into separate islands, Lea and Hutaff, but it closed due to a storm in 1998, creating the hyphenated island. Rich Inlet to the south separates Lea-Hutaff from Figure Eight Island.

In 2018, 80 privately held upland and oceanfront acres on Lea Island not previously sold to Audubon were offered for sale. The acreage is accessible only by boat and has no services. The asking price was $4 million.

The parcel of the composite island originally known as Hutaff Island is still privately owned but open to the public. Efforts are continuing to expand Lea Island State Natural Area, but at what price? In 2018, $4 million was the starting point.

Access

The islands are reachable by boat.

Search Lea Island or enter nc.audubon.org
/conservation/lea-hutaff-island-iba.

HAMPSTEAD

Hampstead has surged over the past couple of decades; development has spilled east over the coastal plain woods between US 17 and the Atlantic Intracoastal Waterway. The residential growth is largely unseen from the highway that has sprawled from a crossroads, where NC 210 intersected US 17. The still-unincorporated community is home to more than 4,000 residents. New homes, some quite large, pepper the roads that wind east toward the water. There are several residential golf course communities, and many homes have waterfront lots on coves that are fingers of the sound west of Topsail Island.

George Washington may very well have stopped at Hampstead during his southern tour in 1791. South of town, beside the right-of-way, the Daughters of the American Revolution have designated a live oak tree as the site of his encampment. NC 210 turns to the west at Hampstead.

Search Visit Pender or enter www.visitpender.com.

Best phone number for tourism information: 910-259-1278.

POPLAR GROVE PLANTATION

The manor house at Poplar Grove Plantation dates from 1850, built by Joseph M. Foy on the grounds of the 1795 home built by his father, James Foy, that was destroyed by fire. The younger Foy became a pioneer in peanut cultivation and rebuilt the family fortunes through these 685 acres during the Reconstruction era. The house and grounds exemplifies antebellum plantation architecture and lifestyle and is one of the few plantation complexes remaining in the state. The house is on National Register of Historic Places and is one of a small number included in the National Park Service Gullah Geechee Heritage Corridor, a planning and guidance program assist-

What's behind the Breakers?

Breathe easy, parents! It is not a falsehood to tell children that the waves crumpling at their feet are made by a great wave machine. The truth is that most waves are products of the wind.

There's a catch, of course: the wave-building wind may not be the same zephyr sending beach balls down the strand. Imagine a becalmed sea, hundreds, perhaps thousands of miles away. A breeze gusts the ocean's surface, pushing the water into ripples and creating an effect similar to when you blow on the surface of a bowl of soup. The breeze continues, and the ripples, gathering energy from the wind, pile together and build into waves that travel across the sea to froth at your feet. The friction of air moving over water is sufficient to begin an ocean wave, but the effectiveness of the wind to forge waves depends on the average velocity of the wind, the duration of the wind, and the fetch—the reach of open water—that the wind traverses. The stronger the wind, the longer it blows, and the greater the distance of open ocean across which it pushes the water, the greater the waves that reach the shore.

Wind is not predictable or simple, and neither are waves, although all waves have some characteristics in common.

Each ripple spawned by wind has a steep windward side that acts as a sail. Should the wind gust too sharply, the top of the youthful wave shatters, spilling over its leading surface or exploding in spray. A stormy coastal day reveals a frothing sea, because the wind shears the crests of waves and spits them about.

Waves can hint at their origin by the way they approach the beach: sharp, peaked waves spilling whitecaps as they march landward before breaking with a "groan" are probably young waves created by a nearby offshore storm. A wave that rolls into a crest that uniformly pipe-curls over and breaks with a roar before pummeling the surf zone is ending a journey from far away.

Occasionally, a remarkable diamond-like pattern may be seen in the arriving waves. This is a wild sight, slightly abstract and, despite its contrast to the typical march of waves, overlooked. The diamond pattern occurs when intersecting groups of waves originating from distant, separate compass points do not march straight into shore. The groups are called wave trains. Each has its own rhythm, wavelength, period of repetition, and height. When separate wave trains intersect and continue their individual tracks, the eye sees a diamond pattern of crests.

When a wave train overtakes another, the separate crests may combine to form a large single wave or the crest of one may combine with the trough of the other, minimizing the effect. Surfers and body surfers quickly learn that every fourth or fifth wave (or some other count) is larger than average—that's the one to wait for! The larger wave is probably the combined overlap of two different wave trains.

In a boat offshore, waves are noticed and felt as swells, which travel at an average rate of 3.5 times their period, which is the distance between successive crests in seconds. Thus, a wave with a 20-second period travels at about 70 miles per hour. (The longest period of swell ever reported was 22.5 seconds, corresponding to a wavelength of 2,600 feet and a speed of 78 miles per hour—a serious wave.)

The wind can blow in any direction, and waves can begin from any direction. Why, then, when they arrive at the beach, do they usually break mostly parallel to shore? Well, waves refract or begin to "bend" as soon as the depth of the water is about one-half their wavelength. In addition, the wave responds to shallows by shortening its length, increasing its height, and reducing its speed, just like a person running uphill who chops his steps, lifts his knees higher, and slows down.

The most dramatic evidence of this phenomenon is at Cape Point, the spit of land extending southeast into the ocean at Cape Hatteras. The anglers lining the two sides of the spit witness the spectacular clash of waves, which originate far out at sea. As the leading edge of these waves reaches the first shallows of Cape Point, the faster-traveling edges, which are in deeper water to either side of the spit, refract around the shallows, bending until you witness a spectacular head-to-head explosion of water.

The movement of water at the edge of land will always be one of the most enthralling and restful images on earth. The mystery of waves, their possible origin, the transoceanic crossings, the shapes and patterns that never repeat, will always be the attraction of the beach—a product of the great wave machine that sends beach balls bouncing away . . .

ing in the preservation of the cultural heritage of slaves and their descendants in the coastal Southeast.

The plantation grounds are open to the public, and there is a fee for the guided tour of the manor. In addition to the house, there are several outbuildings open to the public, including a tenant house, kitchen, blacksmith shop, salt works, and turpentine display.

Access

Poplar Grove is beside US 17 in Scott's Hill.

Search Poplar Grove or enter poplargrove.org.

New Hanover County

EVENTUALLY, after much colonial and antebellum whittling and shifting of boundaries, New Hanover County stabilized as the high, dry ground bounded by water—the Cape Fear River on the west, the Northeast Cape Fear River and Island Creek on the north, and the Atlantic Ocean on the east. This saltier limit extends south from Rich Inlet, between Lea-Hutaff and Figure Eight Islands, to a compass heading that once passed through the now-extinct (i.e., filled-in) Corncake Inlet, south of Fort Fisher Recreational Area.

The closed inlet marks the separation between New Hanover, with its river-backed headland, and the Smith Island complex in Brunswick County, frequently referred to by the eponymous resort name Bald Head Island. As of 2017, it was possible to walk to Bald Head Island from Fort Fisher and to do so with dry feet. All told, New Hanover County has approximately 27 miles of beach between these north and south boundaries. Not all of these oceanfront miles are easily accessible, for many different reasons.

New Hanover is the smallest and most populous coastal county because Wilmington, the state's ninth largest city, sits smack in the middle of the county and spreads east from the east bank of the Cape Fear River all the way to the Atlantic Intracoastal Waterway. It is really easy for residents to drive to the beach after a day of work downtown. In fact, many live on or very near the oceanfront. The influence of a vibrant Wilmington pressures the accessibility of the available coastline.

The population of Wilmington is growing steadily, spilling cross-county from the historical riverfront boundaries into the native longleaf pine forests. Much of the growth has been residential communities. Commercial and office development serving the residential communities border the major highways (US Routes 421, 117, 76, and 74) leading to the oceanfront communities. The result is a tedious gauntlet to drive (albeit with plenty of services) in order to reach local beaches. River Road, the historic route from Wilmington on the east bank of the Cape Fear River, south of Sanders Road, still passes through the once-dominant coastal landscape of longleaf pine forest and freshwater marshes.

The towns of Wrightsville Beach, Carolina Beach, and Kure Beach are well-established, self-sufficient communities with a varying degree of dependency on tourism. Wrightsville Beach, closest to Wilmington, feels and looks more like a suburban enclave. Over the years its relationship to Wilmington has been similar to Virginia Beach's relationship to Norfolk. Farther south, Carolina Beach is more "resort-beachy." While year-round residency is increasing, the streets are quiet and parking free and easy between Labor Day and Memorial Day. Kure Beach, more distant still, is a grand place that is upgrading nicely to provide access to the surf and solitude and comparative quiet after summer season.

Balancing the needs of community residents with the demands of a tourism-based economy prompts an ongoing civic dialogue in many communities about "who we are or want to be." This is a challenge in the county, particularly in those areas not inside the city limits. While there is not a clear-cut Mercedes/four-wheel-drive divide, there is sufficient difference between user groups that "who has access to the beach" becomes a policy issue. In the shoulder and high summer season, public parking fees leave no doubt about a community's attitude toward day visitors. Except for established state recreation areas, the public beach in New Hanover County is far from free.

More than half of the 27 miles of oceanfront occurs on three barrier islands: from north to south, Figure Eight, Shell Island/Wrightsville Beach, and Masonboro Island. While the islands have almost uniformly exquisite beaches, the islands themselves are completely different in character and accessibility. Slightly more than 5 miles in length, Figure Eight is a low-density exclusive private island for homeowners and their guests; 4-mile-long Wrightsville Beach/Shell Island, a historic playground for Wilmington, is a densely, handsomely developed resort and residential beach; and 8.4-mile-long Masonboro Island is in the North Carolina Coastal Reserve and a National Estuarine Research Reserve Site. It is undeveloped and only accessible by watercraft.

Heading south from Wilmington, US 421 crosses Snows Cut, the 1.75-mile-long channel of the Atlantic Intracoastal Waterway gouged between 1929 and 1931 by the U.S. Army Corps of Engineers to connect Myrtle Grove Sound with the Cape Fear River. The channel lopped off the southern tip of the county from the mainland, creating a fourth island, at one point promoted as "Pleasure Island," an obvious reference to the oceanfront and recreation opportunities. It includes Fort Fisher State Historic Site and the communities of Carolina Beach and Kure Beach, along with Carolina Beach State Park and Fort Fisher State Recreation Area.

Before Snows Cut, this was a peninsula of the mainland, and though it's now technically an island, it remains an ever-narrowing neck of land between the Cape Fear River and the Atlantic Ocean. From Snows Cut south, there are no barrier islands, a characteristic of the North Carolina coast.

While the northern portion of Carolina Beach is a barrier spit or peninsula, the southern portion is solid mainland peninsula and remains so south through Kure Beach to Fort Fisher. There is a difference in the oceanfront; the dunes are smaller because the land is actually a modest bluff. This is particularly noticeable at Kure Beach.

The remaining miles of oceanfront in the county occur in the communities of Carolina Beach and Kure Beach, at Fort Fisher Historic Site, and at Fort Fisher State Recreation Area. The two resort communities, which have a mix of residential housing as well as some oceanfront hotels, account for about 6.5 miles of developed and accessible beach—3.5 in Carolina Beach and 3 in Kure. Fort Fisher State Recreation Area is the big beach draw because of the extensive parking, the updated bathhouses with restroom, and the lifeguarded beach.

Wilmington is a coastal destination of a different sort; it is a city, rich in mercantile history and blessed with an abundance of architectural character. It has also had an astonishing renaissance that began in the 1980s. Do the show titles *Dawson's Creek* or *One Tree Hill* stir memories? Much filming has occurred in the Wilmington area, where the creative forces of North Carolina's film industry made a base.

The resurgence of the community has generated growth, and Wilmington, once 10 miles from the nearest beach, has marched nearly right up to all of them. The town is filling up the middle of the county between the Cape Fear River and the Intracoastal Waterway and is now spreading north into the dense, dark, and often soggy forests of northern New Hanover County.

New Hanover County also includes two components of the North Carolina National Estuarine Research Reserve, Masonboro Island and Zeke's Island. Masonboro Island is a 6-mile-long low barrier south of Wrightsville Beach, accessible by boat.

Zeke's Island is at the end of US 421, beyond the Fort Fisher/Southport ferry dock, and contains a 4-mile-long barrier spit that extends south from the Federal Point access area. Because of these "free" beaches (though admittedly they are not readily accessible), in New Hanover County there is quite a balance in the types of beach experience available to visitors.

Some of the high ground in the county was not high enough. Floodwaters from Hurricane Florence in 2018 brought havoc to parts of Wilmington and New Hanover County, areas that had remained untouched for decades by rising waters and high winds. The rainfall record for a year was shattered in one week, and necessary food and supplies could not reach the city. The effects of Florence will linger and shape future growth decisions.

For Your Bucket:
Tour historic Wilmington
Dine on the Cape Fear River
Go for a river cruise
Visit the uss *North Carolina*
Visit Masonboro Island
Visit Carolina Beach State Park
Hang out on the Carolina Beach boardwalk
Fish the Kure Beach fishing pier
Walk to Bald Head Island
Ride the ferry to Southport and back

Access

The beachfront communities provide access; parking, metered or otherwise, can be problematic or expensive during the declared vacation season.

There is a large regional access with parking, restrooms, showers, and a dune crossover south of Fort Fisher Historic Site. It is clearly signed.

The county maintains a 24-acre park, Snows Cut Park, off of River Road on the northwest side of US 421, the Wilmington side of Snows Cut.

Search Wilmington Beaches or enter www.wilmingtonandbeaches.com.

Best phone number for tourism information: 866-266-9690.

Access locations: search NC Beach Access; click the NC DEQ Beach and Waterfront Access Map link; at the bottom of the second column, click "Go to Beach Access Locator."

WILMINGTON

This city-by-the-river continues to recast itself, as it has done repeatedly since becoming a major mercantile center in the early nineteenth century. It is on a rousing upswing, digging into its trade history from distant decades to repurpose its commercial and architectural heritage into an inviting place to be. This ongoing civic commitment is making the downtown walkable and entertaining. "Older" Wilmington—from Eighth Street to the Cape Fear River—hums with an ever-confident energy: that of a city shaping a future around and within its past (and with a reminder from Hurricane Florence to be mindful of Mother Nature).

The excitement flows downhill to the river, and the outlook from there is upbeat and onward. The Cape Fear River, and the commerce it generated beginning in the eighteenth century, made Wilmington the state's largest and richest city by the fourth decade of the nineteenth. Money poured in; buildings and houses went up—many created by architects and builders from northeastern cities introduced to wealthy Wilmington residents through mercantile trade connections. The buildings that survived the several fires that savaged the city in the nineteenth century make walkable Wilmington a treasure trove of architectural variety in government and mercantile buildings, churches, and near-palatial homes.

Wilmington's place in North Carolina's history is secure. There are more historical markers here than in any other city in the state (including one noting the birthplace of Whistler's mother). Commerce has grown on these riverbanks since the early 1730s, and for several years in the eighteenth century it served as the state capital. Until 1910 it was the state's largest city.

Historically, the economy of the city was based on mercantile trade such as the production and shipping of naval stores from nearby pine forests. The secure harbor made Wilmington the only reliable natural deepwater port in the state.

The commercial heart still draws from the river, and the street to walk is Front Street. The Cotton Exchange, between Grace and Walnut Streets, is a boutique crafted out of old cotton warehouses. It provides a multilevel descent to public parking along cobbled Water Street and the promenade along the Cape Fear River. The backdrop to the setting is the magnificent uss *North Carolina* at berth across the river.

The Wilmington Railroad Museum, next to the convention center on 505 Nutt Street at the north end of the downtown, occupies the renovated Atlantic Coastline Station. This is a starting point for gaining some historical perspective: the museum tells the story of the 161-mile-long Wilmington to Weldon Railroad, which linked the Cape Fear River to the Roanoke River in Roanoke Rapids. In 1840 it was the longest continuous length of track in the world.

Riverfront Park between Market and Princess Streets is a gathering place that has a farmer's market in season. Nearby is the new-to-look-like-old Riverfront Information Center, a first stop for guiding pamphlets and directions. Nearby, one can catch a ride on the Wilmington Trolley Company for narrated rides through the expansive historic district.

Pedestrians and trolley (or horse-drawn carriage) riders will quickly take in the city's handsome environment. One block east and south of city center—Market Street and Front Street—moss-draped trees shade sidewalks and houses and floral gardens surround houses exhibiting amazing architectural variety. A hallmark of the city fabric is the eclecticism of its buildings, a vestige of fashion, taste, and individual competitiveness that drove building construction in the nineteenth and early twentieth centuries. Wilmington's wealthy wanted to make their mark, and architecture became the billboard declaring their arrival and success.

Wilmington's historic district spreads from the commercial downtown to include close, quite old residential neighborhoods. At the south end of the Downtown Riverwalk, at Water and Ann Streets, is Chandler's Wharf, a concentration of shopping and dining in heritage buildings where suppliers, or chandlers, outfitted ships. The riverside restaurants have outdoor seating on expansive decks a step or two above the Cape Fear. The shops across Water Street from the restaurants tuck into the foot of the inland bluff. The higher elevation is where early residents built their lavish homes.

The historic residential area is a short uphill walk from the river, and the street grid extends inland from its banks. The 1825 Governor Edward B. Dudley mansion is at 325 Front Street on the corner with Nun Street. Dudley won the first statewide gubernatorial election in 1836 and was the president of the Wilmington and Weldon Railroad. The Dudley mansion is one of several fine houses along Front Street. The number of historical markers in this area makes walking a good option, though the guided tours can deliver much of the information on those markers. Two blocks from the Dudley Mansion, at Orange Street and Second Street, is the Children's Museum of Wilmington (admission) and three historic buildings, including an 1804 Georgian-style building that was built as a Masonic Lodge. Across Orange Street, at 102 Orange Street, is the Mitchell-Anderson House (1738), the oldest surviving structure in the city. This is just a close-in taste of the town's fabric; wander north and east to uncover the rich history of the black community, a history prominently noted on the visitor guide map to Wilmington.

More is yet to come: in 2017 Wilmington removed a 1960s elevated parking deck for the RiverPlace, a mixed-use commercial/residential development with frontage on Water Street. Archaeologists moved in quickly to document subterranean features and recover nineteenth-century artifacts.

The Cape Fear River, central to the city's story and a placid setting for its downtown innovation, also offers a great point of view. Take a river cruise or hire a water taxi to cross to the USS *North Carolina*, at berth in a slip on the west bank. Make the time to visit the memorial there, and the time will be easily filled and well spent.

The single-mindedness of beach-bound vacationers frequently leaves Wilmington a lost opportunity for exploration, even for a side trip. The city center is easily reached from areas west and north of Wilmington, though: follow the routing for US 17 (I-40 becomes College Road when it crosses US 17). The route travels over Market Street and carries you to the heart of the city; the tree-planted median signals the destination. Approaching Wilmington from the south, follow US 17/74/76 to cross the Cape Fear River. After the crossing, exit right onto Front Street or turn left onto Third Street. Either route leads to city center.

Search Wilmington Beaches or enter www.wilmingtonandbeaches.com.

Best phone number for tourism information: 866-266-9690.

FIGURE EIGHT ISLAND

Figure Eight Island is the northernmost barrier island in New Hanover County. It is a low-profile island; the higher upland portions of the northern half are wider and more wooded than its southern half. On the west it is backed by the extensive marshes of Middle Sound.

Figure Eight Island is private—a gated community—and exclusively developed with some large, extraordinary homes. A site-sensitive development of nearly 450 homes fills the island. Only homeowners and their guests clear the mainland guardhouse to cross a private drawbridge over the Intracoastal Waterway and then travel onto a causeway through the marsh and onto the island. The security and isolation have great appeal to privacy-conscious vacationers. Properties are available for rental.

There is no doubting the quality of the island's location and the care taken with the land planning. The roads thread atop a sparsely vegetated spine, with side streets that serve marsh-front or oceanfront houses. Particular care was taken to preserve much of the natural vegetation at the island's north end, adjacent to Rich Inlet, which has been set aside as a preserve for island residents.

The southern half of the island features several "neighborhoods" sited on spurs protruding into the sound formed around lagoons with boating access to the sound.

The island tussles with erosion. The channel of Rich Inlet on the north end has shifted, paring sand from the beach and threatening some houses. The south end of the island, which looks past Mason Inlet to Shell Island, began accreting sand in a low, wide fan at an astonishing rate in the late 1990s as the inlet practically sprinted south. Though beneficial to Figure Eight, the migration had catastrophic effects on Shell Island property owners.

In 2002 the inlet was moved 3,000 feet north, providing substantial relief to Shell Island residents, and it has been comparatively stable since that relocation.

Search Figure 8 Island to find several sources for property management and/or sales on the island.

WRIGHTSVILLE BEACH AND SHELL ISLAND

This 4-mile-long island is unique among barrier island resort communities in North Carolina. Its architectural character makes this evident. Handsome, permanent homes stand shingle-to-shingle on cottage-sized lots. The town beckons with an attractive and lively vibe. The off-season is a slowdown, not a slump: joggers stride the streets, and in the late afternoon beach parking lots fill with sunset seekers. Surfers work the waves, and the broad gentle foreshore hosts walkers even as chill winds blow.

The beach here is wide and flat and has long been favored by families with small children because of the gentle wave action. The south end of the island has held a magnificent dune field signed as part of the Masonboro Island Component of the North Carolina National Estuarine Research Reserve. It was battered by Hurricane Florence but will rebuild slowly.

Since the late nineteenth century—10 years before its 1899 incorporation—Wrightsville Beach has been tethered to Wilmington: by train, then trolley, then car. The proximity became its history.

A commuting habit that began in an eastbound pursuit of intermittent

$and Dollar$

Beach nourishment promises to be an increasingly expensive coastal issue of the next decade. The subject is contentious and the debate is sharp.

Beach nourishment is the process of replacing the sand on a beach from a source outside of the beach system. The process is straightforward. Typically, sand dredged from a borrow site (sometimes offshore, sometimes from inlet channels) is pumped as a wet slurry and deposited on the ocean berm. While each beach nourishment project is unique, the basic process extends and elevates the beach. Doing so provides a place for people to walk and spread their towels, and it also provides an additional buffer and measure of safety for oceanfront property.

The last point hits local governments and citizens in the pocketbook. For years North Carolina law prohibited the use of hardened structures such as terminal groins or jetties to be built on the beaches. (The lone exception to date is Fort Fisher State Historic Site.) Beach nourishment remained as one of the few options available to oceanfront property owners to ameliorate the effects of chronic erosion caused by rising sea level or to repair storm damage. The other options are relocation or loss of property.

In 2011 the North Carolina General Assembly repealed the 30-year-old ban on hardened structures. The legislation allowed for the construction of four "test" terminal groins (rock structures placed at or very near inlets). Figure Eight Island, Ocean Isle Beach, Holden Beach, and Bald Head Island submitted applications to the U.S. Army Corps of Engineers. Bald Head was approved and constructed the first part of their project. The other three applications are still in the permit process. In 2015 the General Assembly passed a law allowing two more municipalities to apply: North Topsail Beach and Emerald Isle are the communities considering proposals.

These are expensive projects. While they are typically successful in arresting erosion for a targeted area, terminal groins, if not properly designed, interrupt the natural movement of sand along the face of the beach, sometimes depriving another location of natural replenishment.

Beach nourishment is not as permanent, but it isn't inexpensive, either, costing between $2 and $5 million per mile of beach. Current trends seem to indicate that any given nourishment project may only be an interim response to the intractable problem of rising sea level.

Nourishment projects are carefully defined and are designed to weather-in and mimic the local natural sand beach. A 2002–3 project from the eastern end of Emerald Isle provides some examples. Installed during the winter before the 2003 vacation season, the project widened the beach by approximately 180 feet. Based on the average annual tidal rise, the project started at a point on the beach that was 7 feet above mean sea level, then tapered gradually seaward from there (starting higher creates a drop-off where the new sand meets the water).

The final cost was $3.78 per linear foot, or slightly under $2 million per mile. By the summer of 2004, the project had weathered in nicely despite some initial misgivings over the quality of the source material, which included large clam shells and gray color (typical coastal sand is tan to brown because of the oxidized shell and clastic grains matter).

The problem of source sand can sour users on a project quickly and/or cause it to fail. If the sand size of the source material differs too much from naturally occurring material, it will not remain in place for the designed life of the project, which is typically eight years.

Emerald Isle has an extensive beach monitoring program that enables a targeted nourishment schedule. Subsequent nourishment projects at different locations along the 13-mile beach took place in 2004, 2005, 2007, and 2013. Storm damage to the beach initiated many of these projects. Federal Emergency Management Agency funds helped with some of the costs. Still, Emerald Isle has spent $41 million since 2003 to keep sand between houses and sea and provide a place for visitors to enjoy. This proved an effective buffer when Hurricane Florence assailed the coast in 2018.

Beach nourishment is old news along the coast. There are 326 miles of shoreline in the state, and slightly less than 75 miles are actively managed, possibly increasing to 85 miles if pending projects are approved.

Historically, the federal government has paid a substantial part of the expense, but this is changing. Federal budgets are becoming much less generous, so in 2017 an advisory group proposed a beach nourishment fund to assist local communities in paying for nourishment projects. The North Carolina General Assembly established the fund but has not endowed it — yet. What appears to be clear is that while sea level is rising, federal funds for nourishment are diminishing.

The funding debate is intense and acrimonious. Those opposed see a taxpayer-funded subsidy benefiting property owners and rewarding unwise behavior that is environmentally harmful. They contend that long-term projected costs will be greater than relocating or buying and removing the threatened structure. Proponents reply that the real beneficiary is the public; that only publicly accessible beaches receive nourishment; that the cost-benefit ratio is more than favorable, given the tourism economy; that it is the most manageable and least expensive option because of existing land values; that environmental damage, if any, is brief and minimal; and that nourished beaches restore nesting habitat that had vanished.

What seems certain is that beach nourishment will continue to be needed at increasing costs. In the future, the federal government may no longer be willing (or able) to provide the subsidy it has in the past. In anticipation of reduced federal money, resort communities faced with eroding beaches are increasing property taxes and imposing occupancy taxes in an effort to stockpile sufficient funds to undertake projects on their own. The cost will be staggering. North Topsail Beach, ineligible for federal monies because it is in a CoBRA red-line zone (a designation that is being reviewed), is looking at $25–30 million in 2004 dollars for its 6-mile project. Homeowners would have to pick up the tab.

At some point, whether in time or in dollars, the issue of rising sea level, coastal erosion, and beach nourishment will prompt a reform in coastal development policy. It is a matter of dollars and sense.

pleasures-by-the-sea has reversed for many to become a westbound ride to the office. Wrightsville Beach looks more like "home" than "away"—a neighborhood by the sea, not a vacation resort. But it is both. There are homes and hotel rooms to rent in this handsome, occasionally pretentious island community. It's wonderful to visit, but even better to belong.

Wrightsville Beach is "cottagey" in feeling, regardless of the height of the buildings. Even at the high-rise zoned lands of the Shell Island portion, the prevailing perception is "low," perhaps because the dune system is wide enough to visually balance the mass of the larger buildings.

The community capitalizes on the commutable distance by encouraging year-round visitation, astutely providing easy access to the oceanfront. The summer population can swell to nearly 50,000, so it's easier to visit when school is in session.

Since 1889, when a rail line began steadily chugging across Banks Channel bringing bathers to its shores, Wrightsville Beach has been the

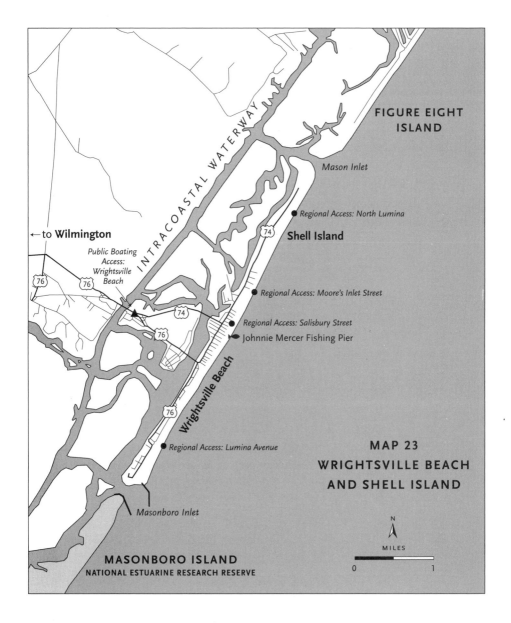

FIGURE EIGHT
ISLAND

Mason Inlet

INTRACOASTAL WATERWAY

← to **Wilmington**

Public Boating
Access:
Wrightsville
Beach

76

76

74

● Regional Access: North Lumina

74 **Shell Island**

● Regional Access: Moore's Inlet Street

● Regional Access: Salisbury Street

76

74

■ Johnnie Mercer Fishing Pier

Wrightsville Beach

76

● Regional Access: Lumina Avenue

**MAP 23
WRIGHTSVILLE BEACH
AND SHELL ISLAND**

Masonboro Inlet

MASONBORO ISLAND
NATIONAL ESTUARINE RESEARCH RESERVE

N

MILES

0   1

place of choice for Wilmingtonians to live and play. It incorporated 10 years later and promptly had to rebuild after a hurricane welcomed the new city to life by the sea.

Rebuild it did. A local power company, Tide Water Power, turned the railroad into an electric trolley.

Its president, Hugh MacRae, built an entertainment pavilion at the last trolley stop, named it Lumina, and rimmed it with lights, and so Wrightsville Beach bathed in the joys of living and playing by the sea.

Early on this streetcar access made it a beach for anyone. Tide Water Power subdivided the beachfront, began building sturdy cottages for common, everyday folks in 1907. In 1911 John Quince Myers purchased one such house, and it stayed in his family until 1954.

If you want to see what oceanfront living was like 100 years ago, then stop in the Wrightsville Beach Museum of History at 303 South Salisbury Street; the museum is in John Quince Myers's oceanfront cottage. This splendid museum, small but ambitious, captures the story of the early years of the resort and features an exquisite scale model of the 1907 Oceanic Hotel, the 1897 Seashore Hotel, and the 1905 Lumina—Wrightsville Beach at the turn of the twentieth century. In 2018 the museum added the 1924 Ewing-Bordeaux historic cottage to its portfolio of Wrightsville Beach's past.

In 1934 a fire swept the north end of the island, clearing out boarding-houses, homes, and hotels.

Again, they rebuilt.

Then, in 1954, Hurricane Hazel, a Category 4 storm, crossed right over the island at high tide. And the oceanfront houses rebuilt again.

In 2018 Hurricane Florence made landfall here and the community fared well, a matter of cleanup rather than rebuild.

Every time it has had to right itself from the toss of a storm, Wrightsville Beach has carried forward bits and pieces of its prestorm days in the form of architectural detailing and its original city form. The houses look sturdy, permanent, and lived-in.

Shell Island, now a part of Wrightsville Beach, was a distinct island as late as the early 1960s, separated by Moore's Inlet (its location is marked by a street with that name). During segregation Shell Island was a historically black resort. In 1965 the intervening Moore's Inlet was filled in, and the combined geography became one community. "Shell Island" is still used in local conversation.

A Holiday Inn (locals cynically nicknamed it "Holiday Inlet") once stood in the approximate location of the old Moore's Inlet channel. Hurricane Fran so damaged the motel that it was razed and a new one constructed in its place.

The island narrows near the site of the old inlet, which restricts development to the east side of Lumina Drive. Extensive salt marsh is visible to the west. The only beachfront high-rise construction within the corporate limits of the island is on what was once Shell Island. These taller buildings obscure the view of the ocean, and revised zoning laws adopted in 1974 confine high-rise and midrise construction to those buildings you see today.

Lumina Avenue passes the Shell Island Resort and loops out at the north end of the island in a tight turn-around. (No parking is available at this turnaround, but there is a pay-parking access lot at the south edge of the Shell Island Resort.) The area north of the turnout is a dedicated bird sanctuary and one of the most dynamic headlands in the state.

In the early 1990s, the dune/beach complex extended more than a quarter mile north from a previous parking area in this location. The waters of Mason Inlet lapped between Shell Island and Figure Eight Island to the north. Within a few years, the fast-migrating inlet eroded the extensive headland and chewed at the scant beach protecting the Shell Island Resort. An emergency dredging and relocation of Mason Inlet three-quarters of a mile north created a tidal-flat buffer for the Shell Island headland that has been designated the Mason Inlet Bird Sanctuary. Audubon North Carolina manages the sanctuary, including the tidal shoals and the eastern half of the sandy spit extending north from Shell Island Resort. The relocation of the inlet is still holding.

It also resulted in shoaling the Intracoastal Waterway at the mouth of Mason's Creek. Homeowner Associations representing 1,044 property owners from Figure Eight Island and the north end of Wrightsville Beach are funding the associated maintenance costs for the 30-year life of the project. There is no intention of maintaining Mason's Creek as a navigable channel, and recreational boaters quickly learned that it shoals rapidly.

There are two routes over one drawbridge to Wrightsville Beach: US 74 and US 76 cross the Intracoastal Waterway to Harbor Island following the early streetcar route. The roads fork at a roundabout; US 74 continues north to the Shell Island portion of Wrightsville Beach, terminating at the Johnny Mercer Pier. US 76 winds to the south end of the island, where it runs out of room at the South Wrightsville Beach Access. There is a highway sign that affirms the obvious.

After a visit it is easy to see how Wrightsville Beach beckons—much as the Lumina Pavilion did in the big band era.

But the community extends a decidedly mixed message with its extremely expensive, heavily enforced public parking policy. Public beach access is available for paid parking, and the summer rates have been as high as $2.50 per hour. Even at this price point, parking is hard to come by.

Access

There are public pay parking lots at the following locations: Jack Parker Boulevard, South Lumina Parking Lot (near the Oceanic Restaurant), Wynn Plaza Parking Lot, East and West Salisbury Street Parking Lots (adjacent to Johnny Mercer's Pier), Ocean View Parking Lot, Moore's Inlet Parking Lot (beside the Holiday Inn), North Lumina Parking Lot, and the North Wrightsville Beach Parking Lot (adjacent to Shell Island Resort).

Park in designated parking areas or lots with meters. Parking is enforced in most lots between 9 AM to 6 PM seven days a week, but may vary. Confirmation helps avoid citations.

Parking fees may be paid in cash or by approved credit card at the parking Pay-Station, or through an account on www.paybyphone.com.

For parking information: search Wrightsville Beach or enter www.town ofwrightsvillebeach.com and use the "Visitors" drop-down menu.

For tourism information: search Wilmington Beaches
or enter www.wilmingtonandbeaches.com.

Best phone number for tourism information: 866-266-9690.

MASONBORO ISLAND NATIONAL ESTUARINE RESEARCH RESERVE

The large sign by the dunes at the south end of Wrightsville Beach announces that you are entering part of the Masonboro Island component of the North Carolina National Estuarine Research Reserve. The namesake island is visible south across the frothy waves of Masonboro Inlet. While there is no visible "line in the sand," the southward migration of the inlet may have slipped across the legal border separating the two islands.

Masonboro Island is a wonderful addition to natural North Carolina. This 5,653-acre, 8.4-mile island is the largest of the state's four components of the National Estuarine Research Reserve. Land and marsh acquisition began in 1985, and the island was officially designated part of the system in 1991.

The undisturbed barrier island is an astonishing anachronism in this rapidly developed section of the coast. The Army Corps of Engineers constructed a jetty on the island's north end to stabilize Masonboro Inlet, and this construction is the only artificial structure on the island

The low, essentially dune-free profile indicates that Masonboro is an "overwash" island. Storm surge rushes over the island and moves sand into the marsh, rolling the island landward.

The wide beaches and the solitude they provide are a haven for loggerhead turtles and piping plovers, two endangered species that can nest in comparative safety along the undeveloped shores. There are approximately 453 acres of natural dune and upland habitat and additional acreage of dredge spoil islands adjacent to the Atlantic Intracoastal Waterway, which comprises the western boundary. Between the dunes and the Waterway are extensive marsh and tidal flats; in fact, these wetlands comprise 87 percent of the reserve's total acreage. By all standards it is considered a pristine barrier island environment that has benefited from lack of easy access.

In 1952, the artificial opening of Carolina Beach Inlet for easier Atlantic Ocean access severed the island from mainland access by vehicle. This proved to be a blessing for the island, restricting visitation to boaters; that is still the case today. Recreational anglers and beach lovers frequent the island seeking the solitude of the expansive marsh and a lengthy undeveloped beach.

While the island has never supported a settlement, it may be that this was the first New World land sighted by a European explorer. Some historians believe that the island noted by explorer Giovanni da Verrazano several miles north of the mouth of the Cape Fear River in a 1524 report to his sponsor, Francis I, included present-day Masonboro Island.

Access

Access is only by boat or kayak. There are no facilities; bring everything needed for a visit. Camping is permitted according to reserve regulations.

Search Masonboro Island Reserve or enter www.nccoastalreserve.net
and use the "Reserve Sites" drop-down menu.

Best phone number for tourism information: 910-962-2998.

SNOWS CUT PARK

New Hanover County maintains a 24-acre park on the north bank of Snows Cut just west of the US 421 Bridge over the Atlantic Intracoastal Waterway, which passes through Snows Cut, linking the Cape Fear River and Myrtle Grove Sound. The address of the park is 9420 River Road. To reach the park from the north, exit US 421 onto River Road and turn right immediately before the Intracoastal Waterway Bridge. The park has four boat-launching ramps, restrooms, picnic shelters, tables, grills, and a gazebo.

Search Snows Cut Park or enter www.parks.nhcgov.
com and use the dropdown menu, Locations.

Best phone number to reserve a shelter: 910-798-PARK (7275).

PLEASURE ISLAND

This is not an island that can be pinpointed on a map, even though Google Maps can drop a marker. Instead, it is a very handy way of organizing and marketing some of the most accessible tourist locations within New Hanover County.

In the 1930s, when the U.S. Army Corps of Engineers excavated Snows Cut, a passage for the Intracoastal Waterway spanning between the Cape Fear River and Myrtle Grove Sound, it created an "island" south of the new waterway, which became locally known as Pleasure Island. The newly (and barely) separated peninsula, pinned between the Atlantic Ocean and the Cape Fear River, includes some of the best recreation resources in the county: the resort communities of Carolina and Kure Beach, Carolina Beach State Park, Historic Fort Fisher, and the Fort Fisher State Recreation Area.

The Pleasure Island Chamber of Commerce is organized to provide the marketing and tourism services for this length of coast, which features includes the most easily accessible lengths of beach in the county.

US 421 crosses the Atlantic Intracoastal Waterway from the north. It is locally renamed to Lake Park Boulevard as it enters Carolina Beach. The Pleasure Island Chamber of Commerce office is on the west side of the highway at 1121 North Lake Park Boulevard. You can avoid heavy summer traffic by turning right onto Dow Road, the first intersection after you cross over Snows Cut. Dow Road is a two-lane road bordering Carolina Beach State Park, and summer traffic is lighter here than on US 421. Turn left on Harper

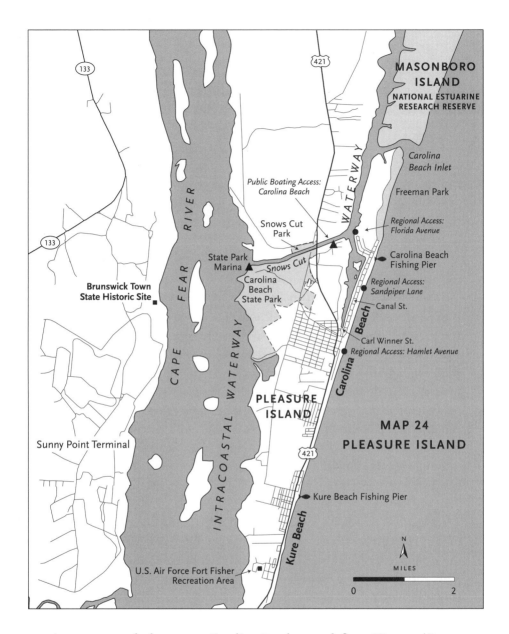

Avenue to reach downtown Carolina Beach, turn left on SR 1539 (Ocean Boulevard) for southern Carolina Beach, or continue to Avenue K, which ends in the center of Kure Beach.

Search Pleasure Island NC or enter www.pleasureislandnc.org.

Best phone number for tourism information: 910-458-8434.

New Hanover County   319

Access

The individual municipalities provide access. For a rule of thumb, sleep north and swim south; the farther south on US 421, the more convenient the access.

CAROLINA BEACH STATE PARK

Carolina Beach State Park is on Pleasure Island's northwest corner just off of Dow Road, a quick right turn off of US 421 after crossing Snows Cut. The landmark for the signed turn is a water tower. Turn right onto SR 1628, which leads to the park.

The high-intensity nearby resort environment is a foil for this 761-acre park bounded by the Cape Fear River to the west, Snows Cut to the north, and Dow Road, which bisects the peninsula. The park offers campsites and boating access to Snows Cut and the Cape Fear River and, importantly, preserves some of the unique natural features of the coastal plain.

Carolina Beach State Park protects some of the most biologically diverse plant communities in the entire state park system. The network of interpretive trails threads among 13 different plant communities. One of these is the native longleaf pine savannah bordering the entrance road of the park. Once characteristic of much of New Hanover County, it is carefully sustained by using controlled burns, a process that mimics how fire would naturally work in an uninhabited longleaf pine forest.

Two trails to seek out, among the many in the park, are the Sugarloaf Trail and the Fly Trap Loop.

Sugarloaf Trail skirts south from the park marina along the east bank of the Cape Fear. Birdlife is one joy of the trail: discreet hikers are likely to see wading birds such as egrets and herons and perhaps catch a glance of a kingfisher along the salt marshes and sandy riverbank. After an easy mile-long walk along a packed-sand trail, hikers arrive at the Sugarloaf, a large relic sand dune from the Pleistocene age, nearly 55 feet above sea level, that is stabilized by live oak trees. Sugarloaf has long been a navigational landmark for Cape Fear sailors—it appears on maps drafted in the mid-eighteenth century. Farther along the trail there are several limestone sink ponds, formed when the underlying coquina rock collapsed after being dissolved by groundwater percolation and the new surface depression filled with water. The trail loops back to the marina, and spur trails return to the camping area.

Fly Trap Loop leads through boggy ground populated by the carnivorous Venus flytraps, sundews, and pitcher plants, which prefer the high moisture and spongy organic soil in limited areas of the coastal plain. The Venus flytrap is found only within a 75-mile radius of Wilmington and nowhere else in the world. If you call the park in May, the rangers will be glad to tell you when the flytraps will flower, a point in their life cycle that makes these diminutive predators more visible.

The remainder of the park is generally a combination of evergreen shrub savanna and sandy ridge vegetation. The juxtaposition of these strikingly varied environments is readily seen in the short Fly Trap Loop. In mid- to early spring, the flowers of the sweetbay magnolia, which prefers the dark soil of the wetter areas of the park, perfume the trails. In mid- to late summer, the fragrant flowers of loblolly bay, an upright broadleaf evergreen tree, are in full bloom. In the drier sandy ridge habitats, wiregrass and longleaf pine join blackjack oak to form the familiar Sandhills associations.

Access

The park is open at 7 AM and closes as early as 6 PM in the winter months and as late as 10 PM in the summer.

The park provides camping and boating access to the Cape Fear River and Intracoastal Waterway. The tent/trailer campsites may be reserved online or by calling; groups may reserve sites too. There are restrooms and a central bathhouse but no utility hookups.

The marina has 44 slips available for daily, weekly, or monthly rental. A full-service store and snack bar at the marina stocks items such as insect repellent, sunscreen, sunglasses, flares, and fishing tackle. The marina also has restrooms.

There is also a boat-launching ramp and parking for vehicles with trailers.

Search Carolina Beach Park or enter www.ncparks.gov
and use the "Find a Park" drop-down menu.

Best phone number for tourism information: 910-458-8206.

Campsite reservations: 910-458-7770.

Blue Skies for the Brown Pelican

There were brown pelicans in the early 1960s, and then there were none for nearly two decades. Now they are back, steadily increasing in numbers and pushing their home range north. These magnificent birds have permanent roosts (the brown pelican does not always migrate) on dredge spoil islands as far north as Oregon Inlet, a historic first. It is all the more remarkable because the species hovered on the brink of extinction in the 1970s. The brown pelican is a companion story to the resurgence of many raptors following the banning of DDT in the early 1970s.

And *how* they are back—flying gracefully, elegantly, wondrously lazing and dipping, gliding by the beach. To see a squadron pass, wing to wing or in an echelon grouping, feather-to-froth above the waves, is to witness the deliberate passage of great, dignified kites. So effortless is their habit of flight that pelicans appear to be magically suspended, pulled past the beach by invisible strings. They rule the skies above our coastal waters.

If you aren't sure you have ever seen a pelican, here is the first clue: the birds are huge. They're the largest birds you are likely to see at the coast. A pelican flies with great dignity, pulling its head back on its shoulders, tucking its nearly 1-foot-long beak into its chest. It is, in a word, unconcerned, and certainly above it all.

That the pelican has grace in the air seems impossible given its awkward, practically prehistoric appearance. The overlarge bill that is its meal ticket cuts into its appeal. You cannot use words like "cute" or "cuddly" to describe them. Surprisingly, though, pelicans can be adroit, nimble, and beak-bashingly brave when hungry.

The second best thing to a pelican fly-by is a dinnertime at the wave trough. Pelicans are picky eaters, feeding almost exclusively on mullet, menhaden, and silversides (a small baitfish)—not that you'll ever see. They feed opportunistically, with the subtlety and elegance of a dropped brick.

Pelicans fold their wings, tip their tail feathers up, and drop, no, *crash* into the water from heights of 30 feet or more. It is a teeth-jarring spectacle to witness and would crumble the hollow bones of a pelican except that they are protected by all-natural bubble wrap: air sacs under their skin that also help them to bob to the surface like a cork when their beaks are full. Dinner comes up in the scoop sack beneath the beak, the water is squeezed out, the fish is swallowed whole. The pelican rises and, if still hungry, crashes the lunch counter again.

It's quite a show because brown pelicans have a wingspan of nearly 7 feet. Ordinarily, their flying habit is so lazy as to be hypnotic, but when the dinner bell rings, it becomes reckless abandon. There's a sudden climb, a precipitous plunge, and a satisfied push back from the table.

The brown pelican's recovery was rapid once it got underway. The key was the banning of the pesticide DDT, which persisted in the food chain. When pelicans retained high levels by eating contaminated fish, the residual systemic DDT reduced calcium in their eggshells, resulting in nesting failure because of crushing. Today, the threat removed, the bird flourishes in North Carolina because of suitable nesting habitat.

In the early 1980s, brown pelicans began nesting on older dredge-spoil islands with grassy cover in Pamlico Sound. Adults construct nests about 1 foot high made of grass. Usually they lay two or three eggs in spring that hatch in a month. The parents feed the chicks regurgitated fish. Volunteers who help biologists band the new chicks report that the rookery islands are aromatic to a fault and can linger in laundry for two wash cycles.

Happily, the recently established pelican colonies seem permanent. There are an estimated 5,000–6,000 nesting pairs (2017), and the population is considered stable. In spite of its nonchalant flight, the brown pelican is doing much better than just sliding by.

CAROLINA BEACH

A well-designed boardwalk, updated and improved in 2015, has created a classy and enticing place at the up-tempo resort of Carolina Beach. The oceanfront center of action, unique in the state, is elegantly enhanced by the arbor-covered elongated walkway that spans from the Hampton Inn in the south nearly the full length of the oceanfront hotel district. To cross the dunes, to stroll by the sea, to have a seat and rest awhile—even just to shower off the sand—go to the boardwalk.

This is not gentrification of a place for years known for its buzz, jump, and pop. The Carolina Beach boardwalk is not only a promenade; it's a finishing touch that organizes the oceanfront. It frames the action—waves to the east, beach party to the west. The town persona is still neon and beach music, and the boardwalk does not tamp the energy down. Turquoise, tangerine, and all the collegiate colors paint the mood of this resort city.

The clear oceanfront center of action are the several blocks either side and between Cape Fear Boulevard and Harper Avenue. There is a lively urban density to this central area, where awnings hover over narrow alleys and ornamental streetlights illuminate the crowded walkways. Here the streets are so narrow that cars have to crawl. There is just a lot to do here—live-music nightspots, miscellaneous vendors, whatever. It doesn't matter what the shops sell: the attraction is the compression of the space and the jostling it forces. Carolina Beach has the feel of a carnival midway. It needs the fuel of coconut oil, night breezes, and crowds to feed the bounce. The boardwalk comes alive at night, especially during the annual Beach Music Festival, when shaggers shuffle into town in a dance-loving mass.

Something is working right for the town—a Courtyard Marriott sporting a slightly retro look anchors the southern end of the center and fits right in despite its mass.

Carolina Beach has been a resort/entertainment destination since the late nineteenth century. The town incorporated in 1925. There are remnants of that era: the median of Harper Avenue once sported trolley lines that brought bathers to the beach from distant places. US 421, routed over Lake Park Boulevard, is the main thoroughfare; after passing the Harper Avenue turn toward the city center, it veers east to the oceanfront, behind a row of houses. The namesake Lake Park is on the west side, and the residential development of mostly single-family homes continues to the city limits at Alabama Avenue.

One block north of Harper Avenue is Carl Winner Street, an important demarcation in the resort. North of Carl Winner Street the oceanfront is actually similar to a barrier island separated from the peninsula by Myrtle Grove Sound. South of Carl Winner Street, Carolina Beach is on the peninsula that spans west to the Cape Fear River.

The barrier island section is mostly residential, single-family, and multifamily houses. Myrtle Grove Sound is the center of boating and fishing activity for Carolina Beach. Since the mid-1980s the small cottages on approximately 50-foot-wide lots have been steadily replaced by midrise condominiums. The taller buildings, narrow streets, and limited on-street parking provide an urban feeling. These newer buildings screen the oceanfront, which is not visible until nearly the end of Carolina Beach Avenue. (There are several long-established motels and hotels north of Carl Winner Street close to downtown.)

This area becomes crowded during summer. Driving to the north end of

Carolina Beach Avenue and returning by way of Canal Street can be tedious. The limited parking fills up quickly, and easy access is the province of the residents and renters.

In recent years the pent-up energy has spilled out onto a terrific resource: Freeman Park, the undeveloped, four-wheel-drive portion of the barrier island managed by the town. The place is an incredible destination for sunbathing, fishing, camping, hanging out, and, during the October 1–March 1 off-season, horseback riding.

The entrance to Freeman Park begins at a guardhouse/toll booth where the pavement of Canal Street and Carolina Beach Avenue ends. The undeveloped barrier, with designated campsites, is framed by Carolina Beach Inlet and the Atlantic Ocean. The 1952 opening of the inlet created the park and cut Masonboro Island off from vehicle traffic. Since 2004 it has been managed by the city as a natural resource.

Vehicle owners must purchase permits to drive into Freeman Park. Different permits are available for day use, for holiday weekends, and for annual use. As with any park, local regulations restrict the vehicle access as well as visitor behavior. It is a win-win all the way around.

Freeman Park and easy ocean access was the big gain from opening the inlet, but that artificial breach has altered the replenishing natural flow of sand from north of the inlet. As a result, the north end of Carolina Beach has wrestled with erosion. A rock revetment reinforces the dune line in front of several houses at the north end. (In 1996 Hurricane Fran washed away much of the sand, exposing the revetment. Hurricane Florence revealed it again.) The beach has a very wide, low dune line and a fairly gentle slope. Carolina Beach Avenue angles east at Starfish Street, and erosion has decreased the width of the beach approaching the Carolina Beach Fishing Pier.

South of Harper Avenue, Carolina Beach looks entirely different. This is the "high ground" and the site of traditional cottage homes, rooming houses, apartments, and small motels. It is more relaxed and inviting than the north end of town, a feeling reinforced by Carolina Beach Lake Park, a freshwater lake set aside and developed as a city recreation area. Much of this area flooded during Hurricane Florence.

Access

There are regional access locations at Carolina Beach Avenue North and Pelican Lane, Carolina Beach Avenue North and Sandpiper Lane, and Carolina Beach Avenue South and Hamlet Avenue. Carolina Beach Avenue South and Atlanta Avenue are the southern town limits.

There are 500 parking spaces within walking distance of city hall, and a fee for all-day parking.

Search Carolina Beach or enter www.carolinabeach.org
and use the "Visitors" drop-down menu.

Search Pleasure Island NC or enter www.pleasureislandnc.org.

Best phone number for tourism information: 910-458-8434.

KURE BEACH

In 2001 Wilmington Beach and Hanby Beach, two contiguous unincorporated areas of New Hanover County, were annexed by Carolina Beach to the north and Kure (*Cur*-ree) Beach to the south, respectively. The Carolina Beach city line is the centerline of Alabama Street. Houses on the south side of Alabama Street are in the Kure Beach section that previously was known as Hanby Beach. Also at Alabama Street, South Lake Park Boulevard, the route of US 421, changes names to Fort Fisher Boulevard North.

In Carolina Beach the state-name streets intersecting South Lake Boulevard signal the approach to Kure Beach. (The "state" streets are intersected by the "fish" streets, named for local game fish.)

Expanded Kure Beach is looking good even at the cost of a quirky north-end landmark, the LaQue Test Center. This was a highly successful (established in 1935) long-term metal weathering test center that exposed structural metal, such as air-conditioner covers and window frames, to the sea elements.

Handsome homes cover the oceanfront location just as the road makes a gentle bend inland. The homes are certainly a much classier introduction to the historic town center than the test site was, but they lack the double-take impact of the "hubcaps-hung-out-to-dry" strangeness of the earlier scene.

Kure Beach dates from 1947, spreading south from where Avenue K intersects with US 421, the stoplight! There is an oceanside extension of Avenue K leading to the Kure Beach Fishing Pier, the oldest pier in the state. This nexus of business includes some shops, a small café, and a convenience store. This is downtown Kure Beach. Atlantic Avenue runs north oceanside from the Kure Beach Pier, with a fine view of the wide, gently sloping

The public beach adjacent the Kure Beach fishing pier is lifeguarded and open for the business of play. (Photo by Bill McKenzie and Tammy Harrell)

beach. A town pavilion overlooks the sands; it an entertainment site during the vacation season.

The community has a wonderful old-timey feeling; it has its own character, distinct from Carolina Beach. Kure Beach homes are not grand, but simple. Even the many new houses reflect an architectural idiom in keeping with that simpler stylistic tone. The town is solid, and the cottages are upgrading with new style that seems content to fit in rather than stand out. The selling point here is the ocean. Kure Beach signals that newer is better than older and comfort does not have to be ostentatious.

Kure Beach sits on a mainland bluff that has protected its cottages from storm damage. Still, it has taken its thrashings: prior to the 1954 landfall of Hazel, a Category 4 hurricane, Atlantic Avenue was two blocks away from the waves. In 2018 Hurricane Florence chiseled uncomfortably close to the foundations of several multifamily units approaching Fort Fisher State Historic Site. The storm took a lot of sand away and left too little a margin of hope.

L. C. Kure constructed the pier in 1923, then promptly rebuilt it the following year after it collapsed. The pier has been rebuilt several times since then because of hurricane damage (repaired again after 1996 Hurricane Fran; it weathered Hurricane Florence), but it continues to serve the many anglers who want to fish amid a sense of history and perseverance. A won-

The colorful cottages of Kure Beach. (Photo by Bill McKenzie and Tammy Harrell)

derful grizzled group hangs out on the pier for hours in the worst of weather waiting for the summer and fall king mackerel runs. By listening in, you can learn a lot about fishing and a lot about what's wrong with the town, state, world, and so on.

The western city limits of Kure Beach extend to the Cape Fear River through the maritime woodland west of Ninth Avenue and Dow Road, the edge of the developed resort. Most of this area will stay undeveloped because it is a required buffer zone between the town and Sunny Point Army Terminal, a military fuel/ammunition depot across the Cape Fear River. South of town center, at 858 Fort Fisher Boulevard South adjacent to the Fort Fisher Trading Post, paired brick columns marking the Fort Fisher entrance flank the road. These are far in advance of the Fort Fisher Historic Site but signal the approach to the U.S. Air Force Fort Fisher Recreation Area, a complex of cottages available for U.S. Air Force personnel.

On the left just before the Fort Fisher State Historic Site is a condominium complex called The Riggings, vacation housing under assault by severe erosion caused in part by a rare natural outcrop of coquina rock north and seaward of their property. The outcrop is a state natural heritage site, and that designation prohibits nourishment of the eroding beach. "Temporary" sandbags (now present more than 20 years) protect the buildings.

In July 2004 the Federal Emergency Management Agency tapped its

New Hanover County

funds for predisaster mitigation for $2.7 million of the $3.6 million required to purchase and demolish The Riggings pending condominium association approval. The owners turned down the offer to accept the money and rebuild across the street.

The coquina rock outcrop, rare in North Carolina, is plainly visible at low tide.

Access

Beach access is labeled and plentiful. Parking is available at the oceanfront ends of Avenues E through N.

Search Kure Beach or enter www.townofkurebeach.org and use the "Recreation & Tourism/Visitor Information" drop-down menus.

Search Pleasure Island NC or enter www.pleasureislandnc.org.

Best phone number for tourism information: 910-458-8434.

FORT FISHER STATE HISTORIC SITE

Fort Fisher State Historic Site is 3 miles south of Kure Beach center and features a serene entry: the road passes under the wandering limbs of a salt-sculpted live oak forest. On the west side of the roadway are the visitor center and the remaining earthworks and reconstructions of the fort. The compelling site is the sea, visible through the coiling, rough bark of the live oaks.

Fort Fisher was the southern counterpart of Fort Macon on Bogue Banks in Carteret County, with an important difference: Fort Fisher was an earthwork fortification. Confederate forces constructed it to pair with Fort Caswell to protect the Cape Fear River's navigable waters. Confederate forces succumbed to a merciless assault here on January 15, 1865, one of the largest land-sea battles ever fought on U.S. soil.

The relentless attack by the Union Navy pales when compared to the assault by the sea. Only 10 percent of the original earthworks remain. The original embankments extended south and were seaward of the existing Fort Fisher State Recreation Area parking lot! The rubble-armored shoreline east of the Daughters of the Confederacy monument (previously moved inland) is the approximate location of the Confederate headquarters inside the fort.

Name That Wave

Anyone who has been walloped unexpectedly by a wave knows that not all waves are alike. There are four identifiable types (there is no "sneaky" wave, however), and each one looks and acts differently when it gets to the beach.

Bubbles and turbulent water bubbling down the face of the wave identify **spilling** waves. These waves seem to bubble away over a long distance, the result of a shallow, sloping bottom.

Collapsing waves are usually low and very close to the beach; the lower half of the wave plunges abruptly, and the wave plays out up the beach. It makes a *plop* or *ploosh* sound when it collapses. These usually occur where the beach profile is short and steep.

A **surging** wave peaks noticeably, but then the bottom moves rapidly forward to push the water up the beach, sort of flipping it onto the sand. The wave seems to pulse forward.

A **plunging** wave is a surfer's wave: the crest curls over, creating an air pocket, and then plunges into a trough. Plunging waves are the most spectacular and, in our mind's eye, the true beach wave. They occur when a swell approaching shore reaches a water depth 1.3 times the height of the wave.

At this point, the wave has shortened and its height has increased, but there is insufficient water (because of the shallow depth) for the swell to continue. The water droplets at the top curl over and crash from lack of support.

There is a personal sense of waves being "big," but what does that mean in real measurements? It's possible to guesstimate the height of breaking waves in the following manner: walk toward the ocean, and stop when you reach a spot on the beach where the top of the breaking waves is level with the horizon. This makes you part of the yardstick.

To guesstimate the wave height, compute the height measured between your eye level and the lowest point on the beach where the water recedes after a breaking wave (whew). This dimension is equal to the height of the breaking wave as measured between its peak and trough. It's a mouthful, but not so challenging. Just remember that your eye level is approximately 5.5 inches less than your height, and add the resulting number to your best estimate of the height difference between the low point of the beach and the point where you are standing.

What surprises me most about this little exercise is that our personal frame of reference for a "big" wave is usually a wave size much less than our height. Waves feel a lot bigger than they really are.

The live oak–lined entrance of Fort Fisher State Historic Site.
(Photo by Bill McKenzie and Tammy Harrell)

The rock armoring of the coast to protect the remnants of the fort received special authorization from the North Carolina General Assembly. At
the time it was the only exception to state law prohibiting permanent structures to thwart erosion.

The cause of the erosion may be the coquina rock outcrop about a quarter mile north. Coquina is a hard limestone composed of the fossilized shells
of a small bivalve. It may have been formed between 10,000 and 2 million
years ago. This outcrop, the only one in the state, is protected as a natural
heritage site. The rock disrupts the normal north–south flow of sand, creating mild erosion to the north and pronounced erosion at the fort.

Admission to the fort is free. The visitor center houses artifacts such
as battle and commemorative swords, and the grounds have an interpretive
walk with exhibits. There is a restored gun emplacement, Shepherd's Battery, with a fully functional heavy seacoast cannon that fired a 32-pound pro-
jectile. The fort has several functioning period weapons that were in place at
the fort sometimes demonstrated at special public events. North Carolina's
Underwater Archaeology Branch maintains an underwater research laboratory at Fort Fisher. This office is instrumental in developing the preservation
and restoration techniques necessary to deal with artifacts recovered from
underwater archaeological sites.

Boardwalk trail along the Cape Fear River at Fort Fisher State Historic Site.
(Photo by Bill McKenzie and Tammy Harrell)

Access

The fort is open April 1–October 1, 9–5 Monday–Saturday, 1–5 on Sunday. The hours are shortened November 1–March 31. You can get to the coquina rock outcrop by walking north on the beach at low tide.

Search Fort Fisher or enter www.nchistoricsites.org/fisher/.

Best phone number for more information: 910-458-5538.

FORT FISHER STATE RECREATION AREA

The Fort Fisher State Recreation Area is the big oceanfront playground at the southern tip of New Hanover County. Nearly the entire peninsula between the Atlantic Ocean and the Cape Fear River from Fort Fisher State Historic Site south is set aside for primary recreation use and preservation of the resources. The great attraction is more than 4 miles of magnificent beach. Including adjoining preserves, there are acres of dunes, maritime forests, islands, marshes, and estuarine waters that are free for exploring.

New Hanover County

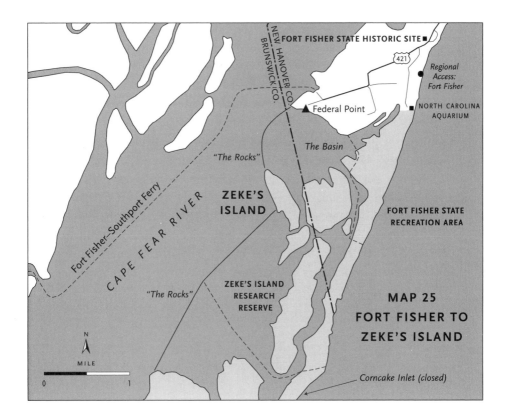

MAP 25
FORT FISHER TO
ZEKE'S ISLAND

A major regional access facility with nearly 200 parking spaces, restrooms, showers, refreshments, and a dune crossover is just south of Fort Fisher. The dune crossover leads to a glorious beach restricted only by the willingness to walk. The beach has summer lifeguard service.

The dune crossover at the access area elevates you above the vegetation in the trough lying behind the primary dunes and provides an educational stroll more than 150 feet long, ending at the gazebo shelter overlooking the waves. Salt-sheared wax myrtle and sea oats/beach grass are the predominant cover along with blanket flower, dollar weed, and other dune-loving plants. The monument at Fort Fisher is visible to the north; looking south, the barrier spit stretches to the horizon.

The recreation area is great for surf fishing, too, and a dune crossover ramp for off-road vehicles sees frequent use by those who love to fish in comparative isolation. They travel south to the barrier beach of Zeke's Island Reserve, a component of the North Carolina Estuarine Research Reserve.

The beachfront narrows to a barrier spit south of the access area, backed by the waters, marshes, and islands of Zeke's Island Reserve. Corncake Inlet, a secondary outlet for the Cape Fear River, used to end the spit; that inlet is now closed, and the shoaling makes it possible to walk the 6 miles to Bald Head Island from Fort Fisher State Recreation Area.

In 2004 North Carolina imposed restrictions to all-terrain vehicles on the barrier strip because of threats to nesting sea turtles and other wildlife. The current policy allows properly permitted vehicles access to the barrier strip 24 hours a day between September 15 and March 31. At all other times, vehicles must exit the beach one-half hour before the park closes. The park gates are locked at closing time.

US 421 continues west to Federal Point following the general bowing of the mainland to the terminus of the highway at the Fort Fisher/Southport ferry dock and the North Carolina Wildlife Resources Commission boat ramp at "the Basin" of Zeke's Island Reserve.

Access

The major access is clearly signed from US 421. The general hours are dawn to dusk year-round. In summer there are lifeguards at the beach, near the access area.

ATV access to the spit south of the regional access site is restricted to permitted vehicles. Permits are $15 weekdays and $25 weekends. An annual pass is $60, a family pass $100. Buy permits at the park office with cash, check, or money order.

Search Fort Fisher State or enter www.ncparks.gov
and enter Fort Fisher in the search window.

Best phone number for more information: 910-458-5798.

NORTH CAROLINA AQUARIUM, FORT FISHER

Rivers flow down to the sea, and the journey of the Cape Fear River from its upstream Piedmont origins to its outfall is a major feature of the Fort Fisher Aquarium's Cape Fear Conservatory. Exhibits present the habitats and habitants along the route, following the changing ecology deep into the Atlantic Ocean.

The walk by the river exhibit showcases the trees, shrubs, and vines of

New Hanover County

the upriver swamps and rare ecosystems such as Carolina bays, home to carnivorous plants such as Venus flytraps.

Here you can go eye-to-eye with a shark—friend or foe? The 20,000-gallon shark tank exhibits these sleek, machine-eyed predators, and additional tanks with other large game fishes offer further educational highlights here. There is more than just a fishy world waiting to be discovered, as the aquarium hosts interactive programs throughout the year, including several behind-the-scenes tours. The program schedule varies.

The aquarium is carefully tucked into the upland region of the Fort Fisher Recreational Area. Like its counterparts in Manteo and Pine Knoll Shores, it presents and explores the mysteries and wonders of the ocean. Exhibits concentrate on the marine and terrestrial life of the southern coast of North Carolina. Multiple programs are offered throughout the year, and the 200-seat auditorium stays busy with daily lectures and films.

Access

The aquarium is open 9 AM–5 PM daily. It is closed Thanksgiving Day, Christmas Day, and New Year's Day. Admission charged.

Search Fort Fisher Aquarium or enter
www.ncaquariums.com and select Fort Fisher.

Best phone number for more information: 910-772-0500.

FEDERAL POINT

Federal Point is the end of the road for US 421. It is a loosely applied term that includes the Fort Fisher/Southport ferry dock, the nearby boat ramp and parking lot, the elevated Battery Buchanan Civil War gun emplacement, and some of the undeveloped flats south of the road touching the waters of "the Basin" of Zeke's Island Reserve. Historically, Federal Point may have been the most southeastern part of the mainland.

A short trail leads to "the Rocks," and a short climb leads to the top of the Battery Buchanan gun emplacement, which has a commanding view of the Cape Fear River.

Access

Park carefully at the boat ramp turnout or off of the highway in the obvious pullovers or at the parking area of the ferry dock.

ZEKE'S ISLAND NATIONAL ESTUARINE RESEARCH RESERVE

The northern border of Zeke's Island National Estuarine Research Reserve begins at the traffic turnaround or the boat ramp at the end of US 421. A trail from there leads to a breakwater known as "the Rocks," the landmark for the preserve's western boundary. The bay inside the rocks is called "the Basin." It is possible to walk the Rocks to a small, sandy spit that is high enough to support some shrubby growth and is the namesake Zeke's Island. This is only advised on the ebbing tide and with great caution; the rocks are slippery with algae. (Wear old clothes, carry water and bug spray, and *be careful*, as emergency help is not readily available.)

Other portions of Zeke's Island are more easily accessible. The preserve includes 1,653 acres of islands, a barrier spit, marsh, tidal flats, and shallow estuarine waters. The rock-rimmed basin slowly filling with sediment is a unique feature. It was included in the National Estuarine Research Reserve Program in 1985.

The three islands—Zeke's, No-Name, and North Island, with their attending flats—are the important components of the reserve. Zeke's Island is 42 low acres, with some high ground where live oaks and red cedar trees grow. North Island, once a barrier island south of New Inlet and now parallel to the barrier spit, has about 138 acres. No-Name Island, southeast from Zeke's Island, has about 3 acres. Extensive marshes and tidal flats spread out from each of the islands. The beach barrier spit has about 64 acres of dunes and uplands and extends to Bald Head Island.

The complex is important to nesting sea turtles and several shorebird species. Bird life thrives in the abundant tidal flat and includes herons and brown pelicans. Its comparative isolation supplements Slip Island and Battery Island, important rookeries nearby in the Cape Fear River.

A gun emplacement was on Zeke's Island during the Civil War. The Army Corps of Engineers constructed the Rocks between 1875 and 1881, extending them from Federal Point along Zeke's Island to just north of Smith Island. (The Rocks are 30 feet wide at the submerged base.) The intent was to reduce shoaling in the Cape Fear River channel from historical New Inlet. The construction effectively closed New Inlet and resulted in the slow silting of the Basin. Zeke's Island subsequently accreted and became a fishing center and the site of a turpentine factory. The great hurricane of 1899 destroyed the wharf and fishing operations.

New Inlet migrated south and eventually shoaled completely, and a lengthening spit of sand has been added south of Fort Fisher Recreation Area.

Access

The barrier spit of Zeke's Island is an approximately 3.5-mile walk south from Fort Fisher State Recreation Area. Boating or kayak access is best from the boating access parking lot at Federal Point. It is possible but NOT ADVISABLE to walk the Rocks to Zeke's Island.

Search Zeke's Island or enter www.nccoastalreserve.net and use the "Reserve Sites" drop-down menu.

Best phone number for tourism information: 910-962-2998.

FORT FISHER TOLL FERRY

The Fort Fisher/Southport toll ferry dock is on the west side of US 421 at Federal Point. Riding the ferry is one of those marvelous interludes in a day trip that only a car ferry ride can provide. This not a quick hop for an evening across the river: daily departures stop at 6:15 PM from Southport and 7 PM from Fort Fisher. This daytime connector crosses every 45 minutes between April 1 and October 31. Departures begin at 5:30 AM weekdays, 7 AM on Saturday and Sunday. A bird guidebook and binoculars turn a pleasant ride into a wildlife adventure.

The ferry replaces about 40 miles of driving and sometimes shares the river with impressive freighters entering or leaving the port of Wilmington. The passage takes about 30 minutes and offers excellent views of Zeke's Island, Bald Head Island, and Oak Island. Like a mariner, you can mark the transit with two familiar landmarks: Old Baldy, the lighthouse on Bald Head Island, and the newer Oak Island light that replaced it. Between and beyond them are the open ocean and the hazardous Frying Pan Shoals.

One particularly intriguing site on the west bank of the Cape Fear is the

Intracoastal Interstate

Wherever you go to the beach in North Carolina, you will cross the Atlantic Intracoastal Waterway. There is no way to avoid it, and even less reason to notice it much unless you're crossing a body of water by means of one of the high-rise bridges linking the barrier islands to the mainland.

Yet this remarkable ditch represents one of the more ambitious and successful civil engineering projects ever completed by the U.S. government. It provides a safe, protected waterway route for light boats and barges not suited for the open ocean. If you are a boater and like lengthy, varied cruises, the Intracoastal Waterway in North Carolina has to be a magical trip. If you are going to the beach, however, it is a hurdle.

The waterway is an old idea. George Washington surveyed a canal route through the Dismal Swamp in the mid-1750s, and a completed canal in 1803 led to boomtown years for Elizabeth City. Other early barge/canal projects connected the Neuse and Newport Rivers north of Beaufort in the early nineteenth century, to shorten the commercial route between that city and New Bern.

The German U-boat attacks during World War I made a sheltered sealane a necessity, and the project was pressed to completion by 1936. It had immediate impact along its route. At Oak Island, for example, the waterway actually impeded access to the coast because it made an island. The project lopped the tip off the mainland south of Wilmington at Snows Cut, which linked Myrtle Grove Sound and the Cape Fear River. This made a Pleasure Island of the mainland resorts of Carolina Beach, Kure Beach, and Fort Fisher.

The waterway reaches 3,000 miles from Massachusetts to Brownsville, Texas, using both natural waterways and artificial canals to provide a continuous navigable passage. Approximately 330 miles are in North Carolina. From Virginia to Morehead City, the waterway is considerably inland from the barrier beaches. From Morehead City south, however, the Intracoastal Waterway is directly landward of the barrier beaches. This part of the coast is where you are most likely to be aware of the inevitable crossing.

Since the 1970s, there has been an improvement in the crossings. Modern four-lane crossings have taken the place of the old swing bridges. The faster, higher-capacity crossings fulfill the need for better hurricane evacuation. This minimization of the waterway has provided an unexpected bonus:

a cure for "seasonal vexation disorder," the agonizing waits at swing bridge crossings while pleasure craft motor on beneath the open bridge, indifferent to the annoyance of idling cars.

The waterway is less than 90 feet wide at most crossings, but that was enough to make it a very effective moat. Some crossings, such as Coinjock in Currituck County, became legendary, if not notorious. The entire Eastern Seaboard seemed to back up on the north side of the waterway, waiting for the bridge to drop back in place and the crossing warning arms to lift on holiday weekends. When the bridge opened, it was like waving the green flag at a NASCAR race, and it sent fuming tourists roaring to the beach. In the early 1980s, a barge rammed the bridge, jamming it, causing traffic of all kinds to grind to a halt until repairs were made.

The most intractable bottleneck was between Morehead City and Atlantic Beach, particularly before the new bridge at Cape Carteret opened. In the summer, Bogue Sound waterway traffic was nearly as endless as automobile traffic on the causeway. The bridge would flip open and shut like it was part of a pinball machine. Traffic would snarl westward on US 70 to the Morehead City limits on weekends. Waiting to cross Bogue Sound had the same inevitability as April 15 and was regarded with the same affection.

You have a few more years to snag a "nostalgic" bridge on busy routes. The waterway routes the length of the Alligator River in Dare and Tyrrell Counties, and the long bridge over the river on US 64 still must lift for boating traffic, which, thankfully, is comparatively light at that location. There is the Beaufort Channel Bridge east of Swansboro, also lightly used, and the swing bridge that carries NC 50 into Surf City. Perhaps the bridge of legend was the narrow Pontoon Bridge serving Sunset Beach, gone but certainly not forgotten. It figuratively was a bridge to another era of family vacations where good things awaited those who were patient and patient and patient.

That's the landlubber's point of view. If you look at the waterway through the eyes of a boater, it's a different experience indeed. In North Carolina, it provides many of the public boating access sites serving the sounds and ocean. Many of the North Carolina Wildlife Resources Commission boat ramps are located along its length, usually within easy access to coastal highways. Communities on the waterway close to inlets frequently have private marinas that use it to advantage. Calabash, for example, is a fishing community on Calabash Creek with access to Little River Inlet by means of the waterway. Throughout its length, the waterway offers excellent crabbing from piers or banks. Fishing can be good, to, depending on where you are along the waterway's course.

Towns along the waterway, such as Belhaven, Beaufort, and Southport, have their own tourist traffic that comes to call by boat. These places pick up a decided cosmopolitan air during the fall and spring migrations of yachts traveling between northern and southern coastal ports.

It is hard to think of the Intracoastal Waterway as a "working road," but that is its primary purpose. Currently it is troubled. The Army Corps of Engineers is having difficulty securing funds for dredging maintenance, and at some inlet crossings, such as Lockwood Folly Inlet, the waterway has shoaled to one-third of its proposed navigation depth (it's supposed to be dredged soon).

The Intracoastal Waterway was born of necessity for coastal security; today its security is no longer a necessity.

abandoned brick cone of Price's Creek Lighthouse, visible slightly downriver from the large commercial docks. Shortly after passing the Price's Creek Lighthouse, which was once used to help navigate the channel to Wilmington, the ferry docks in a sheltered slip just a few miles north of Southport. You've ridden a ferry, crossed a river, and landed in Brunswick County, the southeasternmost county in the state.

Crossings are $5 for a passenger car, $2 for bicycles.

Search Southport Ferry or enter https://www.ncdot.gov
/divisions/ferry and click "Routes and Schedules."

Best phone numbers for tourism information: 910-457-6942
(Southport) and 910-458-3329 (Fort Fisher).

New Hanover County

Brunswick County

BRUNSWICK COUNTY, the southern- and westernmost oceanfront county in the state, borders on South Carolina and is nearly separated from the rest of North Carolina's coast by the Cape Fear River. North of the county, North Carolina's coast is a series of islands arcing north and east, increasingly east to its extreme reach at distant Rodanthe. Relative to the rest of the coast, Brunswick County's beaches are so far west that Bird Island, the westernmost land in the county, is nearly due south of Raleigh.

The county has more than 50 total miles of gently sloping oceanfront accessible from five different islands, and on most of these miles the beaches have a southern exposure.

Bald Head Island, a private resort carved out of the Smith Island Complex east of the Cape Fear River, has an oceanfront with a more southeast–northwest alignment.

West of the Cape Fear River, the four remaining Brunswick Islands—Oak Island, Holden Beach, Ocean Isle Beach, and Sunset Beach—align in a gentle arc that bends from southeast to southwest. The tanning benefits are obvious: to face the beach is to face south, leading to the wry observation that the sun rises on the left and sets on the right.

Complementing the tan-favorable compass alignment of the islands is a barely sloping nearshore that means generally gentle surf. These wide, flat, child-friendly beaches are the foundation of the county's popularity as a family destination. In marked contrast to the higher-wattage appeal of nearby Myrtle Beach, South Carolina, the Brunswick Island communities build their vacation appeal around simple, traditional oceanside and soundside pleasures. The individual island beach resorts offer a smattering of amusements. These are beaches for sandcastles and beach books and sunshades. Off the islands there is shopping and a great deal of golf, but from one island end to another, the vacation tone is set by footprints in the sand.

The tidal rivers and inlets that define the islands separate the county naturally into communities that easily affiliate because of geography. Mainland Southport and St. James, and Oak Island, with its paired communities of Caswell Beach and Oak Island, are easily accessible to each other and work together, served by the Southport–Oak Island Chamber of Commerce. Thirteen-mile-long Oak Island, the lengthiest island, is almost completely residential and one of the county's population centers. Southport, a historic port, is charming in appearance almost to disbelief: live oak–shaded residential streets, a harbor filled with boats and restaurants, and a modest, easily managed commercial center—if you can find a place to park. It's a small town with big appeal for its honest hominess.

The Lockwood Folly River and its wetlands form the physical barrier between Southport–Oak Island and the smaller communities west of the river: Shallotte, Holden Beach, Ocean Isle Beach, Sunset Beach, and Calabash.

Three island communities—Holden Beach, Ocean Isle Beach, and Sunset Beach—have incorporated parts of the mainland, but life on these islands exists apart from their mainland adjuncts. Crossing the high-rise bridges that lead to the three islands is stepping back in time. It's 40 years ago with internet service.

Brunswick County continues to be one of the fastest-growing counties in the state in terms of population-increase percentage. It's a trend driven in great part by the balmy winters of the coastal South, where daytime winter temperatures average in the mid- to high 50s. It is also a county making its mark as a golfing mecca, proudly proclaiming that it is the state's "Golf Coast." Residential golf course community development has driven much of the population increase.

US 17 is the major highway serving the county, routing from Wilmington southwest past Calabash on its way to Myrtle Beach, South Carolina. To reach the island communities, visitors take the once-unhurried two-lane roads that thread the still-rural county en route to the resort communities.

NC 133, which links Wilmington and Southport, is the older, venerable shore route that passes by two county attractions on the way to Southport: Orton Plantation and Gardens and Brunswick Town State Historic Site. Orton Plantation is an eighteenth-century rice plantation with extensive formal gardens. The plantation has been closed since a descendent of the original builder purchased the plantation and began renovation.

Brunswick Town State Historic Site, the historical heart of Brunswick County, was laid out in 1725. The British army razed it in 1776 for resistance against the Crown, and it was never resettled. Visitors can walk the sand beds of streets long gone to see house foundations overlooking the Cape Fear River.

Brunswick County is also a botanical wonderland, possibly hosting more species of plants of restricted distribution than any other county in the state. The diversity of habitats ranges from marsh and maritime forests to Green Swamp, a huge Nature Conservancy preserve of pine savannahs and carnivorous plants.

One of the newest natural features open to the public is Boiling Spring

Lakes Plant Conservation Preserve, a 5,000-acre reserve in the burgeoning community of Boiling Spring Lakes. It offers an unusual peak into the wilds of Brunswick County. Hurricane Florence in 2018 hit Boiling Spring Lakes especially hard, collapsing the dam that formed Patricia Lake, which bordered part of the preserve off of NC 87.

For Your Bucket:

> Book a weekend on Bald Head Island
> Explore Southport
> Join in the 4th of July at Southport
> Climb the Oak Island Lighthouse
> Kayak Big Jim Davis Canal
> Bicycle "Olde Holden" Beach
> Play a Brunswick golf course
> Walk to Bird Island
> Visit the Kindred Spirit
> Eat at Calabash—repeatedly

Search Southport Oak Island or enter www.southport-oakisland.com.

Best phone number for tourism information: 800-457-6964.

Also enter www.nc4thofJuly.com.

For information on Ocean Isle, Holden Beach, and Sunset Beach, search NC Brunswick or enter www.ncbrunswick.com.

Best phone number for tourism information: 800-795-7263.

For information on Brunswick Town State Historic Site search Brunswick Town or enter www.nchistoricsites.org/brunswic/brunswic.htm.

SOUTHPORT

Any approach to Southport sets high expectations for a waterfront community and then delivers. Street-side trees are large and old, a universal statement of both what a community values and longevity in place. The trees give way to a small commercial gathering of one- and two-story brick buildings with enterprises marketing to a mix of residents and tourists. The big deal here, the shaping element underpinning Southport, is a block to the east: the Cape Fear River. Southport is a river town, and the compact center and residential streets taken together are indisputably charming. It's a small-town watercolor to be painted again and again.

Southport perches high on the riverside, 26 feet above sea level. Bay Street parallels the Cape Fear shoreline on the natural bench or shoulder well below the town center, where Moore Street (NC 211) and Howe Street intersect. Walk along Bay Street to see the spiritual heart of this water-based village, where marinas, seafood markets, and restaurants have prime waterfront locations.

The sea breeze—genuine marshy air—affirms the waterfront's mix and match of business and entertainment that time and self-reinvention have cobbled together. People flock to the waterfront to dine and celebrate. They hire charter boats or tie up their sailboats at the marina. No more than a block away, residential porch lights signal home. If this description of Southport strikes you as over-the-top or romanticized, then read *The Old Man and the Boy*, by Robert Ruark. This gentle, nostalgic text draws heavily on the author's boyhood visits with his grandfather, J. B. Ruark, a Southport resident. (A historical marker on Howe Street commemorates the book.) The residential streets that grid inland from the riverfront are lined with two-story, handsomely proportioned wooden houses. In summer, the shaded sidewalks can be musical with crickets and cicadas.

Moore Street, the road into town from the Fort Fisher/Southport ferry dock, passes by a serene *Our Town* cemetery, where moss-draped live oaks shelter the gravesites. Tree-shaded homes line the river right to the city common spaces and waterside park and pier, the heart of the waterfront. East of this promenade passes the ocean traffic of cargo ships, a vivid part of Southport's riverside panorama. The Cape Fear channel aligns so that incoming vessels approach as though they would beach at the waterfront. Similarly, outgoing vessels slide quickly and silently out to sea.

Southport's commanding location over North Carolina's only natural, stable deepwater channel has figured prominently in its history. The two-story Georgian brick building in a parklike setting on Bay Street is the original officers' quarters of mid-eighteenth-century Fort Johnston. The fort was built in 1748 to protect against privateering from French and Spanish vessels.

Whigs burned the original fort in 1775, chasing out Royal Governor Josiah Martin, who fled by British vessel. The federal government rebuilt the fort in 1794–1809. Confederate forces seized the fort in 1861 because of its strategic setting. (Along with Fort Caswell on Oak Island and Fort Fisher across the river, Fort Johnston kept the port of Wilmington open for most of the Civil War.)

Today the officers' quarters serves as the Southport Visitors Center and the place to stop for a copy of the Southport Historical Society's Southport Trail, a 1-mile self-guided walking tour of the community.

The North Carolina Maritime Museum–Southport is adjacent to the visitor center at 204 East Moore Street. It's rich in detail. There is a stunning exhibit of scale models that show the evolution of sailing ships, from merchants to men-of-war. The mercantile, military, and river history that swirled around Southport are meticulously and engagingly presented. The noted "gentleman pirate" Stede Bonnett, captured here on September 26, 1718 (subsequently hanged in "Charles Towne," South Carolina, on December 10, 1718), and piracy generally are the subjects of another exhibit. So, too, is the tragic story of the oil tanker *John D. Gill*, which was torpedoed by a German submarine off of Southport on March 12, 1942. The museum quickly and handsomely fills in the background of Southport's strategic and historical importance, belied by its laid-back atmosphere today.

One natural note: Battery Island, southeast from Southport in the Cape Fear River, is a preserve managed by Audubon North Carolina. The locally known sandbar, closed to human access, has enough feathers in early spring to give it lift. The 100-acre island serves as the nesting ground for nearly 15,000 white ibises and 500 pairs of other shore-wading birds. Seasonally, Audubon North Carolina will sponsor guided bird-watching boat tours, but the island is not open for visitation.

There is a wonderful public pier extending from Bay Street into the Cape Fear River. There are two gazebos on the pier and, weather permitting, a lot of young people trying their luck at fishing.

The Cape Fear River drains into the Atlantic offshore from Southport, the state's most dependable and greatest natural harbor. Southport is also the home port for the Harbor Pilots, who guide the ocean vessels through the local shipping channel.

An important footnote: Southport hosts the North Carolina Fourth of July Festival, a fete the town has been holding for more than 200 years. Stars and Stripes over Southport!

Search Southport NC or enter www.southportnc.org.

Search Southport Oak Island or enter www.southport-oakisland.com.

Best phone number for tourism information: 800-457-6964.

Lighthouses

North Carolina's lighthouses have guided mariners for more than two centuries. These towers are true landmarks—structures identifiable during daylight by their color or painted pattern and by night by their unique lighted signal. In this era of global positioning system navigation, the lighthouses stand tall as working reminders of the state's maritime history. Discovering how tall is a joy that awaits any ambitious traveler—all four major lighthouses are open for climbing for a nominal fee, though hours vary. A tip: get in line early, especially for the full moon climbs!

Six lighthouses serve the coast, marking, north to south, Currituck Banks, Oregon Inlet, Cape Hatteras, Ocracoke Inlet, Cape Lookout, and the Cape Fear River.

North to south, the first light is the redbrick tower at Corolla, known as the Currituck Beach Lighthouse, which was first lighted on December 1, 1875. The 162-foot-tall tower owned and operated by the private nonprofit Outer Banks Conservationists, Inc., is open for climbing to the 150-foot-high focal-plane catwalk. Outer Banks Conservationists, Inc., received the deed for the lighthouse in 2003, based on their long history of restoration and site management. The group charges a small fee to ascend the tower and uses the proceeds for the restoration of the lightkeeper's quarters and the grounds. It is one of the best restoration stories on the Outer Banks. At night, the lighthouse signals with a 20-second flash cycle (on for 3 seconds, off for 17 seconds). The light can be seen for 19 nautical miles.

South of the Currituck light is the horizontally striped frustum of Bodie Island Light Station, which has served Oregon Inlet since 1872. Its beacon is visible 19 miles at sea, and its repeated signal—2.5 seconds on, 2.5 seconds off, 2.5 seconds on, 22.5 seconds off—pulses from a focal plane height of 156 feet above the sandy base. The restored lightkeeper's quarters now serve as a visitor center for Cape Hatteras National Seashore. In 2013, following restoration to the cast iron stairs, the park service opened the lighthouse for climbs; more than 214 spiraling steps ascend to the focal plane deck. Pause before hiking and gaze up the elegant spiral of the weight-restricted stairs. It is quite a view.

The Cape Hatteras Lighthouse, at 208 feet tall, is one of the tallest brick lighthouses in North America and a cause célèbre among lighthouse aficionados. The two beacons inside—once whale oil lamps—make one full rotation every 15 seconds, which is visible as one flash every 7.5 seconds. Built in

1873, the black-and-white barber-pole-striped light replaced an 1802 tower. Although it was 1,500 feet from the ocean when it was built, the ocean was 50 yards away by 1999.

In February of that year, contractors separated it from its foundation, placed it on rollers, jacked it up, put it on tracks leading 2,899.57 feet to its new home, and moved it there. They moved it in July and relit it the following November. The coast guard maintains the light, but the tower belongs to the National Park Service, which carefully controls the ascent up the 257 steps, the equivalent of climbing a 12-story building. Tickets to climb can be purchased at the headquarters building on the lighthouse grounds. The original lightkeeper's quarters is not a museum.

The Ocracoke Lighthouse, dating from 1823, is the oldest continually operating lighthouse in the state. The squat, stucco tower is 75 feet tall, and the focal plane of the light is at 65 feet, visible 14 miles out to sea. At one time it served the state's busiest inlet (Ocracoke) and port (Portsmouth).

The Cape Lookout Lighthouse, south of Ocracoke on South Core Banks in Cape Lookout National Seashore, guards the entrance to Morehead City, warning mariners of the treacherous waters to the southeast known as Cape Lookout Shoals. Placed into service in 1859, this lighthouse became the model for the other majestic beacons along the coast. Its diamond-patterned black-and-white markings are incorrectly thought to be a mistake. Although its pattern seems to be more suited to Cape Hatteras because of its offshore Diamond Shoals, the lighthouse board did specify in 1873 that the Cape Lookout Lighthouse be "checkered." Now the solar-powered (with multiple backups) and LED array "flashes" once every 15 seconds, replicating the historical intervals of the rotating twin beacons. Visitors who make their way to the island may climb the lighthouse (conditions permitting) for a fee. It takes 207 steps to reach the top.

The oldest lighthouse standing in the state is the Bald Head light on Smith Island, constructed in 1795. Although it is no longer illuminated, the tower once signaled the entrance to the Cape Fear River, North Carolina's only natural deepwater channel, ominously guarded by the shifting sands of an offshore sandbar known as Frying Pan Shoals.

Shortly after construction, the Bald Head light became obsolete because the Cape Fear channel shifted much farther north, to a new inlet south of present-day Smith Island. A new lighthouse was authorized by Congress and placed in service in 1816, and the Bald Head light was retired. Eventually, the inlet shoaled, and the channel shifted again to the southwest of Smith Island. By 1848 a new pair of lights (no longer evident) on Oak Island became the primary navigational aid to the mouth of the Cape Fear.

On May 15, 1958, the current Oak Island Lighthouse was placed into service. Initially, this was one of the most powerful beacons in the world, visible 24 miles out to sea. A replacement lighting mechanism reduced the range to 16 miles. The flash activates 4 times at 1-second intervals followed by 6 seconds of darkness.

The distinctive daymarks—black on top, white in the middle, and gray at the bottom—are actually finished into its concrete surface instead of being painted. The nonprofit Friends of Oak Island Lighthouse owns and operates the tower. Tours and climbs are carefully scheduled in the summer.

SMITH ISLAND COMPLEX

The stone tower of Old Baldy, the lighthouse on Bald Head Island, is visible from the Southport waterfront by looking past the foreground marshy islands to the northeast headland of the mouth of the Cape Fear River. Built in 1817 (but decommissioned in 1903), it is the oldest standing lighthouse in the state, pre-dating the still-active Ocracoke Lighthouse by six years.

This early need for a lighthouse hints at the treacherous waters at the mouth of the river. Giovanni da Verrazano called attention to the area in 1524. It would later appear on a 1590 map labeled "Promontorium tremendum," which loosely translates "Dreadful Promontory"; subsequently the associated river was named the Cape Fear. Imaginative sailors later christened the island forming the northeastern bank of the channel as Baldhead, acknowledging the easily visible tall sand dunes marking the entrance by day.

They sailed on by. Not so today, even though Bald Head Island is accessible only by ferry or boat. People but no cars are allowed on the island. A golf course designed by George Cobb threads the middle portion of the island. The homes are substantial and expensive; vacation rentals are priced accordingly. The development is low rise and low density; in the wooded sections of the island, houses are discreetly sited. In addition to the open space provided by the golf course and its surrounds, a 174-acre parcel of magnificent upland forests has been set aside as part of the North Carolina Coastal Reserve.

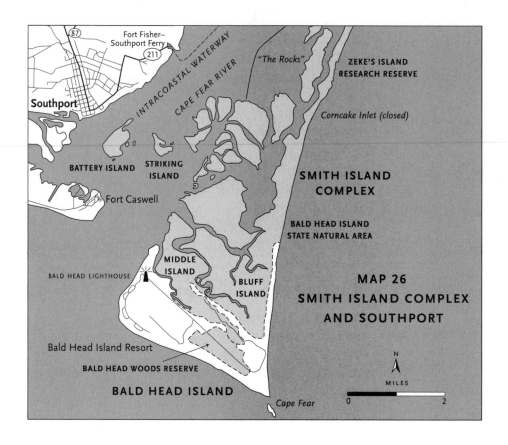

Oh, yes, and there's a combined 14 miles of east- and south-facing oceanfront.

The name Bald Head applies to the largest of three parallel sand ridges in this extraordinary maritime mosaic. Early state maps called this Smith Island for Landgrave Thomas Smith, who acquired it in 1690. By the time the state wished to construct a lighthouse here to serve the Cape Fear River, Benjamin Smith (the namesake of Smithville, later Southport, and perhaps an heir of Thomas) grazed sheep and cattle on the island.

The civic-minded Smith offered 10 acres as a site for the lighthouse in 1789 so long as his grazing rights were protected. By 1794 the General Assembly signed off on the grazing rights; the light was constructed and promptly deemed inadequate. By 1817 another lighthouse, the present-day "Old Baldy," had been constructed. This was the guiding light for the Cape Fear River entrance until it was decommissioned in 1903, replaced by the Cape Fear Light, a taller cast iron light tower at the eastern end of the island.

In turn, this light was decommissioned in 1958 following the construction of the Oak Island Lighthouse. The foundation of this later light is visible today on the island. Old Baldy towered through its bicentennial in 2017 as the state's oldest standing lighthouse, pre-dating the Ocracoke light by six years.

The entirety of the Smith Island Complex, which encompasses more than 12,000 acres of varied coastal ecological zones, is the northern limit for the semitropical vegetation native to the Sea Islands of South Carolina and Georgia. An immense expanse of tidal waters and salt marsh extends upriver from the maritime forests and higher sand ridges of Bald Head Island. Bald Head Island is as far south in the state as one can walk. It is close enough to the coast-hugging flow of the Gulf Stream to be nearly a world unto itself. Resident and nonresident migratory wildlife, including alligators, shelters in the habitat niches. Except for the 2,000 acres of Bald Head Island Resort, some of which is protected in a private reserve, nearly all of this acreage is protected by public or private agencies.

The 1,260-acre Bald Head Island State Natural Area, which protects a mix of these varied habitats, was established in 1979. Within the resort, the Bald Head Conservancy is a management partner with North Carolina's Division of Coastal Management in overseeing the 174-acre Bald Head Woods Reserve, part of the North Carolina Coastal Reserve system.

Corncake Inlet, now closed and considered historical, once separated Bald Head Island from the barrier spit belonging to the Zeke's Island component of the North Carolina National Estuarine Research Reserve. In fact, the boundary between New Hanover and Brunswick Counties was surveyed through the now-closed inlet. Now that the inlet is filled, it is possible to walk from Fort Fisher Recreation Area in New Hanover County to Bald Head Island and Cape Fear in Brunswick County.

On a coast that is extraordinary for its astonishing number and variety of islands, Bald Head is itself extraordinary. It is accessible only by the ferry that runs round-trip from Indigo Plantation in Southport or by private boat.

Access

Although Bald Head is a private resort, it offers villa or cottage rentals and accommodates day trips. Daily ferry departures are from Indigo Plantation north of Southport. There is a fee.

Search Bald Head Island NC or enter www.baldheadisland.com.

The village website is www.villagebhi.org.

BALD HEAD ISLAND STATE NATURAL AREA

The North Carolina Division of Parks and Recreation manages the nearly 6,000-acre state natural area composed of labyrinthine tidal creeks, marsh, bays, and uplands between Bald Head Island and Fort Fisher. Several owners granted the Nature Conservancy title to 9,000 acres of marsh and 1,000 acres of uplands and dunes in the 1970s. The conservancy in turn turned the title over to the State of North Carolina. The tract includes Bluff Island, one of three upland ridges (the other two are Middle Island and Bald Head Island) that, along with marshes, comprise the Smith Island Complex.

The Bald Head Island Conservancy actively participates in the management of the natural area.

Access

Access is by boat only.

Search Fort Fisher State Park or enter www.ncparks
.gov/fort-fisher-state-recreation-area.

Phone: 910-458-5798.

Enter www.bhic.org or contact the Bald Head Island
Conservancy, PO Box 3109, Bald Head Island, NC 28461.

Phone: 910-457-0089.

OAK ISLAND

Oak Island is the longest and easternmost of the Brunswick County Barrier Islands. The island forms the western headland of the mouth of the Cape Fear River and shelters Southport from the open ocean. Thirteen miles to the west, the island extends its reach to the channel of Lockwood Folly Inlet. The Atlantic Intracoastal Waterway connects the two inlets flowing between the mainland and the northern side of the island.

There are two communities. Smaller, traditionally residential Caswell

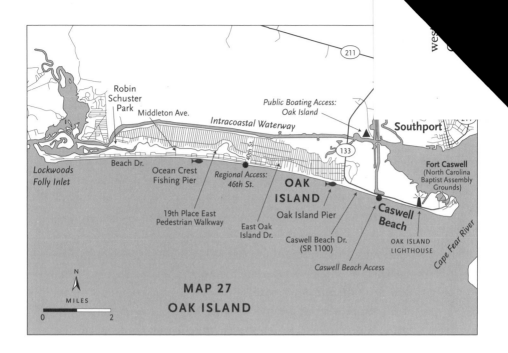

Beach occupies the eastern end and the namesake town of Oak Island that formed with the 1999 merger of Yaupon Beach and Long Beach. The town of Oak Island has a dual character that reflects the island's unusual geography.

The east end of the island is the North Carolina Baptist Assembly grounds, which includes the weathered ramparts and old buildings of Fort Caswell. There is also a U.S. Coast Guard station and the Oak Island Lighthouse, the operating lighthouse marking signaling the entrance to the Cape Fear River. The lighthouse is visible from Southport, as are some of the buildings at the Baptist Assembly grounds, but the Southport vantage is only a small portion of the lengthy island.

Oak Island has an extensive ridge of high ground, and the western half of the island is divided by a substantial tidal creek named Big Jim Davis Canal. This drains the center of the island into Lockwood Folly Inlet. Because of the canal, the western half of the town of Oak Island has a split-tail shape cleanly dividing it into a beachfront barrier and an upland forest ridge that has both canal and Intracoastal Waterway frontage.

NC 133, also known as Long Beach Road, is one of two roads that bridge the Intracoastal Waterway from the mainland. The road leads south from the intersection with NC 211 approximately 2.5 miles west of Southport. On the side of NC 133, just south of the junction, is the Southport/Oak Island Chamber of Commerce welcome center. It is a good first stop for information about the attractions and accommodations of the island communities.

The highway crosses the Intracoastal Waterway over a high-rise bridge. Below the bridge on the mainland are the rusting ruins of a menhaden-processing plant, whose pungent odor used to signal the arrival to Oak Island. The bridge provides an elevated glimpse of the island. It is a tree-covered landscape, and there is only a hint of housing peeking through the treetops in the distance. The bridge ends in a tree-covered section of Oak Island, and the route proceeds to a traffic light.

Be ready for the name change from Long Beach Road to Country Club Drive; and if you do not turn at the light, the route makes a sweeping curve east into the residential community of Caswell Beach. The U.S. Coast Guard station, the Oak Island Lighthouse, and the North Carolina Baptist Assembly grounds are at the end of the road.

A turn right, or west, at the traffic signal will put you on the primary road of East Oak Island Drive, which passes through the commercial district of Oak Island before continuing to the western end of the northern half of the island, between Big Jim Davis Canal and the Atlantic Intracoastal Waterway. Ocean Drive, which routes parallel to the beach one row of houses back, may be reached by turning south on any street between McGlamery Street and SE 74th Street or by turning south as directed by the sign at SE 58th Street in the Oak Island commercial center.

Search Oak Island North Carolina or enter www.oakislandnc.com.

Search Southport Oak Island or enter www.southport-oakisland.com.

NORTH CAROLINA BAPTIST ASSEMBLY GROUNDS/FORT CASWELL

A turnaround at a guard house marks the end of the public Caswell Beach Drive. The eastern end of Oak Island beyond the gates belongs and serves as the North Carolina Baptist Assembly, providing a coastal retreat and year-round gathering place for that denomination. The grounds beyond the gate include the barracks and fortifications of the many iterations of Fort Caswell, named for North Carolina's first governor, Richard Caswell. The Army Corps of Engineers built the fort between 1826 and 1838. Originally constructed as an irregular pentagon, it was never fully staffed until seized by local militia after North Carolina joined the Confederacy, and it remained a guardian of the mouth of the Cape Fear until captured in 1865 by conquering Union troops. Prior to its capture, Confederate forces ignited a powder magazine, destroying one side of the fort and shattering another.

During the Spanish-American War and the First and Second World Wars, this point of land was again garrisoned and fortified against coastal invasion. The fortifications visible on the island are a mishmash of additions and improvements added to the brick portions of the works, which date from the Civil War. After World War I the fort was sold, then repurchased and reinforced for World War II. The property was again offered for sale in 1949 and entered its current service in that year. The property is marked by concrete bunkers that dot the seaward side of the headland, vestiges of the twentieth-century fortifications.

Many of the structures in current use at the assembly grounds are refurbished U.S. Army barracks and outbuildings. The architecture is unmistakable, and the orderly layout of the buildings and grounds leeward of the revetments confirms the longtime importance of this piece of ground to military planners.

This is a private facility operated by the Baptist State Convention of North Carolina.

Search Fort Caswell or enter www.fortcaswell.com.

OAK ISLAND LIGHTHOUSE

Constructed in 1957, the Oak Island Lighthouse went to work in May 1958. It replaced the Cape Fear Light, a metal tower light on the east end of Bald Head Island. That light had previously supplanted the still-visible landmark "Old Baldy" in 1903.

The Oak Island Lighthouse is a starkly efficient form, not the conical shape characteristic of older lighthouses. The paint scheme is a banding of dark at the top (to show against the daytime sky), white in the midsection, and gray at the base.

Although the tower height is 153 feet, the operating light is 169 feet above sea level, because the structure is built on a natural mound. The light flashes four times every 10 seconds. The 36-inch antiaircraft arc lights initially installed made it the brightest lighthouse in the United States and the

Sea Oats (*Uniola paniculata*)

Sand dunes are a movable story, a single frame in the cinema of wind, water, and sand. Sand dunes are ephemeral to geologists yet formidable to us. They are a barrier island's first line of defense against storms, standing as a malleable response line that reduces a storm's impact by making it expend energy before it pushes inland.

Nature builds sand dunes with wind, time, and available sand. People use sand fences or heavy equipment to trap sand and create dunes faster. Both nature and people, however, rely on sea oats (*Uniola paniculata*), the rugged pioneering plant adapted to the worst combinations of salt, wind, and drought, to help hold these castles of sand in place.

Sea oats are coarse, pale green grasses that form tough clumps that die back to the surface of the dune each year. The plants thrive on tough circumstances growing at the back reach of the tides, a sun-seared, grainy, and restless piece of real estate. They stake a claim on the harshest, most demanding environment on a barrier islands and then thrive. It is such an inhospitable outpost that sea oats practically stands alone.

In mid- to late summer, sea oats sends up stems more than 3 feet tall that bear clusters of oat-like seed spikelets. The resemblance to edible grain is obvious, hence the descriptive common name. These plumes ripen to a golden color in September, usually a glorious contrast to the polarized light of the cobalt skies of early autumn. The plant waves its flag against the sea even as the traditional tropical storm season advances.

The true value of sea oats is not what you see above ground but what "grows on" beneath the surface. Spreading via underground stems, sea oats can colonize over the top of a dune. Meanwhile, below the surface sand, it drops anchor. Sea oats spreads vigorously through the core of the dune by means of an insinuating root system. It literally threads through the mass of sand. If sand covers up a plant, it sprouts lateral roots and volunteers new foliage above the taller dune surface. The root network is plainly visible where waves have sliced off part of oat-covered dune, exposing the interior. By this arrangement, the sea oats and the dune can survive all but the most damaging storm surge.

Ironically, the storms that could destroy sea oats also provide the means for its survival. Studies reveal that sea oats seeds germinate best after a period of soaking in salt water. In other words, waves harvest the seeds, wash them in the waves, and spit them back up on the dunes again, a curiously macabre recycling of the plant and, in some instances, the very island.

Sea oats are so important to the beach that the law prohibits harvesting the strands—you may not pick sea oats at any time. As sea oats go, so go the dunes. As dunes go, so go the islands. As you go, leave the sea oats behind.

second-brightest in the world. Newer lights dimmed the show in 1962, and in 2010 the lighthouse received new wiring and 1,000-watt halogen bulbs to replace the older incandescent bulbs. Importantly, it is bright enough and distinctive enough to signal the mouth of the Cape Fear River 16 miles at sea.

The Oak Island Lighthouse is owned by the Town of Caswell Beach that obtained the deed in 2004 as a part of the Federal Land to Parks Program in that year. The Friends of Oak Island Lighthouse, a private 501(c)(3) nonprofit established by the Town of Caswell Beach to maintain and provide public access to the structure, is staffed by volunteers. (The U.S. Coast Guard maintains the beacons). In addition to the lighthouse, the town also received a parking area and beachfront property.

Groups must make appointments as much as four weeks in advance during summer to take a guided climb of the structure. The lighthouse lacks a spiral stair and instead is served by a series of ship's ladders and landings to negotiate the 131 steps the observation deck.

It's a popular stop, and the Friends of Oak Island Lighthouse are presently securing funds and permission to install a larger parking area to serve the many visitors.

The very ornate Gothic gingerbread building across the street from the entrance to the U.S. Coast Guard station is the old lightkeeper's quarters, dating from an earlier era. It was auctioned, moved, and "rescued and restored" to become a private residence. It still looks the part of a period piece of architecture.

Search Oak Island Lighthouse or enter www.oakislandlighthouse.org.

Inquire about tours by writing OakIslandLighthouse@gmail.com.

CASWELL BEACH

NC 133 is the primary route south to Oak Island, crossing over the Atlantic Intracoastal Waterway on the G. V. Barbee Bridge. The road plunges off the bridge, entering the Town of Oak Island; commercial ventures to the west and a row of tall trees with a golf course beyond on the left. At the traffic light intersection with East Oak Island Drive, the state highway becomes SR 1100, locally referred to as Country Club Drive.

The road begins a gradual curve east past the municipal building of the Town of Caswell Beach. The entry into the town is subtle but best marked by the vivid development known as Oak Island Villas on the ocean side of the road. Country Club Drive continues its gentle bend to the east, and as the villas recede and dunes appear on the ocean side, the golf course Caswell Dunes appears to the north. Yaupon Way is the entry road to that development, and at this intersection Country Club Drive continues east as Caswell Beach Road. The salt sculpting of the roadside vegetation and ocean views confirm that the road will parallel the south-facing beach beyond the dunes of Caswell Beach.

Caswell Beach is a quiet, restful constant on Oak Island.

There are around 400 permanent residents who live in this community, which seems more like a big neighborhood rather than an incorporated municipality. There are few physical changes to the community because land use is fulfilled. (The town did acquire the Oak Island Light House in 2004.) Visitors and newcomers should become familiar with local regulations about golf cart use on local roads and the use of bicycle lanes. Caswell Beach seems neutral about tourism, neither inviting nor uninviting, offering limited overtures to visitors. There are new stylish homes available to rent in the communities east end; the beach is gorgeous and the traffic non-existent. Caswell Beach beckons and belongs to golfers, book readers, and bicyclists. The town has no commercial or entertainment district.

The town limits embrace extensive salt marsh on the northern edge of town, part of the golf course, the Oak Island Villas, and the 2.5 miles of beach. Caswell Beach Drive, running very close to the narrow beach, is the primary access for both the oceanfront and second-row homes at the town's east end. It passes a reserve area where a discharge pipe for cooling water used by the Brunswick Nuclear Power Plant passes beneath the road, the Oak Island Lighthouse, and the U.S. Coast Guard station before ending at the North Carolina Baptist Assembly. After this restricted area, there is a neighborhood access site on the oceanfront with parking. Do obey the No Parking signs posted elsewhere.

Search Caswell Beach NC or enter www.caswellbeach.org.

Access

There a large access location with parking marked on Caswell Beach Drive just west of the lighthouse.

TOWN OF OAK ISLAND

The approach to Oak Island from the mainland is the same as that to Caswell Beach, across the Atlantic Intracoastal Waterway. Trees frame the dark waterway waters which are sometimes furrowed by private boats. It is a tranquil picture that rolls by as the road settles into the Town of Oak Island. There is a residential golf course community on the left and some light commercial enterprises on the right, or to the west. There is little hint of the resort community beyond.

The "beyond" begins at the traffic light with a turn right or west onto East Oak Island Drive. This begins the passage along the island's upland spine after passing through a commercial district that is transitioning from an older era of tourism to a more contemporary appeal. It is nearly 10 miles from the traffic light to the western end of West Beach Drive. And there is more island still beyond the turn around.

It's a long drive along an outstanding beach and one that is recovering from oceanfront challenges. In September 2016, Hurricane Matthew flattened a substantial dune line and shaved away massive widths of beach. A subsequent nourishment program has restored much of the beach-towel frontage (though the dark-colored sand threatened successful sea turtle nesting on a strand that has historically attracted large numbers of nesting turtles). The dunes began a gradual rebuilding. As one resident stated, the dunes did their job by absorbing the storm surge energy, but the brunt of that assault withered them.

People and houses usually recover faster than the strand itself and this is the case here. Beachside Oak Island is a handsome, settled barrier beach community with houses and cottages for rent and residency. This is slightly less than half of the Oak Island story as many folks take advantage of the close proximity of water for boating or surfing to live in the upland island woods.

Approximately 7,500 people reside full time in one of two different environments: a wooded residential subdivision and a beach cottage resort.

As mentioned in the Oak Island description, Big Jim Davis Canal, a navigable waterway that leads to Davis Creek and the Lockwood Folly Inlet, splits the western two-thirds of the island. Between the canal and the Intracoastal Waterway there is a grid of numbered streets in a coastal plain pine and hardwood forest. Some of the homes are waterfront on the canal or the waterway. Yacht Drive, one block south of the waterway, winds nearly the length of the island.

On the ocean side of the canal, Oak Island is a barrier island beach and a nearly completely developed cottage resort. The houses are signed, cleverly named, and elevated for flood safety. The most prevalent architectural character reveals this has been a destination for a long time. Upgraded residences are filling in more and more.

The Swain's Cut Bridge, which opened in 2010, carries Middleton Avenue across the Intracoastal Waterway past the headwaters of Big Jim Davis Canal to intersect with Beach Road. This is a more direct way on and off the western half of the town.

Navigating Oak Island for the first time can be tricky. Heading west on East Oak Island Drive from the intersection with Long Beach Road, the first 10 cross streets are named. Thereafter, all such streets are numbered. The first numbered street is 79th Street, and subsequent streets are numbered in descending numerical order until First Street, one block before Middleton Avenue. On the ocean side of East Oak Drive, the streets have the prefix SE (southeast), and on the Intracoastal Waterway side, the prefix NE (northeast). On the ocean side of the canal, the corresponding numerical streets have only the prefix E (east).

Middleton Avenue marks the change from East Oak Island Drive to West Oak Island Drive. Importantly, Middleton Avenue spans from Beach Drive along the oceanfront over the canal leading to the Swain's Cut Bridge. West of Middleton Avenue crossing streets are numbered in increasing numerical order. Streets leading to the canal have the prefix SW (southwest), while streets leading to the Intracoastal Waterway have the prefix NW (northwest). The corresponding streets on the ocean side of the island have the prefix W (west).

Confusing as this may be, it is not a problem when renting on on the oceanfront or one or two rows back.

There are a few key streets: SE 58th Street leads to Beach Driv runs behind the oceanfront row of houses. The turn off of East Oak Dr clearly signed. SE 40th Street is the last street before Big Jim Davis Canal divides the western half of the island. The canal is not bridged until Middleton Avenue, 40 blocks west. That's all there is to it.

In a brief orientation, the first 15 streets—McGlamery Street through 79th—were originally Yaupon Beach. It is charming; tree cover extends nearly to the oceanfront. The setting is soothing; the houses settle amid live oak and the town's namesake tree, the yaupon holly.

Any turn seaward from East Oak Island Drive on these roads leads to the water and an intersection with Ocean Drive, which travels behind the first row of houses and businesses for approximately 15 blocks.

East Oak Island Drive burrows deeper into the island's length and carries the burden of also serving the commercial center for the island. A sign marks the turn on SE 58th Street that leads to Beach Drive and ocean access sites.

Every third street from 58th Street to 40th Street connects Oak Island Drive and Beach Drive. There is a regional beach access parking area at the oceanfront terminus of SE 46th Street.

There are a couple of neat features nearly hidden in the town's length, such as a walkway over the canal, accessible from East 19th Street on the south shore and SE 20th Street off of East Oak Island Drive.

The Oak Island Memorial Waterway Park at NE 52nd Street and Yacht Drive has a nature center, a woodland walk, and a gazebo at the Intracoastal Waterway.

Tidal Way Trails Park at SE 31st Street is next to the Oak Island Recreation Center at 3003 East Oak Island Drive. The park has a small boardwalk and a canoe-launching site on the canal with a gazebo and picnic tables. This features a canoe/kayak only launching site.

At the west end of the island, West Beach Drive forks amid extensive development. The left fork leads to a gorgeous beach front parking turnout with a self-guided walk through the dunes. The right fork leads to parking area on the tidal waters of Lockwood Folly Inlet, a treasured location for anglers.

Access

The named streets of old Yaupon Beach offer limited parking serving the beach. The city provides some parking at their renovated Yaupon Beach Pier on Womble Street. Beachside parking is plainly signed off of Beach Drive.

Search Oak Island NC or enter www.oakislandnc.com.

Search Southport Oak Island or enter www.southport-oakisland.com.

Phone: 800-457-6964.

GREEN SWAMP/BOILING SPRING LAKES PLANT CONSERVATION PRESERVE

The forests beside NC 211 and NC 87 are a green blur at beach-bound speeds . . . so much scruffy pine forest or swamp wasteland. Surprisingly, much of this acreage is considered a botanical wonderland, showcasing some of the most botanically diverse plant communities in the state. The North Carolina chapter of the Nature Conservancy has two extraordinary preserves in Brunswick County, Green Swamp and Boiling Spring Lakes Plant Conservation Preserve.

Green Swamp is a 17,424-acre expanse of pine savanna and upland evergreen shrub bog accessed by a parking area 5.5 miles north of Supply on NC 211. The swamp has been designated a National Natural Landmark by the U.S. Department of the Interior.

What looks barren and unpromising to the eye is actually one of the richest plant habitats in the state, and it harbors the greatest number of carnivorous plants found in the country. The density and diversity of plant species within the swamp rank it as one of the finest unaltered habitats in the state.

A kiosk at the trailhead explains access rules and the types of habitat and plants to be seen.

In the town of Boiling Spring Lakes are the 5,000-plus acres of the Boiling Spring Lakes Plant Conservation Preserve, comanaged by the North Carolina chapter of the Nature Conservancy and the Plant Conservation Program of the North Carolina Department of Agriculture.

An interpretive trail leads through a sample of this mix of habitats that includes the xeric Sandhill community (similar to Pinehurst/Southern

Pines), the Pond Pine Woodland community, and the Pocosin (elevated bog or swamp) community. Each is characterized by different soils, varying soil moisture levels, and the unique plant and animal associations that adapt to those conditions.

A self-guided flyer keyed to the plant communities explains their importance as one moves along the trail. It is an enriching walk in a very subtle woods.

In September 2018, Hurricane Florence's torrential rains caused the dam retaining water in Patricia Lake, the defining water feature of Boiling Spring Lakes, to fail. This also washed out a road serving many of the residents on the eastern side of the community. Part of Boiling Spring Lakes Plant Conservation Preserve is near and partially adjoins the lakebed. Reconstruction plans are not known at this time.

Access

There is a parking area for Green Swamp 5 miles north of Supply on US 211.

Boiling Spring Lakes Plant Conservation Preserve is off of NC 87 in Boiling Springs. The trail begins at the community center, which is plainly signed.

LOCKWOOD FOLLY INLET

Lockwood Folly Inlet, the outlet of the Lockwood Folly River, separates Oak Island and Holden Beach. Recreational boaters consider this dark tannic inlet one of the state's most scenic tidewater rivers. The slowly flowing waters thread through a maze of Spanish moss–draped cypress and live oak trees.

The river headwaters are west of Boiling Spring Lakes. From there it flows northwest before looping underneath NC 211 a few miles east of Supply. Hurricane Florence charged these waters to overflow the banks on the way to the inlet.

Recurring shoaling vexes the inlet and limits safe navigation on the Intracoastal Waterway between Oak Island and Holden Beach. The seaward passage through the inlet is subject to the same forces. As recently as 2016, the U.S. Coast Guard removed some navigation buoys because they no longer marked a viable channel. The inlet was subsequently dredged and returned to service, but funding for future inlet maintenance is not guaranteed.

Extensive flats and bordering marsh channels make the inlet attractive for anglers nonetheless.

Sunset Harbor on the east bank of the Lockwood Folly River provides the closest boating access.

SHALLOTTE

Shallotte is a commercial hub of southern Brunswick County and the gateway town for the burgeoning beach and golf retirement communities that are expanding on the mainland. The town grew outward from a US 17/Main Street crossing of the headwaters of the Shallotte River that winds to its inlet between Holden Beach and Ocean Isle Beach. Shallotte serves as a shopping area for the island communities of Holden Beach, Ocean Isle Beach, and Sunset Beach. The recent expansion of retail and business services on the mainland west of these oceanfront communities has reduced reliance on Shallotte retailers. Shallotte still has centrality to Holden, Ocean Isle, and Sunset Beaches, such that it is the headquarters for a distinct Tourism Development Authority serving the North Carolina Brunswick Islands.

Today US 17 bypass has alleviated north–south traffic over Shallotte's Main Street, but inland state travelers headed to Holden Beach and Ocean Isle Beach find that the most direct route passes through Shallotte. The beach roads, NC 130 to Holden Beach and NC 179 to Ocean Isle, pass through coastal pine forests and travel near several golf course retirement communities before crossing the Atlantic Intracoastal Waterway to the islands.

Search Shallotte or enter www.townofshallotte.org.

HOLDEN BEACH

The grand view from Holden Beach Bridge as it curves and descends to intersect Ocean Boulevard West provides a visual hint of the town's adopted motto, "The Family Beach." The island is spacious and uncrowded and has a decidedly small-town appearance—comfortably spaced cottages line the streets. This is not a resort in the tonier sense of that word, but is a place where people come to be by the sea. Holden Beach is settled; it grew slowly and steadily with evident thought to retaining the low-key character that at-

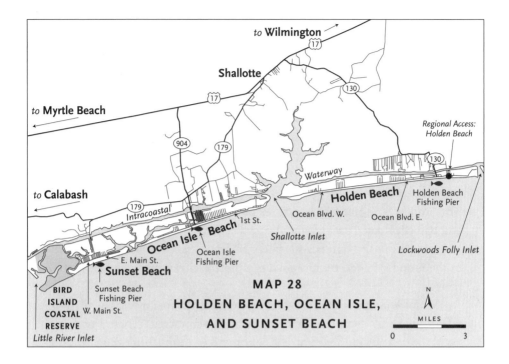

to **Wilmington**

17

Shallotte

130

17

to **Myrtle Beach**

Regional Access:
Holden Beach

904   179

130

to **Calabash**

179   *Intracoastal*

Waterway

Holden Beach   Holden Beach
Fishing Pier

Ocean Blvd. W.   Ocean Blvd. E.

1st St.

Shallotte Inlet

Ocean Isle ↑ **Beach**

Ocean Isle
Fishing Pier

Lockwoods Folly Inlet

E. Main St.

↑ **Sunset Beach**

**BIRD
ISLAND
COASTAL
RESERVE**

Sunset Beach
Fishing Pier

W. Main St.

MAP 28

**HOLDEN BEACH, OCEAN ISLE,
AND SUNSET BEACH**

N

MILES

0   3

Little River Inlet

tracted vacationers initially back in the late 1940s and 1950s. The 8 miles of south-facing oceanfront, low beach profile, and gentle wave action have made it a magnet destination for families. It became an island of family second homes instead of island real estate development. That those homes may be for rent is secondary to why they were built originally. Ample public access crossovers make it easy for non-oceanfront visitors to head to the sands.

Places this simple and wholesome do not remain undiscovered, and Holden Beach is not a well-kept secret. Instead, it has turned out to be a well-publicized one. In 2004 *National Geographic Traveler* picked Holden Beach as one of its top family beaches in the nation. Stephen P. Leatherman, renowned as "Dr. Beach," favors Holden Beach for its laid-back atmosphere, citing personal safety and minimal traffic in addition to the natural attributes. Indeed, the town itself publishes the "Olden" Holden Bike Tour on the town website, www.hbtownhall.com, encouraging visitors to casually wheel the island and see some of the locations and buildings prominent in the community's nearly nine decades of slow growth as a beach destination.

The reason for the measured growth is straightforward: it took multiple generations of the Holden family to come up with a vision that fit their times. It has been a family affair since 1756, when John Holden acquired the island and mainland acreage. Since that time, it has been used to graze farm animals, as a base for fishing. There has been a menhaden plant and a coast guard station on the island, and it has always served as fishing grounds for the family. In the 1930s, the dredging of the Atlantic Intracoastal Waterway provided a clean, unvarying separation from the mainland, limiting access to boat or ferry crossings. Gradually the Holden family built a hotel and a pavilion for entertaining and expanded ferry access, encouraging the construction of more houses, a process that accelerated greatly when the bridge opened.

Since the 1950s, the Holden family has quietly developed the island. The present high-rise bridge assures both easy access and easy evacuation and had stimulated second-home construction somewhat. But it certainly has yet to bring any significantly tall or midrise buildings, hotels, or motels to the island. Holden Beach remains almost exclusively single-family cottages.

As for marketing, the island was touted with this description: "You won't find much to do except swim, fish, and sunbathe." There's nothing wrong with knowing that upfront, and there's not much on the island to contradict that declaration.

In summer, Holden Beach fills up but never seems tightly packed. About 500 homes serve permanent residents. In summer, the population grows to 10,000.

Most of the services are along the mainland causeway leading to the bridge—tackle shops, gift shops, dry goods merchants, restaurants, sundry stores, and service stations. There are still commercial fish and shrimp business along the Atlantic Intracoastal Waterway that are open to the public.

After crossing the high-rise bridge, it is a short drive to the east end of the island, which has a fabulous extended headland adjacent to Lockwood Folly Inlet. Beach erosion at this end of the island was threatening several homes in 2017, and there has been some effort to armor the beach west of the inlet. This is a great place to grab a parking spot—and there are several along North McCray Street. The reward is the solitude of the point. Plentiful shoaling of the inlet and the gentle beach gradient create tidal pools that are excellent for younger children.

The drive along West Ocean Boulevard from the bridge terminus passes several locations where the island is narrow and backed with marsh and there are only houses facing the road on either side. The island also has several locations where solid ground extends a lengthy block to the Atlantic

Intracoastal Waterway and has been neatly gridded width houses. There will be some cottages in these locations that might be annoyingly distant from dune crossovers to the oceanfront.

Access

Parking for beach access is improved but can be problematic for some locations.

There is no parking on Ocean Boulevard, the main street parallel to the ocean. You may park on side streets, but your vehicle must be completely off of the pavement. Getting permission from the adjacent property owner is advised.

There is a regional access area under the high-rise bridge, with 90 parking spaces, restrooms, cold showers, and dune crossovers a short walk away.

There is also a large parking area at the east end of the island in the 300 block of McCray Street, which has parking for 50 cars.

Parking and dune crossovers are at Heritage Harbor, Dream Harbor, and Colonial Beach Streets, Avenue D, Avenue C, Avenue B, Avenue A, Holden Street, and Ferry Road.

Search Town of Holden Beach or enter www.hbtownhall.com.

Search Brunswick Islands NC or enter www.ncbrunswick.com.

OCEAN ISLE BEACH

Ocean Isle Beach is packed with vacation houses, cottages, and condominiums, particularly the middle third of the island, where finger canals penetrate perpendicularly from the Atlantic Intracoastal Waterway into the island's interior. The canals provide waterfront boating access for canal-fronting properties that are shoulder-to-shoulder along the man-made waterways. The canal streets extend to First Street, the primary oceanside road serving the oceanfront houses.

First Street reaches the length of the island, providing ocean access and a glimpse into island's character. Ocean Isle Beach is aspiring: the newer houses that pepper the vintage oceanfront are trending upscale. The newest homes and multifamily buildings showcase a shift away from the simple oceanside cottages of earlier decades. First Street makes an easy, attractive

Water in Orbit

Why, if waves march toward the beach, does the water not continue to slosh into the dunes? This simple question has a charmingly simple answer. While waves move through water horizontally, the actual water molecules move very little. Passing waves move floating objects back and forth, up and down, but never transport them very far. Divers who see seaweed swaying with passing wave action observe a similar movement.

Waves are motion—energy—passing through a medium—the ocean. The actual particles of water in a wave move in a circular orbit, as shown in the diagram. This circular pattern of water-particle movement was first observed by 1802 by the German-Bohemian physicist Franz Gerstner.

As a wave approaches a droplet, it carries the droplet in the direction of transport along with the crest of the wave. Then the trough of the wave follows, and the droplet moves against the direction of the wave for almost the same horizontal distance. During the swell, the droplet is elevated and subsequently "dropped" as the swell passes and the trough approaches. In fact, the water particle returns to almost its original position.

The diameter of the circle is, of course, equal to the height of the wave. When a wave approaches shore, there is insufficient room for particles to make their circular path. The orbit flattens, and the droplets tarry at the top of the swell, pushed higher and ever forward with no support beneath them. The circle is broken, and the wave breaks on the sand.

passage in part because the houses do not loom over the street and many homeowners have landscaped extensively. The fanning fronds of the many palmettos soften the road's appearance, as do the tall salt-tolerant shrubs between houses.

That the island is so populated with vacation homes (only 660 call it home year-round) is no surprise. It was the plan of Odell Williamson, who bought the island after World War II, to develop a family beach resort. He started with a superb location. Ocean Isle Beach has the same east–west orientation as its neighbors and a gentle, tan-all-day, south-facing beach. Ocean Isle Beach has an easy gradient for most of its length. The dune line was chiseled by Hurricane Matthew in 2016 but is recovering. The foreshore is wide and appealing.

Causeway Drive intersects with First Street at the Ocean Isle Pier and a public parking area. Within two blocks are some services and a few of the attractions that contribute to the family atmosphere of the island: one block east and north is the Museum of Coastal Carolina, which offers an introduction to the coast's natural history; restaurants and sidewalks parallel the beachfront along East First Street. The walks are busy with joggers, walkers, and strollers. There are two hotels several blocks to the west and another, quainter resort hotel on the east oceanfront.

The east end is the major playground for Ocean Isle Beach. There are numerous places to park, including many that are not officially marked but that are obvious locations to pull completely off the road. This end of the island, like other inland headlands in this part of Brunswick County, contends with chronic inlet migration and erosion. Shallotte Inlet is migrating west, and Ocean Isle Beach fights a wearying, seemingly endless battle of attrition as the inlet carves in that direction, slicing under the front row of cottages.

The inlet movement has dramatically stopped East First Street at High Point. Similarly, East Second Street ends farther east at Charlotte Street, and East Third Street is being notched back at Columbia Street. Finally, at East Fourth Street there is a beach access area that leads to the magnificent wild east end of the island and its prime fishing and shelling.

Ocean Isle Beach's west end has a concentration of multistory condominiums and vacation villas. There is still some open land, but no parking or beach access is permitted. The 13-story high-rise tower The Winds dominates this end of the island. Just beyond the tower, privately owned Ocean Isle West maintains a gated entrance closing off access to the west end of the island and Tubbs Inlet.

Ocean Isle Beach is up-front about parking: there are marked places at the end of streets perpendicular to the ocean nearly every six blocks. Even on the most crowded days, there are usually a few spaces available at the east end of the island.

Access

Causeway Drive ends at a central parking location adjoining parking for the pier.

The following streets have neighborhood access sites: Monroe Street, Concord Street, Newport Street, Raeford Street, Leland Street, Goldsboro

Street, Chadbourn Street, Winnabow Street, Greensboro Street, and Beaufort Street.

Use common sense about parking in unmarked locations: pull completely off the pavement, and do not block drives, sidewalks, flowerbeds, or side streets. Dune crossovers are located at the south ends of High Point Street, Shelby Street, and Driftwood Drive.

Search Town of Ocean Isle or enter www.oibgov.com.

Search Brunswick Islands NC or enter www.ncbrunswick.com.

SUNSET BEACH

The sun has set on the drawbridge days at this delightful, low-key getaway island, the westernmost of the Brunswick County vacation archipelago. The drawbridge—an anachronistic means of reaching the island—was an honest greeting to the Sunset Beach atmosphere, which floats somewhere between three and four decades ago. This is a simpler place—walk the beach, read a book, make sandcastles with your children, throw a line in the surf. One neat fact: the beach is growing wider.

Nature is steadily *adding* sand to this 3-mile-long island. Today some "beachfront" houses are 600 feet away from the water behind an undulating field of dunes. Extended boardwalks cross the dune field and descend to the foreshore. It is a beautiful sight.

When you park your car at Sunset Beach, it is the end of one trip and the start of another. Between the beachfront homes and the Atlantic Ocean is a long walk, and this is a good thing.

The island floats in its own little world. The mainland nearby is attracting newcomers to golf course communities and commercial development. Not so Sunset Beach. It remains blissfully happy in its place in the sun, listening to the crumple of waves on its distant (from the oceanfront houses) shores.

In 1999 Hurricane Bonnie blew through and closed a steady tidal trickle off the west end of the island called Mad Inlet. This closure welded about 135 acres of high ground called Bird Island to Sunset Beach. Bird Island and 1,300 acres of surrounding marshes promptly became part of the North Carolina Coastal Reserve, and Sunset Beach was blessed with access to a special sort of place for Sunset residents and guests.

The town has constructed a boardwalk at the west end of town that

Sunset Beach has one of the most expansive sand dune fields on the coast.
(Photo by Bill Russ, courtesy of VisitNC.com)

makes a steep ascent over the primary dunes. The beach has a gentle gradient and is one of the finest strands in the state. While there is little isolation on Sunset, there is plenty of serenity. There are no traffic sounds—no sounds at all, really, except those of the edge of the sea.

Yes, there is a pier and a few sundry shops. The causeway from the highrise bridge is handsomely landscaped and sentried with attractive goosenecked streetlights. The road seems to end at central seaside gazebo—a great big welcome to a still-small town, a simple beach community.

Access

There are 25 unimproved access points at First through 11th Streets and 27th through 40th Streets. Parking is permitted at all access locations even though no parking spaces are specifically provided.

Search Sunset Beach NC or enter www.sunsetbeachnc.gov.

Search Brunswick Islands NC or enter www.ncbrunswick.com.

Town hall phone number: 910-579-3808.

BIRD ISLAND

The complex of marsh, high ground, and oceanfront that is Bird Island has slightly less than a mile of beachfront due west of Sunset Beach. Beach walkers amble along the ocean, ever westward, and cross the low flats that once were Mad Inlet. Walkers will look toward the dunes and eventually see there, nestled in a cover of beach-grass-covered dunes, a simple mailbox and bench, the items collectively known as the Kindred Spirit. Inside the mailbox is paper and pen. It is the opportunity to share in the common humanity and emotional epitaphs of those who have come before you or left too soon.

This former island, with its thickly knitted forest and extensive sand flats and dunes, was the last privately owned barrier beach in North Carolina. Strollers can walk to Little River Inlet, the nominal physical demarcation between North and South Carolina. In fact, the island was the starting point for the 1735 survey line between North and South Carolina, but inlet migration has fudged the exact boundary.

Greensboro resident Ralph Clay Price, son of Julian Price, the driving force behind the now absorbed Jefferson-Pilot Corporation, had the money and the dream to own an island. He bought it sight unseen in the late 1950s: the southern and westernmost island in North Carolina, approximately 1,150 acres. He then built a bridge from Sunset Beach crossing the shallow creek known as Mad Inlet. The island has been without access since the 1960s, when arsonists burned the bridge that Price built. The arsonists also spread tacks in the road to slow fire trucks rushing to the conflagration. The Price family never reconstructed the bridge. When Ralph Price died in 1987, he left the island to his wife.

In early 1992 Mrs. Price initiated new development plans for the island and applied for a permit to the Division of Coastal Management to rebuild the bridge to the island. This began a struggle between preservationists and the family over the fate of the island. In 2002 North Carolina completed the purchase of nearly 1,200 acres of upland, dunes, flats, and marsh. It is now a part of the North Carolina Coastal Reserve.

And so the Kindred Spirit belongs to everybody. (In 2018, the North Carolina State Legislature approved plans to purchase 35 acres of property next to the preserve to thwart a planned development. If the purchase succeeds, the state will add this upland acreage to the preserve.)

Access

Public access is primarily by walking from Sunset Beach.

Search Bird Island Reserve or enter
www.nccoastalreserve.net and select Reserve Sites.

CALABASH

Calabash is synonymous with seafood dining, indulgence, or maybe over-indulgence. The buzz is about traditional Calabash seafood: lightly breaded, quickly deep-fried, amply apportioned, and nominally priced. Hush puppies, sweet tea, coleslaw, and a potato accompany the entrees. Why is it so hugely popular? In part it is southern culture, but cooked correctly, Calabash style is also tasty. The touch is light, not oily or greasy.

Seafood dining here has gone on for a long time. In the 1940s, Calabash was a small tidal river town where two local families, the Becks and the Colemans held outdoor oyster roasts for folks. The outdoor roast evolved into an indoor restaurant. Eventually the two families opened "rival" restaurants. The competition was friendly because the families were (and still are) related.

The Calabash reputation spread by word of mouth, and one nationally known entertainer took a fancy to one of the restaurants and to the young woman in charge. Though flattered by the attention, she would not give her name. The good-natured entertainer said he would make her famous anyway. Hence Jimmy Durante's enigmatic close: "Good night, Mrs. Calabash, wherever you are."

Today more than 20 restaurants feed the national reputation that Calabash developed in late 1960s and 1970s. Word of mouth drives recommendations. It's tough to choose a place to pull up a chair, so talk with locals or research online reviews. Take the time to wander the docks and walk the town. Calabash began as a fishing village, and the docks are the historical heart of the community.

One key to summertime and weekend dining in Calabash: arrive early or risk leaving late.

Search Calabash Dining for online reviews.

Search Brunswick Islands NC or enter www.ncbrunswick.com.

With Mollusk Aforethought

That glimmer of color in the sand, the rounded form emerging from the foam of a wave, is an abandoned home. For every shell that whispers sea sounds in our ears, there are others inspiring words of wonder in our minds. Mollusks are probably the most refined architects in the animal world.

A mollusk is a soft-bodied creature that comes in six basic body styles, or classes. Three of those body styles produce the shells that we might reasonably expect to find on North Carolina beaches. Two mollusk classes—the Gastropoda, or snails, and the Pelecypoda, or bivalves—have the most species by far and generate nearly all of the shells. (The tusk shells, members of another class, are found only infrequently.) The snails have one-piece shells with one opening; the bivalves are hinged shells such as oysters, clams, coquinas, and scallops.

A shell is first and foremost armor, developed to protect the mollusk's soft body parts. (Other shell-less mollusks such as squids and slugs have other survival strategies.) Why are there such differences in design and pattern? Probably in response to the environment in which the creature lives, and perhaps whimsy as well—why should there not be variety for its own sake?

Most importantly, each different shell shape is a different animal—the shell is both the visual cue and defining taxonomy for creatures infrequently seen and morphologically very similar when caught outside their homes. In other words, you must judge a snail (or a clam) by its cover.

A shell's shape, color, and pattern of ornamentation provide clues about where it lives. Ornately structured shells (murex, for example) live in calmer, lower-energy waters where waves won't damage the shell's ornate protuberances. The streamlined channel whelk (evocative of the Guggenheim Museum in Manhattan) is aptly named for its high-energy home turf, where its smooth shell contours offer minimal resistance to wave action. Offshore from the churning barrier islands, below the effective level of daily wave action at the seafloor, more ornamentally inclined shell builders find water-motion levels compatible with their shell construction and are likely to flourish undamaged.

The ocean is tough on shells exposed to its tumbling action and the lapidary effect of the sand, which in North Carolina is composed of continental shelf sand and shell debris. A shell cannot resist the grinding effect. If there is no creature inside to replenish the worn surfaces and keep the shell anchored or moving upright, it degrades rapidly. Even the durable, thick-walled helmet shell and whelks can be tumbled to pieces in as few as three weeks. Bright shells, vibrant with color and comparatively unscathed, are probably very recently abandoned. A lingering fetid odor provides the ripest clue of a recent vacancy.

Like any other creature, every mollusk adapts to a particular ocean environment. The type of seafloor, the water temperature, the wave action, and the other creatures that share the neighborhood play a part in which species will live successfully. Here's a general principle, though: sandy or muddy ocean bottoms are more accommodating to bivalves, because they can bury; harder seafloors typically support larger numbers of snails, which are mobile.

The evolutionary change that turned a two-piece fortress into a one-piece armored personnel carrier set some mollusks in motion. Snails inch across the ocean floor on their "foot," grazing or hunting less-agile bivalves. Bivalves, on the other hand, must hide through burrowing or coloration. Bivalves are more general feeders; snails are specialty diners, and some, such as the Atlantic oyster drill, are efficient enough at feeding on their prey that they threaten oyster populations.

The Molluscan lifestyle produces extraordinary architecture, from humble bungalow to exuberant gingerbread Gothic, each of which, although resembling the neighbors, has a "personal" touch. Every shell creature takes a basic "floor plan"—the shape of the shell, the general color scheme, and the coloration pattern—and then does a personal home makeover. The individualization is akin to painting the trim on a house.

The workhorse for each shell-producing mollusk is an organ known as a mantle, a fleshy, cape-like covering lining the inside of the shell and wrapping around the remainder of the mollusk. The mantle makes the shell. The mollusk extracts calcium and magnesium carbonate from its food, and to a limited extent from the water, and gives the minerals in solution to the mantle. The mantle serves as the paintbrush, spreading the liquid carbonates (and other minerals) on the inside of the shell. After deposition, it rapidly crystallizes into complex, rigid lattices that make up the shell. The spots, bands, and checkers of color are deposits of waste material into the shell lattice.

Mollusks experience periods of growth followed by rest. This shows in the shell in the form of ridges of enlarging dimension emanating from the hinge of the bivalve or the axis of the coil in snails. While the ridges of a shell reflect periods of growth, they are not annual measurements such as the concentric rings of a tree. The periods of shell growth may correspond to seasonal change but do not correlate on a calendar basis. No one can accurately determine a mollusk's age from its shell, but it is possible to get a good idea of periods of feast or famine.

None of this changes the fundamental reason people look for shells, and that is because they are pretty and free and fall under the "finders keepers" rule.

Acknowledgments

The opportunity to revisit *North Carolina Beaches* came in 2016; the travel to research this update started the following year. It continued until my ever-patient editor, Lucas Church, blew the whistle in the summer of 2018.

This edition is written to help readers choose from among all the equally enticing and alluring coastal locations — to know before they go. Sand and surf are a given, but matching vacation expectations to atmosphere, attitude, and attractions improves the chances of a memorable holiday. *North Carolina Beaches* helps to do just that.

I have received generous help from many professionals during this effort. I give particular thanks to Greg "Rudi" Rudolph, Carteret County Shore Protection Manager. He is also a member of the Coastal Resources Science Advisory Panel and chair of the Coastal Resources Advisory Council. Thanks also to Daniel I. Rubenstein, director of the Program in Environmental Studies of Princeton University, for sharing his knowledge of the Shackleford Banks horses.

Karen Sphar of the Southport–Oak Island Area Chamber of Commerce and Mitzi York of the Brunswick County Tourism Development Authority were repeatedly helpful. Marshall Morris was a fine driver, and Bill McKenzie and Tammy Harrell of Wilmington assisted with photography.

Anyone who visits our national seashores, national wildlife refuges, state parks, historic sites, and aquariums will appreciate the personnel's professionalism and willingness to help and educate. My effort was greatly eased by their generosity of time and knowledge.

Special thanks to Mark Simpson-Vos, Wyndham Robertson Editorial Director of the University of North Carolina Press, who encouraged me to come around again; to my sister, Meredith M. Babb, director of the University Press of Florida, who is a consistent guiding voice in publishing; and to

Lucas Church, who cheered me on. I have special appreciation for the sharp eye and immeasurable patience of Christi Stanforth, the copyeditor, and for UNC Press assistant managing editor Jay Mazzocchi, who provided guidance during production.

My wonderful companion and wife, Ginny Boyle, wholeheartedly encouraged my playing in the sand. Every wanderer needs an anchor, and she anchors me.

Taft's Poem

For Taft Lee Morris
February 2, 1979–February 4, 1989

Once,
The silver sea slip foamed around your ankles
And high above your sun-towed head the man-birds roared,
And rolling split the sky.
We built castles
And the sea pulled them in
And laughingly
We built them again in brash defiance.
We hallowed pools for your splashing and small fish
Caught to stock your private puddle-sea.
To this mooring, you brought ropes,
Tangled, tentacled, frondlings, and with sticks and boat bones
Secured your palace of sand.
You came to this at three
And I, at thirty-three,
Had not grown enough to know you.
A thousand questions flowed
And I of answers stood silent for one.

Your gentle mother told you
Your spirit will live forever.

You knew and smiled.
I know now and cry still.

For once,
The silver sea slip foamed around your ankles
Slid past your toes and ebbed,
Leaving forever your palace of sand
Grain by grain
Behind.

Glenn Morris
February 7, 1989

bivalves, 374–75

Black River, 285

Bluff Island, 352

Bodie Island, 37, 97, 101–2, 108, 110, 113, 116

Bodie Island Lighthouse, 26, 80, 98–99, 103, 347

Bodie Island Visitors Center, 26, 99, 103–6

Bogue Banks, 13, 44, 111, 205–7, 209, 216, 232–37, 238–40, 243–44, 246–49, 252–55, 257–58, 275, 282, 329. *See also* Atlantic Beach; Emerald Isle; Fort Macon; Indian Beach; Pine Knoll Shores; Salter Path

Bogue Inlet, 256–57, 265–66, 268

Bogue Sound, 1, 205, 208, 228–30, 233, 244, 256, 339

Boiling Spring Lakes Plant Conservation Preserve, 362–63

British Sailors' Cemetery (Ocracoke), 163, 177

brown pelicans, 322–23, 336

Brown's Island, 273

Brunswick, N.C., 11

Brunswick County, 3, 265, 290–91, 302, 340–44, 351–52, 362, 364, 369–70

Brunswick Town State Historic Site, 343–44

Buxton, N.C., 2, 44–45, 48, 98, 131–34, 136, 137, 139, 143–44, 166, 186, 191; Portsmouth ferry, 181–82

Buxton Woods Coastal Reserve, 143–44

Buxton Woods Nature Trail, 139

Caffey's Inlet Life-Saving Station, 53, 155

Calabash, N.C., 290, 339, 343–44, 373

Camp Davis, 264

Camp Glenn, 232

Camp Lejeune Marine Corps Base, 5, 231, 258, 264, 266, 273–74

Canadian Hole, 131–33

Cape Carteret, 205, 208, 233–34, 237, 253, 256–58, 268, 339

Cape Fear region, 9

Cape Fear River, 8, 9, 11–12, 175, 208, 285, 302–6, 308, 317–18, 320–21, 324, 328–29, 332, 334–36, 338, 342–44, 346–50, 352–53, 357

Cape Hatteras, 3–4, 8, 12, 14, 111, 134, 142, 144, 147, 154, 175–77, 206, 220, 299, 347–48

Cape Hatteras Bight, 118, 140, 145–46

Cape Hatteras Lighthouse, 8, 26, 97, 99, 111, 132, 135–38, 142, 347

Cape Hatteras Light Station and Visitor's Center, 135, 137, 140

Cape Hatteras National Seashore, 4, 26, 44–45, 47–49, 57, 72–73, 95–103, 108, 112, 131–32, 137, 143–44, 158, 162, 172, 177, 180, 190, 205–6, 242, 347; beach access, 14, 24, 140; campgrounds, 125

Cape Kendrick, 122

Cape Lookout, xv, 3–4, 37, 103, 111, 166–67, 175, 189–94, 197–200, 205–6, 212, 214, 218, 220, 232, 249, 257, 275, 285

Cape Lookout Lighthouse, 190, 193, 215, 220, 348

Cape Lookout Light Station, 191–92, 198, 207, 215

Cape Lookout National Seashore, xv, 4, 13–14, 24, 26, 44, 118, 167, 180–81, 185, 189–93, 201, 205, 207, 211, 215–16, 220, 234, 239, 348; beach access, 26, 167, 216; driving to, 13–14, 26; ferries to, 26

Cape Lookout National Seashore concession ferries and cabins, 212

Cape Lookout National Seashore Visitors Center, 14, 26, 44, 189–203

Cape Point, 2, 97, 99–100, 111, 119, 134–36, 141–42, 145, 147–48, 165–66, 299

Cape Point Beach, 140–42

Monument to a Century of Flight, 58

Moore's Inlet, 314, 316

Morehead City, N.C., 11, 205, 207–8, 228–34, 237, 240, 243, 254, 258, 264, 273, 283, 338–39, 348

Myrtle Grove Sound, 303, 318, 324, 338

Nags Head, N.C., 69–74; beach access, 47; beach cottage historic district, 50, 72–73, 77

Nags Head Woods Ecological Preserve, 69, 71, 187

National Estuarine Research Reserve. *See* North Carolina National Estuarine Research Reserve(s)

National Estuarine Sanctuary Program, 5

National Marine Fisheries Service, 259

National Oceanic and Atmospheric Administration (NOAA), 5

National Ocean Service, 55

National Park Service: and beach access, 26, 108–9, 127, 160, 164, 170; campgrounds, 26, 103, 126, 136–37, 145, 169, 176, 348; ferry licenses, 182, 197; and handicapped access, 4, 61, 198

national wildlife refuges, 17, 89, 91, 96, 119, 187, 123

Native American Museum (Frisco), 134, 144

Native Americans, 9–10, 17, 31, 58, 92–93, 134, 144–45, 232, 255, 281

Nature Conservancy, 31, 69–70, 76, 226, 281, 343, 352, 362; land acquisitions, 31, 226, 281; land ownership, 31, 70, 76, 343, 352; state acquisitions from, 69, 362

New Bern, N.C., xv, 11, 13, 237, 290, 293, 338

Newport River, 227, 231

Newport River Regional Access Area, 228

New River, 264, 267, 273–75

New River Air Station, 5

New River Inlet, 265–67, 273–75, 279–80

New Topsail Inlet, 287, 295

No Name Island, 336

North Banks, 30. *See also* Currituck County

North Carolina (battleship), 145

North Carolina Aquarium(s): Fort Fisher, 334; Roanoke Island, 88; Pine Knoll Shores, 249

North Carolina Baptist Assembly Grounds (Oak Island), 353–54

North Carolina Center for the Advancement of Teaching, 172

North Carolina Coastal Reserve(s), 5, 61, 85, 139, 281, 303, 349, 351, 370, 372; Bald Head Woods, 302, 305, 310, 334, 336–37, 342, 344, 349, 350, 351, 352, 355; Bird Island, xv, 111, 342, 344, 370, 372–73; Buxton Woods, 98, 139–40, 143, 186; Emily and Richardson Preyer Buckridge, 85; Kitty Hawk Woods, 60–62; Permuda Island, 281, 283

North Carolina Coastal Resources Commission, 281

North Carolina Department of Transportation, 6, 20, 113, 151, 182

North Carolina Division of Coastal Management, 3, 351, 372

North Carolina Division of Marine Fisheries, 259, 260

North Carolina Division of Parks and Recreation, 352

North Carolina Ferry Service, 152, 172, 211–13, 215, 219

North Carolina Historic Shipwreck Preserve, 74

North Carolina Maritime Museum (Beaufort), 11, 156, 207, 223–24, 346

North Carolina National Estuarine Research Reserve(s), 31, 225–27, 304,

309, 351; Currituck Banks, 31; Rachel Carson, 226–28; Masonboro Island, 304, 309, 316; Zeke's Island, 304, 351
North Carolina Wildlife Resources Commission: fisheries management, 159, 259–61; fishing and boating access sites, 66, 334, 339; game, 285; land management, 259
North Core Banks, 181, 190–91, 193, 197, 211–12
North Island, 336
North Swan Beach, 27
North Topsail Beach, N.C., 264–67, 275–81, 292, 310, 312
North Topsail Shores, 279

Oak Island, 352–54. *See also* Caswell Beach; Fort Caswell
Oak Island, N.C. (town), 359–62
Oak Island Coast Guard Station, 353–54, 357–58
Oak Island Lighthouse, 355, 357
Ocean Isle Beach, N.C., 310, 342–43, 364, 367–69
Ocean Sands, 33
Ocracoke, N.C., 6, 13, 44, 97–100, 108, 124. *See also* Ocracoke Village
Ocracoke Beach Day Use Area, 169
Ocracoke Campground, 168–69
Ocracoke Inlet, 10, 163–64, 169–70, 173, 181, 190–91, 193, 195, 347
Ocracoke Island, 44, 97, 118, 149, 150–52, 158–62, 169, 178, 180–82, 196; Cedar Island ferry, 99, 183; Hatteras ferry, 151–52, 158; Swan Quarter ferry, 183
Ocracoke Island Visitors Center, 26, 180
Ocracoke Light Station, 175–76
Ocracoke North End, 164–65
Ocracoke Pony Pen, 165–68
Ocracoke Preservation Society Museum, 173–74, 180–81

Ocracoke Toll Ferry, 182–83
Ocracoke Village, 99, 152, 160, 171, 182
"Old Baldy" Lighthouse, 337, 349, 350–51, 355
Old Topsail Inlet, 287, 296
Onslow Bay, 205, 220, 275, 285
Onslow Beach, 264, 267, 273, 275, 281
Onslow County, 263–83, 286, 292
Ophelia Inlet/Drum Inlet, 191, 197–98, 212
Oregon Inlet, 108–10, 112–17, 130, 152, 155, 169, 195, 290, 322, 347
Oregon Inlet Campground, 106
Oregon Inlet Coast Guard Station, 114–15
Oregon Inlet Fishing Center, 108, 114, 155
Oregon Inlet Jetty, 113–14
Oriental (shipwreck), 117
Orton Plantation and Gardens, 343
Outer Banks, 1, 7–9; highways, 13
Outer Banks Center for Wildlife Education, 17, 38
Outer Banks History Center, 88–89
Outer Banks National Scenic Byway, 96
oystering, 260

Pamlico Sound, 10, 84, 131
Paradise Bay, 255
Pea Island, 86; north end, 99
Pea Island Cookhouse Museum (Manteo), 86
Pea Island Life-Saving Station, 91
Pea Island National Wildlife Refuge, 91
Pea Island Drive, 119–21
Pender County, 284–300
Permuda Island, 281
Permuda Island Coastal Reserve, 281–83
Perquimans County, 77
Pine Island Club, 41
Pine Knoll Shores, N.C., 246–47
piping plover, 118–19, 185, 226

Swan Beach, N.C., 27–29
Swan Quarter, N.C., 67–68, 99, 183, 188, 291; Ocracoke ferry, 100, 135, 149, 151, 210
Swan Quarter National Wildlife Refuge, 159, 183
Swansboro, N.C., 167, 258, 267–69
Swash Inlet, 193–94

Taylor Creek (Beaufort), 222–23, 225–26
Teach's Hole (Ocracoke), 161, 178
Theodore Roosevelt State Natural Area, 236, 239, 248–49
tides, 67–68, 184
Topsail Beach, 275–78, 285–88, 292, 293–96, 311–12
Topsail Island, xv, 232, 264–65, 275–78, 280, 285–87, 290, 292. See also North Topsail Beach; Surf City

U.S. Army Corps of Engineers, 53, 310; dune and beach, 65; channel dredging, 318
U.S. Army Research Pier, 46, 55
U.S. Coast and Geodetic Survey, 68, 277
U.S. Coast Guard, 5, 101, 123–24, 128, 152–56, 177, 239, 353–54; maintenance of lighthouses, 37, 137, 357; Ocracoke Station (retired), 114; Oregon Inlet Station, 109
—active stations: Fort Macon, 238–40; Oak Island, 355, 357
U.S. Fish and Wildlife Service, 4, 116, 210, 296; Alligator River refuge, 50, 85; Back Bay refuge, 27; Cedar Island National Wildlife refuge, 210–11; Currituck refuge, 30–31; Lake Mattamuskeet, 158; Mackay Island refuge, 22–23; National Wildlife Refuges Visitor Center, 89, 91; Pea Island refuge, 116–17; Pocosin Lakes, 158; Swan Quarter refuge, 159

U.S. Life-Saving Service, 12, 17, 53, 225
—historic sites: Caffey's Inlet Station, 74; Cape Lookout Station, 156; Chicamacomico, 123–25; Durant Station, 148, 156; Kill Devil Hills Station, 155; Kitty Hawk Coast Guard Station, 155; Little Kinnakeet Station, 98, 128, 156; Oregon Inlet Station (retired), 5, 109, 155; Pea Island Station, 120, 155; Portsmouth Island Station, 156; Wash Woods Station, 29, 155; Whalebone Junction Station, 53, 100–101

Virginia, 14, 18–21, 166
Virginia Beach, Va., 21, 302
Virginia Dare Trail, 47, 59, 61, 77–78

Wanchese, N.C., 81–83, 93–94; water access, 21, 149, 230; fishing industry, 148, 152, 159, 183, 224, 274
Washington Baum Bridge, 71, 80–82
Wash Woods, 29, 155, 202
Wash Woods Life-Saving Station, 29, 155
Waterside Theater (Roanoke Island), 49–50, 82, 92
Waves, N.C., 107, 121, 125–27
waves, ocean, xvii, 55, 133–34, 141, 201–2, 298–99, 330, 368
Whalebone Junction, 53, 71, 75, 79–81, 96, 99, 101
Whalebone Junction Information Center, 100–101
Whalehead Club 19, 38–41
White Oak River, 267–69
Wilmington, N.C., xv, 11, 13, 302–3, 305–8, 326, 337; port of 337, 346
Wilmington Beach, N.C., 305, 308, 316, 326. See also Carolina Beach
Wimble Shoals, 121–22, 126
wind kiting, 133
windsurfing, 49, 99, 131–34, 215
Wright brothers, 35, 58, 61–68

About the Author

Photo by Melinda Fine

A visit to Currituck County in 1962 whetted Glenn Morris's curiosity about the North Carolina coast. His fascination grew through multiple visits to different coastal locations from his hometown, Greensboro.

He attended Princeton University, then received a master's of landscape architecture from North Carolina State University. He joined *Southern Living* in 1976, serving as landscape editor and then outdoor living editor. As a free-lance writer, he contributed to multiple newspapers and magazines, including *Southern Living, Coastal Living,* and *The State.* He is the author of *Small Gardens,* in the Taylor Weekend Gardening Series (1999), and *Country Roads of North Carolina* (1995).

The Raleigh resident returned to his lifelong appreciation of the North Carolina coast with the 1993 publication of *North Carolina Beaches: A Guide to Coastal Access* by UNC Press. This updated 2019 edition looks anew at wonderful old places in a different era.

Other **Southern Gateways Guides** you might enjoy

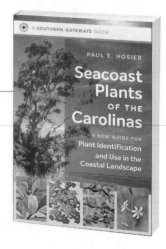

Seacoast Plants of the Carolinas
A New Guide for Plant Identification and
Use in the Coastal Landscape

PAUL E. HOSIER

Published in association with North Carolina Sea Grant

The must-have guide for plant lovers along the North Carolina coast

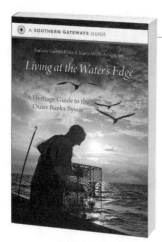

Living at the Water's Edge
A Heritage Guide to the Outer Banks Byway

BARBARA GARRITY-BLAKE
AND KAREN WILLIS AMSPACHER

A unique guide to the byway's people and places

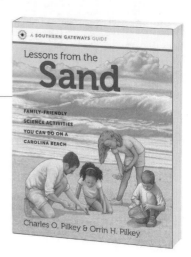

Lessons from the Sand
Family-Friendly Science Activities You Can Do
on a Carolina Beach

CHARLES O. PILKEY AND ORRIN H. PILKEY

*Fun ways to learn about the beach and
its surrounding environment*